THE GERMAN HISTORIANS AND ENGLAND

A STUDY IN NINETEENTH-CENTURY VIEWS

THE GERMAN HISTORIANS AND ENGLAND

A STUDY IN NINETEENTH-CENTURY VIEWS

CHARLES E. McCLELLAND
University of Pennsylvania

CAMBRIDGE
AT THE UNIVERSITY PRESS
1971

Published by the Syndics of the Cambridge University Press
Bentley House, 200 Euston Road, London N.W.1
American Branch: 32 East 57th Street, New York, N.Y.10022

Library of Congress Catalogue Card Number: 79-154514

ISBN: 0 521 08063 0

Printed in Great Britain
at the University Printing House, Cambridge
(Brooke Crutchley, University Printer)

To the memory of Hajo Holborn

CONTENTS

ACKNOWLEDGEMENT

The history of ideas is now established as a legitimate approach to the past. Unlike other daughters of Clio, however, it has often had to struggle to assert its personality, techniques, and virtues. Political history, for example, does not have to be defended against charges of being airy, speculative, or irrelevant. The history of ideas has to answer accusations that it veers between hagiography (of those who established commonly accepted views of man and the universe) and the recounting of errors (which had best be forgotten). The methods of the history of ideas are less fixed than those of economic or social history. Yet despite all its weaknesses, it lives on.

The explanation for its vitality lies partly in a heightened curiosity about ideas which have been called into question. A general European *crise de conscience* since the late nineteenth century forced the careful examination of received ideas and their creators. It would be hard to find a land where this crisis was more keenly felt than Germany itself. The subsequent transfer of deep concern with the history of ideas to American soil, often by exiles from regimes which attempted to stamp out ideas, has nurtured the discipline.

Anyone who knew the late Hajo Holborn will know what I mean by saying this book would have been impossible without him. His wisdom, insight, and encouragement constantly sustained my labors, just as his humor, courage, and commitment to high intellectual values presented his students and friends with an unforgettable example for their lives. He upheld the standard of the history of ideas erected in Germany by his teacher, Friedrich Meinecke.

Many other teachers, colleagues, and friends aided in the creation of this work. Hans W. Gatzke, Henry A. Turner, Jr., and Franklin L. Baumer of Yale University, Arno J. Mayer and James H. Billington of Princeton University, and John L. Snell of the University of North Carolina read earlier drafts and offered many helpful criticisms. I am also indebted to Felix Gilbert, Andreas Dorpalen, John L. Gillis,

Lamar J. R. Cecil, Wolfgang J. Mommsen, Karl Dietrich Bracher, and Fritz Fischer for advice and encouragement along the way. Other colleagues at Princeton University and the University of Pennsylvania have offered me countless useful suggestions.

Grants from the Woodrow Wilson Foundation and Princeton University made possible two research trips to Germany in 1965–6 and 1968. I owe much to the personnel of the university libraries of Hamburg, Freiburg im Breisgau, Tübingen, Heidelberg, Frankfurt am Main, Göttingen, and the Free University of Berlin for generous help in my research. I am particularly indebted to the archival personnel of the *Deutsche Staatsbibliothek* in East Berlin for their assistance. German state archives which kindly placed their holdings at my disposal include the Württembergische Landesbibliothek and Württembergische General-Landesarchiv in Stuttgart, the List-Archiv in Reutlingen, the Bundesarchiv in Koblenz, the Politisches Archiv des Auswärtigen Amtes in Bonn, and the Preussisches Geheimes Archiv in Berlin.

The thanks which I owe to my wife, Muriel, cannot be fully expressed here. A scholar in her own right, she took the time to read each draft carefully and always offered the most reasoned and valuable criticisms. Her political scientist's eye for economical statements and clarity has given this work whatever readability it has.

Even the best advice, whether stylistic or substantive, cannot eliminate all errors; for these I alone take responsibility.

CHARLES MCCLELLAND

Philadelphia, March 1971

PART I

INTRODUCTION

which I sought in letters, articles, and books, often proved hard to ascertain. The change of a government in London, Palmerston's latest note on Schleswig-Holstein, or the significance of reform legislation doubtless got discussed at the scholars' *Stammtisch* or club and might sometimes stray into a letter; but, until late in the century, historians seldom commented in print on current English events. Even in critical years when the direction of English diplomacy deeply affected Germany, her historians barely mentioned England in their letters and articles: policies made on the Seine or the Neva aroused more hopes and fears in such crisis years as 1848 and 1859, for example, than those made on the Thames.[1] The very lack of evidence here suggests that the Germans thought of England more in symbolic terms than in immediate, practical ones.

Flexibility also seems useful in deciding which authors to include. If one defines 'historian' too narrowly, one excludes such economists as List and Schmoller and such social theorists as Marx and Huber. The criterion, to be meaningful, must include writers who influenced the German interpretation of England and English history. Some of the names are unfamiliar today, yet, with few exceptions, they all enjoyed international esteem in their time. As for the geographical distribution of the sources, one can say that virtually all the historical writings about England came from cities and university towns – most, from North Germany; some, from the medium states south of the Main. I have excluded Austrian historians because they wrote little about England and because they moved in a somewhat different cultural stream. England certainly did not have the same intense symbolic meaning for the Austrians.

Underlying the choice of a chronological presentation is the assumption that the political thoughts and needs of each succeeding generation conditioned how German historians described England. In order to heighten the contrast between generations enough to make their historical writing usable as a document in the history of ideas, I have had to resort to the seemingly unfair practice of seeking out the fundamental prejudices of each author in each generation. Nineteenth-

[1] For example, perusal of Hans Rosenberg's *Die nationalpolitische Publizistik Deutschlands vom Eintritt der Neuen Ära in Preussen bis zum Ausbruch des deutschen Krieges*, 2 vols. (Munich and Berlin, 1935), covering a very critical period in German foreign relations, reveals how small a role England played in the thoughts of leading political writers – including many historians – compared to other great powers.

The historians sought to attain their political goals by direct political action, as in 1848; but they also believed in educating their fellow Germans to a level of political sophistication sufficient for responsible citizenship. German reformers from Stein onward realized this need. The usefulness of the past as a lesson to the present, not mere antiquarianism and pedantry, inspired succeeding generations of German scholars to raise history first to a 'science', then to a distinguishing hallmark of German thought.[1] Throughout most of the nineteenth century, when historical studies attained increasingly high plateaus of 'critical' and 'scientific' method, one could still classify German schools of history chiefly by the way they used the past to teach a political lesson. For this reason their histories are more than obsolete and long-winded volumes gathering dust on our shelves: they are historical documents in themselves. They show us what one of the most influential intellectual elites in Germany thought of the world around it and, allowing for some distortion and an inevitable 'culture lag', what their educated middle-class readers must have absorbed into their own thoughts.

Since the object of this study is to trace the German ideas of England rather than describe the evolution of a special fragment of German historiography, I have defined 'historian' and 'historical literature' loosely. The numerous 'histories of England' written in the nineteenth century reveal much, but their scope necessarily remained fixed by the canons imposed by scholarship and publishers. In many cases I have drawn upon even broader works, such as the 'world histories' favored in the early nineteenth century, when no other printed source of a historian's attitudes exists. Shorter pieces, such as articles, often reveal views on topics of contemporary interest outside the scope of more formal monographs and general histories. I have also examined the letters and personal papers of the historians where available. Secondary materials have usually only grazed this topic; in addition, biographies of all but the greatest nineteenth-century historians, when they exist at all, are usually brief, eulogistic, and uninformative.

Despite the enormous collective bulk of the primary materials, some information is represented only feebly. The immediate reactions of German historians to contemporary English politics and developments,

[1] For an evaluation of the massive impact of historical thought on German intellectual development in the nineteenth century, see Karl Mannheim, 'Historicism' (1924), in his *Essays on the Sociology of Knowledge*, ed. by Paul Kecskemeti (New York, 1952), pp. 84–133.

fickleness of the newspapers I did consult quickly discouraged making newspapers a main source. After consulting memoirs of public figures (business and military men, statesmen, scholars, and literati) and surveying the literature printed about England, I gradually came to realize that the overwhelming majority of pertinent writings, the bulk of ideas about England, came from one clearly recognizable group. Consistency and breadth of viewpoint set the men in this group off from the journalists with their oscillating reactions to day-to-day events. This group also thought and wrote more about England than poets, philosophers, or statesmen because, in a sense, it was a part of their intellectual or academic duty to do so. To study this group meant to follow a clear thread through the maze of German intellectual life. Empirical sampling of the sources thus revealed what logic could have suggested: that in a century dominated by historicism, the historians themselves are one of the best sources for intellectual trends.

Most of the historians belonged to the influential cultural elite composed largely of professors. German historians looking back at the last century from the vantage point of this one have wistfully noted the high place in the life of the nation which professors then enjoyed. In the century before 1918, Meinecke wrote, 'the politics of scholars [*Gelehrtenpolitik*]...were nowhere else so sharply and clearly developed and were nowhere else so closely bound up with the decisive movements of national history as in Germany'.[1] Once they had become politicized by the revolutionary events at the beginning of the nineteenth century, many German professors took up the cause of reconciling the young national culture, which they helped create, with the German political system, which functioned largely without them. The nation might be the child of the poets; the states, children of monarchs and bureaucrats; but the idea of the nation-state was the darling of the professors, as their disproportionate presence in the Frankfurt National Assembly of 1848 showed. 'The will of the bourgeois class to have its way in politics, to make the nation unified and powerful in the world,' Meinecke concluded, 'was directed and nourished to an incalculable degree by the politics of scholars.'[2] And of all the scholars, the historians contributed disproportionately to the political leadership of the German middle class.

[1] Friedrich Meinecke, 'Drei Generationen deutscher Gelehrtenpolitik', *Staat und Persönlichkeit* (Berlin, 1933), p. 136. [2] *Ibid.*, p. 137.

proaches. Diplomatic histories tell of the relations between the Foreign Office and the German courts, at least in crucial times; the reaction of German public opinion to Anglo-German relations has also been described in part;[1] German views of English culture and the influence of that culture have received some attention (but not nearly enough).[2] Scholars have pursued much more diligently the attitude of the English toward Germany than vice-versa.[3] Sources of these studies have ranged from newspapers to diplomatic archives to the writings of poets and philosophers. Even these sources have not always been used wisely, and the results have frequently fallen short of definitive coverage.

This study offers such broad coverage of the entire period when England meant most to German thinkers. Like earlier students, I have been forced to limit my investigation to manageable proportions, to seek a compact body of source material. In addition I looked for the most meaningful sources. Almost at the start I saw that the German press offered neither compactness nor consistency: censorship, the low standing of journalism among the professions, the rare expression of editorial opinion in the early nineteenth-century press, and the

[1] These works concentrate on Anglo-German relations chiefly after 1848 and focus heavily on newspapers and interest groups as sources of public opinion: Bernadotte E. Schmitt, *England and Germany, 1740–1914* (Princeton, 1916), a general treatment; Raymond J. Sontag, *Germany and England; Background of Conflict, 1848–1894* (New York, 1938); Eber Malcolm Carroll, *Germany and the Great Powers, 1866–1914. A Study in Public Opinion and Foreign Policy* (New York, 1938); and Pauline R. Anderson, *The Background of Anti-English Feeling in Germany, 1890–1902* (Washington, 1939). Werner Eugen Mosse, in *The European Powers and the German Question, 1848–71* (Cambridge, 1958), discusses chiefly English attitudes; so does Kurt Meine, *England und Deutschland in der Zeit des Überganges vom Manchestertum zum Imperialismus, 1871–76* (Berlin, 1937).

[2] See, for example, Franz Muncker, *Anschauungen vom englischen Staat und Volk in der deutschen Literatur der letzten vier Jahrhunderte*, 2 vols. (Munich, 1918–25); Percy Ernst Schramm, 'Deutschlands Verhältnis zur englischen Kultur nach der Begründung des neuen Reiches', *Schicksalswege deutscher Vergangenheit*, ed. by Walter Hubatsch (Düsseldorf, 1950), 289–319; René Wellek, *Confrontations. Studies in the Intellectual and Literary Relations between Germany, England, and the United States during the Nineteenth Century* (Princeton, 1965).

[3] See, for example, Manfred Messerschmidt, *Deutschland in englischer Sicht. Die Wandlungen des Deutschlandbildes in der englischen Geschichtsschreibung* (Düsseldorf, 1955); Manfred Schlenke, *England und das friderizianische Preussen, 1740–1763. Ein Beitrag zum Verhältnis von Politik und öffentlicher Meinung in England des 18. Jahrhunderts* (Freiburg i.B., 1963). Klaus Dockhorn has also investigated the impact of German thought on England in his books, *Deutscher Geist und angelsächsische Geistesgeschichte* (Göttingen, 1954) and *Der deutsche Historismus in England* (Göttingen, 1950). Less exhaustive but more suggestive is Percy Ernst Schramm's article, 'Englands Verhältnis zur deutschen Kultur zwischen der Reichsgründung und der Jahrhundertwende', in *Deutschland und Europa* [Rothfels *Festschrift*] (Düsseldorf, 1951). Even the German historical view of France has been described in Heinz-Otto Sieburg's *Deutschland und Frankreich in der Geschichtsschreibung des 19. Jahrhunderts*, 2 vols. (Wiesbaden, 1954–8).

with respect such vulgar matters as commerce and industry. By the eve of the French Revolution, however, German intellectuals went so far in agreeing that England symbolized the best form of government, the most progressive economic policies, the best international posture, the most interesting literature, and even the most admirable human characteristics that one can justifiably speak of 'Anglomania'. Germans probably felt more sense of kinship with the English people than any other in Europe – a fact which sheds light on the development of German national consciousness through the process of confrontation with foreign cultures. To a remarkable extent, German thinkers defined German national characteristics not in contrast, but in comparison to the English, by seeking the similarities rather than the differences.

From this time on, and well into the century, England continued to represent well-defined symbolic qualities to German thinkers. These qualities cannot be explained as the sole product of normal cultural or political exchange, geographical contiguity, or the improvement of information and communication, though all these played some role. Clearly German thinkers cast England in a role incomparably more meaningful than that of most other neighboring lands, such as Sweden, Russia, or Italy. Only France was a symbolic subject charged with comparable meaning. Even when the Anglo–German rivalry arose in the late nineteenth century, England remained a charged subject, though negatively.

Why should this be so? The answer is important not only to an understanding of Anglo–German relations, but of the relations between other 'model' and 'modernizing' polities in the contemporary world. The Germans' lively interest in England stemmed from more than purely intellectual causes. It was bound up with struggles for political power, class interests, the cause of national integration, and economic modernization. The nature and intensity of German opinion about England is a subject which goes to the roots of German nationalism, liberalism, and conservatism.

Despite the inherent importance of the problem, however, the changing attitude of German thinkers toward England has not been fully investigated. The vast scope of research necessary to describe and analyze it fully explains the lack of comprehensive treatments. What literature there is exhibits a variety of partial and limited ap-

CHAPTER I

PROLOGUE

'Image' is a widely understood concept today, thanks to the merchants of flattery who have developed advertising into a major industry in America and Europe. Yet before commercial exploitation diluted and popularized the concept, intellectuals for centuries shaped symbols and myths in a similar, if more honest way. When European thinkers began to accept the nation-state as a normal form of political organization and a legitimate object of human allegiance, they also began to build complex symbolic models, aggregates of accepted perceptions which defined the 'character' of the emerging nations of Europe. Sometime during the eighteenth century, such a process took place among certain German intellectuals, and England became a symbol invested with exemplary qualities and surrounded by emotional charges. Of course Germans had written about England before then and still write about it today. But the symbolic value in older times was weak and diffused: by contrast, from the late eighteenth century until just recently, the word 'England' suggested something else to German intellectuals – a complex of values, associations, aspirations, and feelings.

There was little reason for England to represent anything special to German intellectuals before the eighteenth century. Before then, Germans thought little about the country, which seemed remote, isolated, and not very important. The features of English life which interested continental intellectuals from the eighteenth century on – the libertarian political constitution, empiricism, the leading position in the development of commerce and industry, and her unique literature – either had not existed before or had to await recognition until the stage was set. Such events as the victory of the moderns over the ancients and the emergence of a wholly new type of secular, independent intellectual first made it possible to regard the state or art of modern England (rather than Greece or Rome) as models and to treat

century historians set great store by their own objectivity, but this study must discount it from the start. Clearly the German historians were children of their times; inescapable contemporary concerns guided the questions they asked, the materials they chose to use, and the form of their books. Yet their prejudices are fruitful aids to those who wish to understand them better. As Peter Gay recently put it, 'When literate and cultivated men make what seem to us Philistine judgments, their inconsistency – which was not an inconsistency to them – should provide historians with a window to the inner recesses of past convictions.'[1] To seek the presuppositions of a generation is to deny neither the idiosyncrasies nor the greatness of individual historians.

Defining just how long a generation lasted and which dates marked the beginnings of new interpretations of England must remain flexible, too. In each group of intellectual contemporaries there are outriders and laggards, and the work of some men spans more than one generation. I have found that units of about fifteen years best fit the transition of thought from one generation to the next throughout most of the nineteenth century. Chapter divisions correspond roughly, but not precisely, to these transitions, except in one case – the period from about 1870 to 1885, which produced too little important literature on England to warrant a full chapter. Instead I have offered a separate chapter on Treitschke, justified on two grounds: because he changed his views on England more dramatically than any other historian and because he stood out in a generation which produced fewer historians of England than any other. Perhaps his generation turned its eyes so little toward England because, as Srbik has suggested, it focussed its attention on German unification, the inward-looking transition between the outward-looking cosmopolitanism of the Enlightenment and the later, equally outward-looking world-awareness of the period of overseas expansion.[2]

The meaningful unit of study for this subject is a long one, punctuated at the start by the political collapse of the ancient *Reich* and Prussia under Napoleon's blows and at the end by Germany's grasp for world power. These political events, more than anything else,

[1] Peter Gay, *The Enlightenment* (New York, 1966), p. 211.

[2] Heinrich Ritter von Srbik, *Geist und Geschichte vom deutschen Humanismus bis zur Gegenwart*, 2 vols. (Munich and Salzburg, 1950–1), II, 28. For stimulating but less sympathetic observations on bias in European textbooks, see Edward H. Dance, *History the Betrayer. A Study in Bias*, 2nd edn. (London, 1964).

exercised the greatest influence on the attitudes of the German intellectuals toward England. In order to cover it in a limited space, I have had to hold to a minimum description of historical background, diplomatic relations, and public opinion in the broad sense. I have generally not fully analyzed the sources on which historians drew nor the impact of their writings upon the public. Aside from the limitations of space, there are good reasons for excluding both these topics from this investigation. As the accessibility, codification, and printing of English sources improved in the later part of the century, scholars had more to draw upon and tightened their grip on accurate details;[1] yet in many cases greater knowledge did not lead to a more objective evaluation. As for impact on the public, one encounters the danger of saying *post hoc ergo propter hoc*. Quantitative data on the size of a given edition are very hard to ascertain, and an 1810 edition of 1,000 copies might be as 'influential' as an 1870 edition of 5,000. Reviews also help little, for the more popular journals, established in quantity only late in the century, rarely reviewed scholarly works, and the reviews of respectable work on England appearing in scholarly journals were usually written by authors included in this study. Even when scholars addressed themselves to a wider audience through articles, they usually chose prestigious national journals which influenced the elite rather than the mass; thus their impact on the public often moved through indirect channels and therefore defies exact measurement.

In reading through a staggering number of historical works, I have consistently sought answers to certain questions. Most deal with attitudes toward political institutions and great men; some, with such prominent cultural features as England's religious and ethnic heritage; some others, with economic and military themes. The questions were not formulated arbitrarily, however; to a large extent the nineteenth-century historians suggested them by the way they dwelt upon certain themes, and after a few preliminary readings I found myself asking other authors for their views on the same subjects. Sometimes I received no answers, but even silence is useful in showing that a subject had ceased to interest historians. The frequency of use of certain slogans connected with England also indicated attitudes which were

[1] For elucidation of this and other historiographical details, see the authoritative works of George Peabody Gooch, *History and Historians in the Nineteenth Century* (Boston, 1959); Eduard Fueter, *Geschichte der neueren Historiographie*, 3rd edn. (Munich, 1936); and Srbik, *Geist und Geschichte*.

sometimes inarticulate. Such normative words as 'free' and 'Germanic' were used more heavily at one time than at others; neologisms such as *Selfgovernment* and *Parlamentarismus* revealed changes of thinking about England for which a new vocabulary became necessary. Their choice of words, being largely a subconscious process, indicates not only how they thought but how they felt about England.

Feelings and half-articulated ideas reveal as much about attitudes as the most sophisticated critical analysis. Sometimes openly, sometimes indirectly, many German historians revealed that they felt so close to English traditions that they vaguely confused their loyalty to German traditions. That is, by stressing what was common to both Englishmen and Germans and overlooking what divided them, they long put off the confrontation with English national uniqueness which a fully developed national consciousness ultimately demanded. Despite Herder's admonition that each nation follow its guiding genius as expressed in its language, his contemporaries and later generations tended to forge their national self-image only in contrast to Latin, particularly French characteristics. The need for an ally against French power was thus not the only reason for praising Britain; German authors, the creators of modern German literature in the eighteenth century, also needed the encouragement to strike out against the dominance of French taste and fashions. In Shakespeare and Ossian they found the encouragement they needed, the reassurance that a 'barbarous' Germanic tongue could express the loftiest sentiments. Thus the German fascination for England, like the later turn against her, was bound up in the first stirrings of German national consciousness.

CHAPTER 2

THE EIGHTEENTH-CENTURY BACKGROUND

In the 1780s it was still possible for a British traveler to leave Dover and, after a brief sail of seventy miles to Ostend, to set foot on territory ruled by a German prince. From there he could travel overland for many days, in fact nearly 1,000 miles, before leaving territories ruled by German princes, so vast was the extent of the Empire. Yet if he did make such a journey, he would have been unimpressed by the Holy Roman Empire of the German Nation, the only title which covered all the lands he traveled through. He would have had to pass through innumerable borders and tariff lines, deal with a bewildering variety of currencies and measures, and appreciate the profound differences between life in ecclesiastical principalities, free cities, kingdoms, electorates, and the estates of imperial free barons. He would have quickly discovered the political meaninglessness of the imperial title and might have agreed with young Hegel's observation that, since a state cannot exist without power, the German Empire simply did not exist. If our traveler roamed through the north, he might have been puzzled to find himself in German territories ruled by the monarchs of England, Denmark, Sweden, or Russia. Given this situation, it was hardly surprising that German patriotism was not necessarily the same as German nationalism: loyalty to one's city, to pretentious little dynasties, to one's church or, for a few learned spirits, to the enlightened ideals of a supernational humanity was more common than loyalty to some unreal abstraction known as 'Germany'.

German intellectuals, sharing in the West European Enlightenment, felt their kinship for humanity and cosmopolitan ideals most strongly. To be sure, the final decades of the eighteenth century began to produce thinkers and movements which ultimately loosened Germany's intellectual ties to the West.[1] But before then, the German republic of letters had been unable and largely unwilling to override the political and confessional atomization of Germany and produce rich and independent national cultural traditions. Since the tragedy of the Thirty Years' War, the West – France and England – had acted as donors of literary, political, and economic models. Reflecting the cosmopolitan interests of the Enlightenment, Germans took over the historiographical traditions of Gibbon, Hume, Voltaire, and Montesquieu. So-called cultural history, emphasizing literature and economics as well as politics, typified German historical writing in the late eighteenth century as much as it did French and English. It was natural for men of learning to absorb the admiration for England expressed in many internationally known writings of the English themselves and of French Anglophiles such as Voltaire and Montesquieu. The two Frenchmen enjoyed a following in Germany, but they were almost the only French historians who deeply impressed the Germans. The British could boast of at least three men whose works found an audible echo across the North Sea. Hume's Tory interpretation of English history long remained fixed in the minds of German historians, who either copied it or felt obliged to attack it. Robertson's Scottish history inspired the first German 'national' history of the Enlightenment by M. I. Schmidt (1763–94). Gibbon, too, was much read in Germany.[2]

Yet an uncritical plundering of foreign books for favorable sentiments about England does not fully explain the German attitude. Other opinions were available, particularly those produced in France by both radical and ultraconservative opponents of British constitutional doctrines.[3] Nevertheless most German writers, after the cool deliberation characteristic of writing in the Enlightenment, demonstrated a decided preference for things English. Their enemies and ridiculers described this preference as 'Anglomania', an unjust epithet if one compares their mild prejudice to the passion of some later generations. Still, a posture which struck many contemporaries as unwarranted and

[1] See Hajo Holborn, 'Der deutsche Idealismus in sozialgeschichtlicher Beleuchtung', *Historische Zeitschrift*, CLXXIV (1952), 361.

[2] German historians also drew heavily upon Adam Smith in the late eighteenth century. See Wilhelm Treue, 'Adam Smith in Deutschland. Zum Problem des "politischen Professors" zwischen 1776 und 1810', in *Deutschland und Europa*.

[3] See Frances Acomb, *Anglophobia in France, 1763–1789* (Durham, N.C., 1950). Many of the French arguments for and against English practices and 'national character' recurred in German writings later on.

exaggerated admiration for England above any other land requires some explanation.

A large branch in late eighteenth-century German Anglomania sprang from literary roots. After the mid-eighteenth century the influence of English culture in Germany was probably more important than French, if only because German literature, in its search for independent forms, tried to shake off the grip of French models. The experimental and self-consciously anti-French movement of *Sturm und Drang* (Storm and Stress) discovered Milton, Shakespeare, 'Ossian', and Shaftesbury. Other authors imitated the English poets of the eighteenth century and London's literary weeklies.

Increasing wealth and ease of travel, closer trade connections, and mutual political interests made travel to England more common for Germans than ever before, as the swelling of travel literature in Germany after 1750 attests.[1] The strength of Anglomania in Germany may well have derived from the exuberance of recent discovery.

The content of that discovery was as much determined by what German travelers wanted to see as what they actually saw. As Ralf Dahrendorf has pointed out, '...travel does not modify people's opinions very significantly; it merely provides them with words to express what otherwise might remain not only unsaid, but also unthought. Travel provides arguments'.[2] Undoubtedly political arguments supplied one of the main reasons for curiosity about England: Germans could discuss and study English political institutions freely, whereas they were blocked from thinking or experimenting politically at home. Even this kind of political theorizing based on foreign models was largely limited to 'university towns, imperial cities, or state capitals in the domains of the more tolerant of absolutist rulers'.[3] Germans made voyages of body and mind to sharpen their political understanding on foreign, and particularly English models.

If one moves from generalization to the narrower field of historical writing during this period, one finds a similar pattern. History was just becoming a separate discipline at the end of the eighteenth century, and its association with moral philosophy, classical philology, and

[1] Robert Elsasser, *Über die politischen Bildungsreisen der Deutschen nach England* (Heidelberg, 1917), *passim*.

[2] Ralf Dahrendorf, *Society and Democracy in Germany* (Garden City, New York, 1967), p. ix.

[3] Frederick M. Barnard, *Herder's Social and Political Thought* (Oxford, 1965), p. 6.

theology lingered on. It is much harder to say who was a historian in this period than later on, since specialization in one discipline was uncongenial to eighteenth-century intellectual life. It is also hard to find systematic discussion of England, for the age preferred universal histories based on an encyclopedic knowledge of secondary sources rather than specialized immersion in a narrower range of primary documents. In its infancy critical history stumbled often on the overgrown paths of legend, so that myths the Germans had picked up from English and French historians often persisted unchallenged.

Both the emergence of a distinct historical science with its own method and subject matter and the systematic introduction of England as a political model owe much to one institution. The channels through which English influences moved are still imperfectly charted, but one may certainly identify the University of Göttingen as the principal agency for impulses entering German intellectual life from England in the later eighteenth century.[1] What Hamburg was to British commerce and Hanover to British foreign policy, Göttingen was to British political ideas and historical method – a gateway to Germany. Göttingen, significantly enough, was also the seat of the first academic historical school.[2]

Göttingen was a new university, founded in 1737 and unencumbered by the pious traditionalism and corruption which paralyzed many North German universities. The fact that the Elector of Hanover was also the King of Great Britain and Ireland did not automatically mean that British liberties predominated; but it did mean that a strong landed aristocracy, only loosely controlled by an absentee ruler, could develop its interests much as it wished. Because the Hanoverian nobility played an active role in matters of state, '...the upper classes sought to obtain political knowledge on the English pattern by study and travel instead of pursuing a military education'.[3] The university met this desire by developing political and legal studies. It also developed philology and the classics, essential to a gentlemanly education, and these disciplines later became fused with political and legal studies

[1] See Goetz von Selle, *Die Georg-August-Universität zu Göttingen 1737–1937* (Göttingen, 1937), p. 183ff.

[2] Elsasser, *Bildungsreisen*, p. 1ff.; also Fritz Stern, *Varieties of History* (New York, 1956), p. 17; and Herbert Butterfield, *Man on His Past* (Cambridge, 1955), p. 39ff.

[3] Friederike Fürst, *August Ludwig von Schlözer, ein deutscher Aufklärer im 18. Jahrhundert* [*Heidelberger Abhandlungen zur mittleren und neueren Geschichte*, vol. 56] (Heidelberg, 1928), p. 11.

into the new school of academic history. Not only did the Göttingen professors enjoy considerably more freedom of expression than those at other German institutions; the official tendency to guard against the doctrines of monarchical absolutism and to hold up for admiration a political system based on aristocratic rights nudged the professorate into a positive judgment about the English constitution.

Göttingen quickly achieved a superior international reputation, which assured it a steady stream of talented teachers and students from all over Protestant Germany. Most of the leading eighteenth-century historians studied or taught there. Considering the generally pro-English bias of the institution, it is not surprising that so many of its alumni and professors were Anglophiles. The degree to which they idealized England, and particularly English constitutional and economic conditions, varied, but Anglophobe graduates and teachers from Göttingen were rare. The idealization of England was not, however, as much a mania at Göttingen in the last two decades of the century as detractors indicated. The older scholars there, while portraying England in flattering colors, by no means dwelt upon it to the exclusion of other nations. Furthermore, the older the scholar, the cooler was the tone of praise for England.

A few examples may suffice to indicate the tenor of historical writing about England in the late eighteenth century. Justus Möser, August Ludwig von Schlözer, Johann Wilhelm von Archenholtz, and Johannes von Müller[1] all wrote about England before 1789 and had all arrived at middle or advanced age by the outbreak of the French Revolution. All (except Archenholtz) were famous historians; Möser and Schlözer were Göttingen alumni, and Schlözer taught most of his life at Göttingen. Müller, a Swiss by origin, had his own reasons for preferring English liberty to the sort of regimentation which the Swiss observed and feared in neighboring France. Archenholtz, a Prussian officer turned traveler and publicist, had spent ten years in England and popularized recent British history.

If one word could summarize what these historians most admired in

[1] Justus Möser (1720–94) was a high official of the Bishopric of Osnabrück, one of the earliest German patriotic writers, and a critic of the French Enlightenment. August Ludwig von Schlözer (1735–1809) was a professor at Göttingen and an early authority on Russia. Johann Wilhelm von Archenholtz (1743–1812) was a Prussian officer who later became a leading North German publicist and popular historian. Johannes von Müller (1752–1809) was the leading writer of patriotic Swiss history in the eighteenth century. For further information, see Biographical Appendix.

English history, it is 'freedom'. Englishmen seemed to enjoy more political and personal civic liberty than any other Europeans. German historians seemed to regard the English as a nobler species because they had always fought for their rights. The historians, brushing aside the counterargument that English government came close to anarchy, were content to be impressed and misled by Montesquieu. The English constitution seemed to incorporate classical principles of harmony and balance in government at a time when precisely those principles were being struck down by princely absolutism in the German states. Before 1789, German thinkers were usually content to stop short of discussing institutions in greater detail than Montesquieu. Like Schiller, they bathed in the refreshing but harmless springs of *Freiheitspathos* (enthusiasm for freedom). It sufficed to know that the English were the freest people on earth. 'Before the outbreak of the French Revolution, no discussion of freedom got beyond theory or poetry...'[1]

The typical description of English political institutions in the pre-1789 period can be found in the writings of Schlözer, the irascible scholar-adventurer who opened up the vast field of Russian history to Europe. His broad range encompassed lectures and books on history, politics, statistics, trade, and exploration, and his remarks on England played a relatively small role in his works. After lecturing at length on the various forms of government, including mixed forms, he completed his lecture series on constitutions with a Montesquieuan ideal type. 'This ideal of a supremely fortunate form of government', he said, 'is of course more than just an ideal: England really has it, and Rome had it in its first epoch, although only partly.' On the other hand, Schlözer's partisanship fell short of advocating the adoption of such a constitution: 'accident, directed by good sense, favored by conjuncture', not 'philosophy' had brought it about.[2] Schlözer implied that luck and history, rather than human will, shaped constitutions. As a man in the Enlightenment tradition, Schlözer stressed freedom of the press (he was the editor of the enormously popular journal *Staatsanzeigen*), education, and the devotion of the monarch to the well-being of the people, but not radical copying of other nations. The power of the British press and the person of George III, whom

[1] Selle, *Die Georg-August-Universität*, p. 201.

[2] August Ludwig von Schlözer, *Allgemeines Staatsrecht und Staatsverfassungslehre* (Göttingen, 1793), p. 155. This book, although published after 1789, represents the thoughts and lectures of decades before.

Schlözer ranked with Frederick the Great and Joseph II as enlightened rulers, thus elicited favorable judgments from him.

Other scholars could agree that Britain was the freest modern state without citing the ideal balance of monarchic, aristocratic, and democratic functions, without praising freedom of the press, and without being advocates of the Enlightenment. Justus Möser viewed England as the leading representative of aristocratic, racially inherited, and historically developed Germanic freedom. As a consistent foe of contemporary French thought (and of French foreign policy as well), Möser defended 'the historical and concrete integrity of customs and institutions...' against 'the doctrine of sovereignty and the theoretical individualism of the Enlightenment...'[1] Like Montesquieu he opposed the innovating, anti-traditional, and socially leveling tendencies of enlightened despotism and preferred the peculiar common-law liberties supposedly passed down through Germanic tribal life to the present.[2] Möser hoped to preserve these liberties, then under steady attack in Germany, and called on patriotism to defend the heritage. In this sense he could be called 'the discoverer and creator of the German concept of nationality'.[3] England not only offered a splendid example of resistance to French imperialism and French notions of absolute royal sovereignty; she offered living proof that Germanic traditions, developed to their full potential, could be superior to the 'Latin' heritage presumably carried on by France. If only Germany would see this and return to developing her native Germanic traditions, she, too, could achieve greatness. Möser in effect sharpened German national consciousness by pointing to the threat from French culture and the positive example of England. In that way, his concept of German nationality arose 'by English suggestion'.[4] For this early German nationalist historian, admiration for England was bound up with defining German nationality in the first place.

Möser's own life offers ample reasons for his conservatism, his appeal to cleanse German law of imported Roman elements, and his praise of England. He represented the interests of the aristocracy of Osnabrück, a large ecclesiastical principality in northwestern Germany.

[1] Leonard Krieger, *The German Idea of Freedom* (Boston, 1957), p. 79.

[2] Srbik, *Geist und Geschichte*, I, 135.

[3] *Ibid.*

[4] Carlo Antoni, *Der Kampf wider die Vernunft. Zur Entstehungsgeschichte des deutschen Freiheitsgedankens*, tr. by W. Goetz (Stuttgart, 1951), p. 129.

Because the Westphalian settlement had arranged for alternating Catholic and Protestant prince-bishops, the upper classes of Osnabrück had been able to frustrate much of the governmental rationalization which was so common in other German states with settled successions. The ruler during most of Möser's career in Osnabrück's government was Frederick Duke of York, for whom George III acted as regent during his minority. Möser thus had occasion to travel to England on official missions while acting as the middle-man between the Osnabrück aristocracy and the absent English ruler. It was natural for Möser to defend Osnabrück's corporate liberties with arguments drawn from the sophisticated world of English politics. What impressed him about England – and impressed his aristocratic clients in Osnabrück as well – was the security of status, political power, and property enjoyed by the English landowning class. Aristocratic privileges were balanced by duties to the community and limited by 'honor' and tradition. The 'corporations' which governed English as well as Osnabrück politics, Möser thought, had a life of their own, grew organically, and involved men with citizen-rights in the affairs of state. To be sure, Möser did not advocate copying the details of English government;[1] but he did advocate adopting its 'spirit'. The 'organic' principle, which Möser found as much in English law as in Shakespeare or the English garden, should be raised up against the 'mechanical' principle exemplified in French bureaucratic absolutism, Molière, or in the geometric gardens of Versailles. Möser's message came out of season; but his combination of 'organic' and history-minded conservatism, his opposition to the extreme claims for reason in the Enlightenment, his national consciousness, nebulous racism, and Anglophilia proved a potent brew for the generation to be discussed in the next chapter.

Yet another interpretation of English freedom was offered by Johannes von Müller. He stressed the role of the bourgeoisie in the development of England's free institutions, a fact which helps to explain the enormous popularity enjoyed by his precritical historical writings among the German middle class. Growing up in Schaffhausen (Switzerland), like Schlözer the son of a cleric and a restless seeker after

[1] Justus Möser, *Sämmtliche Werke*, 7 vols. (Berlin, 1798–1820), VII, 194. For an evaluation of the prime importance of the 'corporate' English constitution to Möser's conception of history and the state, see Peter Klassen, *Justus Möser* (Frankfurt/Main, 1936), p. 210.

broader horizons, he soon escaped from the narrow intellectual confines of his native town. Unlike Möser he appreciated the Enlightenment: Locke, Hume, and Adam Smith were liberating influences on him. Although he was meant to study theology (like so many German historians!), his work at Göttingen, especially with Schlözer, turned him toward history. He spent the rest of his energetic but unstable life in Germany, serving a series of governments in diverse administrative posts and writing history books. Throughout the vagaries of his career, he held to one consistent theme: the celebration of liberty in a sentimental tone. Müller's dramatic sense and lack of critical keenness resulted in such colorful, enthusiastic, and factually shaky works as his *History of Switzerland*, the basis of Schiller's play *Wilhelm Tell*. His references to England shared the same zeal for liberty and underdeveloped critical sense.

Müller followed Montesquieu and Möser in explaining the origin of English liberty in racial terms, but he liked to single out the little people, the farmers and the townsmen, as the truest bearers of a Germanic spirit of liberty. The drive of the third estate against 'Norman' tyranny, rather than the static balance of Montesquieu, underlay the success of the English constitution. The development of that constitution, in Müller's accounts, was nothing less than the story of liberty in Europe from 1215 to 1688. The baronial revolts ending in such concessions as the Magna Charta, he believed, constituted the 'restoration of Anglo-Saxon freedom' and guaranteed not just aristocratic privileges but the liberty of all men.[1]

Whoever blocked the unfolding of this Germanic liberty received Müller's scorn. He described Henry VIII, for example, as the greatest tyrant of his age. The 'indwelling spirit of liberty' in the English people, he explained, had temporarily succumbed in the Wars of the Roses, and thus public opinion lay helpless before Henry. Those aspects of Henry's reign which Müller could not disapprove – notably the English Reformation – were ascribed to the energy and genius of the people alone, not to the monarch.[2] Elizabeth, on the other hand, escaped censure: 'The Queen could do anything she wished, because she wanted only what was fitting for the spirit of the times.'[3] A good

[1] Johannes von Müller, *Vierundzwanzig Bücher allgemeiner Geschichten, besonders der europäischen Menschheit*, new ed., 3 vols. (Tübingen, 1810), II, 214, 291. This major work originated in a lecture series about 1780 but was published posthumously.

[2] *Ibid.*, III, 57, 91.

[3] *Ibid.*, p. 91.

ruler, Müller believed, was one who had the confidence of the people.

Müller further reflected bourgeois opinion by passing over the turbulent events of seventeenth-century England, which he interpreted more as religious than as constitutional issues. The usefulness of revolution to gain rights had not yet dawned on German middle-class thinkers. What did fascinate them, however, was English trade, naval, and foreign policies. The policy of Britain and many German states had long agreed on resisting French power in Europe. In the last great European war before the revolution, most of North Germany had joined Britain in resisting the Bourbon–Habsburg alliance of the Seven Years' War. Out of this long struggle emerged a consciousness of German–English *Waffenbrüderschaft* (brotherhood in arms) later deepened in the coalitions against the French Revolution. Neither German sympathy for the American Revolution nor occasional British naval abuses of neutrality could completely efface this feeling of comradeship with England.

Müller, like most other German scholars, approved the British commercial empire, and he filled his volumes with its trade statistics. He did not question British sea power at all, believing it necessary to the balance of power and, therewith, the peace of Europe. There was no mention of British *Handelspolitik* (trade policy) and no accusation of the ruthless exploitation of naval power to gain commercial supremacy.[1] At worst Müller warned that *Handelsgeist* (commercial spirit) *might* overwhelm the free English spirit someday, and that British foreign policy had sometimes been inconsiderate of the needs of other peoples.[2]

Möser, Schlözer, and Müller treated England well, but usually in passing and not without a tone of reserve. A more dedicated writer of Anglophile literature, an adventurer who virtually made a living from praise and description of Britain, was Johann Wilhelm von Archenholtz. Although his noble birth and formal training channeled him into the Prussian officer corps, an injury during the Seven Years' War and his gambling debts forced Archenholtz to retire. He took up traveling and, after protracted stays in Italy and England, published

[1] *Ibid.*, p. 500.

[2] *Ibid.*, p. 505. On this page may be found the only sharply negative remarks about England in the entire work; they are vague and unclearly expressed, and may have been added to the 1810 edition as a concession to Napoleonic censorship.

a highly successful description of both countries.[1] The success of this enterprise encouraged Archenholtz to continue his new literary career: among other things he wrote a history of the Seven Years' War and founded a periodical devoted to England, *Annalen der brittischen Geschichte*. Drawing on Montesquieu, Voltaire, and his own observations, Archenholtz described England as the freest country in the world, where the liberty of the individual knew no bounds but the just laws of the land. Although a nobleman, Archenholtz was also a freemason: he praised the democratic traits which gave merit such a high place in society, respected trade and the useful arts, and tempered royal prerogative and aristocratic privilege. All complaints about British vices and evils, he thought, were the children of continental envy. And, like almost all German authors, he praised the freedom of expression which so invigorated English letters and political life.[2]

The striking similarity between the otherwise diverse writings of Möser, Schlözer, Müller, Archenholtz, and indeed of most German commentators on England before 1789, lay in their acceptance of the flattering views which the English held of themselves. Observations were so uncritical that England virtually meant all things to all men. The English example could be used to support arguments for noble privilege or democratic rewards to talent, for agrarians or commercial men, for improving the position of the crown or for surrounding it with checks. The paths were many, but they converged on the English conception of freedom from arbitrariness, abuse, and excessive prying by royal officials. Everyone from Möser's Osnabrück landowners to Archenholtz's Hamburg merchants echoed the cry of freedom from the irrational abuses of the *ancien régime*. England, which had done much to shape the philosophy and political thought of the Enlightenment in its own image, reaped the rewards of its spread over Europe. And even as the first stirrings of hostility to the Enlightenment could be felt in the writings of Möser, as the sanctity of each nation's idiosyncrasies was being preached by Herder, England did not suffer: the threat to German *Eigenart* (individuality) came not from 'blood-related'

[1] Johann Wilhelm von Archenholtz, *England und Italien*, 2 vols. in 3 (Leipzig, 1785). I have used a later English edition, *A Picture of England* (Dublin, 1791) for quotations in this work. Archenholtz's book enjoyed enormous popularity, as the numerous pirated editions and translations of the book show.

[2] See *A Picture of England* for comments on English liberty (pp. 1–20), royal prerogative (20ff.), democratic temper and hatred of hypocrisy (24f.), justified national pride (32f.), moral character (35), religious toleration (101), and commercial greatness (124).

England, but from the 'Latin' colossus across the Rhine. For the groping nationalism of Möser and his younger admirers, England offered a way of combining political conservatism with the potentially revolutionary idea of a unified national culture. The English experience showed them that such a culture could be reconciled with the 'particularism of socially and juridically closed corporations' based on ancient Germanic liberties.[1] When the French Revolution tried to consolidate the nation at the expense of historical corporate rights, it made the English example – as the Germans interpreted it – a more controversial issue.

[1] Antoni, *Kampf wider die Vernunft*, p. 129.

PART II

THE GERMAN VIEW OF ENGLAND IN THE REVOLUTIONARY AND NAPOLEONIC PERIODS

CHAPTER 3

THE CHALLENGE OF THE FRENCH REVOLUTION

The revolutionary events which began in Paris in May of 1789 touched German thought long before French armies revolutionized German reality. 'Perhaps no event provoked such unanimity as the French Revolution,' Droz has written of the German reaction.

> Even down to certain princely courts people passionately followed the revolution's triumphant march... The aristocracy remained favorable, since they believed what was happening in France was the bridling of absolutism... As for the German intelligentsia, it saw in the first measures taken by the constituent assembly the realization of everything which an age of light had counseled and prepared, the consequence and the crowning of the humanitarian work of the century.[1]

The high Prussian bureaucrats who dined regularly together in the Berlin *Mittwochgesellschaft* (Wednesday Society) agreed that the French were merely applying the best traditions of Frederick the Great to the ills of France. The great German Enlightenment revues, such as Schlözer's *Staatsanzeigen* (with its then enormous circulation of over 4,000), Nicolai's *Allgemeine Deutsche Bibliothek*, Biester's *Berlinsche Monatsschrift*, and several others were filled with news and commentary on French events. Many German intellectuals actually moved to Paris in order to witness the great upheaval taking place there. Archenholtz, for example, moved his entire family in the summer of 1791. So great was the interest in the revolution at home that he decided to found a new revue in Berlin, *Minerva*, devoted chiefly to reportage on the revolution. It was an immediate success. Even Friedrich von Gentz, later a tireless advocate of reaction, began his literary career with a modest defense of the revolutionaries.[2] For the

[1] Jacques Droz, *L'Allemagne et la Révolution Française* (Paris, 1949), p. 42.
[2] Paul Sweet, *Friedrich von Gentz, Defender of the Old Order* (Madison, 1941), p. 17.

moment France, rather than England, dominated German political thought.

As in their admiration for England, the Germans did not fully understand the French events which they witnessed. Furthermore, only a scattered handful made the leap from enthusiasm for the French revolution to demands for a similar radical and popular movement in Germany. After the first sweet taste of freedom from royal tyranny, symbolized by the fall of the Bastille, German enthusiasm for the revolution itself began to wane, first among the aristocrats, who noted the French abolition of feudal privileges, later among the moderates (including Archenholtz), who deplored the fall of the Feuillants. Few German observers would unhesitantly defend any constitution more radical than that of 1791. With the appearance of Burke's *Reflections* in Germany, unanimity about the revolution had ceased. In the 1790s publicists at opposite extremes called for united opposition to the further course of the revolution or for a Franco-Prussian alliance against England to secure peace and freedom in Europe.[1] And finally, when England and France went to war in 1793, German feelings about the revolution and its works could no longer be separated from their feelings about England's attempt to curb them.

The revolution, and later the Napoleonic invasion, had a decided impact on German judgments of England in both quantitative and qualitative ways. The amount of written discussion increased markedly due to England's moral and financial leadership of the struggle against the French Revolution. The neutralization of most of North Germany between the signing of the Treaty of Basel (1795) and the Franco-Prussian war of 1806 meant that Germans could travel freely to England to gratify their heightened curiosity.

The qualitative changes were even greater. Either as a result of the French Revolution or of older intellectual currents now swollen and channeled by the confrontation with the revolution, German intellectuals accelerated the growth of a system of values capable of offering an alternative to the 'western' Enlightenment. Given the middle-class origins and support of the Enlightenment, it is not surprising that ideas of practical reforms directed at the social and political institutions of Europe formed an integral part of 'enlightened' thinking. When the

[1] Droz, *L'Allemagne et la Révolution*, pp. 85–93. The idea of an alliance came from the publicist Andreas Riem, one of Germany's most vocal Anglophobes.

revolutionary governments of France attempted to implement some of these ideas, however, they were driven to use increasingly forceful methods, thereby demonstrating the toughness of traditional practices, the self-defeating inhumanity of violent change, and, in the eyes of many, the impracticality of the revolution's principles. French invasion and Napoleonic dictatorship in Germany further discredited not only France, but also the natural law, rationalism, and cosmopolitanism of the 'foreign' Enlightenment.

Out of this intellectual ferment arose various tendencies of thought identified by later generations of scholars as romanticism, nationalism, historicism, and conservatism. All these labels cover a variety of thinkers, so there is always an objectionable imprecision in using them. Also, the major German thinkers with whom these tendencies are associated wrote even before the revolution, so one must not insist on a catastrophic causation of these intellectual currents.[1] Yet to explain the increasing interest of the German public in the writings of Möser, Herder and the nationalist, romantic poets, academic historians, and Edmund Burke, one must turn to the revolution and its assault on the German old regime for part of the explanation. Did these changes in the viewpoint of many Germans tend to alter the quality of sentiment about England?

A further effect of the revolution and the keen curiosity it aroused in Germany was an increase in the sophistication of German writers in political affairs. Germans have usually been depicted by western parodists and serious historians alike as 'unpolitical', a charge borne out at first glance by their tenuous and blurred understanding of the English governmental system they professed to admire. The charge is a bit unfair, since it implies acceptance of western political systems as the inevitable goal of all European societies. The real question, then, is not whether the Germans became more 'political' as a result of watching the overthrow of the old regime, but to what degree they expressed their political thoughts and expectations in western terms. German political scientists, legal scholars, historians, and publicists had to come to grips with the revolution. The great historians of the

[1] As Arthur Lovejoy has pointed out in his *Essays in the History of Ideas* (New York, 1960), p. 235f. *et passim*, there are many romanticisms, some of them predating the revolution. Historicism must be dated at least as early as Vico, and conservatism, as the late Klaus Epstein has shown in *The Genesis of German Conservatism* (Princeton, 1966), also became an articulate ideology before 1789. See also Fritz Valjavec, *Die Entstehung der politischen Strömungen in Deutschland, 1770–1815* (Munich, 1951), pp. 39ff., 302ff.

Enlightenment could no longer satisfy the younger generation's demand for profounder analysis of political systems. Schlözer, for example, had thought it sufficient to classify governments by the number of men who exercised power, somewhat as Linnaeus classified plants.[1] The generation of students who had stampeded into his lecture hall had passed by 1790. The next generation, seeking more profundity, stampeded out again. One of these students, later a famous historian in his own right, testified equally to the advance of student sophistication and the pique of the disillusioned when he charged that all of Schlözer's famous expertise on the United States came out of one English book.[2] The political knowledge which pleased the pre-revolutionary students no longer sufficed.

The difference in the experience of generations during the years of French revolution and Napoleonic invasion was acute: while the writers of the Enlightenment continued to think and write in the abstract, lucid, and passionless fashion they had always employed, younger authors seemed more engaged and more willing to surrender clarity for the sake of trying out new ideas. New combinations of content and style appeared among historical works. In harmony with the new-found respectability of the irrational encouraged by romantic *belles lettres*, many historians and political thinkers began to dispute the underlying tenet of both the Enlightenment and the French Revolution – that only the rational is real.

All these mental changes accompanying the German confrontation with the French Revolution and the collapse of the *Reich* raised grave doubts about the conception of England formed up to then by German historical thinkers. Did England still have a right to be called the freest European state, once the French Constitution of 1791 and the Rights of Man had been proclaimed? Could one admire an England which suspended the most cherished rights of Englishmen (such as habeas corpus) in the struggle against the Rights of Man? Could a naval power that molested neutral shipping and blockaded the continent under the Orders in Council be tolerated or encouraged? Such questions arose even among the admirers of England in the two decades on either side of 1800. On the other hand, men harking back to Möser's ideas pondered on the strength of a country with deeply-rooted and

[1] Schlözer was actually deeply impressed by the Linnaean system when he taught and studied at the University of Uppsala. See Fürst, *August Ludwig von Schlözer*, p. 23.

[2] Friedrich von Raumer, *Lebenserinnerungen und Briefwechsel* (Leipzig, 1861), p. 39.

loyally defended traditions, no matter how eccentric, uncategorized, and irrational they might be. Had not the French Constitution of 1791 failed to take root? Was it not, after all, the 'good old laws' and unequal – but familiar – rights which Germans craved? Could these not be restored by jumping backwards over the intervening period of enlightened absolutism and establishing continuity with ancient customs passed down from the Germanic tribes? Was there not a meaningfulness in the past, in history, which surpassed frail human understanding? Were not the English to be encouraged and emulated in their attempts to contain the advance of French rationalism? These questions aroused increasingly passionate debate as the initial enthusiasm for the French Revolution yielded to disillusionment with the Terror and the Napoleonic revolution from above on German soil itself. And finally, as in all conflicts, there were many who remained indifferent or aloof, men like Schiller who, disillusioned by both French and English behavior, greeted the new century in 1800 with the lament, 'Two powerful nations wrestle / For the sole possession of the world, / To swallow all countries' liberty / They brandish the trident and the thunderbolt.'[1]

Probably the most striking example of the eroding effect of the revolution on German Anglophilia came from Archenholtz. As we have seen, Archenholtz had been in the vanguard of popularizers of English affairs in the 1780s. In the nineties, however, his fascination with revolutionary France brought about a total revision of his ideas on England. By 1798 he claimed that the British had completely changed their national character, had lost all understanding of freedom, and had fallen into immoral slavery.[2] Archenholtz's exasperation with England soon led him to cease publication of his *Annalen*. Although he ultimately despaired of French extremism, he never recovered his previous love of Britain.

Archenholtz's bitterness reflected to some extent the views of his adopted city, Hamburg, which suffered economically from the Anglo-French wars and blamed most of the suffering on England. But elsewhere in the German states, particularly in the larger ones which tried to resist the challenge from France, political events in the first decade

[1] Friedrich Schiller, *Sämmtliche Werke*, ed. by Gerhard Fricke and Herbert Göpfert, 5 vols. (Munich, 1958–62), I, 459.

[2] See Friedrich Ruof, *Johann Wilhelm von Archenholtz* [*Historische Studien*, No. 131] (Berlin, 1915), pp. 30, 95, *et passim*.

of the nineteenth century produced a different view of England. A crisis comparable to that faced by Florentine humanists in the early fifteenth century[1] gradually gripped some parts of the German intelligentsia. It would be only a small exaggeration to say that many of the German historians sought in the virtues of England what the Florentines had sought in ancient Rome. The civic virtue of the Romans and the English appeared comparable to such Prussian officials as Barthold Georg Niebuhr and Ludwig von Vincke.[2] Furthermore, England served not only as a source of ideas for the creation of civic virtue but also as a direct defender of the old order on the international level. The concept of a hereditary brotherhood in arms, inherited from the wars of the eighteenth century, could be invoked as well.

Generally the reaction of German historians to all these disturbing questions about England was strongly in her favor. Men like Archenholtz, who persisted in denigrating England even after they had become disillusioned with the outcome of the French Revolution, were relatively rare. This is not to say that pro-French elements vanished from the German world of letters; as long as French power determined the fate of at least the western part of the former German Empire, many publicists fell in line with French attitudes toward the British arch-enemy or maintained a superior indifference to the Franco-British struggle. Nor had the discipline of history, whether academic or amateur, achieved the dominant position it was later to attain in German intellectual life. In short, to study what historians wrote about England at this time is to concentrate on a body of opinion which was probably less universally accepted than later in the century or during the earlier period when the writings of historians just happened to coincide with the prevailing Anglomania. What is important about the historians' views at this time lies not necessarily in their representativeness, which can be disputed, but in their significance for the future. For out of the Anglo-French struggle of these years grew the philosophical, political, and ideological connection between Anglophilia and historicism that was to last for many decades into the nineteenth century.

[1] Hans Baron, *The Crisis of the Early Renaissance*, 2nd edn. (Princeton, 1966) brilliantly discussed the impact of political insecurity on literary production in Florentine society.

[2] George P. Gooch, *History and Historians*, p. 14. Barthold Georg Niebuhr (1776–1831) began as a Danish and Prussian civil servant but ended his career as a history professor at Bonn, having made important contributions to the new historical method and the history of Rome. Ludwig von Vincke (1774–1844) was a Westphalian aristocrat and influential Prussian civil servant. (See Biographical Appendix.)

This alliance can be explained partly from the circumstances in which the major historians writing about England found themselves. A majority of these men had studied at Göttingen, which, as ever, remained a locus of English studies and pro-English sentiment. Several of them were great amateurs who pursued history as a sideline to their activity as government officials. Without exception they came from the professional or clerical middle class or the petty nobility, and as teachers and administrators they continued to serve the state in some capacity: they were not a 'free-floating intelligentsia' totally independent of the favor of patrons. They were not likely to advocate the dissolution or overthrow of the states in which they worked; on the contrary, they bent most of their scholarly efforts in support of a healthy respect for historically-developed human institutions. In some cases – though not all – their motives for admiring England were dictated largely by the conjunction of international relations, that is, by the struggle against Bonaparte. No European country at the time offered such clear proof of the viability and continuity of historically-developed community life as England.

Within this general area of consensus, however, lay a variety of differing interpretations. For most German historians writing before 1815, freedom still represented the foremost characteristic of England. Since a French form of liberty had arisen, however, a clearer and more sharply political definition of liberty emerged from the comparison. Spittler, Gentz,[1] Niebuhr, and Vincke all agreed that England remained the leading model of a free state. Considerable variety characterized their reasoning on how such freedom could exist; the men closest in temper to the middle class, e.g. Spittler, explained English liberty as the child of Parliament and bourgeois virtue; at the other end of the spectrum, Gentz explained liberty as the product of a wise aristocratic conservatism and continuity.

I

Before the French Revolution had long been under way, Ludwig Timotheus von Spittler published his *Entwurf der Geschichte der*

[1] Ludwig Timotheus von Spittler (1752–1810) taught philosophy and history in his native Württemberg and in Göttingen before assuming high office in the Württemberg civil service. Friedrich von Gentz (1764–1832) became a leading Berlin publicist and later, after campaigning with his pen against the French Revolution and Napoleon, a leading adviser to Prince Metternich. (See Biographical Appendix.)

europäischen Staaten (1793). As one might expect from a Göttingen professor, he combined the cool, 'philosophical' tone of the Enlightenment with a favorable picture of Britain. But one can also note from his work a greater intensity of interest in England. In volume alone, the passages dealing with England outweigh by a full third those devoted to any other nation. Admittedly Spittler treated the medieval period with inexcusable haste, and he devoted a third of his second edition (1809) to a qualified defense of British policy since 1793. Despite these biases, though, the book contained the most judicious and balanced presentation of British history produced in Germany in the late eighteenth century. Spittler's thoroughness and his considerable attention to England marked significant changes compared to the older Schlözer, whom Spittler displaced in popularity at Göttingen.

In spite of the noble 'von' in his name, Spittler came from a clergyman's family of the small-town middle class of Württemberg. He, too, took the well-beaten path followed by so many German historians in the founding years of academic history: despite modest means he got academic training by studying theology; that led via philosophy and philology into history. Spittler studied at the strict Tübingen *Stift*, a college for impecunious would-be pastors which turned out such great alumni as Hegel, Hölderlin, and Schelling. Ten years before the French Revolution he was appointed *Professor für bürgerliche Geschichte*, a title containing ironic ambiguities. One translation, the one intended by the university, would be 'civic history', and Spittler did specialize in the past of the German states, especially of his native Württemberg and his adopted Hanover. But the term, which can also be translated as 'bourgeois history', well describes Spittler's viewpoint. Even when he gave up teaching to become a high civil servant in Württemberg, the large political role of the towns and the active parliamentary life there gave him no cause to suppress his opinions.

His background helps explain why Spittler placed greater emphasis on institutions than many of his contemporaries and considered the rise of freedom in England to be inseparable from the growth of representative bodies and the middle class. He thus rejected Möser's theory connecting liberty to land ownership. For this reason, Spittler saw the wealth of a supposedly strong middle class and the poverty of the English crown as the main reasons for the flowering of English culture and the rise of Parliament. Spittler had little use for revolution, however: he usually took the side of the king against mass uprisings, but his distaste for revolution sprang more from a love of order than from royalistic prejudice. Even England's suspension of much-needed reforms during the revolutionary wars seemed to him necessary 'in order not to give any room to this age's whim to change things frivolously'.[1] As a representative of the older moderate, middle-class *Aufklärung* (Enlightenment), Spittler maintained throughout the revolutionary period the same cool, dispassionate tone characteristic of the period before 1789. Even when praising British liberty, he shunned 'enthusiasm'.

If one catches flashes in Spittler's works explaining the much-praised English form of liberty as more the fruit of the diligent and peaceful work of bourgeois reason than of bitter revolutionary battles, one can find clear confirmation in the works of two other Göttingen professors. Johann Gottfried Eichhorn and Arnold Hermann Ludwig Heeren,[2] like Spittler, came from Protestant clerical families, studied theology, and then, via philology or philosophy, came to teach history at their alma mater, Göttingen. The major difference lay in Heeren's place of origin: unlike the Württembergers Spittler and Eichhorn, he came from Bremen, a town with important overseas trading connections and hence conscious of commercial and naval matters. Under the influence of Montesquieu (of whom he was the foremost German disciple) and Adam Smith, Heeren inaugurated a sociological and economic approach to history. Eichhorn, on the other hand, specialized more in diplomatic history. Significantly, neither of these men, already mature at the time of the French Revolution and generally sympathetic to the English cause, drew attention to the English revolutions of the seventeenth century. Instead, they almost ignored the inner structure of English domestic institutions and the ideology of English liberty to concentrate on defending the maritime and diplomatic role of England against French charges of naval despotism.

To be sure, both men regarded the English constitution *since* 1689 as perfect and thought England had been more free than any other nation even before then; but neither was especially interested in the

[1] Ludwig Timotheus von Spittler, *Entwurf der Geschichte der europäischen Staaten*, 2nd edn., 2 vols. (Göttingen, 1809), I, 454.

[2] Johann Gottfried Eichhorn (1752–1827) was a Göttingen professor of philosophy who lectured on history as well. Arnold Hermann Ludwig Heeren (1760–1842) taught philosophy, then history at Göttingen. (See Biographical Appendix.)

domestic political side of British life. Eichhorn, for example, simply omitted any discussion of the events of 1640–60 in his voluminous *Weltgeschichte* (1814). Heeren, who at least touched on the history of Parliament before 1688, found it too stormy for precise discussion: the dispute between Parliament and the Stuarts, for example, appeared as a mere religious quarrel among wild and unenlightened fanatics similar to the Mountain of the French Revolution.[1] Nor did they see in parliamentary politicking any special guarantee of liberty: they, like many other Germans (and some Englishmen!), found fault with the alternation of parliamentary groups in power. Heeren even called the ministers' constant search for a majority 'the seed of decay', and both thought sudden changes in government made Britain a less than trustworthy ally.[2]

What gave England her fame as the foremost land of liberty, both men agreed, was her attempt to guarantee Europe's freedom as diligently as her own. Heeren qualified this belief somewhat, for he thought England before 1689 was too involved in religious squabbles and insular matters to play a major role on the continent. Only with the advent of the 'liberator of Europe', William III, had England begun to exercise a 'beneficial influence' on world politics.[3] Heeren praised every English wartime leader of the eighteenth century. The merits of English foreign policy exceeded the few faults such as the subsidy system and misuse of maritime law in wartime.[4] Eichhorn, on the other hand, saw not even these minor flaws. Eichhorn believed that England was fighting and had always fought only for the balance of power and the preservation of Europe from universal monarchy; Heeren, on the other hand, saw desire for colonial gains as the motive of English foreign policy for at least the previous century, though the side results had benefited Europe. Eichhorn attributed the British rise at sea to the combined greed, aggression, and ineptitude of the other naval powers. He referred to Britain as 'a cliff in the sea, proud Albion', which alone could 'threaten [France] from the other side and hold it back by its greater natural moral power'.[5] Heeren's greater sobriety about *all* English history did not make him any less partisan

[1] Arnold Hermann Ludwig Heeren, *Handbuch der Geschichte des europäischen Staatensystems* (Göttingen, 1809), p. 167ff.

[2] *Ibid.*, p. 241f. Johann Gottfried Eichhorn, *Geschichte der letzten drei Jahrhunderte*, 6 vols. (Göttingen, 1804), II, 240.

[3] Heeren, *Handbuch*, pp. 141, 221, 387.

[4] *Ibid.*, pp. 409, 469.

[5] Eichhorn, *Drei Jahrhunderte*, II, 305.

for the immediate English cause, however. If Heeren attempted no apology of English commercial drives, he at least refrained from heaping abuse on them.

Both Eichhorn and Heeren considered trade, shipping, and, consequently, naval power as 'natural' to England, as though it were automatically produced by geography and climate. Eichhorn, ignoring such evidence of English maritime weakness as the dominant position of the medieval Hansa, found evidence of this 'natural' inclination in the remote middle ages. The many deviations from 'nature' were written off as unenlightened policy. Heeren had the wisdom to place England's rise to great naval power chiefly in the eighteenth century; but he also thought this development natural. Only the anarchy of the later middle ages and the religious squabbles of the seventeenth century, he thought, had impeded the inevitable. Current British trade policy was wise and 'reasonable', Heeren believed, and deserved to be emulated by all other nations.[1]

II

Spittler, Eichhorn, and Heeren clung with somewhat increased tenacity to older Anglophile formulae in the face of new controversies brought up by the French Revolution. This reaction was fairly typical of the older generation of historians, especially in Göttingen. But younger writers, who had grown up in the turbulent world of changing intellectual values, became more passionate and unqualified in defense of England. For some of them, Burke became not only a mentor in political theory but, by association, an interpreter of British history as well. When Friedrich von Gentz translated Burke's *Reflections* into German, the book became an instant literary sensation. Baron vom Stein and his friends August Wilhelm Rehberg and Ernst Brandes, all Göttingen alumni,[2] spread the new gospel of slow 'organic' change as the answer to sweeping French 'mechanical' reforms. They employed Burke's philosophical conservatism and the English unwritten constitution as their most persuasive auxiliaries.[3] Burke's *Reflections* confirmed and strengthened the conservative yet patriotic message they had absorbed

[1] Heeren, *Handbuch*, p. 328.

[2] Brandes, incidentally, was Curator of Göttingen for a time.

[3] See von Selle, *Die Georg-August-Universität*, p. 189ff., and Epstein, *The Genesis of German Conservatism*, p. 567ff.

from Möser. Many other men made famous by their dual struggle against Napoleon and for a new Germany followed Stein's example of studying England. All shared in the new patriotism generated by the shame of the German states' collapse beneath the onslaught of France. Aside from Vincke, Niebuhr, and Gentz, whom we shall discuss below, one must mention the Prussian officials Hardenberg, von Schön, and Wilhelm von Humboldt. The pattern followed by these men in acquiring a deep interest in Britain was essentially similar. After an initially tolerant attitude toward the French Revolution, they became increasingly disenchanted in the 1790s. Study of English institutions and, above all, of Burke was augmented in most cases by a trip to England during the eleven years of North German neutrality (1795–1806). All gained a positive impression of Great Britain; many returned excited and deeply impressed by what they had seen; a few, like Gentz and Niebuhr, even made propaganda for England in the press and among continental diplomats. This was not always politically wise, especially since censorship made publication of avowedly pro-English works somewhat hazardous, especially in Prussia. After the final conquest of North Germany by Napoleon in 1806 and even during the preceding period of neutrality, German governments often suppressed pro-English statements lest the French be offended. Prudent men sometimes thought it best not to publish laudatory remarks about England; Vincke's *Darstellung der inneren Verwaltung Grossbrittaniens*, for example, was written in 1807 but could appear in print only in 1815.

Of all the German propagandists for England between 1789 and 1815, Friedrich von Gentz started earliest (with the translation of Burke in 1793) and remained the most dedicated. Since he lived by his pen, he eventually accepted money from the British government for his services.[1] The son of a well-connected Prussian civil servant, young Gentz overcame the tedium of his own bureaucratic career in Berlin (1785–1802) by gracing the pages of local journals with brilliant articles and the salons of Berlin society with his wit and tact. He evidently enjoyed social climbing and was eventually rewarded with a patent of nobility. After the *succès d'estime* of his Burke translation,

[1] Although Gentz accepted British grants, his conversion through Burke came before his sustenance on pounds sterling. In this regard he was perhaps less venal and less unprincipled than many other German journalists.

he became one of the leading pioneers of political journalism and popular history in the Berlin of the 1790s. He ransacked British history for arguments in his often tendentious essays and articles instead of studying it for its own sake. Nevertheless, Gentz's propaganda for England was refined and based on historically sound foundations. In 1802, after falling increasingly from official favor as a result of the Prussian government's anti-British drift, Gentz left Berlin, made a trip to England which impressed him enormously, and entered Austrian service as an anti-Napoleonic propagandist under the influence of his English impressions. While he was in England, high statesmen had both flattered his ego and filled him with their opinions and information during interviews. He had talked with more leading British statesmen than many of the foreign secretaries of the continent. His private letters show that his enthusiasm for what he saw in England in the first decade of the nineteenth century was genuine and articulate.

Barthold Georg Niebuhr pursued a career somewhat similar in its beginning in state service and its end in historical writing and political journalism – except that Niebuhr achieved higher standards as a historian than Gentz. Niebuhr was also the son of a well-to-do (but middle-class) family. His father was an explorer and scholar in Denmark. After studying in Holstein and serving in the Danish Finance Ministry, Niebuhr took a prolonged trip to England (1798–9) which deeply impressed him. He served six more years in the Danish finance service, then joined the Prussian government in 1806 on the invitation of Baron vom Stein. Though offered the Prussian Finance Ministry under Hardenberg in 1810, he left government service and began the lectures at the new University of Berlin which eventually led to his *Roman History* and his reputation as 'the first commanding figure in modern historiography'.[1] His good understanding of things British contributed to Niebuhr's selection as chief Prussian plenipotentiary in subsidy negotiations with England during the Wars of Liberation in 1813. He continued to align himself with Prussian policy thereafter and was rewarded with the Embassy to the Holy See, a delicate post in the light of Protestant Prussia's newly-established rule over the Catholic Rhineland. During his researches into early Roman history and during his later years of writing in Bonn (1823–31), Niebuhr

[1] Gooch, *History and Historians*, p. 14.

claimed to have been helped in understanding Rome by studying the 'new Rome', Great Britain.[1]

In the critical years of Napoleonic sway in Europe, both Niebuhr and Gentz felt compelled to defend England both for her foreign policy and her internal institutions. On questions of British military and diplomatic aims, both present and historical, they were much more vehement than Heeren, Spittler, or Eichhorn. They declared that England traditionally sought only to defend Europe's liberty; French propaganda notwithstanding, she did so with no calculation of commercial profit and even at great cost to herself. Gentz also claimed that England was upholding Europe's freedom by leading the struggle against France and the revolution. Any sacrifices in liberty at home (for example, the suspension of the Habeas Corpus Act) were justified by the great fight for freedom in Europe. In Gentz's opinion, French aggression had started the great series of European revolutionary wars and had kept them going.[2] Gentz and Niebuhr dismissed French charges that Britain opposed the revolution as a pretext to erect a trading and naval monopoly. Niebuhr, in an unprinted *mémoire* of 1806, vehemently denied that Britain was fighting France simply to gain colonial and industrial supremacy in the world; in fact, as a financial expert he thought the British were straining their economy to dangerous extremes in an unselfish attempt to keep Europe free. Justice, claimed Niebuhr, characterized all wars waged by Britain, with the possible exception of the Dutch conflicts of the seventeenth century. 'The prosperity of England is advantageous to the independent powers of the continent,' he wrote, 'and its greatness contains no menace for them... It is quite certain that England has never carried on an unjust war against these powers.'[3] England's policy had always been to resist French tyranny, and even if the protection of English commerce played a role, that same commerce 'pulled the north of Europe out of poverty and barbarism'.[4] Finally, touching colonialism, Niebuhr declared that India and the other colonies responsible for British wealth and power had benefited endlessly from British rule. He saw only anarchy and

[1] *Ibid.*, p. 16.

[2] Friedrich von Gentz, 'Über Ursprung und Charakter des Krieges gegen die französische Revolution', *Ausgewählte Schriften*, ed. by Wilhelm Weick, 5 vols. (Stuttgart and Leipzig, 1836–8), II, 254 *et passim.*

[3] Niebuhr, 'Mémoire sur la guerre entre l'Angleterre et la France', *Nachgelassene Schriften B. G. Niebuhrs nichtphilologischen Inhalts* (Hamburg, 1842), p. 423f.

[4] *Ibid.*, p. 424.

ignorance as the alternatives to wise British domination. Gentz and Niebuhr's defenses of English colonialism, at a time when it raised doubts among the English themselves, underlined the lack of any sense of Anglo–German overseas competition in the historical writing of these and succeeding decades.

What really set apart the younger generation of Anglophiles, represented by Niebuhr and Gentz, from the older branch was not this sort of defense of British foreign policy, however. Much more characteristic was their deeper interest in British domestic institutions. It was here, on the grounds of England's ancient laws and customary (if irrational and non-uniform) social relationships, that they defended England most vociferously against the challenge of the French Revolution. When Gentz wrote his letters from London in 1802, he fell into organicist rhetoric to explain England's superiority: 'harmony is the secret of her greatness'.[1] He meant that 'a certain composure, an orderly progression from one matter to another, an evenness, apportionment, order, and quiet' characterized English life in contrast to the turmoil, uncertainty, and violence on the continent.[2] The order and prosperity resulting from a 'harmonic' national life impressed Gentz more than the personal liberties enjoyed by the English citizen. British freedom, he thought, like all true freedom, confined itself to the limits set by authority and the rule of law. England thus demonstrated that liberty could coexist with order and deference. It was this lesson, rather than constitutional dogma, which Gentz tried to preach. Though the constitution itself was 'an object of justified admiration', Gentz cautioned against copying British laws before 'severely testing to see if one's fatherland is mature enough for a British constitution'.[3]

Niebuhr reached much the same conclusions about English history. He believed that Britain's 'true' freedom, based on respect for law, grew stronger as Napoleon trampled out liberty in the rest of Europe. Dictatorial powers seemed as necessary to wartime Britain as they had been to ancient Rome, and strong monarchy, assuring the rule of law, thus guaranteed true freedom.[4] Like Gentz and the Prussian reformers, Niebuhr tended to bypass the institution of Parliament, to seek the

[1] Friedrich K. Wittichen, ed., *Briefe von und zu Friedrich von Gentz*, 3 vols. (Munich and Berlin, 1909–13), II, 392. Letter dated 22 November 1802.
[2] *Ibid.*, p. 393.
[3] Friedrich von Gentz, 'Über politische Freiheit', *Ausgewählte Schriften*, II, 18.
[4] Niebuhr, 'Die katholische Frage in Irland', *Nachgelassene Schriften*, p. 348 *et passim*.

true pillars of the English state where Möser had sought them – in the landed aristocracy and the 'country squires'. In 1815 he warned against allowing these classes to decline, for, as he wrote in the preface to Vincke's *Darstellung*, aristocratic institutions of local self-government were far more essential to English liberty than the central legislative body. 'Freedom rests disproportionately more upon administration (*Verwaltung*) than on the constitution (*Verfassung*),' he thought.[1]

This distinction between administration and constitution was fundamental in the thinking of the Prussian reformers who followed the lead of Baron vom Stein, and explains why men who were essentially 'reform conservatives'[2] could admire the political structure of a country which had long passed as the liberals' ideal. As conservatives, as men touched with the new respect for the relevance of the past preached by Möser, they sought to reach back over the century and a half of centralization; as reformers, they sought a way to breathe new life into the Prussian state after the disaster at Jena, to give the Prussian populace some reason for wanting to go on being Prussians. For both these reasons they welcomed the idea of English self-government, described for the first time in some detail[3] by Ludwig von Vincke, a Prussian official who fled to England during the Franco–Prussian war in 1806 and returned to impress his views on Stein, Niebuhr, and others. The purpose of introducing the spirit of English self-government into Prussia, as in the form of Stein's *Städteordnung*, or municipal law, was to strengthen a sense of citizenship among the responsible populace by giving them a part in administering their own affairs. Their hope was to spread loyalty to king and country, commonly regarded as an English trait, beyond the circle of royal bureaucrats. Vincke also wished to break down the rigid Prussian class structure by stripping all but the eldest sons of noblemen of their special privileges. For all the liberalizing tenor of these plans, however, the reformers went far back into history, or rather back into a past half historical and half mythical, for their justification. Niebuhr and Vincke, and probably the other Prussian reformers, shared Möser's idea that self-government was essentially

[1] Niebuhr, 'Vorrede zur *Darstellung der inneren Verwaltung Grossbrittaniens*', *Nachgelassene Schriften*, p. 462.

[2] For a discussion of this form of conservatism see Epstein, *The Genesis of German Conservatism*, pp. 7–10.

[3] Ludwig von Vincke, *Darstellung der inneren Verwaltung Grossbrittaniens* [written 1807] (Berlin, 1815).

a Germanic system which had lived on in England after its demise on the continent.[1] A strong, free landed class, checking the ambitions of central government by levying and spending its own taxes, represented the ideal.

III

The revival of such terms as 'Germanic' indicates some interesting coincidences in the German attitude toward England after about 1800 and broader intellectual trends in Germany. It was a period of great intellectual confusion, when medical charlatans and magicians appealed to many well-educated Germans, when Rosicrucianism flourished, and when all sorts of new ideas of a cosmic and organicist type, ranging from Herder's *Volksgeist* (spirit of the people) to Lamarck's 'biology', were being formulated and discussed. Goethe was pondering the development and morphology of plants, trying to understand their development rather than classifying them in the endlessly monotonous descriptions in the fashion of a Linnaeus. The Grimms and other philologists were pursuing investigations of language, which Herder had taught was the highest expression of the *Volksgeist*, and positing the 'Aryan' origins of the European languages. The role of heredity and its exact nature were far from being settled, and the dogma of heritable acquired characteristics seemed to have the upper hand. Under the circumstances it was hard, if not impossible, for intelligent laymen to sort out such questions when thinking of England. Clearly they put a higher value on German kinship with England than would have been warranted by the common origin of the two languages. England came to be spoken of more and more in terms which usually obtain only in blood-related families. Möser's murkily racial viewpoint on England now began to develop into a major factor in evaluating it. The stress of the romantic historians on the middle ages further contributed to a sense of closeness between English and German traditions, which had indeed been closer then than at the end of the eighteenth century. The reason for the revival of the concept of Germanic community at precisely this time of uncertainty and reform may have something to do with the increasing acceptance of Herder's concept of *Volksgeist*. Being true to the *Volksgeist* meant virtually cutting oneself off from certain kinds of political experience which the reformers wished to draw upon. In the

[1] Niebuhr, 'Vorrede', p. 464.

case of English self-government, for example, one could conclusively fall back on medieval German patterns, to corporate *Stände* (estates), free cities, and so forth; but these traditions were hard to update in a realistic way. The most telling argument against them, made by defenders of royal absolutism, was that they were disruptive, almost anarchistic. At this point the English example proved excellent for the reformers on two grounds: it showed that free institutions, especially self-government, did not always make for a weak state, on the contrary; and it represented a continuation of ancient 'Germanic' law which the Germans could safely emulate to some extent without doing violence to their own *Volksgeist*. At the same time, loyalty to the *Volksgeist* could be maintained against the non-Germanic 'French' revolutionary tradition.

The major weakness of the rather romantic, Burkean picture of England drawn by so many German historians during the Napoleonic wars was that it stressed the remote past and the essential continuity of English history into the present. Discontinuities – the Norman invasion, the Wars of the Roses, seventeenth-century turmoil and experimentation – were minimized to make England appear as the living model of slow, organic change-within-continuity. Resistance to the ideas of the French Revolution had brought about a subtle reversal of England's image: from the widely-praised land of freedom in the late eighteenth century, she had become a land of order which, insofar as she served freedom, worked to liberate the nations of Europe from French domination. It was England's foreign policy which now came under discussion when 'liberty' was talked of. (It was thus not accidental that the anti-Napoleonic wars begun in 1813 have usually been called 'wars of liberation' in Germany). Of course English political institutions continued to receive admiration in some quarters, especially after the failure of French constitutionalism; but a subtle shift of interest took place here, too, toward local rather than central organs.

Guido de Ruggiero has pointed out the role which nationalism played in Germany toward the end of the Napoleonic wars as a middle ground linking conservative political theory, which in the writings of Haller and Adam Müller was passing from its pre-theoretical adolescence into a sort of self-confident maturity, and the potentially anarchic individualism of romantic thought. In a broad sense this role existed, but conservatism had no exclusive right to the national idea:

the spectacle of German princes invoking nationalist allegiances in 1813 gave way later to persecution of the extreme nationalist *Deutschtümler* (Germanomanes) as dangerous demagogues espousing a doctrine hostile to the Vienna settlement. Given the general tendency of conservative and romantic historians to admire England, however, one is forced to ask what kind of nationalism it was that could be generous, even over-generous, to another great power. The answer to this puzzle is twofold. First, none of the historians treated in this chapter were nationalists before all else; they did not advocate the unity of the German state and nation with anything like the passion of Fichte. The very minimum of recognition for the nation-state idea granted in the form of the loose Germanic Confederation satisfied them, for it fulfilled the aim of guaranteeing that German subjects would live under German rulers. So much of German national sentiment was focussed on an antipathy for French domination that, once the foreigner was removed from German soil, much of the immediate cause for widespread national feeling was removed. Second, the racial thinking mentioned above allowed German thinkers to define their national identity not in opposition, but in comparison to England. The distinction, made famous by Hegel, between Catholic–Latin and Protestant–Germanic cultural types was very much in the air at this time, and it tended to define the character of culture more in terms of great blocs of nations with similar origins than in terms of exclusive nationhood. This kind of thinking even produced a dream in Niebuhr's mind of 'a great-German, freedom-loving community of states' uniting the German-speaking lands, England, and Scandinavia against the French 'hereditary enemy'.[1] While conceding hatred of the 'Latin' French, the recent spur to German national consciousness, this doctrine emphasized a racially-based cosmopolitanism which served both as a reservoir for international resistance to French power and as an innocuous, non-revolutionary outlet for a form of German nationalism.

IV

The German conception of England, then, was deeply influenced by the French Revolution and Napoleonic invasion. The older Anglophilia

[1] Georg Künzel, biographical essay on Niebuhr in the latter's *Politische Schriften* (Frankfurt/Main, 1923), p. 329.

of the *Aufklärung* underwent a severe test as the French did away with traditional feudal concepts of liberty and created a new kind of political order based on reason. A small band of thinkers, largely associated with Göttingen, fought back with ideological arguments inspired by Burke and the English example and, when they came close to the halls of power after the Prussian collapse, attempted to put into practice some of the ideas they espoused. When the Anglo-French struggle increasingly involved Germany in the early years of the new century, the major historians came out in defense of England's role in European affairs. They turned a deaf ear to French charges that England hoped to exploit Europe and the world in the interests of a selfish naval imperialism serving the interests of a nation of shopkeepers. In keeping with the anti-revolutionary use of English history, German historians of this period shied away from the turbulent political past of England and stressed the beauties and benefits of continuity described by Burke. They associated English habits with a love of tradition and empiricism, a hatred of speculative reason and dull uniformity, and a joy in the infinite variety of human life. All these traits, they believed, characterized the best traditions of German culture as well, for they all went back, theoretically, to a common origin in the misty past of Germanic tribal life. England seemed to prove more clearly than any other state in the world that Germanic traditions could still be drawn upon to yield liberty without a Declaration of the Rights of Man, fraternity without the abolition of traditional social hierarchy, and prosperity without equality.

When the immediate threat of the French Revolution had passed, however, with the expulsion of the invading foreigner, German interest in the liberating foreigner declined markedly. For over a decade after the Carlsbad Decrees, the voices of organic reform fell silent, and England lost her firmest supporters; at the same time, radical reformers, barely tolerated in southwest Germany, justifiably found more to admire in the France of Louis XVIII than the England of George IV. Ten years after Waterloo, there were few signs of any Anglo-German 'love-hate' relationship; indifference was evidently the predominant feeling.

CHAPTER 4

RESTORATION VERSUS CONSTITUTIONALISM AND THE GERMAN VIEW OF ENGLAND

After the flow of French imperial power carried the German historical assessment of England one way, the ebb tide carried it another. Until 1813 England had seemed the only hope for breaking Napoleon's rule. In that year, however, German patriots thrilled to see their own people rise at last to drive out the invader. After the smoke of Waterloo had dissipated, Adam Müller, an anti-Smithian economist, described the resultant change of feeling towards England in Germany thus:

> We erred, during the hopelessness of 1806–12, in taking England to be the actual foundation of European liberty rather than *just* a base and supply point of it; and we estimated the power of political thinking in England too highly, that of the continent too little.[1]

Müller's reaction typified the sort of adjustment in the German view of England made in the light of the new international situation and domestic issues and ideologies. Whereas Britain had led Europe in the wars against revolutionary and Napoleonic France, after 1815 leadership was replaced by a mediating stance. Postwar economic crisis, civil disorder, loud demands for governmental reform, and other troubles which plagued England were met with such controversial measures as the Corn Laws, the Six Acts, and repeated assurances that

[1] Adam Müller, 'Staatswirtschaftliche Verlegenheiten in England und Reform der Geldverhältnisse in Österreich' (1816), *Ausgewählte Abhandlungen*, ed. by J. Baxa (Jena, 1921), p. 95. Only a decade before, however, when Friedrich von Raumer had become acquainted with him in Göttingen, Müller had pretended to be a rich Englishman. Müller was actually an impoverished Prussian, but his choice of national types to ape tells much about the difference in romantic and conservative thinking about England before and after the fall of Napoleon. See Friedrich von Raumer, *Lebenserinnerungen und Briefwechsel*, I, 38ff.

reform was unnecessary. Then, under Canning, British policy abetted revolution in South America and the Mediterranean. At the same time, the hopes of nationalists and reformers in Germany were progressively eroded after 1815.

The impact of these changes upon the historians discussed above varied. Several of these authors either died before Waterloo (Spittler and Johannes von Müller) or wrote no new works dealing with England (Eichhorn and Heeren). Some of the most eager conservative propagandists for Britain during the Napoleonic period (Gentz and Niebuhr) would no longer justify their enthusiasm in the light of new circumstances. On the other hand, other historians who defended the heritage of the French Revolution began publishing their major works only as the quarter-century of wars ended. The revived rationalism of Karl von Rotteck and Friedrich Christoph Schlosser[1] provided a viewpoint for a sharply critical assessment of England.

Neither Gentz nor Niebuhr wrote much about England after 1815. In their sparse comments one senses a reaction of disappointment, if not alarm, to recent developments. Both regarded English foreign policy as dangerous. Gentz, perpetually thinking of the concert of Europe, merely echoed his employer, Metternich, in condemning Canning and British toleration of national liberation movements. The year after the British Coercion Acts of 1817, Gentz still wondered if British freedom – especially freedom of the press – was not, after all, too extensive.[2] Niebuhr also despaired of English foreign policy: the posture of the Foreign Office after 1815 shattered his dream of an international system of 'free Germanic' states. His random remarks attest to prolonged disillusionment. 'After England had emerged from so many years of revolutionary wars with fame and extended territory,' Niebuhr wrote in 1823, 'an infamous period began for her.'[3] Britain's failure to divide or conquer the United States in the War of 1812, the sorry state of public finance, industry, and agriculture, and the mediocrity of recent governments distressed him. In 1824 he seemed to admit that Stein's attempt to introduce the spirit of English local self-administra-

[1] Karl von Rotteck (1775–1840) taught history and law at the University of Freiburg im Breisgau and became one of the most prominent leaders of the liberal opposition in Baden's parliament during the 1820s and 1830s. Friedrich Christoph Schlosser (1776–1861) was professor of history at Heidelberg and one of the most popular historical writers of Germany. (See Biographical Appendix.)

[2] Cf. Gentz, 'Pressefreiheit in England' (1818), in *Ausgewählte Schriften*, v, 61–118.

[3] Niebuhr, 'Über Englands Zukunft', *Nachgelassene Schriften*, p. 426.

tion in Prussia had failed, and two years later he noted that even in England ancient institutions of local government were falling on evil days.[1] For both Niebuhr and Gentz, England appeared weak and indecisive in European affairs and less a model for domestic liberties than before. Although under Burke's influence they still admired English *history*,[2] the recent trends they condemned undermined much of their curiosity and motivation to investigate it. Both died shortly after the new outburst of revolution in France in 1830, Niebuhr's end having probably been hastened by nervous depression and fear about a new age of chaos. The vital nerve of their admiration had been their opposition to Jacobinism and Napoleonic domination; the passing of these threats, rather than changes in England *per se*, determined their revised view.

When men such as Niebuhr and Gentz gave up writing about English history, they left the field largely to a new camp of historians writing in the heritage of French revolutionary political ideology. If the 'historical school' persisted in seeing the English past through the eyes of Burke, this new 'school' judged England by the standards of immutable reason. And by the standards of natural law and the Kantian imperative, they found English history wanting.

Karl von Rotteck, an outstanding representative of this new political historiography, is remembered today more for his political activities than for his very popular and didactic history books. Rotteck's father, a Freiburg doctor, had been ennobled by Joseph II, whose reforming spirit the young scholar always admired. Rotteck's mother being French, he took an early interest in affairs just across the border. The French Revolution, including its democratic elements, left a deep impress on his thought. He spent his life teaching in his native Freiburg in Baden, one of the German states most exposed to French constitutional doctrines. After being appointed Professor of World History to the then Austrian University of Freiburg at the age of 23, a position for which he had not actually been trained, he changed over to teaching *Vernunftrecht* (law of reason) and political science in 1818. From then until the mid-twenties he was elected to represent the university in the aristocratic First Chamber of the Baden Diet, and he even led the liberal faction in the Second (or Lower) Chamber, the

[1] Niebuhr, 'Über die Organisation der ländlichen Verfassung in Preussen'; and 'Über ständische Verfassung', *Nachgelassene Schriften*, pp. 305–9 and 310–15, respectively.

[2] Niebuhr considered writing the first definitive German account of English history for Perthes in the mid-1820s.

most representative parliament in all the German states, until the Diet of the Confederation curtailed his political activity in 1832. Greatly outnumbered, persecuted, often dogmatic in his espousal of the more moderate principles of the French Revolution, Rotteck became one of the idols of the small liberal bourgeoisie scattered over Germany. His books sold in such quantities as to make him one of the most popular of German writers.[1]

Friedrich Christoph Schlosser, Rotteck's contemporary North German rival for the esteem of opponents of monarchical absolutism, was also passionately committed to the political doctrines of the late Enlightenment, including the Rousseauian idea that government should serve the general will. The influence of Rousseau and Kant explains in part why Schlosser, another Göttingen theology student, seemed immune to the Burkean and romantic organicism, based on the English example, which pervaded the atmosphere there in the late eighteenth century. Combining the passion of Rousseau with the stern rigor of Kant, he beat a retreat away from the historicist's sympathy for the past toward a moralist's insistence on judging it. After a series of school posts in Frankfurt, Schlosser, like Rotteck, found the atmosphere in Baden more congenial after reaction had begun to set in throughout the rest of Germany. He taught at Heidelberg, the major university of Baden, from 1817 on. Schlosser had considerably better credentials as an academic historian than Rotteck[2] – and correspondingly less political experience and tendentious animus. On the other hand, his ethical bent, subjective viewpoint, and sympathy for 'the people' made him seem the very antithesis of the uncommitted and archive-oriented Ranke, to whom he was often contrasted.[3] Like Rotteck he addressed himself to a wide audience, which responded by purchasing remarkable quantities of his writings.[4]

[1] One of his biographers claimed that his *Weltgeschichte* had sold about 100,000 copies – an impossible figure for the early nineteenth century, when a brilliantly successful edition was reckoned at 1,000 or 1,500 copies, but one which may have been close to the truth if one counts pirated editions and later reprints. See Richard Roepell, *Karl Wenceslaus von Rotteck* (Breslau, 1883), p. 17.

[2] According to Dr Franz Laubenberger, *Oberarchivrat* of the City Archive of Freiburg-im-Breisgau and an authority on Rotteck, he used practically no original sources; depended on secondary sources and newspaper clippings for his knowledge of England; and, indeed, read very little at all. (Interview of 14 June 1968.)

[3] Ottokar Lorenz, *Die Geschichtswissenschaft in Hauptrichtungen und Aufgaben* (Berlin, 1886), p. 60ff.

[4] Schlosser's *Weltgeschichte für das deutsche Volk*, written in the 1840s and 1850s, was published in a stately fifth edition as late as 1901–4.

From their uncertain sanctuary in politically turbulent but constitutionally advanced Baden, Rotteck and Schlosser aimed their works at readers throughout Germany in the hope of strengthening their faith in the political norms of a new and somewhat insecure liberalism. Their method was to show how bad things had been under the old regime. They concentrated heavily on the internal history of states rather than international relations. Generally speaking, the English model hardly satisfied their demands for a state based on reason, and they were far from holding it up for emulation. Indeed, the French system of the Restoration seemed preferable for its simplicity and retention of many revolutionary reforms. Britain's common law and hoary traditions were too remote, insular, and confused for states shaped by Josephinist or Kantian rationalism. Neither Rotteck nor Schlosser showed that respect for the concrete and the 'historically-developed' which had been the hallmark of the Göttingen historians, and neither made the effort actually to go to England.

Considering that both men applied unbending absolute standards to history, it is hardly surprising that they thought little of English 'liberty'. For Rotteck, liberty was less the battered prize of endless historical struggles than the perfect abstract right of every man. In his *Allgemeine Geschichte* (1812–27), for example, Rotteck regarded the English Bill of Rights less as the culmination of a long development toward freedom than as an insufficient fulfillment of natural liberty – it was only 'a recognition of precious natural right'.[1] Nor did Schlosser in his *Geschichte des achtzehnten Jahrhunderts in gedrängter Übersicht* (1823) pay much attention to freedom, for he dwelt more on abuses than on positive achievements. It was clear to both that British liberty was for the few.

Consequently these two liberals were uninspired by the development of parliamentary institutions in England. Rotteck, for example, instead of dwelling on parliamentary power since 1689, spent much time vilifying the Tudor parliaments as servile agents of the monarch's will. He ignored both the popularity of much that the Tudors did and the gains Parliament slowly made against the dynasty. Rotteck even attacked the sacred lady of German historians: Elizabeth's deeds may

[1] Karl von Rotteck, *Allgemeine Geschichte vom Anfang der historischen Kenntnis bis auf unsere Zeiten*, 15th original edn., 15 vols. (Brunswick, 1844), VIII, 90. The first edition, in nine volumes, appeared in Freiburg (Herder Verlag) from 1812 to 1827. Gooch called it the 'Bible of liberal Europe'.

have reflected the *Zeitgeist* (spirit of the age), as Johannes von Müller had said of her, but the English people, Rotteck said, sinned by not demanding a different *Zeitgeist*. At the height of his moral indignation, Rotteck proclaimed that 'her government, measured by the standards of an enlightened era and a politically emancipated people, appears highly despotic and is comparable, in many ugly traits, to that of Turkey'.[1]

Nor did Rotteck show more enthusiasm for the events of the seventeenth century, particularly the tumult of 1640–60. Following Hume, he despised the 'fanatics' of the parliamentary party and declared that the revolution sprang from unclarity about the rights of the crown. Rotteck scornfully attributed the behavior of the parliamentary party to religious fanaticism.[2] He was neutral in his judgments of James I and Charles I, but Cromwell received no mercy. Rotteck dismissed him as a sly, ambitious hypocrite who violently clamped order onto the deservedly collapsing edifice of English political life. Rotteck's judgments stood in marked contrast to the interpretations of the Puritan Revolution which later generations of German liberals espoused. Only when he reached 1689 did his scorn abate somewhat. He greeted the Bill of Rights as 'the salvation of national liberty' and held William III to be the liberator of Europe. George I was praised as 'wise and peace-loving, capable of dealing with a dangerous situation with strength and moderation'.[3] The anti-militarist Freiburg politician found Walpole so peace-loving and excellent that he justified even his bribery.

Schlosser, on the other hand, singled out Walpole for pillorying. Although admitting that the minister's peaceful policy had spared England from the 'evils which weighed upon the rest of Europe', Schlosser regarded his system of bribery as a 'wound inflicted upon the public morality' of all Europe.[4] In demoralizing power Walpole's system could only be compared to the 'machine state' of Frederick the Great or the worst writings of the French sensualist philosophers. Schlosser approved the changes of 1689, but only because they seemed to support the principle that 'the people, not blood, make a king'.[5] For the Hanoverian kings, however, he had nothing but contempt.

[1] *Ibid.*, III, 186. [2] Cf. *Ibid.*, VII, 290ff., and VIII, 69ff. [3] *Ibid.*, III, 177.

[4] Schlosser, *Geschichte des achtzehnten Jahrhunderts in gedrängter Übersicht*, 2 pts. in 1 vol. (Heidelberg, 1823), pt. 1, p. 182f.

[5] *Ibid.*, p. 12.

English readers of the *Geschichte des achtzehnten Jahrhunderts* could console themselves only with the observation that if the English did poorly in Schlosser's pages, the French did even worse.

Despite their differences about the eighteenth century, Rotteck and Schlosser used much the same terminology, especially in the two significant subdivisions of constitutional and foreign policy development. If Rotteck could revile the parliaments of the sixteenth century as a 'crawling slavish pack'[1] and those of the seventeenth as both penny-pinching and chaotic, he spared all notice to those between the Glorious Revolution and the late eighteenth century. Then, when the French constitution fashioned the principles of reason into a political system, the English constitution appeared to 'suppress the truth'; the suspension of civil rights and the increased powers of the executive and military all disgusted Rotteck. 'True patriots', like Fox, Rotteck's hero, had been silenced.[2] The unreformed Parliament of the eighteenth century, Rotteck said, was a mere 'theatre'. What good fortune British public life enjoyed derived from freedom of the press, one of the few English freedoms appreciated by this persecuted political writer.

Rotteck was puzzled indeed by that constitution. The alternation of governing and opposition parties seemed wrong. How could right be done, he asked, when the opposition, instead of grouping together to block individual bad laws, usually opposed the government without regard to issues? This objection, derived from the workings of the little German parliaments established after 1815, bedeviled German liberal thought long after 1815, as we shall see in the next chapter. Rotteck's comments gave clear evidence that the concept of 'his majesty's opposition' remained mysterious in Germany.[3]

Schlosser's opinion of the constitution followed similar, if less articulate, lines. On the other hand, he thought English government of the eighteenth century was unique because responsible men carried it on and 'constitution and law' protected its integrity. He also believed that British politics had become increasingly 'democratic' until the reaction in the 1770s. At the same time Schlosser, who mistrusted

[1] Rotteck, *Allgemeine Geschichte*, VII, 155.

[2] *Ibid.*, IX, 176ff. Also see Rotteck's review of George Custance, *Gedrängte Übersicht der englischen Verfassung*, in Rotteck's *Gesammelte und nachgelassene Schriften*, ed. by Hermann von Rotteck, 5 vols. in 3 (Pforzheim, 1841–3), I, 93–102.

[3] The term itself was coined in England in 1826 and achieved general recognition by about 1850. See Archibald S. Foord, *His Majesty's Opposition, 1714–1830* (Oxford, 1964).

large concentrations of capital, deplored the rise of a moneyed class over the 'free landowner' and, like Rotteck, disapproved the most recent constitutional developments. He attempted no analysis of the institutions involved in it, however, but preferred to glide away from any concrete discussion.[1]

Both Rotteck and Schlosser agreed that British foreign policy rested upon the selfish needs of *Handelspolitik*. Schlosser denied that England owed her international status to her constitution or her freedom. It was rather the British army and navy which had raised Britain since Cromwell, Blake, and Monk. Nor was the cause of liberty the mainspring of British foreign policy: the English fought at home to maintain Parliament and to resist royal oppression, Schlosser thought, but abroad they forced men to pay tribute to their egotistical mercantile system.[2] Schlosser blamed English influence and continental aping of English fashions for the materialism he so abhorred. 'Sensualism, egoism, commercialism, plenty, money, elegance, and a craving for luxury,' he complained, 'have placed Europe in heavier chains than hierarchy, baronage, or despotism could ever forge.'[3] England, having won control of the sea and world trade, was forging those chains for the continent and herself.

Rotteck's view of English foreign policy darkened when he described England's emergence as an anti-revolutionary power. As long as William III, Walpole, and the elder Pitt had directed Britain's power against the ambitions of *Bourbon* France, Rotteck judged it worthy. Even in peacemaking Britain had shown moderation and wisdom, although he suspected that concern for the balance of power 'could never influence the British government as much as the greed of the tradesmen for profit'.[4] With the American Revolution, however, Rotteck's sympathies evaporated altogether. The continental Armed Neutrality was a fitting, if regrettably short-lived, answer to England's mercantile greed and naval arrogance.[5] Finally, Rotteck said, the birth of the vital French alternative to British 'freedom' – or the perversion of freedom – had stimulated England's diabolical energy. Rotteck blamed England alone for the 'unnatural' 1815 settlement. 'The Union Jack has lost the love and trust of the world by deviating from the

[1] Schlosser, *Achtzehntes Jahrhundert*, I, 184, 336, 339.
[2] *Ibid.*, p. 337.
[3] *Ibid.*, p. 336.
[4] Rotteck, *Allgemeine Geschichte*, VII, 25–8; VIII, 112f., 221.
[5] *Ibid.*, IX, 389.

principles which made [England] somewhat popular before – by mercantile small-heartedness, despotic hardness, and hostility to the spirit of the times.' Rotteck urged, in closing, that Britain reconcile herself with the most powerful force in the world, 'outraged public opinion'.[1]

The opinions of Rotteck and Schlosser about specific events in English history serve to illustrate the new canons of judgment created by admirers of the *aims* of the French Revolution. Granted, Rotteck's fulminations at servile Tudor parliaments and his contempt for religious fanaticism, even among the opponents of tyranny in 1640, fell in with some currents of writing by Englishmen; but Rotteck failed to praise where one of his major sources, Hume, did so. He criticized almost every ruler and major movement in modern English history and ascribed the worst motives to the historical actors. Schlosser outdid even Rotteck in the depth of his rage, although not in the breadth of his subject matter. Instead of seeking in Protestantism a common Anglo-German bond, they reproved the English reformers. Neither followed Möser and Niebuhr by stressing the similar origins in Germanic law of the institutions of the two lands. As late children of the Enlightenment, they were too conscious of their own age to overlook the differences between modern England and Germany. Their South German orientation, in an age still strongly particularistic, also affected their view. In several other ways, Schlosser and Rotteck deviated from the interests of their predecessors. They both emphasized the geographic factors which made England 'different' from the continent, probably to discourage would-be adaptors of 'peculiar' British practice. Both men turned away from England's 'merely historic' liberties and self-government toward interest in British commerce and naval power. Schlosser hated trade and bemoaned the decline of agriculture; Rotteck, more indebted to Adam Smith, did admire and envy English industry, but he thundered against unequal division of the resultant wealth. Rotteck's interest in industrial questions reflected his youth: from his day onwards, historians increasingly had to face the problem of evaluating the English industrial revolution and adjusting their views accordingly.

[1] *Ibid.* Rotteck managed to impress his view upon one of his colleagues, Friedrich W. A. Murhard, the editor in the 1820s of the influential *Allgemeine politische Annalen* published by Cotta. Murhard, who had visited England during the dark days of the Six Acts, helped spread a very unflattering view of England in South Germany throughout the 1820s.

In their critical posture toward England, Rotteck and Schlosser were carrying on the traditions of Enlightenment historical thought with other means. To be sure, they were much more critical than their own rationalist predecessors (Spittler or Heeren, for example), not to mention their rivals in the 'historical school' (Niebuhr, for example). The political and ethical standards of their own day sufficed for the formation of their historical judgments, and it is significant that they hardly bothered with exhaustive research into original sources.

Britain's inaction, her refusal to reform herself or to join wholeheartedly in the restoration, alienated both the left and the right in Germany after 1815. It is too simple to say that 'liberals' detested and 'conservatives' loved England after 1815, for these labels mean little in speaking of restoration Germany. Certainly admirers of the ideas of the French Revolution (not all of whom were Francophiles, however) found that England did not measure up to their standards, and Burkean conservatives who had called for British-style 'freedom' during the Napoleonic occupation now found even the reduced liberties of the High Tory years dangerous. Hegel, who embodied the synthesis of German rationalism and philosophical conservatism, symbolizes this paradox: in one of his few comments on the English scene, he warned against parliamentary reform both because it did not go far enough toward establishing a rational form of government and because it would open the floodgate of revolutionary change.[1]

The usual explanation given by German scholars even today is also too simple: many South Germans may have been Francophiles and

[1] Hegel's love of government by reason made him quite willing to accept the enlightened bureaucratic mechanism of the Prussian state, but he did not speak in the rhetoric of conservatism. His language and faith in reason actually gave him something in common with Rotteck. Both despised England chiefly because its political system was corrupt and inefficient. The essential difference between the Berlin philosopher and the Freiburg radical was that Hegel feared the changes proposed by the Reform Bill more than the evils it sought to remove. Hegel's attack also resembled left-wing criticism in dwelling on English social inequalities. The privileged aristocracy, Hegel maintained, protected its oligarchic rights by its overwhelming control of Parliament. Hegel was ahead of other analysts in seeing that Parliament had the 'substance' of governmental power; the king, rights which were 'more illusion than reality'. (Georg Wilhelm Friedrich Hegel, 'Über die englische Reform-Bill,' *Sämmtliche Werke*, ed. by H. Glockner *et al.*, 21 vols. (Stuttgart, 1958), XX, 507.) 'England is so noticeably behind the other civilized nations of Europe in the institutions of true law,' he wrote, 'for the simple reason that the powers of government lie in the hands of those who possess privileges contradicting all reasonable constitutional law and true legislation.' (*Ibid.*, p. 480.) He maintained that the confusion of uncodified positive law in England was so great that rational measures of correction would merely undermine the whole tottering system and lead to a revolution. (*Ibid.*, pp. 515–18.)

many North Germans Anglophiles, but too many exceptions exist to make this observation an 'explanation'. In the last analysis, opinion about and – more directly – fear of the French Revolution and Napoleonic domination constituted the greatest single influence on the view of England held by German historians who grew up in the era. From this time on, German historiography, even in its moments of greatest objectivity, could not fully escape from politically-charged standards in evaluating England.

PART III

ANGLO-GERMAN FRATERNITY – THE MIDDLE DECADES

INTRODUCTION

That decline of interest or disillusionment characterized German thought about England in the 1820s may be explained by the absence of any reason for strong feelings on the subject. The waves of Anglophilia connected with the German Enlightenment and the international struggle against France had abated, and no cause for admiration or hatred had arisen to replace them. In the 1830s and 1840s, however, new reasons did arise.

The genuine calm of the 1820s gave way to a deceptively false one in the following decades. As Robert von Mohl saw the new situation, 'Things went along in the country...in the traditional and habitual way, with apparent quiet and prosperity. But underneath the surface there was much dissatisfaction, not only with German affairs and the illiberal work of the *Bundestag* (Federal Diet), but with the slow pace of internal improvements...'[1] The French and Belgian revolutions of 1830 had given many Germans hope that constitutional monarchy and national self-determination could triumph in Europe despite Metternich. In response the *Bundestag* sought to stamp out all criticism of the existing order, for the Confederation remained a symbol of German disunity in everything but fear of change. The forces of movement won a few skirmishes in their attempt to substitute the rule of law and parliamentary consultation for bureaucratic absolutism, but their gains were never safe, as the seven Göttingen professors discovered when they were rudely banished for protesting the royal revocation of the Hanoverian constitution. Their moment of power in 1848 ended in disaster as well. During this period the most successful work of opposition-minded Germans lay not in the field of action, but in the field of thought. German thinkers developed conceptual systems fitted to the requirements of the coming capitalist, constitutional, and scientific age. It was in these decades that German

[1] Robert von Mohl, *Lebenserinnerungen*, ed. by D. Korber, 2 vols. (Stuttgart, 1902), II, 15.

constitutionalism grew, if not to full political maturity, at least to theoretical solidity; and that the first great capitalists, economic visionaries, and critics of capitalism emerged.

These new currents in German thought provided renewed impetus to study England, but they were not the only cause. England, too, changed in these decades – perhaps not as dramatically as some historians have supposed, but certainly enough to force contemporary German thinkers to pay attention. How could such reform measures as the amelioration of religious disabilities, the redistribution of Commons seats and enlargement of the electorate in 1832, reorganization of local government, industrialization, and free-trade agitation fail to raise echoes in Germany? The contrast of stagnation in the German states with movement in England – typified by the *Bundestag* passing its repressive Six Acts in the same month as the English Lords approved the Reform Bill – made England appear even more interesting than it actually was. Oppositional thinkers, bored by the sterile political terrain of the Metternich era and the post-1848 reaction – and discouraged by censorship from using domestic political examples – turned with delight to the lush gardens of reformed English constitutional life. The other end of the political spectrum found itself divided more and more about England: not all 'organic' conservatives thought the country lost after 1832, for England had once again demonstrated to them the possibility of peaceful development, of adaptation to new needs without sacrifice of authority and privilege. This conservative approval tended to grow as the English political system resisted attempts at radical change and weathered the storms of 1848. What did this odd agreement of conservatives and progressives mean? As change in both Britain and the Germanies began to accelerate in tempo, a mild confusion and fluidity of attitudes resulted; German interest in England, in any case, took on a renewed intensity and sophistication.

The peace which obtained among most of the great powers until the mid-1850s gave German thinkers less cause to concern themselves with Britain as an ally or enemy. Metternich strongly influenced the foreign policy of most German states until 1848, and this generally meant that relations between them and London were cool and correct, but rarely tense. The end of the personal union of Hanover and Britain in 1837 removed many causes of friction over purely German matters. German–English official relations no longer constituted a crucial issue, and German commentators showed little interest in the subject. The most volatile issue between Britain and the German states lay in the realm of economic policy: protectionists loudly but unsuccessfully bewailed the flood of British goods on their home markets; the anti-protectionist *Zollverein* (customs union), led by Prussia, carried on a campaign in the 1840s to force the abolition of such British restraints of trade as the Navigation Acts and the Corn Laws.[1] The other North German coastal states, however, remained aloof from these attacks on British trade policy.

Even as they lamented British competition, German economic thinkers and businessmen admiringly studied British techniques and sought to learn from British mistakes and avoid the human waste of industrialization. British capital, machinery, and engineering skill helped spark and speed the industrial revolution in the Germanies; from the 1840s on, British working-class misery prodded many German thinkers into an urgent search for answers to what was already called the 'social question'.

To these other factors influencing German attitudes toward Britain one must add the name of one man – Karl Josias von Bunsen, Prussian ambassador to the Court of St James's throughout the 1840s and early 1850s. Bunsen fits the common stereotype of the Prussians who served in that post – he loved England perhaps as much as his own country. He gained a reputation for being helpful to Germans in London. The men he helped most were those who shared his own interest in history; he did much to facilitate research by German historians of England. Their visits to the English archives and libraries became increasingly frequent as the critical method used by Bunsen's teacher, Niebuhr, and by Ranke's seminar forced scholars into the sources.

The adoption of Ranke's[2] selfconscious detachment rarely accompanied the increasing acceptance of his standards in the critical use of sources. Rotteck still enjoyed popularity in the 1840s, and Schlosser's lecture hall remained full until the 1850s. Partisanship about England did not cease with the improvement of sources and increasing use of

[1] For a full discussion of Anglo-German trade relations in this period, see W. O. Henderson, *The Zollverein* (Cambridge, 1939), chs. 4 and 5. For British contributions to continental industrial growth see *Britain and Industrial Europe* (Liverpool, 1954), by the same author.

[2] Leopold von Ranke (1795–1886), who taught most of his life at the University of Berlin, was the most famous and influential German historian of the nineteenth century. (See Biographical Appendix.)

them; but partisanship became better informed. If we seek evidence that Ranke's politically detached manner of writing history had still not swept the field, we may simply note that the three decades after 1830 witnessed the most feverish and politically motivated preoccupation of German historians with English constitutional norms. A second generation of German constitutionalists, succeeding the Rottecks and Schlossers, looked upon England as an elder brother to be emulated or at least admired. This generation included Friedrich Christoph Dahlmann, Karl Theodor Welcker, Robert von Mohl, and Georg Gottfried Gervinus.[1] Significantly, they were joined in their enthusiasm by such aging converts as Rotteck himself. Their views will be discussed in ch. 5.

At the same time, many politically conservative North German observers maintained a nostalgic admiration for Britain by minimizing the impact of reform, as did Friedrich von Raumer,[2] or by stressing other aspects of English life and history than domestic political arrangements. Many North German conservatives ignored constitutionalism and stressed the community of interest, culture, and 'blood' between the English and the Germans. Leopold von Ranke, whose thought categories included such generalized (and often congruent) pairs as Protestant–Catholic, Germanic–Romance, and Spanish/French–English/German, subtly encouraged the notion of 'natural' German–English alliance; he also ecumenically embraced the Church of England, a position wholly in accord with Friedrich Wilhelm IV's projects for cooperation between English and Prussian Protestantism. While Ranke avoided pushing the theme of racial community too far, his friend and fellow-historian Johann Martin Lappenberg[3] cultivated the idea that the best English traditions were of Saxon, and therefore

[1] Friedrich Christoph Dahlmann (1785–1860), who taught at Kiel, Göttingen, and Bonn, was one of the leading historians and political scientists of his era. He was also politically active in the cause of German unity under Prussia. Karl Theodor Welcker (1790–1869) was a leading Baden political leader and professor who collaborated with Rotteck. Robert von Mohl (1799–1875) taught law at Tübingen and Heidelberg and was one of the principal founders of the German idea of the state of laws (*Rechtsstaat*). Georg Gottfried Gervinus (1805–71) was expelled from his professorship at Göttingen in 1837 and thereafter taught and wrote history in an anti-establishment vein. (See Biographical Appendix.)

[2] Friedrich von Raumer (1781–1873) began his career as a Prussian civil servant but went on to become a professor at the University of Berlin. (See Biographical Appendix.)

[3] Johann Martin Lappenberg (1794–1865) was a lawyer, diplomat, and archivist of Hamburg. (See Biographical Appendix.)

of Germanic, origin. Other historians, too, touched upon this theme of inherited similarities, and it had no necessary connection with political conservatism. But it had an unmistakable connection with historicism. Above all, this vague and harmless sort of racist thinking reflected a desire to be associated with British glory. Ranke and Lappenberg's efforts resulted in the first exhaustively researched, thoroughly original narrative histories of England written by Germans; they will be discussed in ch. 6.

Although most German academics writing about England in the 1830s, 1840s, and 1850s were looking up to a politically mature older brother or seeking family resemblances in their first cousins, a minority of outsiders dissented from these views. They looked upon the maturing process of the English state and society with the critical eye of sibling rivals. Except for Friedrich Julius Stahl,[1] the conservative theorist, their feelings were not unmixed, and their attitudes varied extremely at different points in their careers or in their writings. Friedrich List and Johann Gustav Droysen,[2] for example, admired English constitutional norms at the same time they warned against accepting English economic and foreign policies at face value. Victor Aimé Huber[3] underwent the odd transformation from foe of English constitutionalism to warm advocate of the English answer to the 'social question'. Lothar Bucher,[4] beginning at the radical end of the political spectrum, admired England; but as he grew more conservative, he initiated increasingly bitter attacks upon its institutions and policies. Bucher's methods and motives bore a striking resemblance to those of Karl Marx and Friedrich Engels.[5] All three belonged to a generation which began to use 'debunking' and 'unmasking' in the most aggressive

1 Friedrich Julius Stahl (1802–61) was a professor of law in Bavaria before moving to Berlin, where he became a leading spokesman for conservative political forces. (See Biographical Appendix.)

2 Friedrich List (1789–1846) began as a lecturer in his native Württemberg but went on to become a political exile, and American industrialist, then a tireless champion of German protectionism. Johann Gustav Droysen (1808–84) taught history at Kiel, Jena, and Berlin and is remembered as one of the most vocal spokesmen for Prussia's unifying 'mission' in Germany. (See Biographical Appendix.)

3 Victor Aimé Huber (1801–69) spent much of his life studying and teaching literature and history at various schools and universities before discovering, in the last thirty years of his life, the 'social question' raised by industrialization. (See Biographical Appendix.)

4 Lothar Bucher (1817–92) was successively a lawyer and politician; exile and journalist; and civil servant and adviser to Bismarck. (See Biographical Appendix.)

5 Karl Marx (1818–83) and Friedrich Engels (1820–95) were the founders of modern socialism and communism. (See Biographical Appendix.)

way – as an ideological weapon, not simply for the fun of it.[1] Nevertheless, the critical opinions of these men, to be discussed in ch. 7, gained little popularity in Germany; nor did any of these men attack England with enough frequency or intensity to be called crusaders. They hardly succeeded in altering the German view of England.

The orthodox view, while still quite favorable, did undergo some changes in the writings of the generation born between about 1810 and 1830. The German historians of this generation who admired England – and most of them did – were almost without exception political liberals. But they differed from the 'old' liberals of the pre-1848 stamp in being more nationalistic (and more *kleindeutsch*, or 'little German'), and less parliament-oriented in their political demands. They matured when German liberalism was still an academically respectable ideology rather than the tainted congeries of splintered interest groups which it became in Bismarck's empire. The liberal ideological master of this generation, Rudolf von Gneist,[2] bore much of the responsibility for shifting his readers' interest away from British parliamentary institutions to local government. Although no single influence can be isolated to explain their advocacy of a 'Prussian' solution to the problem of German unity, all the young liberal historians to be discussed in ch. 8 owed some debt to older nationalist historians like Droysen and Dahlmann. Their faith in the 'new Germany' which attained political shape in their active years, as well as their diminished faith in English parliamentary government, injected notes of doubt in their praise of England. While still regarding England as a 'relation', they treated it with more distance, with the respect due to an aging favorite uncle from a promising young man.

It is vain to seek the reasons for the differences in interpretation adumbrated here in the class origins of the historians discussed. They came, with few exceptions, from the small-town bourgeois milieu of the professional and public service class. The 'vons' before some of

[1] Karl Mannheim, in *Ideology and Utopia*, tr. by Louis Wirth and Edward Shils (New York, 1936), sees 'debunking' and 'unmasking' as the first form of expression for 'the discovery of the social-situational roots of thought' (p. 39 *et passim*). Bucher, Engels, and Marx attacked English 'hypocrisy' not so much on moral grounds as on political ones: if they could show that English parliamentarism or 'English' laissez-faire economic science was merely an ideological false front camouflaging national or class interests, they could undermine the faith of German followers of these 'ideologies'.

[2] Rudolf von Gneist (1816–95) was a Prussian professor of law, politician, and legal reformer. (See Biographical Appendix.)

their names indicate rewards of title to themselves or recent ancestors for loyal service to the state, not membership in the proud landed aristocracy.

The occupational choices of these historians fell more heavily on the side of university teaching than had been the case before 1830. The authorities on English history were now less often statesmen, in the manner of Möser, Niebuhr, or Vincke, and more likely to be professors with increasingly narrow specialties as time went on. They had much better training in historical technique than previous generations, since history had finally become established as a prestigious, autonomous discipline. As scholars they tended to be more demanding and more scrupulous with evidence than their forerunners. This superior training did much to raise the level of discussion about England and to dispel several naïve traditional prejudices.

Yet the more intensely scholarly cast of writing about England did not necessarily mean greater objectivity, nor did it mean that these scholars shunned such common pitfalls on the path of objectivity as political engagement. It is precisely in their political engagement that the two generations writing between 1830 and 1870 distinguished themselves most markedly from preceding and succeeding historians. Indeed, nearly half the men mentioned earlier were jailed, exiled, or forcibly driven from office because of their political engagement, and only two or three of them never held a political office of major importance. Their deep concern about fundamental constitutional reform and, in rare cases, for social change as well, could not help but influence their view of England, the leading 'constitutional' state of Europe. But one must repeat the *caveat* that no neat polarization into 'right' and 'left' fully corresponds to similarly polarized views of England.

Other facts, such as the religious and regional background of respective historians, may explain some of the attitudes encountered in their writings. Most of them were not strongly religious, for the overwhelming majority were worldly Protestants who looked upon Christian faith as an intellectual heirloom, not as a spiritual guide. They felt most like descendants of Luther or Calvin when attacking Rome, the enemy of spiritual freedom. The Catholic influence on the German historians' view of England was slight, since the Catholic regions of Germany produced so few notable historians at all. The few Southerners who wrote about England generally came from Protestant backgrounds.

It was chiefly the North that provided Germany's historians in these decades: the new Prussian universities at Berlin and Bonn, Göttingen (which temporarily lost some of its lustre after the expulsion of the Göttingen Seven), and Holstein's university at Kiel, where exposure to the Danish–German conflict made *kleindeutsch* nationalists of such men as Dahlmann and Droysen. In the south Heidelberg and, to a lesser extent, Tübingen and Freiburg maintained high standards of scholarship in history, and more southern Germans wrote about England than previously. It was in the universities, where the forces critical of the restoration and the post-1848 reaction were allowed to survive, that these generations of historians formed their image of England. It was there that the constitutionalist professors studied English domestic, especially parliamentary, institutions with an intensity and warmth of admiration born of their own hopes for reshaping the German states. It is to this group that we shall now turn.

CHAPTER 5

ENGLAND AS OLDER BROTHER – CONSTITUTIONALISM AND THE BRITISH EXAMPLE

In 1836 Karl Theodor Welcker, next to Rotteck the leading constitutionalist politician of South Germany, made his first trip to England. This trip, his biographer thinks, 'was of great importance for the extension and solidification of his political views'.[1] Welcker, like many thoughtful political reformers in Germany, had become increasingly disappointed in the French parliamentary system, and he particularly wished to emulate the British practice of ministerial responsibility to Parliament. At about the same time, Leopold von Ranke wrote in his jumbled diary the sort of cryptic summary judgment about England which one almost never finds in his published histories: 'The Middle Ages saw the free institution in the corporation; – we see it in the individual. In England both are united, and thereon lies the stability of freedom.'[2] Ranke is well known for his success in separating his conservative feelings from his published historical judgments; but in his diary he wrote less cautiously. Ranke, who had edited the Prussian-conservative and government-sanctioned *Historisch-politische Zeitschrift* only a few years before, can be regarded as an observer from the side of the political field opposite Welcker. Yet the two men agreed in admiring England.

Ranke's views, as we shall see in the next chapter, were colored by a humanistic conservatism that could admire what was old and unique in each major European society without demanding its universal adoption: each 'people' in the Christian-Germanic world had its own

[1] Karl Wild, *Karl Theodor Welcker* (Heidelberg, 1913), p. 165.

[2] Leopold von Ranke, *Tagebücher*, ed. by Walter Peter Fuchs and Theodor Schieder (Munich and Vienna, 1964), p. 243.

discrete but equal place. Welcker, on the other hand, praised certain things in English history which were of more recent origin and could reasonably lend support to constitutionalist demands for innovation everywhere. Such an attitude was possible for German liberals only after French constitutionalism began to lose prestige in the face of Orleanist royalism and British constitutionalism had gained prestige from the Reform Bill. To urge study and emulation of British political institutions had the added advantage of sounding unsubversive: reform along French lines still smacked of invasion, as it had in the revolutionary and Napoleonic period, but German constitutionalists could urge the adoption of an 'English constitution' without raising the specter of revolution and foreign occupation. The British reformers had dared lay hands on rotting ancient institutions; they had succeeded in rejuvenating the system without unleashing the revolution predicted by Hegel; and this success impressed the German constitutionalists.

A graphic example of the impact which the English reformers had on such young men as Friedrich Christoph Dahlmann, Karl Theodor Welcker, Robert von Mohl, Georg Gottfried Gervinus, and their followers may be found in the way they changed the negative views of older men like Rotteck. Rotteck's vitriolic attacks on England, discussed in the last chapter, had depicted English freedom as hanging by the slender thread of liberty of the press.[1] Rotteck had also contrasted England's inequalities of wealth and privilege with his own ideal of abstract liberty for all.[2] But 1832 brought about a change of degree, if not in direction, in Rotteck's view.[3] After the Reform Bill Rotteck suspended his polemics against England. He evidently believed that the sunlight of rational law was finally thawing away the frozen concepts of historical law and Burkean conservatism. Rotteck summed up his new, grudgingly neutral attitude toward England in his *Staatslexikon* a few years before his death:

It is true that England was raised by a marvelous grace of circumstance to a system of political and civil liberty which, after lengthy and laborious struggles, finally victorious, placed her ahead of all other nations. Nevertheless, so many deformations of historical law or merely of daily practice remained in the system that it could be an object of admiration and even of envy and emulation for the other nations *only before the North American and French*

[1] Theodor Wilhelm, *Die englische Verfassung und der vormärzliche deutsche Liberalismus* (Stuttgart, 1928), pp. 31, 38, 45, 51f., 61, 87, 94.

[2] *Ibid.*, p. 28.

[3] *Ibid.*, pp. 72–5.

Revolutions. Thereafter it appeared to all clear-eyed men in all its comprehensive inadequacy, and only since the recent Parliament reform did it take on a form approximately worthy of modern political theory.[1]

Friedrich Murhard, a South German publicist whose articles about England in the 1820s had breathed the spirit of Rotteck, went even further in revising his opinions. He now maintained that only travel to England could provide a full understanding of English institutions and recommended that European states 'should, above all, send their officials to England if they wish to advance political wisdom in their own lands'.[2]

With no major international questions to divert their attention from the most pressing question of the day – constitutional government in the German states – German liberals began to investigate English domestic life more carefully than before. Almost all the constitutionalist historians having enjoyed legal training, they were well-qualified to dwell on English public institutions more thoroughly than previous historians had. Their accuracy in describing English politics increased considerably from the generation of Rotteck to that of Robert von Mohl.[3] They had a fine feeling for the law which made them admire the English jury system, until then virtually unknown in Germany. As leading publicists, such men as Friedrich Christoph Dahlmann, Robert von Mohl, and Karl von Welcker had to face the bothersome censorship of the Germanic Confederation, so they looked with envy on British press freedoms. All the constitutionalists warmly admired the unwritten English constitution and believed that at least some English institutions of government could be transferred to German soil.[4]

Because the constitutionalists set the pace of political study of England, we should dwell first on the beliefs and assumptions common to them before proceeding to the views of the more conservative political thinkers. The political engagement and didactic purpose of the constitutionalists narrowed their historical focus considerably. Foreign

[1] Rotteck, 'Constitution', *Staatslexikon*, 18 vols. (Altona, 1834–48), III, 763f.

[2] Friedrich Murhard, 'Englands Staatsverfassung', *Staatslexikon*, V, 84–171; the quotation is on p. 88.

[3] Rotteck (born in 1775) of course belonged to an earlier generation than Dahlmann, Welcker, or Mohl.

[4] For a thorough discussion of the views of Dahlmann, Mohl, Rotteck, Welcker, and others regarding the English constitution, with emphasis on their mistakes, see Wilhelm, *Die englische Verfassung*. Friedrich Klenk, *Die Beurteilung der englischen Verfassung in Deutschland von Hegel bis Stahl* (Tübingen, 1930), treats some other men and argues that the constitutionalists understood England rather well.

policy and cultural and economic history receded far into the background of their writings, and their chronological range predictably extended back only to the seventeenth century, when modern constitutionalism arose. Their works tended to analyze rather than narrate: even though some constitutionalists wrote narrative works treating many facets of English history, they chiefly wanted to dissect the British state and analyze the 'division of powers' within it.

The division of powers remained the standard starting point of political analysis among the generation of constitutionalists succeeding Rotteck. Montesquieu, in Bk XI, ch. 6 of his *De l'esprit des lois*, had divided the British constitution into executive, legislative, and judicial branches. He had ascribed monarchical, aristocratic, and democratic properties to the three parts of Parliament (King, Lords, and Commons). German constitutional historians long accepted Montesquieu's description uncritically, ignoring his own warning that he described only the law, not the practice of the English state.[1] Elaborators and commentators of Montesquieu, such as Blackstone and the Genevan DeLolme, in turn became authorities for German constitutionalists. DeLolme had raised up the unwritten English constitution as a counterweight against the democratic tendencies of his fellow Genevan, Rousseau. German historians, who showed no desire to exchange the tyranny of the mob for that of the crown, understandably preferred DeLolme to Rousseau as a political theorist, just as they preferred a 'mixed' constitution to any other kind. Dahlmann, for example, launched the German translation of DeLolme's classic[2] and praised him alongside Locke, Blackstone, and Burke as a keen-sighted and impartial interpreter. All his life Dahlmann accepted DeLolme's picture of a great, strong, balanced constitutional monarchy – a dogmatic simplification at the time DeLolme wrote and an illusion when Dahlmann did.

At the center of this monarchy lay, theoretically, the king himself. All the German constitutionalists of this period except Mohl overestimated the power of the English crown in recent history. They followed Montesquieu in assigning wide powers to the English monarch, overlooking or minimizing the eclipse of the royal veto,

[1] Charles de Secondat, Baron de Montesquieu, *Oeuvres complètes* (Paris, 1892), I, 263.

[2] Friedrich Christoph Dahlmann, 'Vorrede von DeLolme's *Darstellung der Verfassung von England*', *Kleine Schriften und Reden* (Stuttgart, 1886), pp. 111–20. The original work was Jean Louis DeLolme, *Constitution de l'Angleterre* (Amsterdam, 1771).

last used under Queen Anne, and the practical disappearance of the crown's power to name ministers at will. The political naïveté of the pre-1848 generation was compounded by a desire to prove a point: 'the liberals believed they had in England historical proof that the [constitutional] limitation of the crown did not mean its impotence.'[1] They did not see that the second division of government, Parliament, had virtually assumed all important executive functions since 1832, leaving the crown the appearance but not the substance of power.

By citing Montesquieu and relying on their political experience in Germany, the constitutionalists also blocked the path to understanding the legislative institutions they so much admired in England. If the king were as powerful as Montesquieu had indicated, then the grip of a powerful aristocracy on Parliament held little danger: the crown would act as a bulwark against selfish social interests. Dahlmann, whose favorite project was the erection of a two-house legislature based on the English example, lauded the English system of representing the moneyed interest and the 'small aristocracy' (i.e. gentry)[2] together in Commons and leaving the upper house to the great landed lords. Welcker, the co-editor of the *Staatslexikon*, agreed with him. They presupposed a strong king, of course, to guarantee social justice in this system. The most monarchistic of the constitutionalists, Dahlmann, perceived no shift of power to the disadvantage of the king. He regarded the 1832 reforms as a mere pruning of the basically healthy English parliamentary plant rather than an historic break with the past.[3]

As a consequence of overlooking the virtual exclusion of the English crown from executive power by a ministry responsible only to Parliament, few constitutionalists thoroughly understood English partisan opposition. Dahlmann, Rotteck, and Murhard all condemned any opposition organized to seek power instead of justice; they did not recognize systematic opposition as a fundamental necessity of English parliamentary government.[4] Most German theorists then thought in

[1] Wilhelm, *Die englische Verfassung*, p. 97.

[2] German scholars used the same word, *Adel* or nobility, for both lords and gentry; 'small' or 'lower' were used to indicate gentry. Only later in the century did the English term 'gentry' achieve a permanent place in German use.

[3] Wilhelm, *Die englische Verfassung*, p. 76. Also see Friedrich Christoph Dahlmann, *Die Politik auf den Grund und Mass der gegebenen Zustände zurückgeführt* (Göttingen, 1835), p. 84.

[4] Indeed, many Englishmen held similar opinions. See Foord, *His Majesty's Opposition*, *passim.*

terms of a constitutional 'dualism' which balanced the prince and the ministry on one side, the people and the legislature on the other. Opposition in the contemporary German parliaments was widely regarded as defiance of the king (still identified with the very concept of the state) and, potentially, violence against the state itself. An intransigent opposition thus theoretically contributed to anarchy. German political science of the era looked upon the parliamentary body less as a battleground than as a meeting ground suitable for peaceful, constructive cooperation between people and ruler. They invoked the freedom of opposition in Britain not in order to strengthen the rights of interest-oriented factions, of which they disapproved, but only in order to establish the right of parliamentary bodies to check ministerial wrongdoing. They were puzzled when the English opposition, instead of approving the good and censuring the bad acts of royal government, voted indiscriminately against government measures.

In effect, then, the German constitutionalists desired for their small states an idealized version of a system which was ceasing to exist in Britain. They had never understood or accepted the waning system of patronage, which in their eyes meant simple corruption, and they, along with many Englishmen, found the emerging system of party rule obnoxious and aberrant. Because they so much wanted to establish the principle of *loyal* opposition in the German states, and because England offered the most persuasive example of the principle, they could not afford to analyze the system in a realistic way. They consequently failed to establish the vital principle that partisan opposition to the governing ministry need not mean opposition to the crown or the state itself,[1] and their viewpoint profoundly colored the later development of German parliamentary attitudes.

Only one constitutionalist of the pre-March era saw through the confusion of his colleagues over the function of parties in English government – Robert von Mohl. His opinions of Great Britain were more incisive than those of the other liberals. Mohl visited Britain in 1847, but his acuteness owed less to his minute study of British institutions during his trip than to formative readings completed before then. Also, Mohl was younger and wrote later than the other constitutionalists, at a time when analysis of the externals of British constitutional life no longer sufficed for learned discussion.

[1] Dahlmann, *Die Politik*, p. 182.

Mohl tried to alter the basis of instruction in German political science (previously based on the law of the defunct *Reich*) by drawing his sources from the dynamics of the constitutional systems of the west – notably America and France.[1] In the 1840s, however, disillusionment with the manipulation of the French constitutional system by Louis Philippe turned his interest to English affairs. After 1845 he wrote many articles about English personalities and letters – including a review of Lord Henry Brougham's *British Constitution.* Mohl's most important publication during this period grasped the constitutional realities of England more firmly than any previous German liberal and presented them to the German scholarly world in a clear form.[2] Mohl, breaking with the theory of the division of powers, described the government of England as a committee formed from the majority party of both Houses of Parliament. Mohl rejected the current German dualist view, which presupposed a strong king to lead and integrate the state as well as a legislative body to act as a check on the king. Instead, he asserted that the English system contained no dualism between prince and people, but rather one between the factual ruler (parliamentary majority) and the opposition.

Mohl contrasted the English Parliament to the German *Kammern* (chambers) as a creative to a destructive factor in government. No disharmony could arise between government and people in England, he reasoned, because Parliament represented both. And in Parliament itself, despite substantial middle-class gains since 1832, the parties shared such fundamentally similar aristocratic backgrounds that they agreed on all important issues.[3] In England the predominance of Parliament (*Parlamentarismus*) had overcome the dualism between prince and people. In contrast, the 'constitutionalism' of the German states still allowed the king to rule as well as reign, required the ministers to do his bidding, and only gave the assemblies a choice between meaningless monarchical toadyism and futile oppositional pariahdom. In Mohl's opinion, this kind of separation of powers, far from guaranteeing liberty, led to legislative barrenness and the instability

[1] Mohl, *Lebenserinnerungen*, I, 146; Erich Angermann, *Robert von Mohl* (Neuwied, 1962), p. 26f.

[2] Mohl, 'Über die verschiedene Auffassung des repräsentativen Systems in England, Frankreich und Deutschland', *Zeitschrift für die gesamte Staatswissenschaft*, III (1846), 451–95. (Also printed with few changes in Mohl's *Staatsrecht*, *Völkerrecht und Politik*, 3 vols. (Tübingen, 1860–69), I, 33–65.)

[3] *Ibid.*, p. 454.

of the state itself. Mohl fully realized that the English crown had lost most of its power, although he still thought a good king could accomplish much.[1] But in marked contrast to most other German liberals, Mohl admired and respected the essential role of English parties.[2]

There are several possible explanations of the German constitutionalists' misunderstanding the functioning of English central government. Before 1848 they were rarely in a position to examine the workings of English institutions empirically; their political inexperience and exclusion from high office led them to cling to a theoretical and legalistic approach.[3]

The available information suggests that the constitutionalists were better-read than the preceding generations of historians, but their heavy reliance on secondary materials condemned them to many mistakes and anachronisms. Dahlmann's library, for example, contained just over 3,100 titles, of which about 100 dealt in some way with England; few of these were by Englishmen, and even fewer were primary sources. Dahlmann could select his interpretation from among the works of Montesquieu and Schlosser, Guizot and Hallam, DeLolme and Macaulay, but he usually chose a rather conservative appraisal of the English past. When he lectured to his students on eighteenth-century English history, his notes contained pages torn from some century-old chronology of English history, bare facts supplemented by occasional newspaper clippings and the author's own marginalia.[4]

Nor did the constitutionalists always have the chance to travel widely in England, and when they did go, as Mohl complained after his own trip in 1847, they had less time to make full observations than they would have liked.[5] Mohl had already rejected the Montesquieu picture of the English constitution from his pre-voyage readings, so his trip hardly decided his turn away from Montesquieu. Indeed, Mohl's interests, adumbrating those of German political thinkers in the 1850s, had already shifted away from the central institutions toward local

[1] *Ibid.*, p. 453.
[2] *Ibid.*, p. 455.
[3] Fueter, *Historiographie*, pp. 522–3.
[4] For a list of titles in Dahlmann's library, see his *Nachlass* in the *Deutsche Staatsbibliothek*, East Berlin, Kasten 3; for lecture notes on England, see Kasten 9.
[5] Robert von Mohl, letter to his brother Julius, dated Heidelberg, 1 November 1847, in *Nachlass* Mohl, Cod. Hist. Q 506 III 20a, *Württembergsche Landesbibliothek*, Stuttgart.

administration. Nevertheless, the recurrent theme of travel to England in order to corroborate one's theories, rather than to look about without prior prejudices, surfaces even in the writings of Mohl, whose sight seemed so much clearer than that of his somewhat older constitutionalist colleagues. Before leaving for England he explained the purpose of his trip:

I would very much like to see their rural and other lower-level administration, in person and at close range, in order to discover if a means exists there for radically curing our entire bureaucratic mischief [*Schreiberunfug*]...Our administration is unbelievably stupid, because it can no longer do anything but *write*. One thing is clear: [to the objection that improvement is 'impossible'] the answer – that the 'impossible' *exists* in England – is the only decisive one.[1]

It is a tribute to Mohl's scrupulous honesty that he subsequently found the English administrative system weak in many respects and said so; but then he had the advantage of being the foremost German expert on *Polizei*, that is, local administration in the widest sense. Not all scholars who went to England with preconceived notions shed them after empirical observation.

Yet the constitutionalists' misconceptions about the English crown and Parliament resulted from more than their own political inexperience and lack of first-hand knowledge. Given a choice between their own empirical observations and the idealization inherited from Montesquieu, they took the latter; they saw in the English constitution what they wanted to see. Murhard, for example, sometimes sounded as if he knew the difference between English constitutional theory and practice. Nevertheless, if pressed, he insisted on their identity. Murhard knew the argument of Gaetano Filangieri (*La scienza della legislazione*, 1780) and Destutt de Tracy (*Commentaire sur l'esprit des lois de Montesquieu*, 1817) that the division of powers had ceased to function in England. Nevertheless, Murhard rejected their view, arguing that England was powerful and free precisely because a powerful king and a powerful Parliament worked hand-in-hand. If he wished to persuade German princes that more power should be granted to their legislatures, he could ill afford to depict the English king's close cooperation with Parliament as the result of the crown's impotence. Murhard's rational-

[1] Robert von Mohl, letter to his brother Julius, dated Tübingen, 7 March 1847, *Nachlass* Mohl, *loc. cit.*

ization of recent examples of that impotence occasionally overstepped the border of casuistry.[1]

About the third division of the English state, the judiciary, there was less comment among the constitutionalists. They all praised the jury, which to them summarized the best elements of the English legal system. Dahlmann and Welcker, among others, advocated its adoption in Germany.[2] In addition, the three main authors of the *Staatslexikon* (Rotteck, Welcker, and Murhard) regarded the free press as a fourth element of the English constitution. Welcker compared freedom of the press to a watchdog that kept the three divisions of state within their competences. Rotteck and Murhard, who until 1832 believed that parliamentary corruption had undermined the balance and had bought off Commons for the purposes of the aristocracy and the crown, saw in the press and the jury system the only guarantee of English liberty.[3]

The choice of emphasis and the misunderstanding of the admittedly fluid British parliamentary system suggest several remarkable facets of motivation in the constitutionalists' analysis of English politics. By concentrating on the capital and the central institutions, on the purely formal aspects of government, and by glossing over troublesome facts which did not fit into their picture, they reflected their own desires. The recentness of centralized parliamentary institutions in many German states and the resultant disagreement over certain basic fundamentals of political life encouraged focussing attention on the formal principles and institutions which England took for granted. When one adds to this the general praise of juries and press freedoms, one concludes that the German constitutionalists desired, above all, to check the arbitrary exercise of power by princely bureaucracies, not replace these bureaucracies with a full-powered parliament. Impeachment, free speech and press, and limited ministerial responsibility were to be the weapons of an awakened bourgeois intelligentsia against arbitrary government, and these were best developed in Britain. What they did not see so clearly – the development of parliamentary pre-

[1] Klenk, in his *Beurteilung der... Verfassung*, argues that Murhard and another liberal Anglophile contributor to the *Staatslexikon*, the Saxon Friedrich von Bülau (1805–59), recognized the dominant position of Parliament after 1832. His argument falls on the point that neither man assembled his random insights into a coherent theory, as Mohl did.

[2] See Dahlmann, 'Ein Wegweiser durch die Geschichte der englischen Jury' (1846), *Kleine Schriften*, 337–55; and Welcker's article 'Jury' in the *Staatslexikon*, IX, 28–160.

[3] Wilhelm, *Die englische Verfassung*, pp. 45–7.

dominance and government by interest-oriented parties – was something they did not want in Germany. So, with isolated exceptions such as Mohl, they praised a vanishing system in England and ignored the emerging one.

Naturally the degree of admiration for the English political system among German constitutionalists varied with the degree of political radicalism in each man. The warmth with which they advocated adopting an 'English constitution' in Germany varied similarly. Constitutionalists of the natural-law school, for example Rotteck, became scarce in Germany during this period, so that even Rotteck's own colleagues in the *Staatslexikon* project often differed with his low estimate of England's value as a model free country. The political reforms of 1832 had silenced the last criticisms among German left-wing constitutionalists without alarming the organic-minded, continuity-loving moderates. These men, with their high regard for ordered change and historical determination, dominated the new political theory of the 1840s. While putting the finishing touches on the monumental *Staatslexikon*, Welcker probably spoke for most German liberals:

> When one looks upon the totality of English conditions; when one compares that with our dear German ministers, officials, learned pedants, clumsy businessmen; when one contrasts the results for the honor of the fatherland, freedom, and power in terms of all the highest principles of political life, whether for citizens or princes; finally, when one compares England's steady progress and improvement to our daily regression, again in terms of all those highest principles – then all our governmental wisdom seems almost childish.[1]

The most conservative of the constitutionalists, Dahlmann, proved the most uncritical admirer of England. As a young man he had published a paean of praise for the British political system, 'Ein Wort über Verfassung'. During the Napoleonic age, he said, Germans 'glanced out upon their blood relation, England, the only watchtower of freedom left in the great flood, and became aware of their own nothingness'.[2] His article argued that Schleswig-Holstein and England resembled each other in so many respects that the duchies should adopt an 'English constitution'. Dahlmann anticipated no difficulty

[1] Karl Theodor Welcker, 'Englands Staatsverfassung' (1846), *Supplement zur ersten Auflage des Staatslexikons*, II, 230.

[2] Dahlmann, 'Ein Wort über Verfassung' (1815), *Kleine Schriften*, p. 29.

there, for the driving engine behind British constitutional development was, after all, Saxon liberty, and the Schleswig-Holsteiners were Saxons, too! 'Related nationality, a commonly experienced political youth, the penetrating ray of identical faith, and long association can found state structures capable of quite similar constitutions,' he believed.[1] Dahlmann used 'the ideas and the spirit of Savigny and the historical school' to discover 'the principle of organic development and a "unity-building power" in the Germanic essence of the English'.[2]

It has often been noted that Dahlmann's *Politik* (1835) was *the* representative work of North German liberalism in the early nineteenth century, just as Rotteck and Welcker's *Staatslexikon* was the bible of Southern liberals.[3] But, as a glance at Dahlmann's earliest and last writings on England shows, he did not have to undergo any conversion in the manner of the authors of the *Staatslexikon*. The 1832 reforms only reinforced his view that England represented the spirit of organic self-renewal, ordered change, and compromise. Even in 1849, after his own abortive attempt to copy English parliamentary practice in the Frankfurt National Assembly, and after the general disappointment of German nationalists with English indifference to their cause, Dahlmann continued to praise the English example.[4]

England was not an incidental part of Dahlmann's thought – it was a keystone. When his *Politik* appeared in 1835, the most controversial part of the work, the one taken up by friend and foe alike, dealt with the 'English example' of government. The reason for Dahlmann's dependence on foreign models was the contemporary insecurity of German constitutionalists, groping as they were towards a new model for government in Germany. 'Without a foreign model,' one of Dahlmann's later biographers wrote, 'it was simply impossible to get anywhere in politics then.'[5] The French model was already losing favour, so Dahlmann's book reinforced the reawakening interest in England. Typically, Georg Gottfried Gervinus, an admirer of Dahl-

[1] Dahlmann, *Die Politik*, p. 26. Also see Wilhelm, *Die englische Verfassung*, pp. 34, 37.

[2] Wilhelm, *Die englische Verfassung*, p. 36.

[3] See, for example, Wilhelm Mommsen, *Grösse und Versagen des deutschen Bürgertums* (Munich, 1949), p. 39.

[4] Friedrich Christoph Dahlmann, Speech [probably to the First Chamber of the Prussian Landtag], 16 October 1849, in *Nachlass* Dahlmann, Kasten 6.

[5] Hermann Christern, *F. C. Dahlmanns politische Entwicklung bis 1848* (Leipzig, 1921), p. 245.

mann, put down the book with a feeling that he had not used the English example *enough*. 'Notice how much surer and bolder he is in the chapters on education, where he has a good foundation in Germany,' Gervinus wrote to a friend in 1835, 'than he is in the matter of constitutions, where everything is as quivering and slippery as rubber under foot. He should have stood more often on England...'[1]

Gervinus's criticism, which seems a caricature of the dependence of the new political theorists on England, was seriously meant. As if to respond to such criticisms, Dahlmann turned to historical works which would fill in the examples required by the constitutionalists. It is no exaggeration to say that 'Dahlmann placed history in the position of servant to politics; it was supposed to offer examples for his political views...[and] direct fruits for life.'[2] It was in this spirit that Dahlmann wrote his *History of the English Revolution*; as he pointed out in the preface, he believed that this period contained the richest political lessons in all modern history.[3] Despite increasing protests from the conservatives and romantic defenders of German *Eigenart* that one could not transplant foreign institutions, Dahlmann and the constitutionalists continued to write and behave as though they believed in such a possibility. Their optimism rested on firmer grounds than mere mechanical reasoning. England had developed her freedom from her Germanic heritage, they believed; Germany could do the same. Even most constitutionalists, for example Dahlmann, Welcker, and Mohl, emphasized England's Germanic past. Dahlmann, we may recall, argued that institutions like England's would transplant well to Schleswig-Holstein because of the latter's 'Saxon' origin. Mohl regarded Parliament as the finest flower of 'Germanic popular assemblies'.[4]

With an awareness of Dahlmann's pedagogical purpose in mind, the reader can detect interpretative passages in Dahlmann's work which reflect more the thinking of nineteenth-century German constitutionalists than the realities of early-modern English politics. Dahlmann stood in the highly secular and humanitarian tradition of the German constitutionalists in regarding the English Reformation as a purely

[1] Georg Gottfried Gervinus, letter to Georg Beseler, dated Heidelberg, 4 September 1835, *Nachlass* Gervinus, Hdbg. Hs. 2544, *Universitätsbibliothek Heidelberg*.

[2] Christern, *Dahlmanns politische Entwicklung*, p. 229.

[3] Friedrich Christoph Dahlmann, *Geschichte der englischen Revolution* (Leipzig, 1844).

[4] Mohl, 'Über die verschiedene Auffassung...', p. 451f.

political event motivated by the worldly ambitions of the Tudors. A certain distaste for 'religious fanatics' like Cromwell was mixed with the belief that religion, particularly in Cromwell's case, was often a cloak for ambition.

Although Dahlmann regarded Henry VIII as a lustful and arbitrary tyrant,[1] he, like most German historians, had a deep affection for one Tudor – Elizabeth, for it was she who had unified *and* 'constitutionalized' England in a manner Dahlmann would have Prussia emulate. Dahlmann credited Elizabeth for all England's greatness – Elizabeth *and* her willing Parliament. In Dahlmann's eyes, both these factors had made possible the completion of English national unity (symbolized by the unity of the religious factions against a common enemy in 1588). A strong monarchy had welded national unity since the twelfth century, but the vital element in English unity was the traditional spirit of freedom of the Anglo-Saxons, expressed in parliamentary institutions. The defeat of the Armada convinced Dahlmann that a strong monarchy had done its job of forging the English together into a genuine nation-state, enabling England to unfold its parliamentary institutions to the fullest extent. He foresaw a comparable program for Germany, with the Prussian monarchy playing the role of the Tudors.

What Dahlmann wished to avoid in Germany was a Stuart tragedy. Although the Stuarts had long been favorite targets of German constitutionalists, who in turn set the tone of German historiography in this field until Ranke, the traditional interpretation had dismissed the Stuarts as merely abominable kings. Dahlmann shared this view, but he bore down upon the era of the Puritan Revolution in great detail because of its peculiar instructiveness. Dahlmann accepted the Whig theory that there had been a 'constitution' to break and that the Stuarts had broken it. This supposedly arbitrary policy set back by decades the 'natural' growth of Parliament under Elizabeth. The resistance of Commons to the Stuarts appeared to him a conservative movement aimed at restoring traditional Germanic liberties and laws.[2]

[1] Dahlmann, *Englische Revolution*, pp. 50–80.

[2] This interpretation undoubtedly derived in part from theories of Montesquieu and DeLolme about the connection between ancient Germanic law and liberty: fighting for one meant fighting for the other, in Dahlmann's eyes. The notion of fighting for the 'good old laws' of Germanic-feudal origin against a usurping tyrant was common in some of the German states, including Schleswig-Holstein, where Dahlmann had worked in behalf of

Charles I received the blame for the chaos of the 1640s for having driven the parliamentary forces into an inflexible position. Unfortunately, from Dahlmann's standpoint, Parliament had gone on to usurp royal rights, upset the separation of powers, and endanger liberty from another quarter; but the Stuarts were always worse.[1] If Dahlmann's lesson were not clear enough, he made it explicit in his preface; revolution is a terrible sickness requiring centuries of recuperation, but it is the inevitable consequence when kings and ministers crush historic Germanic liberties. This was as much Dahlmann's answer to his expulsion from Göttingen by the constitution-breaking King of Hanover as the standard view of revolution among pre-March North German constitutionalists. One of the reasons for their failure in 1848 was their clinging to legalistic definitions of grievance, rather than to Machiavellian justifications in the name of power. Dahlmann's interpretation of the English revolution, with its typical constitutionalist distaste for disequilibrium in the separation of powers and of 'tyrants' like Cromwell,[2] reflected the rather modest *ständisch* (corporative) demands of the majority Right Center in the later Frankfurt National Assembly. Evidently they wanted to avoid both Stuarts and Cromwells, bypassing 'unnecessary' upheaval in favor of the 'organic development' supposedly embodied in the rest of British history. Thus they viewed the gains of the 'Glorious Revolution' as a restoration of Germanic liberties. Dahlmann, like most of the constitutionalists, found little to interest him in the further development of English political structure after the advent of William III.

If Treitschke is justified in calling Dahlmann's accounts of the English and French revolutions harbingers of the German revolution of 1848,[3] then the aims and ambitions of the 'Parliament of Professors' at

the local notables, and especially in Württemberg. There, according to contemporary ideas, the most 'English' of the German state constitutions existed until the Napoleonic reorganization. On Württemberg see Jacques Droz, *L'Allemagne et la révolution française*, p. 134 *et passim*.

[1] Dahlmann, *Englische Revolution*, p. 202f.

[2] Dahlmann found Cromwell so hard to understand that he hinted the Protector might be insane. He also stubbornly refused to grant Cromwell any credit for establishing English military or naval might or great-power status. All these, according to Dahlmann, sprang from Elizabeth. Tyrants, in the pre-March liberal view, were always weak. See Dahlmann, *Englische Revolution*, pp. 247, 244, 137ff.

[3] Treitschke's picturesque phrase, 'die Sturmvögel der Revolution', translates clumsily as the 'storm-petrels of revolution', the ocean birds which give warning of the approaching tempest. See Heinrich von Treitschke, *Deutsche Geschichte im 19. Jahrhundert*, 5 vols. (Leipzig, 1879–94), v, 409.

Frankfurt come more sharply into focus. Most of the participants left Frankfurt with a deep sense of disappointment and frustration, but the evidence does not indicate that it was directed against the English (or other foreign) models upon which the parliamentarians had drawn. The German historians sitting in the Frankfurt National Assembly (and in the state parliaments) constantly referred in their speeches to English practice as they understood it. Explaining the failure of 1848, some felt German conditions had not been right in 1848; others, that Prussia had not lived up to her assigned role; others still, like Gervinus, that the German middle class had proven incapable of the role assigned to it. But criticism virtually never fell on the ideal of the English system itself. Nor did the constitutionalist historians who played major roles in 1848 believe (as did a later school of German nationalist historians) that British policy toward Germany had rested on implacable hostility to unification. Even at the height of the crisis over Schleswig-Holstein, in which Britain had a strong interest, the constitutionalists blamed anti-German international pressures on Russia and France – even Sweden – before mentioning England.[1]

As a result of the reaction, rather than the revolution, the amount of material written about England by the pre-March generation declined in the 1850s. Few men wished to risk their safety by openly lauding English parliamentary government while the restoration of bureaucratic rule in the centers and *Junker* control of the countryside proceeded. One of the few who did, Georg Gottfried Gervinus, paid for his temerity with a complex and costly trial for high treason.[2] His later work, chiefly the *Introduction to the History of the Nineteenth Century*,[3] reflected the inverse ratio between disappointment in German political

[1] Most of the evidence here is negative. Surprisingly, there is very little mention of English foreign policy even in the 1848 letters and speeches of the German historians. Robert von Mohl, for example, rather offhandedly mentioned the possibility of war over Schleswig-Holstein at the height of the crisis in Frankfurt over the Malmö Armistice. England was far down the list of those states he mentioned as possible enemies. See 'Berichte von Robert von Mohl an seine Frau aus Frankfurt am Main und Gotha, 1848–49', in *Nachlass* Mohl, *Bundesarchiv*, *Aussenstelle*, Frankfurt am Main, N 141–I, dated Frankfurt, 6 November 1848. Mohl, one of the ministers of the Frankfurt provisional government, barely mentioned English foreign policy in his reports. Nor does the correspondence of any other constitutionalist dating from the revolution years touch upon England as a great power, let alone accuse England of hampering German unification.

[2] See the account in Walter Boehlich, ed., *Der Hochverratsprozess gegen Gervinus* (Frankfurt am Main, 1967).

[3] Gervinus, *Einleitung in die Geschichte des neunzehnten Jahrhunderts* (Leipzig, 1853). For this study the fourth edition (1863) is cited.

life and adulation of Britain, which reached its peak in the 1850s. In other ways, however, Gervinus broke away from his former moderate allies and developed constitutionalist ideology beyond the point where Mohl or Dahlmann would follow. That point was democracy.

Gervinus stood accused of 'inciting high treason and endangering public peace and order', because his book attempted to prove the following point:

that, following a definite law of historical development, and in spite of all hindrances and inhibiting factors, democratic tendencies are in the process of steady progress; the attempt is made to spread the conviction that they must naturally and necessarily achieve victory in the modern European states, with the help of violent movements of the masses (in new, destructive revolutions), but also – even more effectively – via the quiet path of undermining with ideas. ...The prize of victory is depicted as the introduction of republican in place of monarchical political forms...and including the overthrow of existing constitutions...[1]

Gervinus replied quite slyly that his book was not 'a political pamphlet written in some personal political tendency of the author' but rather 'a strictly scientific historical work which depicts a tendency of the times and of history'. In the same breath he ridiculed the idea that he preferred democracy to constitutional monarchy: '...in truth, my book says more good things...about constitutional monarchy, as it exists in England, than of any other political form – the political praise heaped on England is the greatest imaginable.'[2]

The truth of Gervinus's real opinion lay somewhere between. Even before the debacle of 1848, he had expressed despair about the ability of the German bourgeoisie to give full support to the efforts of constitutionalist intellectuals for the piecemeal, moderate improvements in government which he so admired in England.[3] Gervinus justified his extensive and controversial work in German literary history as an attempt to convince the German people that its preoccupation with questions of religion and culture was misplaced, since the great ages of religion and German literature had ended. His own failure to convince the reading public of this idea led him to conclude, after

[1] 'Anklageschrift gegen Professor G. G. Gervinus', Mannheim, January 1853, reprinted in Boehlich, *Der Hochverratsprozess*, p. 7.

[2] Gervinus's *Protocoll*, Heidelberg, 28 January 1853, *ibid.*, p. 10.

[3] See Gervinus's most revealing letters to Georg Beseler of 1837 and 1838, *Nachlass* Gervinus, Hdbg. Hs. 2544.

1848, that the lack of *Gemeinsinn*, or public spirit, would permanently frustrate the sort of moderate development he would have liked to see copied from England. The year-in, year-out concern of the leading elements in English society with public matters would never appear in Germany. That is why Gervinus, with all his preference for English constitutional monarchy, felt that a great revolution from below would be the only force capable of dislodging the feudal-bureaucratic order in the German states. Gervinus thus laid out the ideological reasoning behind his *Introduction*, long before it was published, in a private letter:

The question is simply this: whether the example of American democracy or English monarchy has better prospects in the development of our states, indeed of all European states...The English monarchy has my total sympathy now as always; if I give the best prospects to American democracy, please remember that I have always been afraid of such an undesirable turn amid all my constitutional hopes; but after what has happened [after 1848], I would consider it a self-delusion if I did not admit to myself that constitutional monarchy has...lost all its prospects.[1]

Part of Gervinus's inner objection to the American democratic model – as to the Swiss – lay explicitly in their fragility. Even for this critic of the German liberals' tendency to worship *Macht* (power),[2] one of the ultimate problems of democracy remained the fear that it weakened the state.

Gervinus patently stood outside the mainstream of post-1848 liberal thinking, marked off by his belief that a democratic solution lay ahead for Europe. His climb into the ranks of respectable scholarship from his beginnings as the son of a bankrupt tanner forced to enter a clerking career in dry goods also set him apart socially from most of his fellow academic historians. His subsequent experiences, beginning with his expulsion from Göttingen in 1837 as one of the 'Göttingen Seven' and ending with his embitterment with the Frankfurt National Assembly and his treason trial, gave his life a turbulent quality

[1] Georg Gottfried Gervinus, letter to Baron von Rutenberg, Heidelberg, 6 May 1851, in *Nachlass* Gervinus, Hdbg. Hs. 2560. Gervinus's democratic ideology, atypical as it was among the constitutionalist survivors of 1848, has understandably become the object of considerable interest in the DDR.

[2] *Ibid.* For Gervinus's criticism of Dahlmann and others 'seized by the swindling hunger for power, [who would be willing] to disregard the certain crimes of the present for the uncertain glories and virtues of the future', see his letter to Professor Ewald, Heidelberg, 28 April 1867, *Nachlass* Gervinus, Hdbg. Hs. 2549.

unmatched by the careers of other pre-March constitutionalists. Nevertheless, Gervinus held a view of England which contained most of the typical constitutionalist elements in an even sharper formulation. Furthermore, like Mohl and Dahlmann, he held 'race' to be a factor working in history. Not only did he share the common view that 'the original Germanic constitution was developed best among the Anglo-Saxons',[1] he began his scholarly career with one of the first German histories of the Anglo-Saxons.[2] Like the other constitutionalists, he enthusiastically accepted heavy dependence on the English political model. Unlike the other constitutionalists, however, he dealt with problems in English culture – such as religion – in an understanding and respectful way. In his concern for the Germanic and Protestant ties between the German and English traditions, Gervinus came quite close to the position of the conservative Ranke[3] – a marked betrayal of his Anglophobe and Rankephobe teacher Schlosser, and a notable index to the decline of the pre-1830 Rotteck–Schlosser view of England.

In some ways, Gervinus went even further than Ranke. The latter regarded the conflict between religious confessions and between the Romance and Germanic 'peoples' as a dynamic rivalry which usefully checked any liberty-killing universalism. Not so Gervinus! In his view independence, individualism, and intellectual freedom – the major treasures of man – existed only among the Germanic peoples. Religious liberty and the sanctity of the individual, he thought, proceeded from the aristocratic nature of Germanic feudalism.[4] From it he deduced the English love of freedom, the aristocratic traditions which made freedom possible, and the admirable constitutional state and Protestant Church which were the political and religious expressions of freedom. Ultimately love of freedom must lead in England, as it had in America, to democracy.[5] The continent, including Germany, would trail along behind as always. Gervinus reconciled the aristocratic age of the eighteenth century with his democratic ideals: the English aristocracy proved so responsible that it refrained from setting up an oligarchy in the Polish manner. 'On the contrary,' he commented, 'the English state produced at that time the great model for mixed constitutions in

[1] Georg Gottfried Gervinus, lecture notes on 'Politik auf geschichtlicher Grundlage', *Nachlass* Gervinus, Hdbg. Hs. 1405, p. 4.

[2] Georg Gottfried Gervinus, *Geschichte der Angelsachsen im Ueberblick* (Frankfurt/Main, 1830).

[3] See ch. 6.

[4] Gervinus, *Einleitung*, p. 42.

[5] *Ibid.*, p. 49.

the modern age.'[1] The readiness of the ancients to give their lives and goods for the state seemed reborn in England, yet the English state still allowed enormous liberty.[2] This liberty itself struck Gervinus as awesome: law and order were scrupulously protected in England despite the lack of a standing army.[3] From such unsettling incidents as the riots which afflicted Britain immediately after the Napoleonic wars, Gervinus drew the questionable conclusion that the English state was strengthened rather than threatened by revolution, for 'all desires and complaints of the people have so many natural outlets'.[4]

England's love of freedom, Gervinus thought, went beyond her own borders. He emphasized England's anti-Catholic leadership and constant concern for the balance of power. Gervinus was bound to censure Britain for oppressing the American colonies, but he tempered his criticisms with observations about England's good claim to the new world she had developed.[5] His blanket approval of English foreign policy extended even to such an extreme case as Ireland. Here he admitted English harshness, but he blamed Irish sufferings on the very liberty which characterized the English. They were temperamentally unable to follow the Catholic example of repression, and precisely this humanitarianism drew out Irish sufferings indefinitely. 'Protestantism, rooted in resistance against Roman exclusiveness, came into conflict with its own inherent spirit of tolerance even when it was at its most intolerant.'[6] By identifying the English with Germanic freedom and Protestantism, Gervinus could excuse the blackest deeds in English history. His extremism in this regard made him unique even among Anglophile historians.

Gervinus was so partisan about England that he invented ways of excusing policies which contradicted his democratic principles. For example, he declared that the English state had been a republic 'in essence' since 1688.[7] Unlike Rotteck, he judged the tyranny of English kings and the greed of the aristocracy not by an absolute standard but by that of contemporary Europe: judged in this way, England emerged gloriously.[8] In other ways, too, Gervinus discriminated in favor of England. The second volume of his *History of the Nineteenth Century*,

[1] *Ibid.*, p. 84. [2] *Ibid.*, p. 88. [3] *Ibid.*, p. 55.
[4] *Ibid.*, p. 113. [5] *Ibid.*, p. 118.
[6] Gervinus, *Geschichte des neunzehnten Jahrhunderts*, 8 vols. (Leipzig, 1853–66), VII, 489.
[7] Gervinus, *Einleitung*, p. 84. [8] *Ibid.*, p. 86ff.

which treated the European reaction after 1815, omitted mention of England – as if there had been no reaction there.[1]

Gervinus's view of England, like the rest of his lengthy book, was an unfaithful mirror of German historical thought in the 1850s, simply because it developed pre-March constitutionalist ideology leftward. At the same time most of the other pre-March constitutionalists were developing their thought in the opposite direction or swearing off politics altogether. Nevertheless, Gervinus's praise of England contained many elements derived from the constitutionalist vocabulary, and his former allies also thought favorably about England throughout the 1850s. The constitutionalists, from Dahlmann on the right to Gervinus on the left, had always been compromisers at bottom, seeking to erect political institutions able to close the gap between arbitrary princely and bureaucratic power and the politically disorganized 'people', by which they actually meant the educated elite (*Bildungsschicht*).[2] The type of institutions they wished to create – a two-house legislature, a limited monarchy, an independent and unbureaucratized judicature with juries, strong local self-government, and freedom of discussion – had existed longest and most successfully in England. If English institutions did not work satisfactorily when transferred to France, the constitutionalists could still make a case that they would work in Germany, a nation possessing similar Germanic traditions of law and 'spirit'. It was especially this 'spirit', rather than the exact details of English government, which the German constitutionalists wished to borrow – the spirit of community-mindedness, gradualism, and compromise which their countrymen allegedly lacked. Indeed, their love of compromise led them to underestimate the role of partisanship in English parliamentary life, to mistrust parties as such, and to play out a tragedy in 1848 with an English text. Even though American federal or French constitutional practice undeniably influenced the Frankfurt constitution-makers, they were forced to accept these influences because of the nature of their own *national* problem. The behavior of the constitutionalists reflects more the exigencies of nation-building than the ideal of parliamentary development. It had been this latter ideal which had dominated the thought

[1] Gervinus, *Geschichte des neunzehnten Jahrhunderts*, II (1856).

[2] For an enlightening discussion of the constitutionalists' misapplication of the term 'people', see Mommsen, *Grösse und Versagen*, p. 37.

of the constitutionalists in their small states before 1848. Even when some of them – especially Dahlmann – had supported unification of Germany under Prussia, they had done so only on the supposition that constitutional government must accompany or precede unification. The paucity of their comments on foreign-policy matters in 1848 compared to their overriding concern with a good constitution indicates the shape of their curiosity about England. It also explains why they showed so little awareness of a possible rivalry between England and a yet-unborn German national state, despite the crises of 1848 over Schleswig-Holstein. If there was disappointment about Britain's lukewarm position on German unification, it melted away after Louis Napoleon's subversion of constitutional government in France and reaction in the German states left Britain once again as a beacon of political light. The events of the German revolutions thus had no perceptible effect on constitutionalist admiration for England: it had been growing since the 1830s and evidently reached its peak in the 1850s.

The view of the constitutionalists colored the thinking of educated Germans more strongly than that of any other group of historians in the pre-March period. It was they who focussed attention upon the neo-Gothic Houses on the Thames and refined the German concept of liberty with English references. Few voices arose from the conservative quarter to contradict them, and many from the same quarter joined in the chorus of praise. It is to this quarter that we must now turn in order to understand the depth of German adulation of England at mid-century.

CHAPTER 6

ENGLAND AS FIRST COUSIN – RANKE AND PROTESTANT-GERMANIC CONSERVATISM

The rising tide of interest in and approval of English political institutions accompanied the development of an ideology of political opposition among the German constitutionalists from the 1830s onwards. But what of those writers indifferent or hostile to reforms of German political life, those who fundamentally agreed with the order set up in Germany as a result of the Congress of Vienna and restored after successive waves of constitutionalist agitation? One might expect them to take cognizance of the new uses of English history developed by the constitutionalists, to concede to them exclusive use of that example, and to fight back with a negative picture of England. This did in fact occur in the thinking of a few extreme conservatives in Prussia, as we shall see in the next chapter. But actually the most important conservative, 'establishment' historians revered England and added their voices to the loud chorus of praise. This would have been impossible if they had engaged the constitutionalists in direct debate over the same issues in English life and history. Instead, they almost always spoke of different things, of remote periods of history, of cultural rather than political life, of foreign policy rather than the rise of parliamentary power over the monarchy. They avoided the issues raised by the constitutionalists. They drew a picture of another England – an 'old England' capable of warming the hearts of German aristocrats to oppose the 'new England' that agitated the minds of modernizing commercial and bureaucratic elites. Their major presuppositions included a preoccupation with established Protestant Christianity, romantic ideas about the unity of Germanic peoples, and an overestimation of continuity in the historical process. Many authors of this view of England knew the country and its historical sources better than their constitutionalist counterparts: they were drawn to England more by non-ideological interest and sentiment than by constitutionalist ideology. Their political viewpoint colored but did not determine their approach as it did with the constitutionalists.

The central figure among the German historians of England writing in this tradition was Leopold von Ranke. He contributed more to the study of English history in Germany than any other writer – by his own classic study of early-modern England[1] and by training other leading scholars of England, notably Reinhold Pauli (see ch. 8). Ranke's detached and apparently non-partisan approach to English history also contributed to later characteristics of the German view, particularly a tendency to study England chiefly as an actor on the stage of European power politics rather than the leader in European domestic political reform. It is no small irony that the later canonization of Ranke's conservative Anglophile approach led to jettisoning the English domestic political example and focussing on the increasingly tense international relations between Britain and the *Reich* – a formula which fed the fires of late nineteenth-century German Anglophobia.

Ranke's reluctant refusal in the late 1820s to write a major history of England (a project he later took up again) led the publisher Perthes to select a less illustrious author to write the first critically researched history of England in German – Johann Martin von Lappenberg. Like Ranke, Lappenberg came from a bourgeois Protestant clerical family and arrived at an academic career in history by a circuitous route. Ranke had prepared himself for the ministry, and Lappenberg had studied medicine. Both later turned to history, but neither fully shed earlier influences: Ranke retained his Christian-humanist education at Schulpforta and Leipzig; Lappenberg, deep impressions about the continuous development of law from the middle ages, derived from his studies at Göttingen. Lappenberg, indeed, was the last nineteenth-century historian profoundly influenced by Möser, one of the earliest spokesmen for Germanic ideology. Both men had strong personal ties to Britain as well: Ranke married an Anglo-Irish lady, and Lappenberg, who studied in Edinburgh, went through several

[1] Leopold von Ranke, *Englische Geschichte vornehmlich im sechzehnten und siebzehnten Jahrhundert*, 7 vols. (Berlin, 1859–68). All references to this work involve the first edition except for vol. III. The original vol. III was divided into vol. III and IV in the third edition, which had to be used for this study.

agonizing years hoping to marry into a Scottish family. Both maintained contacts and traveled in England. Lappenberg, a Hamburger, felt as strongly drawn to English manners and culture as to German. Finally, both men exhibited strong traits of Christian piety – a characteristic noticeably lacking in the more secular-minded German constitutionalists. Ranke had followed this line from the start, probably as a result of his training for the ministry; Lappenberg, an emotionally unstable person in his youth, because of a dual conversion to Protestant orthodoxy and political conservatism in the early 1820s.

Both Lappenberg and Ranke would be difficult to place in political perspective if one had to rely on their private papers and public utterances – neither one left a very enlightening record. Fortunately the ideas they expressed in their published works echoed the less voluminous comments of a number of other men who stood high in the Prussian establishment during their maturity. The extremes in mid-nineteenth-century German political life have been studied with some competence, but the ideas and opinions of the officially tolerated middle ground have not. As soon as one studies the views of a number of somewhat scholarly Prussian officials, one finds a remarkable correspondence between their general view of England and that of Ranke and Lappenberg, the real scholars. For that reason it would be useful to mention briefly a few other observers from the conservative and pious world of North German letters – men such as Baron Christian Karl Josias von Bunsen, Prussian ambassador to England during most of Friedrich Wilhelm IV's reign; Ludwig von Gerlach,[1] one of the same king's favorites; or Friedrich von Raumer, whose close connections with high Prussian civil servants and the royal family prompted oppositional professors to nickname him 'the lackey professor' of history at Berlin. Several degrees of conservatism separated these men, to be sure; but compared to the constitutionalists, they were all pillars of the existing order in Prussia. Both Bunsen and Raumer held high reputations in the world of German letters; Gerlach's significance lies in the very close correspondence between his views and those of his royal master.

Crudely expressed, a model of the view of these men would begin

[1] Christian Karl Josias von Bunsen (1791–1860) was a Prussian civil servant, prominent private scholar, and collaborator of Niebuhr on the history of Rome. Ludwig von Gerlach (1795–1877) was a highly influential Prussian civil servant, conservative politician, and political writer. (See Biographical Appendix.)

with the assertion that England was a great fellow Protestant power; that this religious similarity had some connection with England's Germanic heritage; that inborn reverence for tradition and Christian piety insured England against revolution and rapid concessions to fleeting demands for change; that the aristocracy still (properly) dominated English life. Honor, dignity, piety, respect for hierarchy, and a sense of responsibility kept the classes cheerfully in their places. This view of England stressed the provinces and the countryside while avoiding mention of the new industrial order. It dwelt lovingly on the hoary traditions and rites of the established church, the prerogatives and duties of the nobleman, and England's 'natural' role as Germany's ally. But Benthamites and proletarians, parliamentary dominance and ministerial responsibility – in short, most of the troublesome or progressive elements in English life – were overlooked. By turning their attention to aspects of English life which the constitutionalists considered anachronistic or irrelevant, by stressing the Protestant-Germanic, natural ally theories which seemed to bind the two nations, these men could evade the glaring chasm between English constitutional practice and the open absolutism of Prussia.

The remarks on England in Gerlach's memoirs reveal much about the interests and blind spots of conservative observers in the pre-March period. Gerlach visited England in 1844 and again in 1852. As a Prussian juridical expert on a semi-official mission for his king, Gerlach studied the central and local courts of law. His interest in Parliament was limited to the House of Lords sitting as a court, although the king himself asked him to gather data on Parliament with a view to suggestions for Prussia's future 'corporate' representative body (the later United Diet). In this light, and considering the crown's project to pattern the Prussian upper house after the English House of Lords in the early 1850s, Gerlach's concentration on the Peers was quite significant. Gerlach admired the spirit of *noblesse oblige* which characterized local self-government, and he undoubtedly considered it a good example for the *Junker* who had judicial powers on their estates. Gerlach paid special attention to the system of entail which guaranteed to many noblemen the wherewithal to be public-spirited. He liked British juries and British legal procedure – but chiefly because of its pompous ancient trappings. His admiration for the Church of England (and especially of Pusey and the Tractarians) went back to a similar love of old liturgy and the externals of religion. Not coincidentally, Friedrich Wilhelm had vague hopes of reforming the Prussian church liturgy, setting up apostolic succession through the Church of England, and making other changes in Prussian Protestantism by adapting colorful English traditions. The almost childish delight in liturgical forms shown by Gerlach played an enormous role in the admiration of many Prussian conservatives for England. On the other hand, Gerlach showed little interest in the role of Commons in government or in socio-economic questions. He visited several factory towns without commenting on them; and after witnessing a strike against Lord Londonderry he merely commented on the good order, intelligence, and piety of the British working class.[1]

To the religious Prussian conservative there was no inconsistency in admiring England while rejecting parliamentary government. Clearly the English landed aristocracy still enjoyed prestige and power, and once the question of who ruled was answered, the question of how seemed less important. The moderate Prussian conservatives could argue away the existence of representative government as a product of peculiar English conditions or point to the corruption which reduced its representativeness.[2] It was parochial and irrelevant in their eyes. What mattered were the eternal and international problems of social hierarchy, religion, and the security of the 'Germanic idea of kingship' against possible future revolutions emanating from France. Some were deluded about the nature of English government: Gerlach, for example, naïvely believed England to be a divine-right monarchy because people cheered 'God save the Queen'.[3] Others, like Bunsen, developed away from a stiff conservatism toward an understanding of the usefulness of representative institutions, but he never regarded such institutions as an equal partner with the monarch. Whether deluded or not about the nature of parliamentary rule, the Prussian moderate conservatives usually evaded the issue as far as possible. Only Raumer departed from his colleagues by mentioning the effects of the reforms of the 1830s and the possible decline of the aristocracy. But he firmly believed that

[1] Ernst Ludwig von Gerlach, *Aufzeichnungen aus meinem Leben und Wirken, 1795–1877*, edited by Jakob von Gerlach, 2 vols. (Schwerin, 1903), I, 351–400.

[2] See the remarks on electoral corruption – made with evident approval – by Gerlach (*Aufzeichnungen*, I, 369) and Friedrich von Raumer, *England im Jahre 1835*, 2 vols. (Berlin, 1836), I, 253.

[3] William Shanahan, *German Protestants face the Social Question* (Notre Dame, Ind., 1954), p. 163, n. 11.

reform would end in strengthening monarchical power. Taking this position of royalist reformer, he rationalized this way: 'The more powerful and manifold the participation of the people and the control of Parliament and public opinion are, the more a people can allow and even require a powerful [royal] administration.'[1] Raumer represented a more *politique*, less religiously charged attitude than Gerlach, Ranke, or Bunsen, but he was firmly anti-revolutionary. He admired England more for its religious toleration than its orthodoxy. Raumer's sunny defense of England against the pessimistic Anglophobe conservatives of the late 1820s put England in the most favorable light.[2]

The importance of Protestantism and England's function as a great power in the thinking of Prussian-conservative Anglophiles appears most strongly in the cases of Ranke and Bunsen. Both men had admired England from their earliest days and had espoused an ecumenical and humanistic Christianity, so admiration for the greatest Protestant power was perhaps natural. What makes both cases instructive was the selection of these men of modest family for high posts in Prussia by Friedrich Wilhelm IV at the outset of his reign – Bunsen as Ambassador to England and Ranke as Historiographer of Prussia. Bunsen was catapulted from disgrace to one of the highest posts in Prussia's foreign service chiefly because the new monarch thought he could pave the way for closer Anglo–Prussian cooperation, especially in the field of religion.[3] To Bunsen, as to the king, religion seemed to stand out as the apex of a solid English pyramid of conservative, paternalistic, aristocratic, and orderly values which they would have liked to shore up in Prussia.

In one of his earliest writings on England, Ranke singled out the piety of the English aristocracy as the distinguishing motivation behind

[1] Raumer, *England im Jahre 1835*, I, 382.

[2] Raumer's comments, like most of his historical writing, consisted largely of anecdotal and rather non-analytical material. I have mentioned him here chiefly because he could combine an attachment to the better traditions of the 'enlightened Prussian police state' (Fueter, *Historiographie*, p. 504) with a remarkably vigorous defense of English history and the English present. His major historical remarks consist of the lengthy sections on England in his *Geschichte Europas seit dem Ende des fünfzehnten Jahrhunderts*, 8 vols. (Leipzig, 1832–50). More contemporary comments are to be found in *England im Jahre 1835*, particularly I, 30, 50, 96, 127f., 129, 132f., 198ff., 218, 253, 258, 328, 367, 382, 392, 491, and 551; and II, 26, 96, 112f., 157, 163, 432, and 542ff.

[3] Bunsen had always been as interested in liturgical reform as in diplomacy, and his major successes included an Anglo–Prussian agreement on Protestant clerical cooperation in Jerusalem. His closest friends in England included leaders of the Broad-bottom movement. For details of his life and tenure as ambassador, see Wilma Höcker, *Der Gesandte Bunsen als Vermittler zwischen Preussen und England* (Göttingen, 1951).

its public spirit and, by extension, its championing the best interests of Europe. 'In England,' he wrote, 'a perhaps narrow, but on the whole manly and self-confident religiosity was formed, one capable of overcoming the conflicts [within the aristocracy].'[1] The religiosity of the English aristocracy appeared as a major reason for the political effectiveness of the class and, ultimately, as one of the 'moral energies' which Ranke believed moved history and gave cohesion to epochs:

> No accidental, raging confusion, no wild flying against each other, no succession of states and peoples is offered by world history, as it might appear on first glance...There are forces, to wit spiritual, life-bringing, creative forces, themselves living, there are moral energies which we see in their development.[2]

This aristocratic religious energy, Ranke thought, fixed the role of England as the greatest Protestant power – the upholder of the European balance of power against the non-Protestant empires – first Spain, then France. Britain's conflicts with other Protestant powers – especially Holland and Prussia – received significantly little attention.

Ranke's *Primat der Aussenpolitik* (primacy of foreign policy) – the belief that a state's foreign relations are more significant in explaining history than internal problems – led him initially to view England almost exclusively as the leader of coalitions for the defense of Europe's liberty. Such an approach resulted in suppressing what would most alarm conservatives – analysis of the contemporary shift of power away from the crown and aristocracy – while comforting them with the hope that England would always protect continental Protestantism and its conservative backers. What Ranke implied, like-minded historians stated flatly. As Raumer put it in the 1830s, 'If someday Russian or French armies marched with inimical intentions on the Oder or the Rhine, the English lion would raise itself from its place of rest and develop a power unsuspected by those who believe England is no longer useful or has no stuffing left simply because she will not dance their tune.'[3]

Although Ranke's great work on English history first appeared in the 1850s, in the 1830s his characteristic viewpoint of later years about English history had already crystallized. As early as 1826 he had accep-

[1] Leopold von Ranke, 'Die grossen Mächte', *Historisch-politische Zeitschrift*, II (1833), p. 13.

[2] *Ibid.*, p. 49.

[3] Raumer, *England im Jahre 1835*, II, 113.

ted Perthes' offer to write one of the national histories for the Heeren series. He refused the volumes on Spain and France, but for a few years considered England because its history, unlike that of France, demonstrated an attractive 'continuity and steady progression'.[1] Because of his involvement with the Venetian *relazioni*, Ranke ultimately resigned from the project in favor of Lappenberg. But he recorded his early views in his famous essay on the great powers. In the 1830s Ranke edited the *Historisch-politische Zeitschrift*. This was a notable departure from his self-proclaimed attempt to separate contemporary politics and history, since the journal survived only with the support of a Prussian government eager to counteract the immediate threat of French revolutionary examples.[2] The Prussian government cannot be called inconsistent for supporting both Ranke's favorable picture of English foreign policy and Hegel's condemnation of the English reform movement: animosity towards France and 'French-inspired' constitutional experiments lurked in the background in both cases.

Ranke portrayed the heroic days when England shook off the Stuarts and guarded the 'genius of Europe' and the balance of power against the ambitious and vain France. England 'before all other European states would have had the calling and the power to oppose the French', Ranke noted.[3] Such a calling was impossible as long as the Stuarts ruled. Fortunately that house 'succumbed to a religious and national movement which served the interests of a threatened Europe'.[4]

Far from taking England to task for working against international law, the interests of Europe, or the goals of Prussia, Ranke blandly defended English policies in the crucial eighteenth century. No historian writing at the same time judged so mildly and favorably. Ranke, for example, approved the development of British naval and commercial power in the eighteenth century. Vast colonial possessions and naval preponderance merely guaranteed, in his eyes, the continued success of the European containment of France's ambitions. France had, of course, held her former gains, 'but for a nation which more than any other flatters itself with the glow of general superiority, this was not nearly enough. She felt only the loss of claims which she had regarded as

[1] Hermann Oncken, *Aus Ranke's Frühzeit* (Gotha, 1922), p. 26.

[2] See Sieburg, *Deutschland und Frankreich*, I, 229.

[3] Ranke, 'Die grossen Mächte', p. 6f.

[4] *Ibid.*, p. 13.

rights.'[1] A French plot to rob England of her colonies, not English injustice and even bumbling, had triggered the American Revolution. As Britain had emerged from the American war unscathed because of her sound policies, France had entered into financial chaos and impotence abroad – the main reasons for the French Revolution.[2]

In contrast to his distaste for that revolution, Ranke found ways of stressing how different the English revolutions of the seventeenth century had been. Constitutional historians of Ranke's generation studied the seventeenth century searching for dramatic examples of royal folly and popular wisdom. Ranke, on the other hand, concentrated his labors on seventeenth-century England not only because diplomatic records – his favorite source – abounded, but also because it seemed an age when religious questions moved the minds of men. The constitutionalists minimized the role of religion in English life. Ranke went in the opposite direction, approaching the era for its dramatic examples of the Roman–Protestant struggle. Constitutional questions were only of secondary importance to him, and when he spoke of freedom, he meant the independence of the Protestant churches from the Papacy. England's struggle was the seventeenth- and eighteenth-century chapter in the perennial rivalry of Romance and Germanic nations, with England playing the role of Germanic-Protestant champion.

Ranke finally set out in the 1850s to describe the nation which, in his view, revered its own traditions more than any other. He desired to write a new kind of English history. When he visited Britain in 1857 and again in 1862, he wrote to his English wife describing the awesome beauty of medieval liturgy in Anglican services. No amount of political radicalism could threaten the traditional piety of the English, he believed, for 'hustings and church *are* England'.[3] In his treatment of such knotty problems as the Puritan Revolution, Ranke similarly stressed the interdependence of politics and faith.

In the beginning of his *Englische Geschichte*, while speaking of the middle ages, Ranke adumbrated his treatment of the seventeenth century by linking religious and political questions. Simon de Montfort,

[1] *Ibid.*, p. 35.

[2] *Ibid.*, p. 37f. Fueter called Ranke's attempt to derive the origins of the French Revolution from international relations one of the great historian's striking failures. See Fueter, *Historiographie*, p. 476.

[3] Ranke, *Sämmtliche Werke*, 54 vols. (Leipzig, 1868–90), vols. LIII–LIV, letter no. 182, dated London, 4 April 1857.

for example, had usually been depicted in German constitutionalist writings as an early crusader for parliamentary government, or at least for corporative resistance to royal power. Ranke showed him in a quite different light, as the initiator of an independent English nationality. Representative institutions merely served to amplify popular discontent with 'all foreign interference',[1] chiefly that of Rome. In a similar way, Ranke was eager to demonstrate that the throne, rather than the people, had shaped the destiny of the constitutionalists' model state. And whereas the writers of the Enlightenment had customarily dismissed the religious forces at work in early modern England as 'fanaticism', Ranke, by taking them very seriously, initiated a considerable revision of the German view of Tudors, Stuarts, and Puritans. Henry VIII, for example, emerged as a popular champion of English independence against Rome: 'this egotistical prince certainly did not follow his own desires, as is generally supposed', Ranke wrote, but '...recognized with quick intelligence all political necessities and followed the lines they indicated'.[2] The 'necessities' of which Ranke spoke were clear: by the sixteenth century 'the time had come to give the English realm an independent tradition and internal order corresponding to her cultural attainments and insular position'.[3] Faced with the problem of Henry's seizure of church property, Ranke overcame his Christian scruples and maintained that the proceeds had gone to support a foreign policy useful to the security of Europe.[4] Whereas most constitutionalists had scolded the Tudor parliaments for their servility, Ranke drew a positive moral from their behavior. 'Having arisen originally in the fight against Rome and having declined in the civil wars [of the Roses], Parliament achieved its full importance again only when it stepped onto the side of the monarchy in the struggle against Rome.'[5]

Ranke's application of the *Primat der Aussenpolitik* to English history furthermore resulted in a flattering new view of the much-maligned Stuarts. Had they not contributed much to the unification of the parts of Great Britain, thereby building the powerful base vital to England's historic role as champion of the Protestant-Germanic world? 'Reconciliation under their authority' of 'quarrelling factions' was the 'chief thought of this family', Ranke wrote.[6] Indeed, James I had touched off resistance by his well-meaning attempt to mediate between Pro-

[1] Ranke, *Englische Geschichte*, I, 79.
[2] *Ibid.*, I, 220.
[3] *Ibid.*, I, 122.
[4] *Ibid.*, I, 222f.
[5] *Ibid.*, I, 300.
[6] *Ibid.*, II, 4.

testants and Catholics, not by breaking some (non-existent) constitution. 'One should not think so little of him', Ranke pleaded.[1] Parliament had been too parochial, and Ranke rebuked it for its inability to perceive England's true interests in a French alliance against Spain.[2] The sittings of Parliament 'breathed a decidedly aggressive spirit'.[3] Nevertheless, Ranke insisted that no comparison between the Puritan and French revolutions should be made, for the former had sprung from religious roots.[4] He implied that the modern revolutionary tradition came solely from France, since political revolution did not fit his concept of continuity in the Germanic peoples.

Ranke's dislike of republicanism and illegitimate rulers led naturally to distaste for Cromwell, whose career Ranke sought to interpret as an unhappy interruption in the organic continuity of English history.[5] On the other hand, Ranke had to accept Cromwell's foreign policy. Although he was a tyrannical monster, 'supreme power in itself was not his goal: it only served to realize ideas of religious freedom in the Protestant sense, civic order, and national independence'.[6]

Only when he reached the fall of the Stuart dynasty in 1688–9 did Ranke abandon their defense, and then for quite different reasons from those of the constitutionalists. The Glorious Revolution was necessary not because of the march of liberal ideas, as the constitutionalists proclaimed, but because 'the ancient independence of the European realms could no longer be maintained unless [Louis XIV] encountered permanent resistance... It seemed England's natural calling to undertake such a role: the traditional enmity which she shared with France, her maritime position, and the preponderance of the Protestant faith in the country made such resistance her European duty.'[7] James II had prevented England from carrying out her world-historical mandate, thus it was a 'European necessity' that he 'abandon' the throne. Ranke virtually ignored the constitutional changes resulting from the Glorious Revolution and instead stressed the happy cooperation of prince and people against the French. He did not complain about the somewhat questionable methods used by the English in their century-long struggle with France.[8]

[1] *Ibid.*, II, 6. On the good faith of Charles I and the excitability of Parliament, see II, 242, 237, 448; III (3rd edn.), 317. [2] *Ibid.*, II, 90f. [3] *Ibid.*, III, 19.
[4] *Ibid.*, III, 122. [5] *Ibid.*, IV (3rd edn.), 4. [6] *Ibid.*, IV, 202. [7] *Ibid.*, V, 278.
[8] See, for example, his unusually fair treatment of England's forsaking the grand alliance to make peace at Utrecht, *Englische Geschichte*, VII, 53.

Ranke selected elements of faith, blood, and foreign policy common to both the North German states and England as the basis of his early-modern history. For the early middle ages, Johann Martin Lappenberg could not reasonably stress faith or foreign policy as the most obvious ties between the two lands. Therefore Lappenberg underscored the Germanic element in English history. This stress followed naturally from the romantics' curiosity about the middle ages and from the implications of German philological science, both of which influenced Lappenberg deeply. Philological studies, which acted as a springboard for nineteenth-century historiography, reinforced the old idea of Germanic racial identity of England and Germany. As Mosse has declared,

> To the growing body of racial theory, philology contributed the actual 'Aryan' distinction. Through an examination of German and English linguistic roots German philologists postulated the theory that both peoples had stemmed from a common root...The two peoples had [supposedly] developed the desirable qualities of self-reliance and independence as a direct result of the migration [from India].[1]

Lappenberg had known many leading lights of the new German literary movement in his youth, including philologists. He corresponded for over forty years with Jakob Grimm concerning things Anglo-Saxon and later declared that the study of English history owed more to Grimm than to any other German.[2]

Lappenberg's long acquaintance with the English and his association with the codifiers of the new historical method in the *Monumenta Germaniae Historica* qualified him for his task. His *Geschichte von England* began a major project in German historiography, a complete and scholarly series devoted to English history and written by leading experts.

Two tendencies of the age appeared in Lappenberg's *chef d'œuvre*: the increasingly detailed and specialized narrative demanded by the new historical method and the choice of the nation-state as a principle around which to organize historical works. The old European-wide, cosmopolitan histories so popular before continued to appear, but the national history became the vehicle for learned writing, increasingly

[1] George L. Mosse, *The Crisis of German Ideology* (New York, 1964), p. 89.

[2] Elard Hugo Meyer, *Johann Martin Lappenberg* (Hamburg, 1867), p. 98f. Grimm replied in kind by toasting Lappenberg in 1863 as 'half Englishman, whole German, and dyed-in-the-wool Hamburger' – a flattering tribute to a dying cosmopolitanism.

leaving the world histories to popularizers. Lappenberg had scholarly reasons for writing his English history, for, as he declared, practically no German works existed on the subject, and the uncritical products of English historians dwelt too exclusively upon recent centuries.[1] Lappenberg's work was good enough to be translated into English, and he became the first German historian to take the field of English history as his specialty.

Nevertheless, Lappenberg's history of England from the earliest times until the death of King Stephen hung together on the thread of bias for the 'Saxon Germanic heritage'. Previous accounts of medieval England, he complained in the preface, often suffered from a pro-Roman prejudice: Hume and Gibbon had misunderstood the middle ages because they had overlooked their fundamentally Germanic character. As if to redress this wrong, Lappenberg brushed aside Roman and Celtic Britain and devoted an overwhelming proportion of the first volume of his *Geschichte von England* to the customs and history of the Anglo-Saxons. The second volume, a much shorter work, was an unenthusiastic chronicle of the Norman period. Even so, the culture of the Normans went unmentioned; the fate of Anglo-Saxon culture under the invaders, on the other hand, occupied one-fourth of the second tome.

Lappenberg described the course of English history as a progression from the barbarism resulting from the Roman withdrawal, to improvement with the coming of the German tribes, through the development of a vibrant independent culture. The Nordic invaders were exculpated from destroying Roman culture, which had vanished already; instead, the Germanic tribes saved the island from anarchy. Lappenberg praised their 'mission' as *Kulturträger* (bearers of culture). 'Upon this ground', he wrote of post-Roman Britain, 'a people would arise, soon to become one of the firmest bulwarks of Christianity, to produce the noblest and wisest rulers,...and to outstrip the power not only of the states of the new [medieval] world, but also that of ancient Rome.'[2] The repression of Germanic culture by the 'Romance' Normans could not last forever. Finally, the Anglo-Saxon traditions of government and the English tongue had reasserted themselves in the seventeenth century by the agency of the revolution against the 'Romanizing' Stuarts and

[1] See Johann Martin Lappenberg, *Vorwort* to the *Geschichte von England*, 2 vols. (Hamburg, 1834–7), vol. I.

[2] *Ibid.*, I, 64.

the rise of a purely English literature in the hands of Milton. Taking over a romantic idea, Lappenberg assumed that the genius of Shakespeare could be explained by an 'unconscious return' to the spirit and language of the Anglo-Saxons![1]

The theme of Germanic cultural and racial heritage remained fashionable and respectable in Germany and even in England until the end of the century,[2] so one need not consider Lappenberg or those who echoed his sentiments as aberrant. A more legitimate problem is the motive behind their sentimental insistence that blood tied them to England. In Lappenberg's case we stand at the crossroads where cosmopolitanism, nationalism, and provincialism met in Germany. The three traditional attitudes toward community membership are by no means mutually exclusive, for they existed side by side even in the minds of many German nationalists. Confusion about the matter of which group one belonged to could be held at bay with elastic concepts such as *das Germanische* (Germanicness). On the other hand, insistence on Germanic qualities, real or imagined, had served to set Germans off from other nations – particularly France – since Möser's day. Germanic myths, as used in Wagner's operas, served to create a vivid sense of differentness in German minds. On the other hand, insistence on the Germanic heritage partook of a certain cosmopolitan generosity by including other Germanic peoples, notably the English, in a community of kindred feeling. The motive behind this generosity undoubtedly lay partly in the need to overcome a German sense of inferiority in the face of ancient Roman and modern French culture. The 'quarrel of the ancients and moderns' still echoed in German writings: could modern culture ever hope to attain the heights of ancient Rome? The question had long since been answered in the positive, but chiefly by the French in the name of *their* culture. A lingering doubt about the ability of Germanic peoples to rise to such heights plagued many historians, but here England came to their aid. If England could be

[1] *Ibid.*, pp. lxxii–lxxiii.

[2] Friedrich Max Müller, a German linguist who became a popular oracle in London in the late 1850s, linked language with race and cited Bopp, the Grimms, and other authorities to make his point. Only in 1888 did Müller admit that evidence did not support his earlier contention, but his change of mind had less effect than his earliest pronouncements. This vague form of racism – with its implication that the Germanic peoples were superior as well as different – still seems mild and harmless when compared to the concrete form it took in the minds of H. S. Chamberlain or Hitler. On Müller see Louis Snyder, *Race. A History of Modern Ethnic Theories* (New York, 1939), p. 67.

called the modern Rome, as it often was, then a Germanic civilization could rise to equal the greatest Latin civilization. Some German historians – the majority of them on the conservative, Protestant church-oriented side of the German house of intellect – consequently stressed England's role as the 'new Rome' as much as its resistance to the real Rome of the Papacy.

The elements comprising the moderate conservative, Protestant-Germanic view of England as a close 'relative' among the peoples had of course lain about for decades. Historians of Ranke's caliber did not so much originate a new approach to English history as refine and perfect an old one. It was precisely the traditional aspect of the Protestant-Germanic view which made it easy to embrace despite unsettling evidence to the contrary. Besides, none of the historians discussed in this chapter was an inflexible reactionary: their conservatism ranged from the sharp-eyed bureaucratism of Raumer through the theologically-tinged passivity of Ranke to the misty nostalgia for medieval splendor in Gerlach. Not even the most reactionary among them, for example Gerlach, utterly opposed *all* change, for organicist political philosophy took issue only with the speed of change, not change itself. The serenity of their arguments and their refusal to engage the constitutionalists in polemics over the true nature of England's political institutions reflected the security felt by conservatives before 1848. They could well afford to view England in much the same way as the late-eighteenth-century scholars of Göttingen, and whatever dissonance arose could still be easily suppressed. Even the constitutionalists often agreed with their assessments of remoter periods in English history, an indication that they themselves were more interested in using assorted English historical examples than in revising all of English history.

To summarize the motivations and suppositions underlying the Protestant-Germanic view of England would be to summarize the mentality of an age. Ranke's case is not radically different from that of the others: religion still held a powerful sway over his thought and colored his political and scientific views. Assuming that God acts through the nations and gives unity to periods with 'leading ideas', the historians' duty remained the search for the divine thread. To the North German Protestants and especially to the anti-Habsburg Prussians, God's will included resistance to universalism – whether ancient Roman, medieval Papal, modern Habsburg, Russian, or French.

Indeed, in Ranke's particular view, the tension between Romance and Germanic, between Protestant and Catholic, between blocks of powers constituted the mainspring of European historical energy. England and North Germany were common defenders of God's plan against French hegemonial ambitions (Ranke made little of England's involvement in the rivalry of Prussia and Austria or of her hegemonic position outside of Europe), thus placing both peoples morally on the right (and same) side.

The bridge between religion, race, and politics bypassed certain thorny political paths, particularly those trod by the constitutionalists. Instead the moderate conservatives followed the course of England's *foreign* politics, its culture, or its church affairs. Skirting the issue of domestic reform in recent English history was possible only by stressing the long-range, backward-looking approach of the historicist and antiquarian. The Protestant-Germanic view never raised questions about Britain's future and rarely looked closely at the recent past.

Among the possible motivations behind this view of England one must exclude at least one: nationalism. Ties to religion and region were stronger in the minds of these men than any national bonds, and men like Lappenberg felt at least as strongly drawn to England as to Catholic South Germany. Psychologically it was more flattering to participate in the achievements of the Protestant-Germanic north of Europe than in those of the German people as a whole. The viability of this approach was enhanced by the absence of any large or enduring conflicts between the German states and England. Even the most acrimonious – the conflict between the *Zollverein* and Britain over tariffs and Navigation Laws – were minor enough to be overlooked. National conflicts could still be looked upon as family quarrels.

The most extraordinary thing about the Protestant-Germanic view of England in the mid-nineteenth century, then, is not its component elements or its inspiration. Not what the view was, but who held it turns out to be the surprise. Many Anglo-American historians have noted the admiration of England among German 'liberals' in this period and have falsely concluded that German 'conservatives' must have been on the other side of the fence about England. But as we have seen, many (though not all) of the officially-sanctioned historical thinkers of Prussia, at least, retained and elaborated a view of England quite similar to that of the Burkean conservative reformers around 1810.

Perhaps the Protestant-Germanic historians consciously averted their eyes from recent British history in order to prevent the collapse of this old view; certainly they distorted and suppressed many uncomfortable facts. Perhaps, on the other hand, England's entry into the path of continuing political reform and democratization was so irresolute, so mild, that it fostered a genuine ambivalence about the course of English history. This latter possibility seems most likely. As long as England marched very slowly on the path of reform, as long as the myth of a community of interests in European power politics could be maintained, the moderate conservative view could be upheld. At the same time, the constitutionalists, by stressing exactly the periods of history and aspects of the state ignored by the moderate conservatives, came up with a different but also strongly positive representation of England. They, too, showed cosmopolitan traits; saw England as a political utopia where change could be accomplished without violence; and appreciated the Germanic (if not the religious) heritage of England. Thus well into the 1850s most German historians from the pro-parliamentary left to the moderate right agreed in praising 'England', even though they were talking about two rather different concepts.

Only on the extreme left and right, and from a few thinkers out of season, arose faint voices to inject in the chorus of praise disharmonious notes. Isolated, ranged against each other in many other questions, and divided about the 'true' nature of England, these critics had little immediate influence on academic or public opinion. Yet they all made some important contribution to later representations of England, for in many cases their heresies eventually became the new pieties of the late nineteenth century.

CHAPTER 7

ENGLAND AS A SIBLING RIVAL–OUTSIDE VIEWS

It would be only slightly unfair, in the context of this study, to pass over entirely a number of writers who deviated from the habit of regarding (and sometimes distorting) English history in the most amicable way. First, these men did not form a group in any sense. No common ideology or motivation linked them. Second, many of them changed their own minds about England in the course of their careers or maintained an ambivalent stance, a 'love–hate' relationship. To some extent this ambivalence was natural, particularly in men who did not devote themselves in any intensive way to the study of England (as many of these were). One could, then, be tempted to put them aside as inconvenient non-experts. Third, they were all men out of season in some respect, whose voices, as in the wilderness, reached few contemporary ears and changed few minds. All of them were, to be sure, committed to major socio-political struggles in Germany during the second third of the nineteenth century, but their contemporaries considered them cranks or extremists, thinkers unacceptable or suspect among the academic establishment.

Nevertheless, these controversial outsiders were significant. In many cases, they achieved late or posthumous recognition as prophets, founders of new views, and raisers of questions about England. The unfashionableness of their ideas during most of their lifetimes serves to indicate how strongly entrenched the ideas of the constitutionalists and the Protestant-Germanic historians were; the vogue of these same ideas later on alerts us to the great change in the climate of opinion in the last third of the century.

The chief motives behind the dissenting views were as numerous as the personalities behind them. An orthodox, but somewhat unsentimental political reaction gave the impetus to Friedrich Julius Stahl.

Disappointed constitutional liberalism led Lothar Bucher to a fixed ideological loathing of England and into employment as one of Bismarck's helpers. Starting from a narrow orthodox, divine-right position similar to Stahl's, Victor Aimé Huber turned to a concern for the 'social question' raised by industrialism and increasing approval of English solutions; a similar motivation underlay the views of Karl Marx and Friedrich Engels, although they approached the same evidence from the opposite political pole. The concern of these three for the working man drove them to study the early implications of English modernization for the German proletarian. Friedrich List,[1] on the other hand, viewed the same process with mixed admiration and fear from the standpoint of the fledgling German industrialists. And finally, the most scholarly of this group, Johann Gustav Droysen, departed from the rosy Rankean view of Anglo-German diplomatic relations as a part of his campaign to glorify Prussia and give it a sense of future national destiny.

The social origins of all these men being roughly similar to those of the constitutionalists and the formulators of Protestant-Germanic ideology, one cannot single out any changes in German society or even the social structure of the established academic professions to explain their different views. All came from modestly comfortable families active in the professions or in small industry. All except Marx and Stahl came from a Protestant background, and Stahl, after his conversion to the church of Luther, displayed a vigorous churchly orthodoxy. List, Stahl, and Huber came from South Germany but did not spend all their adult lives there. List lived and traveled in America and Europe, and both Stahl and Huber were employed in Berlin in defense of Prussian corporate conservatism and Protestant orthodoxy in the 1840s. Marx, Engels, and Bucher formed their deepest impressions of England while living there as exiles. If there is an outstanding element common to all these men, it lies in their unusual development out of conflict-torn early manhood into determined and independent intellectual maturity characterized by strong devotion to a cause. All, except Droysen, forewent promising and comfortable careers because of controversial commitments, and even Droysen made his name by opposing many highly-respected scholarly orthodoxies. It was this

[1] List does not belong by birth to the same generation as Marx or Bucher. I have included him here because his ideas were considerably ahead of his time.

independence (or, as contemporaries thought, perversity) of mind, this refusal to accept the reigning view, as much as the implications of their own social and political theories which led them to depart from the reigning view of English history and affairs.

The beginnings of their development in almost all cases involved some form of political iconoclasm, and as young liberals none of these men had much initial cause to criticize England. True, Marx, Engels, and Droysen owed large intellectual debts to Hegel, but they were not uncritical followers; Stahl had been deeply impressed by Schelling, not exactly an Anglophile. Nevertheless, in their youth they had all joined the opposition to the prevailing political system in the Germanic Confederation. Even Stahl, the later philosopher of uncompromising Prussian reaction, fell victim to the discipline meted out to members of the *Burschenschaften* (student associations), and Huber, who first became interested in English poetry and education in his early manhood, had cheered for the Spanish revolutionaries in 1820. At about the same time, Friedrich List had been forced to flee from Württemberg to America for advocating a constitutional regime based on the English model.[1] Both Marx and Bucher participated actively on the bourgeois constitutionalist side in 1848, and Bucher particularly cited English parliamentary examples in his speeches in the Prussian Assembly. All this made admiration for England quite natural for them. Only later, when they turned from youthful enthusiasms to the characteristic life work for which they are remembered, did they develop highly critical appraisals of England.

The most radical breaks with their own past were made by Huber and Stahl. Both demonstrated the close connection between Christian orthodoxy and political conservatism characteristic of Germany before 1848, with conservatism following from religious conversion. Such returns to the church were not uncommon in this generation. Both men found a refuge in Berlin in the early 1840s, where they propagated a strict Protestant orthodoxy and an inflexible defense of the

[1] List's political views will not be treated in this chapter, but interested readers may refer to the following works for his views: on the 'ideal' English constitution, 'Die Staatskunde und Staatspraxis Württembergs im Grundriss', *Werke*, ed. by Wilhelm von Sonntag, 10 vols. (Berlin, 1931–5), I, I, p. 304 *et passim*; on the rights of opposition, 'Verteidigungsrede vom 17. 11. 1821'. *ibid.*, I, 2, p. 710; on English self-government, 'Vorschlag zur Errichtung von Bürgerrottmeisterämtern', *ibid.*, I, I, p. 318. All these works make clear List's advocacy of the English political system in Germany or at least in Württemberg.

Prussian state against the challenges of the rationalistic constitutionalists. In the course of this defense, both men dissected the English domestic constitution, a subject largely avoided or given a superficial blessing by more flexible conservatives like Ranke. They confronted the constitutionalists head-on while many of their ultra-conservative allies refused to allow themselves to be drawn into debating on the same terms.[1] That is why Stahl's thinking, for example, approached that of an advanced constitutional theorist like Mohl much more closely than did Ranke's: Stahl and Mohl were speaking the same language and arriving at much the same conclusion about English parliamentary development.[2] Only in drawing conclusions for the German states did they differ violently. Unlike the nostalgic admirers of an elitist medieval corporation, who saw their idea partially realized in England, Stahl and Huber recognized the danger to monarchical dominance posed by the British Parliament and sought with only mixed success to alarm other conservatives to the peril. Huber and Stahl apparently feared the introduction of British constitutional practice more than the complacent organic conservatives did, and the former consequently sounded a more strident note in denouncing the British model. What they set out to refute was Montesquieu's concept of balance: in their view, it was foolish to suppose that monarchical authority and representative institutions could be in the long run harmonized. Power, they warned, is indivisible. Both moderate conservatives and constitutionalists argued that such harmony existed in England, although they disagreed on the feasibility of extending the system to other countries. Stahl and Huber attacked the very root of this belief.

Huber denied the applicability of the English constitution to Germany by challenging a basic premise of the constitutionalists: that the undeniably happy state of England flowed directly from its political constitution. He granted the power, greatness, and freedom of the

1 See Victor Aimé Huber, 'Über Friedrich von Raumer's "England im Jahre 1835"', *Beiträge zur Kritik der neuesten Literatur*, No. 1 (Rostock, 1837). Huber's attempt to refute the glowing picture of England presented by Raumer achieved little success. Raumer's book went through new editions while Huber was ignored. His journal *Janus*, published (1845–8) with the aid of secret funds from the Prussian government, failed to arouse enough support to justify its continuation, and his appointment at the University of Berlin inspired great hostility among the faculty, which considered him an unqualified political appointee. Radowitz was instrumental in furthering his career in Berlin.

2 Compare, for example, Mohl's 'Über die verschiedene Auffassung' with Friedrich Julius Stahl, *Das monarchische Princip* (Heidelberg, 1845).

English, but he insisted that social injustice and legal anachronisms not be overlooked. Huber's critique of the 'liberal' and 'conservative' views of England in the early 1840s was quite astute:

> Liberalism seeks and finds in England nothing but what can be labeled with the vague term freedom. The smarter ones interpret that as the very real position of Parliament *vis-à-vis* the crown, but the masses think of nothing less than the right of everyone to do and say what he wants. On our side, however, one thinks of the many historic elements which have survived as the basis of the present, most modern conditions... [We] think of much else that is good, beautiful, and efficient, but also of many cases where appearance covers reality and the antiquated letter obscures the modern spirit...[1]

The rationalism of Hegel's critique of England, the implied invidious comparison with the efficient bureaucratic absolutism of Prussia, and a discounting of the value of old communal structures in English local life reappeared to some extent in Huber's words. Only after his first extensive trip to England did he come about to embrace Burke's interpretation of an organic England. His most telling criticism in the early 1840s attacked the constitutionalist view that the English political system, so chaotic in appearance, did in fact 'work' better than bureaucratic centralism.

Stahl's critique of England owed even more to the Hegelian argument.[2] In the wake of Friedrich Wilhelm IV's confusing statements about a future representative assembly for Prussia, Stahl attempted to define the conservative idea of a popular representation. He rejected the theory of the division of powers. In its place he put two completely different principles of government between which every state must choose: the 'monarchical' and the 'parliamentary'.[3] Like Hegel, Stahl feared that the latter principle, by virtually stripping the king of power, 'gravitates toward the republic'.[4] England was Stahl's primary example of a 'parliamentary' regime. The point of Stahl's article was to lend

1 Victor Aimé Huber, 'Zur vergleichenden Politik. Die englische Verfassung und ihr "it works well!"', *Fliegende Blätter für Fragen des Tages*, VI (1843), p. 18f.

2 Stahl, *Das monarchische Princip*. Stahl and Hegel disagreed about many other things, however, and Stahl spent much of his life supporting the ideal of an aristocratic state against the inroads of the Prussian bureaucracy. That he did not seek to follow the moderate conservative view of England as a model aristocratic state is a tribute to his insight into current English political history rather than a contradiction in his own political philosophy.

3 *Ibid.*, p. 2. Note the absence of a 'constitutional' principle capable of combining the other two forms.

4 *Ibid.*, p. 11.

support to the 'monarchical principle', or the virtual omnipotence of the prince under German constitutional conditions.

The attacks of Huber and Stahl become much more interesting when one realizes that they were not without echoes among certain sections of the liberal academic elite. Droysen, for example, sometimes criticized English government as bitterly as his teacher Hegel. Like Hegel, Droysen admired Prussia's professional bureaucratic administration and rejected the feudal muddle of England's local self-government and corporate Parliament. For all his adherence to many constitutionalist principles, Droysen generally agreed with Hegel's summary of English versus German development: 'What the quiet work of princes over more than a hundred years has done for scientific education, wisdom, and the love of justice in Germany has not been acquired by the English nation from its popular representation.'[1] Droysen himself frowned on the oligarchic role of the 'coarse' English nobility in the English state[2] and perceived between parliamentary realities and Montesquieu's theory a gap overlooked by earlier constitutionalists.[3] For all England's personal freedom, its constitution, even after the Revolutionary Settlement, contained too much *Privatrecht* (private law) and 'irrational arbitrariness' to satisfy German needs.[4] Droysen's comments on English domestic history came at random, however; nor could one paint him with the reactionary colors of a Stahl.

What Droysen had in common with Stahl and Huber was an ominous turn toward admiring and generalizing the checkered development of the Prussian state as an ideal. Stahl and Huber, to be sure, merely wished to turn public attention away from *all* constitutional models – German as well as foreign – and persuade Prussians to accept their own peculiar form of government. In their eyes, 1832 had been England's 1789, so no foreign model could now serve as an enlightened alternative to 'revolutionary principles'. Droysen's aim in cloaking the Prussian state in glamorous myths differed: he wanted to convince even non-Prussians that the Prussian power-state offered the only hope for German unity and greatness. His idea was that 'nationalities which do not attach themselves to a militarily strong great power (like

[1] Hegel, 'Reform-Bill', p. 493. See Johann Gustav Droysen, 'Die preussische Verfassung' (1847), *Politische Schriften*, ed. by Felix Gilbert (Munich and Berlin, 1933), p. 74. Here he praised the superiority of certain Prussian institutions over the English.

[2] See Droysen's *Vorlesungen über die Freiheitskriege*, 2 vols. (Kiel, 1846), I, 50f.

[3] *Ibid.*, p. 53.

[4] *Ibid.*, p. 52; also p. 45f.

Prussia) are doomed'.[1] Unlike contemporaries on all sides of the political spectrum, he carefully scrutinized England's historic role as a great power and found harsh words to disillusion his countrymen about it. Prussian power, not English constitutional models or diplomatic support, would decide Germany's future; indeed, Ranke's rosy picture of historic English foreign policy notwithstanding, that power might have to be used *against* England.

It was chiefly Droysen's appreciation of the brutal side of international relations which induced his sober and sometimes sarcastic comments on England. A Prussian nationalist influenced, like Dahlmann and many others, by experiences on the ethnic frontier of Schleswig-Holstein, Droysen lost patience with the long-term and legalistic constitutionalist path to national unity. The Prussian sword, rather than the pen of liberal jurists, would bring about final unity under Prussia. He saw in the international balance of power, so much admired by Ranke, a hindrance to German unity. England's traditional support of this balance, which since 1815 had kept the German question closed, awoke Droysen's hostility and convinced him that English diplomacy hypocritically disguised the advantage of England as the welfare of all Europe. England had purposely fragmented Germany in the settlement of 1815, and its insistence on the establishment of the Dutch monarchy 'appeared to make possible the paralysis of Germany's commercial development forever'.[2] Droysen rejected the notion that any power, including England, could be Prussia's 'natural ally'; the island kingdom differed from the other powers only in pursuing a policy of commercial instead of territorial encroachment against the German lands.[3] Since the early eighteenth century, Droysen wrote, 'England was on the way to a commercial and oceanic despotism which endangered the material well-being of all other states. England's greatness was founded on...a genuine punic system of small-hearted exclusiveness.'[4]

Droysen's emphasis upon the Prussian-national overshadowed his moderate liberalism just as his distaste for British foreign policy overwhelmed his regard for constitutional, 'free' England. The later willingness of many liberals to sacrifice their high constitutional aims in return for German unification under Bismarck seems foreshadowed

[1] Fueter, *Historiographie*, p 494.
[2] Droysen, 'Die politische Stellung Preussens' (1845), *Politische Schriften*, p. 37.
[3] *Ibid.*, p. 57.
[4] Droysen, *Vorlesungen*, I, 104.

in Droysen's early writings. In the period before 1848, however, his Anglophobia, as well as his preference for questions of foreign policy, made him quite atypical of North German liberals. Droysen's allegations about England's selfish motivations and deceptive methods merely echoed old French propaganda from the Napoleonic era. What was new about his view was its association with a Prussian-nationalist rather than a Francophile-internationalist program. Droysen put historical research to work glorifying the 'Prussian way' in order to extend its allure to other Germans. The conservative defenders of the Prussian model had no such imperial or nationalistic motives, and the pure constitutionalists, insofar as they shared Droysen's nationalist goal, sought unity through political reform, including the drastic overhaul of Prussia. Droysen thus offered a dynamic solution to the German problem which dispensed with foreign models and foreign help, as his critique of England implied. Still, Droysen did little to popularize his insights, so his viewpoint remained obscure in the 1840s. But later he attained honor as a founder of the 'Prussian school' of history, and his ideas on Prussia and England were restudied with greater effect by a younger generation.

The dissenters from the prevailing Anglophile view were not, however, engaged in a vast polemical war. In the 1840s Stahl, Huber, and Droysen all arrived at positions critical of England as a result of their commitment to other ideological causes; they paid little more than passing attention to England; and even then, they often balanced sharp criticism with words of praise. Droysen, for example, shared much of Ranke's belief in the interconnection of religion and race. He flushed with enthusiasm when describing the era of his titanic hero, Cromwell, when 'the Germanic element had carried away victory over the French-Norman ones of the middle ages'.[1] Huber, as we see later, underwent something like a conversion in the 1850s in his views of England.

How much more remarkable, in this light, is the passion of Lothar Bucher. This small-town Prussian lawyer, adamant left-liberal deputy in 1848, and victim of reactionary persecution after the collapse of the revolution, began his long involvement with England as a penniless exile in London. His occupation, as London correspondent of the important liberal *National-Zeitung*, required him to familiarize himself

[1] Droysen, *Vorlesungen*, I, 40.

with English life, especially with the matter dearest to the hearts of the readership, parliamentary proceedings. At first Bucher, burning with resentment against the Prussian reactionaries who had exiled him, strove only to inspire his readers with admiration for a political system committed to freedom at home and abroad. In the mid-1850s, however, his naïve and commonplace reportage gave way to increasing disillusionment. Bucher experienced much the same chilly reception in England as other radical exiles and, despite his efforts, remained an increasingly resentful outsider. To his personal affronts were added the evidence of corruption, bungling, and imperialistic adventurism stemming from Britain's involvement in the Crimean War. His faith, so similar to that of most North German bourgeois liberals, that England championed the liberty of all nations (including Germany), died away. By 1857 he bitterly concluded that England's foreign policy served only English interests. 'England is like Russia,' he wrote, 'having no "principles" but only "purposes".'[1] The real aims and the public justifications of English policy had nothing in common, he decided.[2] Thereafter Bucher delighted in vituperatively lashing English hypocrisy.

Once he decided that English foreign policy rested on selfishness, he had to re-examine his ideas about English liberty. His book on 'parliamentarism' set out to prove the old Hegelian thesis of Britain's progressive enslavement to a dictatorship of the aristocracy working through the agency of an all-powerful Parliament.[3] Self-government and common law, the backbone of English justice, were being trampled by a 'parliamentary imperialism'.[4]

Bucher claimed that Parliament's 'imperialism' furthermore threatened the entire world. Once Bucher had concluded that England was using her enormous power toward other goals than international justice, he began to fear English naval might. 'Germany, with her great unprotected trade fleet, has no interest in seeing a single power dominate

[1] Heinrich von Poschinger, ed., *Ein Achtundvierziger: Lothar Buchers Leben und Werke*, 3 vols. (Berlin, 1890–4), II, 43.

[2] Bernhard Dammermann, 'Lothar Bucher in England', *Archiv für Politik und Geschichte*, VIII (1927), pp. 200–2.

[3] Lothar Bucher, *Der Parlamentarismus wie er ist* (Berlin, 1855). This little book enjoyed scant popularity during the Anglophile 1850s. Mohl complained that 'such a book plays into the hands of a dull arbitrary rule by the bureaucracy or of the raw barbarity of the masses'. [*Geschichte und Literatur der Staatswissenschaften*, 3 vols. (Erlangen, 1855–8), II, 61.] Significantly, the second edition of Bucher's book (1881) enjoyed great success.

[4] Dammermann, 'Bucher', p. 209.

the seas,' he wrote, 'least of all one which exercises such domination as despotically as England.'[1] The former free-trader Bucher concluded by 1860 that 'Manchester' laissez-faire economics had been invented to help England capture control of the world market and that Cobden's pacifism masked cowardice in the face of foreign evildoers.[2] Later he called free trade 'the greatest and most audacious deception ever experienced by the world in the economic and political arena'.[3]

The starting point for Bucher's increasing dislike and mistrust of England was its diplomacy. It was thus not surprising that Bismarck, who also suspected British foreign aims,[4] would give the journalist a minor post in the Foreign Office after his Anglophobe orientation cost him his job with the prestigious *National-Zeitung*. Having become an Anglophobe too soon to suit public opinion, he withdrew into the bureaucracy as one of Bismarck's more shadowy advisors. He used his pen only rarely thereafter, usually when Bismarck required an occasional anti-English pamphlet.[5]

It is difficult to say with certainty what motivated Bucher's radical change of opinion about the nature of England and its history. Certainly the embittered tone and hostile intent of all his later writings suggest a highly personal influence. His own secretiveness and the difficulty of gaining access to his few literary remains in East Germany have resulted in few clues. Yet certainly Bucher came to his new negative view in the teeth of widespread pro-English sentiment in Germany and suffered professionally for it, until the drift of his anti-English course brought him right into the path of his old enemy Bismarck. His ideas remained much the same after the mid-1850s and may be discounted as marginal, no matter how true they sometimes were. Only later, in the 1880s when he suddenly achieved popular success with the same old anti-English phrases, did he become interesting as a barometer.

The major concern of the generation to which Stahl, Huber, Droysen, and even Bucher (though considerably younger) belonged devoted

[1] Poschinger, *Achtundvierziger*, II, 48.

[2] *Ibid.*, pp. 142–3; also Dammermann, 'Bucher', p. 193.

[3] Poschinger, *Achtundvierziger*, II, 216.

[4] See Eva Maria Baum, *Bismarcks Urteil über England und die Engländer* (Munich, 1936), especially pp. 12–14, 16, 18, 21, 24, 40, 44–50; Georg Brodnitz, *Bismarcks nationalökonomische Anschauungen* (Jena, 1902); and Hans Rothfels, *Bismarcks englische Bündnispolitik* (Stuttgart, 1924).

[5] For examples of these, see Bucher's *Kleine Schriften politischen Inhalts* (Stuttgart, 1893).

its most passionate interest to politics – great constitutional and national issues. Those scholarly men who deviated from this overriding interest to probe into such relatively undignified matters as economic affairs counted little in the forum of public discussion in Germany. Young Marx and Engels, formulating their critique of the adolescent capitalist order in the 1840s and 1850s, and old Friedrich List, vainly seeking to further such an order for Germany, were prophets without honor in their own land.

Undoubtedly part of the reason for their initial obscurity and later fame lay in their recognizing the implications for Germany of economic developments in England. List's vision of an industrialized Germany protected from foreign competition owed much to British example. Although some form of tariff wall against English manufactures constituted the means, the end itself remained a desire to reproduce England's industrial system. Marx and Engels, though motivated by a concern radically different from that of the enterprising List, also took their cues from England: Engels received his practical training in industrial management in Manchester, and both founders of dialectical materialism drew heavily on British economic theory and practice in formulating their critique of capitalism. Few Germans had the breadth of vision of these men and saw only feebly, if at all, what List and Marx did. To be sure, the more advanced capitalists of the Rhineland admired English methods and sought to learn from them.[1] But List was almost dead before German businessmen began to study English methods seriously, and they never shared his grandiose plans for rapid and coordinated German industrial development. Marx and Engels, needless to say, alienated their bourgeois audience too much to exercise much influence on it and enjoyed no significant workingman's support until much later in the century.

As 'modernizers' living in a pre-industrial society, List, Marx, and Engels found themselves forced into an ambivalent attitude toward England. They accepted the industrial revolution as desirable (though for different reasons) and recognized England as the leader in this direction. Indeed, this recognition was widespread in Europe after the brilliant Crystal Palace exhibition of 1851. On the other hand, List, Marx, and Engels did not simply urge that Germany copy

[1] See Henderson, *Britain and Industrial Europe*, and Joseph Hansen, *Gustav von Mevissen. Ein rheinisches Lebensbild*, 2 vols. (Berlin, 1906), I, *passim*.

England's industrialization and leave it at that. They cautioned against dark sides as well: List, stressing the dangers to Germany of 'Manchester' free-trade doctrines; Marx and Engels, by painting in lurid colors the fate of the working class under English capitalism.

The root of List's ambivalence toward England lay in the duality of admiration and envy. He 'sought for Germany... a similar economic and political structure',[1] but he also anticipated energetic German competition with England and German thwarting of English foreign commercial policy. List's writings often repeated the same ideas again and again: England is a great country worthy of emulation; but German emulation will get no further until it puts aside its misconceptions about how the English built their industrial and commercial dominance – through protection and state intervention. As List wrote in 1839,

It is true, the Germans sympathize with the English more than any other nation. English morality and religiosity, the English sense of right and justice, English tenacity and efficiency stand in high esteem among the Germans, and the belief that the English have to thank their German blood for these beautiful qualities is very flattering to the Germans. A kind of national pride seizes the German whenever he hears the observations made on the Thames that England's free institutions sprouted in German forests...[The Germans] believe, however, that they can best confirm their kinship by imitating English policy and thereby raising themselves to the same level of commercial activity, wealth, and power as their cousins. They should despise and abhor the example of Portugal as that of a Romance people.[2]

Portugal represented to List the sort of economic dependence which British naval, diplomatic, and commercial power, working together, threatened to make out of Germany. List's great journalistic battle aimed at showing the Germans – and the English, too – that the Englishmen's virtues blinded them to their sole great vice, a ruthless drive to world trade monopoly. That is why, List said, the English nation was fine and humane in most situations, but 'only to the point where the English nation's trade monopoly comes into consideration'. From that point on, List argued, the English, 'like all their predeces-

[1] Ludwig Sevin, 'Die Entwicklung von Friedrich Lists kolonialen und weltpolitischen Ideen bis zum Plane einer englischen Allianz 1846', *Jahrbuch für Gesetzgebung, Verwaltung und Volkswirtschaft*, XXXIII (1909), No. 4, p. 327. For other evidence that England was List's ideal in almost every way, see Heinz Rogge, *England, Friedrich List und der deutsche Zollverein* (Greifswald, 1939), p. 56ff.; and Friedrich Bahr, *Die politischen Anschauungen Friedrich Lists dargelegt an seiner Stellung zu England* (Eibau, 1929), pp. 42–3.

[2] Friedrich List, 'Dr Bowring und der deutsche Zollverein' (1839), *Werke*, V, 159 and 163.

sors, and undoubtedly, their successors, are unjust, devious, insolent, and insatiable in greed – a Harpax among the nations'.[1]

List never adopted a tone of moral indignation about England's self-serving trade policies and hypocritical poses as the champion of international economic liberty, for he expected any nation as strong as England to act in the same way. He intended merely to lay bare the historical fluctuations in economic practice and show free-trade doctrine to be a reasonable policy for only some eras and nations, not all. This aim underlay his *negative* comments. But what of his positive program for Germany?

List steadfastly insisted that politics and economics are interlocked, even though they may not seem to be. This was especially true of England, List thought.[2] Consequently his suggestions for Germany always included a maximum intervention of the government for the protection of commerce. At first, List envisioned a German-led, economically united continent competing with the other great economic blocs – Russia, the British Empire, and the United States. Sea power and colonies, vital to such a 'United States of Europe', would have to be gained against British opposition.[3] Although these ideas were interesting and novel in the 1840s, they had no basis whatsoever in the world of political realities. German trade and manufacturing did grow rapidly in the 1840s, but it would have been practically impossible for German industry to produce the steel, ships, capital, and goods for the kind of neo-mercantilist empire List had in mind, even if the political power and will to create it had existed. German commerce was in no position to declare its independence. As one historian of German trade said, 'Every law passed in London, every decree of a British colonial governor, every new flag-raising of the English had some effect on German trade, and there were surely many Hanseatics in the decades before the foundation of the German Empire who followed the dealings of Commons with greater interest than those of the parliament in Berlin.'[4]

List eventually realized the futility of pitting the infant industrial economy of Germany against the enormous power of England. Con-

1 Friedrich List, 'Die englische Allianz und die deutsche Industrie' (1843), *Werke*, VII, 250. Harpax was a character in Plautus' plays known for cupidity.

2 Friedrich List, 'Outlines' (1827), *Werke*, II, 118f.

3 Sevin, 'Entwicklung', pp. 321, 326.

4 Percy Ernst Schramm, *Deutschland und Übersee* (Brunswick, 1950), p. 414. 'Hanseatics' are inhabitants of the North Sea 'Hansa ports', chiefly Bremen, Hamburg, and Lübeck.

sequently the last dream of this erratic and colorful prophet was a political alliance between the German states and England. Not German protectionism, he now argued, but French and Russian political ambition threatened England. The British would do well to encourage a protectionist *Zollverein* in order to strengthen the German economy. A strong Germany, in turn, would be a dependable ally against French and Russian schemes.[1] List's last mission, an attempt to win over the British government to such an idea, met with failure despite encouragement from Peel and the Prussian ambassador, Bunsen. Shortly after his London trip in June 1846, he returned to Germany and, after weeks of depression, took his own life. The protectionist cause which he championed lost ground steadily to free trade. It was not until protectionism rallied in the late 1870s that a new school of German economists invoked List's memory. This 'historical school' in turn influenced the thinking of general historians with greater success than List had enjoyed among the writers of the 1840s.

If such spokesmen for the small new protectionist manufacturing class were in a minority in the 1840s, the champions of the working class were even more obscure. Engels' *Lage der arbeitenden Klasse in England* (Leipzig, 1845), the work of a young businessman barely out of his teens with almost no formal university training, represented something quite new in German letters: history and politics interpreted for the working class. Other Germans had admired the orderliness, patience, and energy of the English workingman, but nobody yet had drawn him as the paragon of virtue standing out against the somber and evil background of the English bourgeois power structure. Engels' contribution to the *Deutsch-französische Jahrbücher* in the 1840s drew a picture of English life even pithier, harsher, and more damning than his own *Lage.*

Pushing to one side the hoary notion of English freedom, Engels

[1] Friedrich List, 'Über den Wert und die Bedingungen einer Allianz zwischen Grossbritannien und Deutschland' (1846), *Gesammelte Schriften*, ed. by Ludwig Häusser, 3 vols. (Stuttgart and Tübingen, 1850), II, 435–68. List's argument was common to Germans who wished political alliance with England but economic independence at the same time. The denials of English economic historians (Clapham and Henderson) notwithstanding, German businessmen and historians of the nineteenth century were often convinced that England did everything in her power in the 1830s and 1840s to discourage German economic progress. Those who believed in a 'national alliance' between England and the German states often pointed out that an economically strong Germany would be of such great political and military use to England that the latter's losses in the export market would be more than compensated.

declared that 'the English, that is the educated English, by whom the continent judges the national character, are the most despicable slaves under the sun'.[1] He ridiculed German writers for praising the independence and freedom of the English. 'The debates in Parliament, the free press, stormy popular assemblies, elections, and juries do not fail to affect German Michael's timid feelings, and in his amazement he mistakes all the pretty appearance for reality.'[2] The English constitution? It had done much good in its time, Engels remarked with brutal irony – since 1828 it had steadily pursued its noblest mission, its own self-destruction. Public opinion, or rather social prejudice, ruled England with the tyranny of an oriental despot. Prejudices and materialism had replaced thought among the upper classes. 'Everywhere one finds the most barbarous indifference and selfish egotism on the one hand and the most distressing scenes of misery and poverty on the other,' he wrote of London.[3] Engels' attacks on the English liberal economic school bit hard. The effects of its doctrines on English social legislation disgusted Engels, who ironically pointed out how 'advantageous it would be if one could treat poverty as a crime and make poorhouses into penal institutions, as has already happened in England under the "liberal" new Poor Law'.[4]

Engels' experiences and observations in England after his arrival there in 1842 contributed significantly to his conversion from utopian to revolutionary socialism. Marx, because his ideas were already better formed and his situation in society more isolated, benefited much less from his experiences as an exile living in London after 1848. Nevertheless, Marx's poverty drove him to take up journalism for a time during the 1850s, and in this capacity he turned his attention to British affairs. American papers, chiefly the *New York Daily Tribune*, were then radical (and Anglophobe) enough to print the sort of insights on the English scene which Marx offered. As a severe critic of capitalist social organization, he naturally found much wrong with the most advanced industrial society in the world. Marx explained British life in the familiar terms of class struggle and riveted his chief attention on the economy, of

[1] Friedrich Engels, 'Die Lage Englands', *Deutsch-französische Jahrbücher* (Paris, 1844), p. 153f.

[2] *Ibid.*, p. 153.

[3] Engels, *The Condition of the Working Class in England*, tr. by W. O. Henderson (New York, 1958), p. 31.

[4] Engels, 'Umrisse zu einer Kritik der Nationalökonomie', *Deutsch-französische Jahrbücher*, p. 107.

which each minor crisis signaled to him the approaching collapse of capitalism.

For his American readers, however, Marx had to write about the 'superstructure' of society as well, so he alternated political and military analysis with his economic reports. The august proceedings of Parliament and the activities of the British abroad fascinated him, as they did practically every other German. Marx's purpose, however, was to expose the class structure of parliamentary government and the hypocrisy, greed, and exploitative quintessence of English foreign policy.

To Marx the rottenness rather than the excellence of the English political system explained how an aristocratic Parliament could be so surprisingly representative of the nation. 'One is tempted to ask not why English Parliaments [for the last 150 years] were so bad but, on the contrary, how they managed to be so good and... to reflect the real movements of English society.'[1] Only the channels of corruption and bribery, allowing the purchase of votes, facilitated accurate parliamentary representation of the strongest economic groups. As for the political parties, Marx classified them solely by the economic lobby they represented: Tory meant landowner; the Whigs, 'hypocrites in religion and Tartuffes in politics', were 'the aristocratic spokesmen for the bourgeoisie';[2] sooner or later the 'Manchester men' would dispense with the Whig middle men and manage the state directly. Their program, Marx wittily asserted, would be streamlined according to classical economic doctrine: the throne, nobility, House of Lords, army, colonial empire, church, and common law would disappear as '*faux frais* of production' – unnecessary overhead. 'National wars,' he continued, 'are also *faux frais*,' for '...England can exploit foreign countries more cheaply if she trades with them in peace.'[3] The Manchesterians hid their program behind a moderate façade, said Marx, because concessions to their waning opponent (the aristocracy) were cheaper than concessions to their rising enemy (the proletariat, represented by the Chartists). The British constitution, because it excluded

[1] Karl Marx, 'Die Wahlkorruption', *New York Daily Tribune*, 20 August 1852, in Karl Marx and Friedrich Engels, *Werke*, ed. by *Institut für Marxismus-Leninismus beim ZK der SED*, 32 vols. (Berlin, 1957 ff.), VIII, 354. The similarity to the questions raised by Namier is ironic. See in particular Lewis B. Namier, *The Structure of Politics at the Accession of George III*, 2 vols. (London, 1929).

[2] Marx, 'Die Wahlen in England', *Tribune*, 6 August 1852, in *Werke*, VIII, 337, 339, 341.

[3] *Ibid.*, p. 343.

the working class, nevertheless remained 'merely a superannuated, outworn, obsolete compromise between the unofficially but practically ruling bourgeoisie and the officially ruling landed aristocracy'.[1]

None of this harshness abated when Marx broached foreign policy. He dwelt at length on the sufferings of Ireland and the non-white colonies. The case of India convinced Marx that British humanity and respectability were mere masks. 'The deep hypocrisy of bourgeois civilization and its inseparable barbarism are unveiled as soon as we turn our glance from their homeland to their colonies...'[2] Far from being the main foes of reactionary Russia, English statesmen from Fox to Palmerston had tacitly aided continental despotism.[3] In the aftermath of 1848, Marx could not forgive England for failing to back her verbal encouragement of European liberalism with deeds.

The language of criticism used by Marx, Engels, and List had much in common: the techniques of unmasking the 'true' motivation of English policy, the accusation of ruthless economic imperialism not only in faraway continents but in Europe as well, and the biting denunciations of British laissez-faire economic doctrine. Marx and Engels went much further than List, however, for they held nothing in English life to be commendable. For List, English industrial society was desirable but not inevitable: Germans must work hard to copy it but must not be taken in by false English theories of free commerce. For Marx and Engels, this same society was inevitable but not desirable: other European nations would fall prey to capitalism, but the working class must grow strong to smite it down. Lest that class forget its calling, Marx and Engels held up lurid pictures of life under a feudal–capitalist alliance in England.

A third German approach to the complicated issues raised by industrialization in England developed with increasing speed after about 1850. Accepting the political inferiority of the workers, its spokesmen nevertheless saw desperate social consequences as clearly as Marx and Engels. They differed from the Marxist revolutionary conclusion in proposing self-help, the solution of the 'social question' from within the working class. The most successful form urged in the 1850s and 1860s, the cooperative society, owed much of its inspiration to British

[1] Marx, 'Die britische Konstitution', *Neue Oder-Zeitung*, 6 March 1855, in *Werke*, XI, 95.

[2] Marx, 'Die künftigen Ergebnisse der britischen Herrschaft in Indien', *Tribune*, 8 August 1853, in *Werke*, IX, 225.

[3] Marx, 'Traditionelle englische Politik', *Tribune*, 12 January 1856, in *Werke*, XI, 573–6.

models, particularly the Rochdale Pioneers. It is hard to say with certainty how much the leading German advocate of cooperative self-help, Hermann Schulze-Delitzsch, had studied England. In the case of Huber, however, the tie to England is obvious.

Huber, in fact, underwent a sort of conversion from his rather hostile view of England in the 1840s. He had seen and criticized English working-class living conditions in 1844; but at that time he concerned himself chiefly with rebutting the English *political* system on behalf of the Prussian 'monarchical principle'. Unlike the superficial Gerlach, who had also visited Manchester in 1844, Huber diagnosed the state of the working class as close to despair, moral dissolution, and hopelessness.[1] As a conservative, Huber preferred an 'organic' solution for these problems to massive state intervention, as Lassalle later proposed, or to revolution in Engels' sense. And as an orthodox Lutheran, he showed more concern for the moral, educational, and cultural needs of the workers than other proponents of self-help. Gradually Huber noticed a visible improvement in English workers' lives which erased the dismal impression made by English factory towns in the 1840s.[2] He concluded that freedom of association and expression in England, not to mention the system of self-government, provided the necessary foundation for an organic solution to social problems.[3] Associations such as the Rochdale Pioneers, Huber wrote, answered social needs best because, unlike artificial cures imposed by the revolutionary masses or the paternalistic state, they would take root and grow.[4] Naturally Huber remained critical of many sides of English economic and political life, for he was still primarily a reformer. But his writings increasingly cited the English example for Germany to follow instead of avoid. He urged his countrymen 'to strengthen...their trust in the more mature experience of this racially kindred people as well as their trust in the powers of self-healing'.[5]

It is interesting to note that Huber's drift into the Anglophile camp contributed to increasing strain in his relations with his former allies among the Prussian ultra-conservatives. Their protective attitude

[1] See Huber's comments in his magazine *Janus*, No. 23 (1845).

[2] Huber, 'Die Arbeiterfrage in England', *Sociale Fragen*, 7 nos. in 1 vol. (Nordhausen, 1863–9), No. 7, p. 8.

[3] *Ibid.* Also 'Die sociale Hebung der arbeitenden Klassen in England', *Deutsche Vierteljahresschrift*, XXXI (1868), p. 110.

[4] See Huber, 'Die Rochedale Pioneers', *Sociale Fragen*, No. 5 (1868), preface.

[5] Huber, 'Sociale Hebung', p. 99.

toward the artisan class and their blind rejection of industrialization drove a wedge between them and Huber. Huber's purity of motive seems substantiated by his revision of his views on England and his alienation from the conservative circles he had once served with his pen. He had first been brought up in the moderate constitutionalist faith in England; had lost this faith and begun to attack the cherished idol of German constitutionalists; and had finally, in the 1850s, discovered the uses of the English example to support an organic conservative political philosophy.

The case of Huber, like that of Bucher, demonstrates that German voices questioning England in the middle decades of the nineteenth century belonged to extreme and fairly isolated spokesmen. Huber, in his days as a reactionary publicist, and Bucher, in his later career as a disappointed constitutionalist, attacked the English 'model' at its most vulnerable place – the gap between theory and practice of the English state. In their periods as admirers and advocates of the British system, however, they stood in generally high esteem with the educated classes in Germany. Huber's attacks, it might be recalled, had appeared chiefly in a journal which could not even pay for itself in subscriptions; Bucher, when his London reports began to deviate from what the liberal readership of the *National-Zeitung* liked to read, saw his journalistic career evaporate. By the 1850s, attacking England had become professionally hazardous.

Droysen, Huber, and Stahl's attempts to elevate Prussia to the place of honor occupied in many German minds by England constituted one of the new developments in writing about England. The concerns and viewpoints of the economists and social critics constituted the other. Both enjoyed a hot-house existence in the 1830s and 1840s because of reactionary fear of English constitutionalism, the acrimonious Anglo-Prussian commercial disputes, and the righteous indignation of social thinkers about the malaise spawned by industrialization. The concentration on both the immediate issues of constitutional government and industrialization in Germany led as well to an unusually sharp examination of *contemporary* English affairs. When the constitution was discussed, debate was no longer clouded by interminable references to Blackstone and Montesquieu. The social and economic problems facing England were immediate. As a result, the critics of England set a precedent for future generations: immediate observation constituted the best weapon against the obfuscations and myths carried on by many Anglophile historians. Even when they looked back on the English past, as Droysen did, they did not proceed further than the roots of contemporary problems – in Droysen's case, no further than the seventeenth century. This emphasis on the recent and the contemporary served to sharpen the contrast between England and the German states just as Lappenberg's emphasis on the early middle ages had served to diminish it.

The motives of all these men in examining England had in common a certain desire to use England as an example to prove a point. None could be said to have dedicated himself chiefly to the study of English affairs. It would serve Droysen's Prussian cause, for example, if he could dispel the idea that England's foreign policy had always been benignly concerned for the welfare of Europe. It would force German patriots to pin their hopes more on Prussia and less on England; it would also make Prussia's reputation for icy political calculation seem less frightening. Whatever the motive, however, none of these men (except Bucher) approached England primarily in an emotional or sentimental way. Even behind the calculated motive in their attacks, most of these writers held England in esteem on other counts. It is an indication of the strength of adulation for England in the 1850s that even an ambivalent attitude was stamped in Germany as 'Anglophobia'.

The ultimate consequences of the writings of these mid-century outsiders cannot be judged with any certainty. For the time being, certainly, their influence was slight. Marx and Engels, who became most famous by the 1880s, certainly impressed their ideas on all posterity – but more by their great analyses, such as *Capital*, than by the articles and pamphlets of the 1840s and 1850s criticizing England. Indeed the German socialist movement, which claimed the inheritance of Marx and Engels, grew rather fond of England from the 1880s on. List's works, almost forgotten during the free-trade era in Germany, received a reincarnation in the work of Schmoller from the 1870s onward. Likewise Droysen's influence on the 'Prussian school' of historians has usually been considered significant. Bucher even enjoyed a few mild publishing successes in the 1880s, shortly before his death. On the whole, one must conclude that their ideas enjoyed a later vogue attributable in some measure to anti-English feeling in Germany. To explain the latter as an outcome, rather than a promoter of their writings, would be misleading. Some of their ideas and techniques (notably 'demasking') later became academically respectable commonplaces, but not because they had persuaded men's minds from the start. In the 1840s and 1850s, there was every reason to question some of the old clichés about England, especially as Germans became increasingly self-conscious and politically thoughtful. But the climate of hostility characteristic of the end of the century did not yet exist, and the seeds of doubt about England found no hospitable environment in which to grow strong. A sense of rivalry, a belief that Prussian political norms, Rhineland industry, and native diplomatic and military skill could compete successfully with the best England could offer, undoubtedly began in the minds of certain German thinkers as early as the 1830s. Yet the same men who pressed for a lesser degree of German dependence on British models recognized some strong kinship to the 'blood-related' English as a force in their destiny.

CHAPTER 8

ENGLAND AS SENESCENT UNCLE – GNEIST AND THE YOUNG NATIONAL LIBERALS

England, as we have seen, was revered by most constitutionalist historians and political scientists of Germany in the second quarter of the nineteenth century; furthermore, Ranke and a more conservative, sometimes more church-conscious group of historians who passed over the recent British constitution nevertheless found a close kinship between German and English culture and a community of interest between British and North German diplomacy, even if they suppressed evidence of division to do so. Only a small number of writers vociferously criticized the worthiness of the English constitution in the 1840s, and 1850s, and an even smaller band tried to turn attention toward Britain's overwhelming industrial might and social misery. This dissident group clearly belonged, for the most part, to a later generation than the men discussed in chs. 5 and 6. Is there any indication that they represented some new wave, some rebellion against the highly Anglophile viewpoint of their elders?

To this question one must answer no. Their age peers among the academic historians – the men with all the social rewards of both university appointments and membership in the increasingly prestigious society of professional historians – overpowered the voices of such 'eccentrics', amateur historians, and outsiders as Marx, Bucher, or Huber. They dominated the pages of Germany's most impressive journals – the *Grenzboten*, *Preussische Jahrbücher*, and the rest. They also dominated university appointments. The hard work and increasingly sophisticated use of documents and critical method which they made standard in their trade gained for this generation of historians higher prestige than any previous one had ever known. Their view of England, which they spread through the many channels open to them, combined most of the positive elements of both the constitutionalist and the Rankean pictures of England. Typically, these men combined Ranke's interest in the past *per se* with a strongly profiled engagement in contemporary political struggles. Yet, as one would expect from the blending of views of England which derived from vaguely hostile camps, they brought a somewhat new perspective to the interpretation of England.

The experience which obtrusively separated most members of this generation of academic historians from both Ranke and the constitutionalists was participation in the German nationalist movement. Even the students of Ranke, who should have learned to work *sine ira et studio*, could not restrain their pens in the battle of words accompanying the agitation for unification. Nor did they always draw strict lines between their professional historical craft and their contemporary involvements. This same attachment of highest priority to German political unification led to a lessening of zeal for the pure constitutionalist cause, manifested in a gradual transfer of attention from the institutions of parliamentary government at the center to those of local self-government.

The most obtrusive similarity to Ranke and the constitutionalists, however, lay in the continued dominance of political affairs in the thoughts and writings of the younger historians. The economic and social questions brought up by List or Marx barely stirred their imagination. They showed only the faintest perception of even an incipient rivalry between the hoped-for German national state and Great Britain, despite the marked tendency of the scholars who took Prussia's side in the great German debates of the day to lay heavier stress on foreign affairs than had the constitutionalists. On the other hand, the new nationalist scholars respected England's constitution. Despite Chartist agitation in 1848 and considerable bumbling in the Crimean War, England withstood the threats of revolution, reaction, and civil war which afflicted the other respected political models – France and America – in 1848–52 and 1861, respectively. If anything, these blows to the hopes to German progressives led to more intense investigation of the surviving political model in England. As Arnold Ruge, another radical German exile in London, explained, German intellectuals 'were not yet faced [before 1848] with the moral destruction of the continent as they are now, nor were they acquainted with the Anglo-Saxon world into which this destruction has hurled them.'[1] Furthermore, as a reviewer of a recent English constitutional history concluded in 1864:

If the liberal party of the continent wishes to summarize in one slogan the various demands it makes in all areas of political life—for ministerial responsibility, parliamentary control of the budget, firm regulation of the administration, and securing fundamental rights—there is hardly any other one than the cry heard so often and so justifiably: give us an English constitution![2]

A twentieth-century historian of the period wrote, 'Next to England's foreign policy and economic successes, its political institutions called forth in Germany respect, genuine interest, and even boundless admiration, because "the spirit of progress was combined with respect for historic tradition" and because an essential reason for England's freedom and preponderant position among the world powers was seen in them.'[3] Neither progress nor love of tradition alone but their unique combination in the British political system made it seem the ideal solution to Germany's problems.

If one seeks causes for the interpretation offered by this younger generation of men whose major common ideological tie was *kleindeutsch* liberalism, one has a number of appealing choices. The least useful lies in the social background of the individual historians: Rudolf von Gneist, who initiated a significant departure in the interpretation of British political history, came from the same background as Ranke's students Reinhold Pauli, Karl von Noorden, and Heinrich von Sybel.[4] All were born into the highly educated professional middle class: physicians, middle-range civil servants, preachers, and army officers surrounded them as fathers and uncles. All were born on Prussian soil[5] – indeed, all but the Rhinelanders Noorden and Sybel in Berlin.

[1] Paul Nerrlich, ed., *Arnold Ruges Briefwechsel und Tagebuchblätter aus den Jahren 1825–1880*, 2 vols. (Berlin, 1886), II, 121.

[2] Alexander Meyer, 'Englische Pressefreiheit', *Preussische Jahrbücher*, XIII (1864), p. 243.

[3] Reinhard J. Lamer, *Der Englische Parlamentarismus in der deutschen politischen Theorie im Zeitalter Bismarcks (1857–1890). Ein Beitrag zur Vorgeschichte des deutschen Parlamentarismus* [*Historische Studien*, No. 387] (Lübeck, 1963), p. 5.

[4] Reinhold Pauli (1823–82) was a professor of history at Tübingen, Marburg, and Göttingen. Karl von Noorden (1833–83) taught at several German universities, ending his career at Leipzig. Heinrich von Sybel (1817–95) taught principally at Bonn, directed the Prussian State Archives, and was politically active in Prussia. (See Biographical Appendix.)

[5] Catholic South German historical scholarship, primarily involved with church history and still very cosmopolitan, developed no clear-cut view of England as did the Protestants of North and South. The greatest historical scholar of Munich at this time, Ignaz Döllinger, characterized the internationalism and ecumenical spirit of many German Catholic

The 'vons' in their names were acquired by themselves or their immediate forebears for meritorious service to the state and culture.

More important than this similar Prussian background is the similarity of political commitment to Prussia as the destined leader of Germany's regeneration and advance into greater liberty. All these men belonged ideologically to the National Liberal or Progressive parties, even though they usually suspected party alignments as undignified for a scholar. They were politically 'engaged'; most served at some time in the Prussian Diet (Sybel, Gneist), the Frankfurt Pre-Parliament (Sybel), or the *Reichstag* (Sybel, Gneist). Pauli, no parliamentarian, nevertheless worked as private secretary to Bunsen, the Prussian Ambassador to London, and served the Prussian cause with his pen. All opposed the reaction of the 1850s and Bismarck's early anti-constitutional career, although the quality of their devotion to the idea of a progressive, Prussian-led German state was more passionate than their public service might indicate. If driven to an extreme, their belief in Prussia's destiny could logically lead to the same sort of critical view of England held by the 'Prussian school' – rejecting the British constitutional model as inapplicable and regarding in England just another hostile foreign power.[1] In most cases, however, the logical polarization of Prussian–German nationalism and Anglophobia did not, for various reasons, develop beyond certain private doubts.

The intellectual traditions upon which these men drew had altered somewhat since the youth of the constitutionalist generation. Despite

professors of the day by maintaining equally good contacts with France and England. Lord Acton, his former pupil, was his best friend. But beyond strictly ecclesiastical problems, church historians had little interest in England.

[1] The traditional distinction between a 'Rankean' and a 'Prussian school' confuses as much as it enlightens, since a considerable reciprocal influence took place. Both Sybel and Max Duncker studied under Ranke, yet Fueter, in his *Geschichte der neueren Historiographie*, pp. 535–49, places them (with Häusser) in the *kleindeutsch* school. Gooch speaks of the same men as the 'Prussian school' (*History and Historians*, pp. 122–50), and adds Dahlmann and Droysen to the list. Fueter understands by the term 'Prussian school' only Droysen and Treitschke, and explains the distinction between them and such 'national-liberal', *kleindeutsch* historians as Sybel in terms of ultimate aims for Prussia. Fueter notes that the 'national-liberal' group fought to make Prussia-Germany *equal* to other national states; the 'Prussian school', to raise the Prussian 'state-idea' *above* all others. In the following discussion I shall follow Fueter's distinction. Georg von Below, *Die deutsche Geschichtsschreibung von den Befreiungskriegen bis zu unseren Tagen*, 2nd. edn. (Munich, 1924), lumps all these men, plus Schlosser and Rotteck, into the useless category of 'political historians'. Srbik, in *Geist und Geschichte*, I, ch. XII, usually avoids the use of the term 'Prussian school' altogether, subsuming Droysen, Häusser, Sybel, Baumgarten, and Treitschke under the concept of '*kleindeutsch* nation-state realism'.

the signs of a revival in the critical thought habits of the enlightenment in the Germanies after about 1840, these men moved in a different direction, deepening their reverence for historicism. They turned away from the excessively polemical, exclusively political, and thoroughly present-minded approach of Rotteck and the cosmopolitan natural-law constitutionalists. At the same time, they rejected the more extreme antiquarian implications of Ranke's teachings, but their professional training and Prussian parochialism led them on toward historicism. The end result was a reverence for tradition, for the discrete event, and for the great personality which at times conflicted with the generalizing, abstracting, and innovating tendencies of their own liberal ideology.

Another apparent difference between this generation of historians and most previous ones lay in their superior use of critical method, careful documentation, and the other scholarly virtues instituted by Ranke. Their books give a striking impression of hard work, scholarly solidity, and thoughtful judgment. Many naive assumptions and traditional clichés about Britain fell before the critical scrutiny of these men. Surprisingly, however, many other traditional assumptions continued to appear in their writings, and a few new errors cropped up. They and their public simply fell into the habit encouraged by their age of 'progress' (and one by no means broken today): they regarded refined technique and the legendary code of the German professor as a guarantee of objectivity. The biases in their work were certainly less conscious, but they remained. The image of England which they presented to a growing public remained colored with the same emotions, hopes, and fears which had influenced earlier renderings. It also carried unprecedented authority.

Finally one can explain differences in terms of actual changes in England itself. Everybody who had reached middle age in the 1860s could see momentous changes which had occurred in his lifetime alone, changes in population distribution, economic conditions, political forms, moral values, and social hierarchy. Certainly many of the contemporary developments in Britain had an unsettling influence on the thoughts of the historians. They were dimly aware that parliamentary government was going through some sort of change in the 1850s and later; they realized that industrialization was undermining the power of the aristocracy, and that after 1848, until after German unification,

Britain could or would not act vigorously on the continent. Nevertheless, our authors rarely examined the changes and problems they sensed were there: neither they nor the less distinguished contributors to the major influential journals gave their readers careful analysis of British political and social changes. Even when they belatedly awoke to some of the rapid alterations of British life, chiefly in the 1860s, they neither fully grasped what was happening nor – most telling of all – regarded the changes as permanent. If, for example, a constitutional change such as the 1867 franchise reform disturbed them, they would simply close their eyes to its significance.

The reason for the odd half-blindness lies chiefly in the best of the explanations for the motives of these historians. Their commitment to political change in the Germanies placed them in the same need as the constitutionalists: they required the British model for their plans, and they urgently wished it to hold still. In the two decades before 1870, this wish proved increasingly vain. As time went on, as the grip of the traditional rulers in North Germany became unstable toward the end of the 1850s, as the nationalist-liberal cause gained the confidence of more and more intellectuals, it became possible to treat English affairs with some degree of critical objectivity without seeming to betray the liberal cause. The ultimate result of this development was public recognition that the new Prussian–German Empire not only *had* a different sort of constitution from England's, but that it *must* be different if the nation-state were to survive. It is difficult to account for such shifts within two decades unless one assigns a very high place to political engagements as a motive in writing history. Yet it is equally difficult to see the motive clearly because the subtlety of the didactic purpose and the scholarly apparatus screened it.

One further development influenced the writings about England of German historians, though it was a result, not a cause, of their outlook. The influence of specialization and professionalization combined with the preference of the day for a national framework to produce longer, bulkier, and narrower historical narratives as well as monographs largely incomprehensible to the general reader. Men like Pauli and Noorden made their scholarly reputations solely on the basis of their knowledge of England; the members of the 'Prussian school' likewise concentrated almost exclusively on Prussia's history. In order to keep in touch with the public, which they wished to influence, these historians turned to the relatively new but highly respected national journals, such as the *Preussische Jahrbücher* and the *Grenzboten*. Here they could hope to reach and persuade the well-read layman, especially the 'molders of public opinion'.[1] Here one was most likely to find Pauli's views on *German* history or Sybel's thoughts on England. As the century wore on, narrative history of England became duller, lengthier, and more detailed; the debate over the meaning of English history moved largely to the intellectual journals and thereby reached more people.

I RUDOLF VON GNEIST

In addition to environmental and general influences on this group of nationalist, liberal, and pro-Prussian writers, there was a very specific human influence in the form of Rudolf von Gneist. As the recognized leader of German commentary on the English constitution after the later 1850s, Gneist quickly became a sort of prophet: young national liberals excitedly discussed his work and overwhelmingly accepted it. He generated considerable enthusiasm for his own explanation of the English constitution, eventually attempted to adapt it to German conditions, and saw his attempt frustrated by Bismarck. In some ways his departure from the well-worn (if often dogmatic) path of previous interpretations of the English constitution mirrored the fateful division over strategy which sapped the strength of German liberalism in the 1870s.

The number of prominent political scientists whose ideal of the good state was best fulfilled by England diminished little immediately after 1848, but the vocabulary used to analyze the English state became more technical. Until the late 1840s the conceptual framework for discussing the English constitution remained essentially that of Montesquieu. As we have seen, so much confusion resulted that 'both liberals and conservatives could seize upon the English example' for their own purposes.[2] Then Mohl for the liberals and Stahl for the conservatives had perceived the predominance of Parliament over the

[1] Erich Leupolt, *Die Aussenpolitik in den bedeutendsten Zeitschriften Deutschlands, 1890–1909* (Leipzig, 1933), p. 21. Also see Otto Westphal, *Welt- und Staatsauffassung des deutschen Liberalismus: Eine Untersuchung über die Preussischen Jahrbücher und den konstitutionellen Liberalismus in Deutschland von 1858–1863* (Munich, 1919).

[2] Eugen Schiffer, *Rudolf von Gneist* (Berlin, 1929), p. 20.

other branches of the English state. In the 1850s, however, German constitutionalists began to think that the existence and potency of central parliamentary institutions *alone* could not guarantee freedom and political stability: the debacle of the French parliamentary system had demonstrated that. Some additional feature of English political life must explain the enviable stability of the state.

The new answer came from Gneist. This remarkable man, long neglected by competent biographers, exercised an influence upon German scholarly thought about the English state which can hardly be overestimated. He devoted his entire life to the study of English constitutional history, on the one hand, and to political activity aimed at introducing the 'wholesome' parts of English public law into Germany, on the other. As a student of Savigny he was taught that German and English public law have a similar original base. Both men sought in the forms of 'Germanic community life' of early medieval times the foundations of law in both England and Germany.[1] Although Gneist claimed to be impartial and critical, he had a distinctly didactic purpose. He once wrote, 'The history and system of English self-government would have to be treated in a fully unintellectual and disconnected manner if they were to produce no principles applicable to our [German] situation.'[2] The principles of which he spoke proceeded not from parliamentary practice, however, but from British administration, particularly on the local level, in the form of the thousands of 'honorary' officials exercising the authority of local government. Thus he consciously reopened the path laid out by Vincke half a century earlier.

Gneist was bound to go astray sometimes in his pioneering 'walk through the jungle' of administrative history, as he later called it.[3] His basic ideas, once formulated at the end of the 1850s in his major work,[4] reappeared constantly and finally assumed a dogmatic quality, thereby creating some new errors in place of those he sought to extir-

[1] Rudolf von Gneist, *Das heutige englische Verfassungs- und Verwaltungsrecht*, 2 vols. (Berlin, 1857–60), I, 250. Vol. I of this major work bears the title *Geschichte und heutige Gestalt der Ämter in England*. Vol. II is called *Die heutige englische Communalverfassung und Communalverwaltung oder das System des Selfgovernment*. The volumes are often cited separately, and later editions appeared under different titles. The first edition will be referred to here.

[2] *Ibid.*, II, ixf.

[3] Gneist, *Englische Verfassungsgeschichte* (Berlin, 1882). p. iv.

[4] That is, his *Verfassungs- und Verwaltungsrecht*.

pate. One of Gneist's severest critics maintained that 'abstractions and antitheses in a mixture of correct and incorrect observations, the limitless, dogmatic exaggeration of a few temporary phenomena of England's political development, and...subjective generality are typical of Gneist's method'.[1]

Unjust as such severity is to Gneist's pioneering services in a totally new field, the central complaint is legitimate. The Berlin professor indeed sought in English constitutional history a corroboration of some of his favorite theories. One of these, the belief that government and society are necessarily hostile, led Gneist to a highly dialectical view of the state. 'Egoism' he once remarked, 'is the essence of society.'[2] The more classes and special groups in society pursued their selfish interests, the stronger the bulwark of justice, the state, must be to neutralize these conflicting interests. Reviving Montesquieu's theory of checks and balances in a different form, he described an England in which such antitheses as local and central government, private interests and public weal, professional bureaucracy and voluntary officers, and state and society balanced each other.

Gneist's theories grew out of his experience in Prussia in the period 1848–58. The idea of the state as a bulwark against class interests assumed great significance after the recent spectacle of class warfare during the June Days in Paris. In Prussia proper, however, Gneist feared a seizure of the state less by the workers than by the nobility. Lorenz von Stein had influenced him considerably, and he had been prepared in Hegel's lecture room for a dialectical interpretation of society. Furthermore, his personal experience as a minor justice official and as a teacher at the University of Berlin demonstrated to him the evils of class exploitation of the state: both his juridical and his teaching careers suffered because he criticized the monopolistic exploitation of the Prussian state by the landed noble class. Gneist was frozen out of the Prussian court system in 1849, and his appointment as full professor at Berlin had to wait almost twenty years until the political thaw of 1858 allowed his great popularity and acknowledged scholarly competence to be recognized officially.[3]

Thus it is hardly surprising that Gneist opposed class exploitation of the state with the Kantian concept of duty to a higher ethical law.

[1] Josef Redlich, *Englische Lokalverwaltung* (Leipzig, 1901), p. 777.

[2] Gneist, *Verfassungs- und Verwaltungsrecht*, I, 229.

[3] Schiffer, *Gneist*, p. 13.

In Prussia the conflict between duty to the ruler and duty to the constitution became acute during the 1850s. Only the *Junker* class solidly supported the reactionary policies of the Prussian *Camarilla*. Gneist first discovered the great difference between the English and German nobles and knights by observing Friedrich Wilhelm IV's government. Originally few differences had existed. Gneist noted that the *Junker* and the English gentry were both powerful by virtue of their property[1] and that the kernel of English parliamentary government existed still in German law. 'The German *Reichstag* is the English Parliament, and the German provincial diets [*Landstände*] contain fragments of the English lower house. But what was accomplished in England by a strong monarchy and the cooperation of the social estates – harmonic unity – degenerated in Germany into an impotent class structure.'[2]

In other words, the political and economic power of the English upper classes had allegedly been harnessed in the service of justice instead of mere special privileges.[3] An English aristocrat habitually thought of his duty before he considered his rights.[4] Gneist thus accused the Prussian *Junker* of ruthlessly exploiting the state to advance class interests while he excused their English counterparts. The reason for the supposed selflessness of the British ruling class was, according to Gneist, a national character long trained in concepts of duty and 'honor' – concepts last used by Justus Möser a century before to describe the same social group in England.

Gneist explained this training as a product of historical forces. In contrast to anachronistic chroniclers of British 'liberty', he stressed Norman rather than Germanic survivals, military rather than peaceful aspects of English history, the strength of feudal contracts, and the sharpness of centuries-long conflict between strong kings and ambitious nobles. Any kind of representative institutions, Gneist believed, would have been impossible until the full assimilation of the Norman conquerors, for such institutions 'would have placed the power of the state in the hands of one or the other nation, of the Norman or the Saxon nobility'.[5] Gneist, with a nod to Germanic solidarity, sympathized with the Saxons, but insisted on recognizing the indispensable

[1] Gneist, *Adel und Ritterschaft in England* (Berlin, 1853), p. 10.

[2] *Ibid.*, p. 43f.

[3] *Ibid.*, p. 38.

[4] *Ibid.*, p. 42. Gneist's dim view of the *Junker* class precluded any possibility that its individual members might think in unselfish terms.

[5] Gneist, *Verfassungs- und Verwaltungsrecht*, I, 91.

contribution of the Normans to the unity of English military, financial, and judicial systems under strong kings.

In ranging over the medieval landscape, Gneist's sharp eye reduced the traditional high points in the development of liberty for a richer, more complicated panorama. He dwelt less upon the great documents of freedom – for example, on the Magna Charta – than on the historical events surrounding them. The 'corporative' action of the noble class, turned in a nobler direction by their conflicts with the monarchy, already betrayed 'the greatest traits of the English character and the essence of the constitution'.[1]

In the course of these battles between kings and nobles in the late middle ages, England changed from a feudal holding to a modern state. During most of this time, Gneist maintained, royal power had constituted the bulwark of justice for the people against the selfish interests of the baronage.[2] His interpretation of the development of parliamentary institutions under Edward I appears quite modern in contrast to earlier ones. The new clarity of Gneist's historical interpretation of Edward was spoiled, however, by generalizing from it. In his monarchist eagerness to show that even parliamentary institutions must come from above, he declared the English monarchy to have been the usual source of England's free institutions. 'As important as the rights of Parliament are,' he wrote, 'one must not forget that in their origin they were an emanation of royal power.'[3] Gneist sharply denounced the cliché that the English state resembled a 'natural growth': rather it was a product of positive action by the monarch.

Why should Gneist pursue this matter? In the 1850s, only a few years after the abysmal failure of the German liberals to establish parliamentary institutions themselves, such an argument could both excuse the debacle and awaken hopes among the middle classes. For Gneist's interpretation of English constitutional history reduced to a few basic ideas: the admirable English constitution emerged only because the monarchy, on one side, and corporative bodies and independent courts, on the other, had worked out a dynamic balance. Administration by 'corporations' (in the widest sense) and a judiciary bound by a common law encircled the king's will. Upon closer examination these two elements were closely associated with two of Gneist's favorite

[1] *Ibid.*, p. 90. [2] *Ibid.*, p. 99.
[3] *Ibid.*, p. 162. Also II, 205, for a vindication of the Tudors.

concepts – *Selbstverwaltung* (self-administration) and the *Rechtsstaat* (state of laws).[1]

For Gneist regarded *Selbstverwaltung*, at the bottom of the pyramid of state, as both the best guarantee and the precondition of the *Rechtsstaat* at the top. Gneist admired English 'self-government' so much because, operating largely on its own initiative but in accordance with national laws, it constituted a harmonious reconciliation of those otherwise hostile abstractions, 'state' and 'society'. The symbol of this reconciliation was the justice of the peace. Though himself a prominent, and therefore economically 'interested' person, the justice supposedly dispensed impartial law. As a private citizen he might pursue his class economic interest, but Gneist believed that appointment to local public office successfully bound him, at least during his tenure, to represent the state, justice, and the public weal. By contrast, Gneist thought, the *Junker* in Prussia during the 1850s carried on local government solely in the interests of his class. The appointive and even burdensome nature of English local office (which Gneist compared favorably to public office in ancient Rome) was offset by no personal advantage, Gneist thought; only the appointee's honor induced him to shoulder the responsibility.[2]

Once in office, the squire learned the art of government by experience, so that he was supposedly seasoned in law and counsel by the time he entered Parliament. Gneist assumed that this training of Parliament's members on the local level explained its superior wisdom and authority compared to the various short-lived assemblies of republican France. The *Rechtsstaat* required a firm local basis before it could develop central representative institutions. Gneist was capitulating to the 'organic' arguments of German conservatism: new political institutions must grow out of existing ones.

Needless to say, Gneist was hardly describing the changing English system of his own time, when local government was as moribund as Parliament was dominant, but that of the eighteenth century. True, he took note of contemporary changes resulting from the shift of administrative responsibility to the center (in the form of more ministerial

[1] *Ibid.*, I, 163.

[2] Gneist chose to overlook what the Webbs called 'the inequality in the incidence of the obligation to serve', which favored the wealthier and more prestigious local personages. Indeed, he concentrated precisely on the more important local offices, such as Justice of the Peace.

supervision) and the introduction of voluntary and elective local boards in place of obligatory appointments by the crown; but Gneist did not approve them. He explained the changes as a by-product of industrialization, a process which strengthened the powers of selfish economic interests and encouraged them to weaken or take over the state, beginning at the lowest level. Where the administration of money (for example, the poor rates) and of justice were separated, Gneist thought, the purely economic concerns of 'society' would overwhelm the selfless principles of the state. Local election instead of royal appointment to local office invited manipulation by mere class interests. In order to keep administration out of the hands of the new moneyed interest arising in the industrial areas, Gneist reasoned, authority had to be moved increasingly toward the center.

Still, the center could not long be immune to the disease of the roots. Government by a parliamentary cabinet virtually independent of the monarch was too weak to withstand the pressure groups of industrial society once they entered Parliament. Gneist's admiration for English institutions in general made him all the more critical of present 'evils'. He analyzed the problem thus in 1860:

> The justified feeling of shame which the [English] nation must experience in reviewing the government of the past few years and the humiliating role, unworthy of England, *vis-à-vis* foreign countries will hopefully have the beneficial effect of changing a haughty public opinion. It should replace the customary mechanical idea of government-by-parliamentary-committee (cabinet), now widely held to be the only genuinely English form of a free constitution, with the insight that the real essence of that constitution rests solidly upon the institutions of local government [*Communalverfassung*] and the duty of personal service. These must be restored and expanded by king, upper house, and gentry—in spite of public opinion.[1]

Gneist realized what many previous constitutionalists had overlooked – that the British constitution no longer resembled the descriptions of Montesquieu and Blackstone; yet despite his self-assessment as a *Realpolitiker* (political realist), he could not accept the changes made since 1832. He declared public opinion to be wrong – a statement which would have shocked Rotteck. No doubt Gneist was right to maintain that public opinion can be organized and swayed by selfish interest groups; but he was wrong to idealize the unreformed English

[1] Gneist, *Verfassungs- und Verwaltungsrecht*, II, 950.

constitution as a system capable of extracting the passions of men from the administration of justice. Misled by generalizing the merely temporary influence of medieval English kings on the development of the state, he insisted that no state, not even contemporary England, could dispense with a strong king or, once it had been trained in public service, a powerful aristocracy. He had criticized muddle-headed constitutionalists for whom 'past and present, form and content flowed together into a friendly and attractive image, but the image was not especially clear, and only one object had emerged from it with firm outlines – Parliament'.[1] Yet Gneist himself fell into the opposite error of generalizing the viability and operating soundness of English local government from a past model. Government by manipulation of partisan groups, typical of contemporary England, struck him as dirty and unfair.

A party government was capable of respecting civil liberties, administering justice impartially, preserving a respected and even brilliant position for the church, and placing men of unquestionable honor in high administrative office. But it was not capable of fulfilling the duty of the state to educate and improve the lot of the lower classes.[2]

Gneist's theories set German liberalism on a new course. For if the just state could not be attained by imposing the rights (especially the power of the purse) of the people on the monarch, if elective organs of self-government were doomed to exploitation by selfish pressure groups, then it had to be attained by imposing the will of the monarch on the people. In effect Gneist approved of the strong king, the efficient salaried bureaucracy at the important *Bezirk* (district) level, and 'self-administration' by royally-appointed, unpaid officials on the lowest level. Parliamentary power at the center, this new ideology implied, could not come about until self-government had produced enough local notables trained in the ethic and imbued with the experience of public service *for its own sake*. Later on, after the citizenry had been trained in responsibility, one might speak of expansion upwards throughout the governmental apparatus. But it is hard to see in Gneist's system how the power of the monarchy and its bureaucracy would ever be broken. Like the thinking of Stein and Vincke, upon which Gneist drew heavily, these plans intended to strengthen and

[1] *Ibid.*, I, vii.

[2] *Ibid.*, p. 308.

conserve the state; they were far less revolutionary than constitutional safeguards and guarantees to individual rights or parliamentary dominance. Gneist's new form of political 'liberalism' thus furthered several developments in contemporary political thought: it tacitly idealized the monarchy and the bureaucracy, turned passions away from the struggle for a German parliament with real powers, aroused interest in local participation in politics, praised the *British* aristocracy at the expense of the German, and in all this contributed to a new kind of misunderstanding of English political life.

Gneist's views quickly asserted dominance over all discussions of the English constitution. Only two years after the first volume of his *Englisches Verfassungs- und Verwaltungsrecht* appeared, Gneist's ideas dominated the most distinguished liberal political encyclopaedia of the time, Johann Caspar Bluntschli's *Deutsches Staatswörterbuch*, the mid-nineteenth century equivalent of the old *Staatslexikon.* As usual, the entry for England dealt mostly with constitutional matters. But the *Staatswörterbuch* brought Gneist's terms into the consciousness of thousands of German intellectuals. 'Only the daily practice of a very thoughtfully formed community life can make one aware of the fact that the free state consists in the fulfillment of common duties,' the entry read. 'Without that awareness, every presentation of the English state will appear unsatisfactory to us; every parliamentary constitution will remain in fact unsatisfactory.'[1] In the new German liberalism, as defined by Gneist, the stress fell on the duties of men rather than their immunities.

Many younger historians quickly absorbed Gneist's ideas. Pauli wove Gneist's findings into his work.[2] Treitschke, whose views of England will be discussed in the next chapter, enthusiastically accepted

[1] *Deutsches Staatswörterbuch*, ed. by Johann Caspar Bluntschli and Karl Brater, 11 vols. (Stuttgart and Leipzig, 1857–60), IV (1859), 457.

[2] See the following for Pauli's ideas about the English constitution; Reinhold Pauli, *Geschichte von England*, 3 vols. [vols. 3–5 of the Heeren series *Geschichte der europäischen Staaten*] (Gotha, 1851–8), II, 668–83; 'Das Parlament im 14. Jahrhundert'. *Bilder aus Alt-England* (Gotha, 1860), pp. 62–89; *Geschichte Englands seit den Friedensschlüssen von 1814 und 1815*, 3 vols. (Leipzig, 1864–75), II, 126–30; 'Cavaliere und Rundköpfe', *Aufsätze zur englischen Geschichte* (Leipzig, 1869); 'Canning', *Aufsätze*, I, 392. Pauli was picked by Lappenberg, an old family friend, to continue the great history of England in the Heeren series. Well-qualified by nine years of private research in England (1847–55) and well-acquainted with English affairs after serving as Ambassador Bunsen's private secretary, Pauli did a very good job, by contemporary standards. See the glowing revues of his *Geschichte von England* by Karl von Noorden, *Historische Zeitschrift*, XIX (1868), p. 218.

Gneist's findings as his own. Eduard Fischel, a liberal publicist, based an enormously popular history of the English constitution upon Gneist's ideas.[1] Eventually the *Reichstag* itself heard Gneist praise the glories of English administration and warn against the dangers of French models. By influencing the Prussian *Kreisordnung* (county administration system) of 1872, he hoped to bring 'old English' administrative principles to Prussia.[2]

By then, Gneist had begun to insist more sharply on the difference between the 'old' and the 'new' England (roughly divided by the reforms of 1832). Gneistian Anglophiles similarly admired English history, but not necessarily contemporary England. German historians somewhat regarded themselves as holders of a sacred trust – the priests of the cult of the 'real' England, saving English history from the doubtful constructions of 'partisan' English writers. Reverence for English *history* thus increased among German historians along with concern about the conditions which stood at the end of that history. The distinction proved convenient after 1870, when thoughts about England became more ambivalent than ever before.

II THE YOUNG NATIONAL LIBERALS

The outpouring of German books on England in the 1850s and early 1860s included not only Ranke's *Englische Geschichte* and Gneist's *Selfgovernment* (as he later retitled his major work), but books and articles by Pauli and Noorden. Even scholars who normally devoted most of their attention to German history (from the Prussian viewpoint), such as Duncker, Sybel, and Treitschke took the time to write articles about England. Despite the apparent differences in scholarly motivation and objectivity between the Rankean tradition and that of Dahlmann, upon whom the 'Prussian school' drew, one finds little difference between the views of England among Ranke's and Dahlmann's students. In scholarly technique, Ranke's method triumphed completely; in political engagement, Dahlmann had won out. Their students, insofar as they followed the lead of both masters in studying

[1] Eduard Fischel, *Die Verfassung Englands* (Berlin, 1862).

[2] See Heinrich Heffter, *Die deutsche Selbstverwaltung im neunzehnten Jahrhundert* (Stuttgart, 1950), pp. 501–25, 548f., *et passim.* Ironically, the end result of the reform was the opposite of what Gneist desired, demonstrating the irresistibility of the trend toward bureaucratization of local government everywhere in Europe.

English history, combined emphases of both men. Ranke's cosmopolitan fascination with the Germanic heritage of England and the *Primat der Aussenpolitik* was well balanced by Dahlmann's preoccupation with Prussia's uniqueness and the internal political reforms which he hoped would lend Prussia a moral prestige in the battle for German unification. Gneist's influence reduced further the enthusiasm of German scholars for dominant parliamentary institutions.

That scholarly involvement in the liberal, *kleindeutsch* national cause enhanced rather than detracted from interest in England is explicable in terms of the peculiar situation of the 1850s and 1860s. Before the German Wars of Unification it scarcely seemed thinkable that a traditional Prussian monarchy, uninfluenced by 'public opinion', would undertake the task of unifying the nation. Therefore constitutional government, with some more meaningful form of public control than the Prussian *oktroyierte Verfassung* (imposed constitution), appeared to be the first step towards unity; and only Britain offered this. If one can believe the self-criticism of such disappointed Anglophiles as Bucher in this period, most national liberals firmly believed that a concert of liberal movements in Europe would lend aid against the concert of reaction; that England, the freest country, must also be the natural leader of such a coalition; and that the German national movement, because it was constitutionalist, could count on England's support.

Thus Ranke's old ideas of Anglo-German (in this case, Anglo-Prussian) *Waffenbrüderschaft* continued in a more febrile form. Few men foresaw the possibility that German calls for unity might arouse qualms in Britain. This blind spot became especially clear in the public discussions of German naval needs, which were simply not thought of in terms of rivalry with Britain.

A large degree of agreement likewise characterized all the Ranke and Dahlmann students in their discussions of English domestic politics and history. They accepted Gneist's distinction between an 'old' and a 'new' England, increasingly treating the latter as an unfortunate but doubtless short-lived aberration. One of the oddest results of this selectivity was a tendency to avoid analysis of current and very recent British constitutional practice. More and more, the difficulties of 'taking over' the functioning British system at one stroke, a constitutionalist dream which Ranke and older conservatives had ridiculed, dawned on the national liberals. It was no coincidence that deep curiosity about power found its way into investigations of English history, as well. Increasingly the effective use of power, rather than effective distribution of it, became a theme which German historians sought out in English history.

Consistent with their own hierarchy of values, most of the national liberal historians frequently mentioned 'national character' and supposedly constant attributes of English 'character' by way of historical explanation. Since so much of English character was supposed to derive from Germanic roots, careless generalizations lumping together English and German experience and future expectations still slipped by the selfconsciously scrupulous scholarly canons of these authors. Pauli, for example, could write in his *Geschichte von England* of 'the great conflict between monarchy and constitutional state, between Romance and Germanic essence' in English history,[1] as though liberalism were an exclusive Germanic property. On the other hand, Pauli and most of the men his age took a more sophisticated approach to the importance of the 'Germanic heritage'. They recognized the importance of Norman (in their view 'Romance') innovations, as well. Indeed, Pauli believed that English political history unfolded through the interaction of the Germanic idea of freedom with the strong 'state idea' of a series of wise monarchs. Pauli liked to compare the English state to a tree of which the people formed the roots which the monarchs pruned and bent to perfection. For this reason he could appreciate rulers as varied in temperament and aims as Alfred and William the Conqueror.[2]

Despite such insights, however, Pauli and the others could not shake off their preference for the Germanic heritage, as they interpreted it. Pauli consistently championed Saxon versus Norman, baronage versus monarchy, English local interest versus foreign entanglement, merchant initiative versus irrational royal indifference to the economy, austere 'Saxon' religious reformers against the worldly 'Roman' church. Writing of a much later period, Noorden could still characterize the basic issue of the age of William III of Orange as 'a Spanish-Catholic offensive and a Germanic-Protestant defensive.[3] Like Ranke, Noorden

[1] Pauli, *Geschichte von England*, I, 856.

[2] Pauli, *The Life of Alfred the Great*, ed. by B. Thorpe (London, 1873), p. 235. (English translation of *König Alfred und seine Stellung in der Geschichte Englands*, Berlin, 1851).

[3] Karl von Noorden, 'William III von Oranien', *Historische Vorträge*, ed. by Wilhelm Maurenbrecher (Leipzig, 1884), p. 9.

and Pauli apparently felt that such an international alliance based on Germanic race and Protestant religion continued to be 'natural'. Even as secular thinkers, they could not dispense with Protestantism to explain an innate cherishing of freedom, and Germanic habits went a long way toward explaining Protestantism. Sybel went less far in stressing the importance of the Germanic heritage, but he used the same concepts.[1]

At the same time, these men showed a new respect for the very principles they considered un-Germanic, especially in terms of political innovation. Pauli, like many constitutionalists before him, obviously sided with the 'Saxon' desire for liberty, but he had grudgingly to admit that a strong monarch was both necessary and good throughout English history. In subtle and sometimes conflicting statements he demonstrated his own search, not for endless examples of victories for 'freedom' in English history, but for the continual development, in a smooth and orderly way, of 'inevitable' traits. The 'inevitable' meant, broadly speaking, the balanced constitution described by Blackstone, a strong monarchy (with a strong fleet) offset by a watchful Parliament, etc. Not anarchy, nor even perfect individual liberty, but a 'striving after a firm order' characterized English history.[2] Certainly it characterized the ambitions of Pauli and the academic middle class from which he came. Pauli did not go as far as Gneist in stressing the need for a strong monarchy, but his enthusiasm for 'liberty' and parliamentary resistance, let alone dominance, was pale compared to that of earlier constitutionalists.

Nothing better indicates the sharp difference in thinking between the pre-March generation and the era of *Realpolitik* than the gap between Dahlmann's interpretation of Cromwell and that of his former student Pauli. The younger man strongly admired the wilful, powerful Puritan. The victory for Protestantism, national power, order, and commerce inherent in Cromwell's regime were analogous to the aims of the Little German forces. The creator of the New Model Army took more and more power to preserve himself and his troops against

[1] So widespread was this belief in the importance of the Germanic heritage that English scholars, who rejuvenated historical scholarship by drawing on German technique, absorbed these notions as well. Freeman's *History of the Norman Conquest*, for example, set out to prove that 'all merits which make the English constitution excellent were of Saxon origin'. (Fueter, *Historiographie*, p. 492.) See also Messerschmidt, *Deutschland in englischer Sicht*, p. 26 *et passim*, for a discussion of the 'Oxford school' and Germanism.

[2] Pauli, *Bilder*, p. 86.

'political intrigues', not to make himself king.[1] Cromwell's most questionable acts – for example, the execution of Charles I – appeared as concessions made to the radicals in the army to forestall greater excesses.[2] Pauli regarded the later dictatorship as a necessary civilian counterweight to the army. The Protector's dictatorship stepped away from 'inoperable republican ideas' and provided both sorely-needed order and a partial return to good old English constitutional practices.[3] Pauli always saw in law and order the real ruler of England. The Stuarts had breached these principles; Cromwell had defended them first against the dynasty, then against Levellers and other extremists.

Carlyle's work on Cromwell had of course impressed the Germans, and one should not credit Pauli with original discovery. But Carlyle's determination to rehabilitate Cromwell had roots in the same German idealist heritage which formed a part of the national-liberal historians' training. The admiration for the heroic and individual and contempt of the masses which characterized Carlyle's work animated that of Pauli, Noorden, and the new liberals. They no longer conceived of representative political institutions as expressions of popular sovereignty, but in the Gneistian sense as 'the participation in the administration of the state by the propertied classes, who exercise communal self-administration'.[4] Such historical and functional observations made English parliamentary traditions increasingly irrelevant to Germany. On the other hand, glorification of noted 'strong men' in English history, such as Edward I, Henry VIII and Cromwell, introduced the habit of identifying the best elements in English history with *Zwingherren* (despots). Still, the ambivalence and caution of a Pauli in drawing conclusions indicated a fairness of mind, as well as a certain confusion of personal political standards, which Schlosser or Dahlmann would have found peculiar. Furthermore, the tendency of the national-liberal scholars to place acts of power in a sphere of moral neutrality, particularly if they were 'necessary' for an approved cause such as 'unity', found expression in many interpretive nuances: Cromwell, for example, had fairly consistently been rebuked for his cruel suppression of Ireland. Pauli, by contrast, excused Drogheda and other acts of terror because a stern example was needed to insure peace and unity.[5]

[1] Pauli, 'Cavaliere und Rundköpfe', p. 317.
[2] *Ibid.*, pp. 323–31.
[3] *Ibid.*, p. 334.
[4] Pauli, *Aufsätze*, p. 392.
[5] *Ibid.*, p. 326.

Consonant with the national-liberal stress on the goal of a utopian *Rechtsstaat* rather than the violent struggle to achieve it, Pauli singled out one thread from the 'confusion of events': 'Right and law preserved England from ruin and helped her over the revolutions.'[1] Parliamentary institutions, Pauli believed, had survived in England only because they had proceeded from the very font of the old authority: the monarchy.[2]

The national liberals, following an old German tradition, did by and large approve of the resistance of the English Parliaments against the Stuarts. In this they parted ways with Gneist, who believed the new system after 1689 too severely restricted the crown, and outdid Ranke in terms of enthusiasm. But they did not find each new gain in Parliament's power *vis-à-vis* the monarchy worth celebrating.

Noorden, one of the clearest observers of modern English constitutional development in Germany, typified much of the rejection of the 'new England' found among the young national-liberal historians by the 1860s. Like Pauli, Noorden, the other notable Rankean historian of England, pursued the master's stress upon England's Germanic, Protestant foreign policy but added a keen interest of his own in the English constitution. Having begun to study history at a comparatively late age, Noorden produced just one major work of diplomatic history[3] plus some fine articles and lectures on the English constitution. His sober and realistic teachings about the contemporary English constitution approached the truth more closely than those of any other contemporary historian.[4] Noorden recognized not only the predominance of Parliament in all affairs of state but also the dominance of one party. Breaking completely with the Blackstonian theory of the division of power among three groups, he recognized the cabinet as the seat of all real power.[5] Furthermore, he maintained that party politics in modern England were based on power more than reason or principle: issues were used only as pretexts for the opposition to attack and the party to defend the cabinet.[6]

[1] Pauli, *Geschichte von England*, I, 820. Pauli spoke here of the thirteenth century, but his words summarize his general view of revolution and turmoil. See his expanded analysis in *Simon von Montfort, Graf von Leicester, der Schöpfer des Hauses der Gemeinen* (Tübingen, 1867).

[2] Pauli, *Geschichte von England*, II, 187f.

[3] Noorden, *Geschichte des spanischen Erbfolgekrieges*, 3 vols. (Leipzig, 1870–82).

[4] See Noorden, 'Die parlamentarische Parteiregierung in England', *Historische Zeitschrift*, XIV (1865), 45–118.

[5] *Ibid.*, p. 67f.

[6] *Ibid.*, p. 74f.

Noorden might have contributed useful lessons to German parliamentarians if he had insisted that they should pursue these characteristic traits in German practice. Instead, he deplored them. For him, as for most North German liberals, 'the idea of seeing in the dominance of the parties a replacement for the *plenitudo potestas* of the non-partisan but constitutional monarch was... simply unbearable'.[1] In view of the large number of minority and coalition governments in England between 1839 and 1868, one can understand why Noorden, like many other German political historians, perceived a distinct decline in the English state.[2] 'Only in our own time', he wrote, 'has the parliamentary constitution begun to succumb to the laws governing all living things.'[3]

Pauli joined Noorden and Gneist in mistrusting the most recent evolution of the English constitution. 'The attentive observer cannot fail to notice,' he wrote, 'that the English ship of state is today being fitted out in a manner which can hardly be called European, let alone English.'[4] He approved the reforms of 1832 only because they prevented revolution, but he refused to predict what the ultimate result of such tampering with the constitution might be.

The ultimate result of such changes in the German view of the English constitution was surrender of the ringing, if naïve, demand of generations of German progressives: 'Give us an English constitution.' Heinrich von Sybel, writing after the crystallization of the new German Imperial Constitution, attempted to maintain some sort of historical tie, but it was a remote one. The German state needed an English constitution, he argued, but not one of the nineteenth century. Instead, Germany required a Tudor constitution, with considerable monarchical powers to supplant two missing elements of parliamentarism – the two-party system and a body politic educated in the great school of self-government.[5] German national-liberal ideology, which inspired most of the leading historians at the time, rejected the system of 'party rule' which made a two-party system possible. Thus in effect, Sybel could only be holding on to the introduction of self-government in

[1] Lamer, *Der englische Parlamentarismus*, p. 69.
[2] Noorden, 'Parlamentarische Parteiregierung', pp. 87, 116.
[3] Noorden, 'Swift', *Historische Vorträge*, p. 91.
[4] Pauli, *Geschichte von England*, II, vii.
[5] Heinrich von Sybel, 'Das neue deutsche Reich' (1871), in *Vorträge und Aufsätze* (Berlin, 1874), pp. 233, 326.

Germany – an effort which only half-succeeded in Prussia a year after he wrote.

If Britain became increasingly irrelevant to the political needs of Germany's leading academic spokesmen for change, Britain as a great power became more important than ever. Sybel, for example, coupled his plea for British understanding of Germany's retarded parliamentary system with an appeal for Anglo-German cooperation against France. He tried to prove to his 'English cousins' that the German victory over France meant a triumph for the forces of civilization and that Germany sought no expansion. 'The victory of Napoleon [III] in the war', he asserted, 'would have meant the victory of clerical tendencies in half Europe.'[1] In 1871 such appeals were unreal and best explained as habitual reflexes of the two decades before Sedan, when men of the 'Prussian school' as well as Ranke's students had extended and generalized the Rankean postulate of natural cooperation between Britain and the German states. Indeed for many it had become a universal article of faith rather than merely a limited historical rule-of-thumb.

Pauli, with his Rankean credentials and his years of secretarial experience at the side of Baron Bunsen in London, naturally had much to say about British foreign policy and Anglo-German (chiefly Anglo-Prussian) relations. From his earliest writings onwards, Pauli took special pains to underscore instances of successful Anglo-Prussian cooperation as early as the middle ages.[2] With scant attention to such facts as the meaninglessness of the term 'Deutschland' in any diplomatic or economic sense, Pauli repeatedly exaggerated the strength of ties between Protestant North Germany and England and consistently played down contrary evidence. To demonstrate Anglo-'German' cooperation in the eighteenth century, for example, he stressed the Seven Years' War (when Britain had supported Prussia) but not the War of Austrian Succession (when Britain had supported Austria).[3] The distortion of the historical circumstances had a point, however: Germany and England were 'the two *welthistorisch bedeutende* Germanic nations' – those with a mission in world history.[4] They had

[1] *Ibid.*, p. 306.

[2] Reinhold Pauli, *Der Gang der internationalen Beziehungen zwischen Deutschland und England* (Gotha, 1859).

[3] *Ibid.*, p. 32. Also see Pauli's 'Englands älteste Beziehungen zu Österreich und Preussen', *Bilder*, p. 108.

[4] Pauli, *Gang der...Beziehungen*, p. 5.

held the destinies of the world in their hands when they cooperated, as (the last time) against Napoleon. Pauli was confident that they would embark on a more or less permanent alliance again, once Germany attained 'constitutionalism and realism'.[1]

Such short and pointed works as Pauli's *Gang der internationalen Beziehungen* were not mere isolated examples of the combination of historical erudition, judicious slanting, and political propaganda. In the first volume of the *Preussische Jahrbücher* in 1857, at least three historians commented on the 'traditional' Anglo-Prussian identity of interests, and, indeed, that journal maintained only one foreign correspondent in the late 1850s – in London. As one of these authors argues, 'The interests of Prussia and England lie close together. The two states became great in unity... They have never been seriously at odds without one or the other – or both – suffering damage.'[2]

Beyond these merely topical appeals for Anglo-Prussian cooperation, which can be understood better in the light of Prussia's relative isolation in the period after the Crimean War, the leading national-liberal historians wrote scholarly books in such a way as to lend credence to their demands. Throughout almost all the works of this period dealing in some way with British–German relations, the authors sought out examples of friendly cooperation. Where minor frictions had existed, they were silent. And where aspects of English behavior had been heavily criticized by critics of England, they leapt to the defense. For example Pauli, like both Ranke and Gneist, absolved England of guilt in the major case of her turning on a 'fellow Germanic land' (the United Netherlands) in the interest of selfish economic advantage: Holland always came out as the aggressor, despite the inconsistency of Navigation Laws with German liberal ideology.[3] For the eighteenth century, Noorden carried on Ranke's traditions – belief in a Germanic-Protestant community and in the identity of interest in opposing France and the Catholic powers.[4] Even on the touchy problem of Ireland, one which should have touched a nationalist and a student of Swift, he refrained from hostility to England's policy.[5] Noorden's flattering view of English foreign policy elaborated the Rankean conception of England's traditional diplomatic role by concentrating

[1] *Ibid.*, p. 34f.
[2] Max Duncker, 'Preussen und England', *Preussische Jahrbücher*, I (1858), p. 29.
[3] Pauli, 'Cavaliere und Rundköpfe', p. 290.
[4] Noorden, *Historische Vorträge*, pp. 9, 24.
[5] Noorden, 'Swift', p. 89 *et passim*.

on the early eighteenth century, the starting point of Ranke's thoughts on the nature of English foreign policy. His choice of that subject reflected the Rankean stress upon the common Anglo-German struggle against French hegemony.

Fear of France and a distaste for the French Revolution inspired by reading Burke gave impetus to Sybel in defending England against the old charges of French revolutionary propaganda. Sybel attacked the 'endless mass of rumors, inventions, myths, and tendentious lies' about England found in the literature of the French Revolution.[1] 'One reads about the certainty that the secret plotter of the war [against France], the man who misguided Austria and Prussia into this mad campaign and continued to be the soul of the struggle aimed at the total destruction of France, was the English minister Pitt.' Napoleon, too, was supposedly driven into a war to the knife by English 'demands contrary to treaty and by an unbearable commercial tyranny'.[2] Sybel dismissed such allegations as nonsense. 'Pitt clung for years to neutrality, did everything to keep the peace, and tried tirelessly to return to a state of peace after the French declaration of war.' Not British domination of the sea but Napoleonic world dominion made peace impossible.[3]

The charge that England had consciously or unconsciously extended its grasp to the point that one could speak of a world hegemony – maritime, commercial, or diplomatic – had been one of the most effective produced by French propagandists in the late eighteenth century. One would at first expect German nationalists to foresee the possibility of conflict between the claims to prestige, naval power, and markets of England and the new German national state demanded by the nationalists. For those who conceived of a modest German development along the agrarian, land-based, and hierarchical traditions of the old Prussia, such a problem did not necessarily arise. But there were those who insisted that the future German national state must be a great naval and commercial power, as well. How did they view England?

The major spokesman for a German fleet and ocean-bound commerce among the national-liberal historians was Pauli, who had grown up in Bremen, next to Hamburg the leader in developing German overseas trade. Pauli consistently and warmly urged his fellow Germans to copy England in building the means of seaborne commerce and a

[1] Heinrich von Sybel, 'Die Erhebung Europas gegen Napoleon I', *Kleine historische Schriften* (Munich, 1863), p. 245.

[2] *Ibid.*, p. 246.

[3] *Ibid.*, p. 247.

navy to protect it. First, he warned, Germany needed unity under a constitutional monarchy, which would guarantee peace and commercial development and thereby ultimately lead to a navy.[1] Pauli evidently did not think beyond the creation of such a navy to the possible rivalries it would engender, especially with Great Britain. He apparently conceived a German navy as a weapon for the defense of commerce, not (as some critics of British naval might maintained) for the purpose of blocking the commerce of others. Nevertheless Pauli found defenses for the most questionable of English naval policies. His defense of the Navigation Acts has already been mentioned. Not even the most spectacular of modern British punic expeditions, the Copenhagen raid of 1807, drew anything less than a full justification from Pauli.[2] In citing the British navy as a reason for Germany's building one, Pauli stressed positive advantages (glory, freedom, and profit) rather than negative necessity (fear of British hegemony). A Prussian fleet, he assumed, would be aimed chiefly at Russia.[3] Even when describing historic Anglo-German commercial confrontations, such as those attending England's struggles with the medieval Hansa in the fourteenth century, Pauli refused to blame English aggression: the Hansa's own 'stiffness and exclusiveness' had undone it, he maintained.[4] His hope for Anglo-Prussian cooperation in unifying Germany and neutralizing both France and Russia overcame all sense of possible rivalry: even if Germany had a fleet, Anglo-German interests would be too numerous to allow for conflict.[5]

National-liberal faith in English aid to the *kleindeutsch* cause often found expression in the private writings of German historians. When this support failed to materialize, many were incredulous; others, like Pauli, took London's attitude, particularly on the Schleswig-Holstein question in the 1860s, as a temporary aberration.[6] Yet this 'betrayal',

[1] Reinhold Pauli, 'Wie Kriegsflotten entstehen', *Preussische Jahrbücher*, XIV (1864), p. 515.

[2] Pauli, 'Canning', p. 414. The British naval attack was widely regarded as a famous historical outrage.

[3] Pauli, 'Preussen und das Meer', pt. 5, *Preussische Jahrbücher*, IV (1859), 163–78.

[4] Pauli, *Geschichte von England*, II, 647.

[5] Pauli, *Gang der...Beziehungen*, p. 34.

[6] See the following letters in Paul Wentzcke and Julius Heyderhoff, eds., *Deutscher Liberalismus im Zeitalter Bismarcks*, 2 vols. (Bonn and Leipzig, 1925–6), I: Häusser (p. 36); Duncker (p. 47)—both from 1859; Sybel (p. 50, from 1860). Other liberal historians expressed similar views on the idea of an Anglo-Prussian alliance. See letters by Baumgarten (p. 29) and Gervinus (p. 30)—both from 1859. Twesten, though not a historian, spoke for the disappointment of many members of the Prussian school when he deplored England's 'shouting and threats' over Schleswig-Holstein in 1864 (p. 229).

the inadequacy of British zeal, could not go unnoticed. Britain's foreign policy had gradually become a matter of keen concern to this generation of national-liberal historians, a matter of even greater import than English constitutionalism. They had quite obviously come to think that foreign policy has everything to do with domestic traditions, race, and past behaviour. They expected a concordance of British and North German-unionist aims in Europe at least partly because of the Protestant-Germanic 'heritage', the German striving for 'free', i.e. constitutional political practices, and the traditional Anglo-German fear of France.

While the German historians writing about England in the 1850s and 1860s continued to admire and praise their subject as an example, one can conclude that they were beset by doubts by 1870. To anyone who took note of the English suffrage reform of 1867, the ambivalent (which to Germans often meant 'hostile') posture of England in matters affecting German unification, and other manifestations of the times, a certain feeling of disillusionment was inevitable. The dissensions and splits within the *kleindeutsch*-liberal cause itself concerning Bismarck's policies carried over to evaluations of Britain and its history. Privately, the vocal supporters of England gave voice to doubts which they cautiously papered over in their works. As Robert von Mohl, now old and feeble, wrote in 1875 to his brother:

> Our time will probably make for interesting studies someday, and people will write lovely books about it; only it is less comfortable to live in it, especially when one is old...Things have gone fundamentally otherwise than we, in our green youth, foresaw, when we saw in constitutional forms the touchstone of wisdom for all times and chipped away at the remnants of old institutions that seemed to hang on.[1]

'Creeping democracy' and the 'disappearance of authority' most bothered the older Mohl, who now doubted, implicitly, the usefulness of the very parliamentary domination in the English style which he had recognized and advocated a quarter of a century before. Similarly Pauli, in his last lectures in the 1870s, divided the period 1868–present in a most significant way. 'Old England' represented 'parliamentarism, mercantile domination of the seas, predominance of old [political] forms, ascent'; 'new England' meant 'reform, free trade,

[1] Robert von Mohl, letter to his brother Julius, dated 15 March 1875, *Nachlass* Mohl, Stuttgart, Codex. hist. 506, III.

new forms, and decadence'.[1] The young Pauli had written many of his works, as he himself put it, 'not without *Tendenz* (topicality) directed to the parties in Prussia' in the 1850s. Although he had considered seventeenth-century English history most instructive for Prussia,[2] he had also expressed confidence that his model, the English constitution, would survive its nineteenth-century 'deficiencies' precisely because they would 'be worked out in good time'.[3] He thus expressed the belief of most Rankeans in continuity and orderly organic development. But in a letter of 1867, while defending his faith in the reforms of 1832, he confessed to a Scottish friend, 'I have [now] had enough of reforms, just as you have. Who would have thought that a people which for more than fifty years has risen up against those wishing to overthrow the constitution [*sic*] would suddenly be ready to dance to Mr Bright's tune! And that at a time when the destructive leanings of democracy will certainly venture new attacks...'[4] Furthermore, the degree to which even a stout Anglophile like Pauli could be swayed by disappointment in British postures in the Franco-Prussian war was revealed in other letters. While treating British sympathy for France as a temporary misunderstanding, he used the pejorative word *Manchesterpolitik* for the first time in describing British policy – describing a turn of events which contradicted the 'communal tribal interests' he had always postulated as the basis of historic Anglo-German understanding in European affairs.

Other men could be cited to show the quandary of the Anglophile national-liberal historians as they juggled the rapidly developing surprises accompanying German unification, their scholarly duty to describe England 'scientifically', and their political urge to show off those parts of English history which they hoped would be useful to the German national cause. Few generations of politically engaged scholars have had to face the adjustments which they did. Their choices reduced at bottom to three: accept the new Bismarckian state, with all its disappointments, and discourage further talk about the English constitutional model or the English alliance; continue to struggle for a

[1] Reinhold Pauli, notes for lectures on 'Einleitung zu einer Geschichte Grossbrittaniens von 1688 bis auf die Gegenwart', *Nachlass* Pauli, *Niedersächsische Staatsbibliothek*, Göttingen, Cod. MS. hist. 73, VI.

[2] Reinhold Pauli, *Lebenserinnerungen*, edited by Elizabeth Pauli (Halle, 1895), p. 205.

[3] *Ibid.*, p. 94, from a letter of 1848.

[4] *Ibid.*, p. 262f., from a letter of 1867 to James Lorimer.

truly parliamentary constitution in Germany and an Anglo-German alliance aimed chiefly at Russia; or accept Bismarck's constitution and foreign policy while continuing to praise an idealized 'old England' of questionable political relevance to contemporary Germany. Few of the national-liberal scholars could make up their minds which course to follow, but most tended toward the third choice. They had been overtaken by events, and in mixed confusion and pleasure they yielded to Bismarck. Most could not stop writing about England, especially those, like Gneist and Pauli, who had built their reputations on English studies. A few, typified by Treitschke (as we shall see in ch. 9) did make a firm commitment to the first choice, with a vengeance. Few took the second path. All had learned the difficulties of applying English constitutional dogmas (many of which were of German manufacture) to German conditions and longed, with Gneist, for a restoration of 'old England', which they felt *had* been meaningful for German conditions. In effect, the German bourgeois academic elite had to accept the descriptions of Marx: they lost faith in the ability of the British hereditary and capitalist elite to carry on the admired traditions of gradualism in the face of democratic pressures. Naïve and far from the centers of power as they were, they were shocked to discover that English foreign policy could act otherwise than in the framework of the 'hereditary' Romance-Germanic (i.e. Franco-Prussian) confrontation which they had been taught to regard as eternal. Far from worshipping 'power', as Anglo-American historiography has charged, they went on casting Germany in the role of Germanic underdog in the face of a Latin (Franco-Papal) conspiracy and England in its mythological role as supporter of such underdogs.

Given the traditional ideas to which they held so tenaciously, it is hardly surprising to find the German national-liberal historians bending over backwards to give England the benefit of every doubt. Romanticization of 'old England' reached a peak in Germany precisely during the years when a 'new Germany' was arising from the crucible of Bismarck's diplomacy and wars. It was no longer possible to write as though nothing had changed in England: Gneist might stubbornly cling to his ludicrous insistence that the British cabinet was illegal, but he could not refute Noorden and others who showed how radically English government had changed in the last 150 years. Sybel might plead for the English to understand that Germany needed a sixteenth-century 'English constitution', Pauli might plead for a Cromwellian *Zwingherr*, but all had the feeling that the ground of the 'English example' was being pulled from under them by the history of the last forty years. Certainly it was no longer possible to speak of 'England' as an unchanging body of historical principles.

The generations which came after chose one of two paths in dealing with English history. Essentially, the first path meant stressing contemporary England and its differences with the Imperial Germany of Bismarck; the other, retreating along the natural line of a merely professional, narrow, and 'objective' treatment, satisfied the needs of the profession for learned tomes on English history.

Some individuals in the second body of scholars – a significantly small and unimpressive lot in the 1870s and 1880s – need not be discussed.[1] Those among them who wrote during the first decade of the new *Reich* and who later took a stand on the Anglo-German estrangement lie more in the line of this investigation and will be treated in ch. 10. The first body – represented chiefly by non-experts on England – held the stage of scholarly as well as public attention in the 1870s, however. Significantly, few voices among the old national-liberal scholars were raised against them. No doubt one of the reasons lay in their own uncertainty and hesitation. This is not difficult to imagine when one realizes that the leading revisionist of the German view of England was himself a national liberal – Heinrich von Treitschke.

[1] Here I speak of Onno Klopp and Moritz Brosch. The former, a Hanoverian turned Viennese Catholic after 1866, wrote to demonstrate the traditions of cooperation in Anglo-Austrian relations, was supported by the Austrian government, and was almost totally rejected by historians of Imperial Germany. The second was Austrian by birth, a journalist by training, and a scholar treated lightly by the profession in Germany. He was a pure scholar, with no consistent viewpoint on English history and without the magnificent qualifications which would have gained respect in Germany or England. See the cool reviews in the *Historische Zeitschrift* and the *English Historical Review* of Brosch's *Geschichte von England*, 5 vols. (Gotha, 1890–7).

PART IV

THE END OF ANGLOPHILIA

INTRODUCTION

It has long been fashionable, especially among economic, social, and intellectual historians, to cast doubt on the classical periodization of European and German history in the modern era. It is now highly questionable whether such dates as 1789, 1848, or even 1914 really constitute the watersheds of history. Nor has 1871, the founding date of the German Empire, escaped demotion among historians of Germany.[1] Certainly the temptation to choose some less conventional date for the definitive turn in the German view of England is also strong.

Nevertheless, considerable evidence suggests that 1871 was indeed the pivotal year in the change of German views of England. It presented the German historians and social scientists with a *fait accompli* for rejection or accommodation. Most accommodated, even though they expressed enough doubts and reservations to indicate that they were quite disappointed with the result. Furthermore, this disappointment evidently increased with the passage of years. Not only did the constitution of the *Reich* leave much to be desired; the anticipated flowering of a new national culture failed, in the contemporary view, to materialize at all. Not even the German economy, despite its phenomenal statistical growth, satisfied the academic elite, which deepened its scorn for the half-educated captains of industry and its fear of the maladjusted and increasingly socialistic industrial proletariat.

The dilemma of those scholars who had traditionally taken an active part in national political life thus became worse than ever. Prussia had gained control of several major universities – Kiel, Göttingen, Marburg, and Strasbourg – in areas traditionally ambivalent to the aims of Prussia. The Prussian universities, including the new acquisitions, did not show the same degree of oppositional political energy which had characterized German universities before 1871. Although the direct influence of the Prussian state on the limits of academic freedom

[1] See Helmut Böhme, *Deutschlands Weg zur Grossmacht* (Cologne and Berlin, 1966).

in this period is controversial and inadequately studied, several curious phenomena stand out to stimulate inquiry. First, the North German professorate developed the noble illusion that it was 'above politics'. Whether such an attitude constituted an irresponsible abdication of political leadership on the part of one of Germany's foremost elites or a successful defense against quite genuine potential infringements on academic freedom by the nervous state ministers who held ultimate power over the universities has likewise remained unsettled. Second, those who deviated from the cautious political canons of the new academic ethic appear to have been rewarded in disproportionate ways. On the other hand, those who spoke out most vociferously against the *status quo* were sometimes punished by the state, as in the notorious Arons case of the 1890s: the traditional exemption of *Privatdozenten* (unsalaried lecturers) from both pay and civil service regulation was modified to prevent even voluntary teachers from expressing opinions considered inimical to the *Reich*. Similarly, the major historians of England, insofar as they deviated from the reigning view of the imperial government (no matter what they thought of the German *status quo*), found their careers somewhat less than 'open to talent'. Furthermore, even before the 1890s one can perceive a distinct decline in the number and quality of works on England. On the other hand, those, like Treitschke,[1] who found it possible to support the imperial government in every twist and turn of its policy, were rewarded with posts and honors, which caused considerable adverse comment among less committed (but better qualified) scholars. No doubt a certain amount of academic carping is inevitable under any circumstances; but the advocates of a position 'above politics' did not find that the government officials who controlled the German university establishment completely shared their view. And in a time when the old traditions of private scholarship, based on inherited wealth, were fading in the face of an industrial economy, such matters counted more than ever.

The German Empire of 1871 was once regarded by Anglo-American scholars as the dynamic powerhouse of Europe. Not even the lessons of the Weimar Republic, with its many social and particularist challenges to the reigning idea of the German national state, have completely

[1] Heinrich von Treitschke (1834–96) was the most famous German nationalist historian; he spent the majority of his teaching years at the University of Berlin. (See Biographical Appendix.)

eradicated this view. German intellectuals of the Empire obviously felt less secure about the viability of the *Reich*, no matter what the statistics of German power may say to the contrary. Indeed, the most vociferous advocates of German nationalism and imperialism under Bismarck were less convinced than the Iron Chancellor himself of the cohesiveness of his creation. In this light, it is not too heretical to put forth the suggestion that the most vocal nationalists and imperialists – Treitschke, for example – worried most about the instability of the new Germany. This insecurity about the viability of the German state explains many things which have puzzled western observers, such as the strident nationalist tone of Wilhelmine Germany, the demand for *Weltpolitik* (global policy) to turn attention away from the obvious failures of a domestic policy and, finally, the odd transformation of the remaining 'non-political' scholarly admirers of England into scholarly nationalists willing to place their pens in the service of a last-ditch effort to unite non-socialist Germans in a common front in defense of a political system in which they only half believed. For the final irony of the German views of England in the nineteenth century is that the socialists, the sworn enemies of that system, had begun to accept contemporary England, or at least features of it, as a weapon against Wilhelmine Germany.

In all of this, scholarly motives obviously played only a secondary role. Scholarly training may well explain *some* of the changes in the German view of England in a broad shift from generation to generation. Macaulay, Carlyle, the Oxford 'school', and more readily available documentation, to name but a few influences, undoubtedly served to alter many a scholarly point over the years. Yet two facts remain to refute much of their impact on German views of England. To take an extreme case of the first fact: Treitschke bothered little to consult archives (other than the Prussian) in writing his histories, and when he had the chance, as in his trip to England in 1896, he did not use it. Those few scholars who did concentrate on archival materials, such as Liebermann, shied carefully away from materials touching anything remotely connected with the Anglo-German rivalry. The second fact is that those scholars who did conscientiously study English archives – and incidentally contributed major findings to English historiography – often went through astonishing revisions of their own views based entirely on the contemporary climate of opinion. The best and most thoroughly documented chief explanation of most German historical views of England went back to domestic political motives in the period 1871–1914. The exceptions to this conclusion confirm the hypothesis: those who wrote *entirely* in a scholarly vein avoided a confrontation, insofar as possible, with the scholars who insisted on discussing English history *in relation to Germany.* They retreated more and more into the historical areas of greatest irrelevance to the present and even there refused to deal with the matters of dispute which their colleagues brought up. Such behaviour constituted a new tradition in the German historical view of England. Their refusal was admirable and even-minded in many cases, and it is hard to doubt their intellectual integrity. But given their indifference to the debate about England, especially after 1896, one can conclude that they followed to the letter the implications of the German academic illusion of being 'above politics'. The German view of England, including that formulated by the most widely read historians, simply passed by the best and most scrupulous users of original sources.

It is possible to discern two eras of differing approaches to English history after 1871. In the earlier, between the establishment of the *Reich* and the serious launching of German *Weltpolitik* in the 1890s, interest in English history dropped off markedly. At least compared to the 1850s and 1860s, far fewer major works and articles appeared, and a generation gap opened between the remaining experts on England (all but Noorden born by 1830) and the generation of historians born in the 1850s and 1860s. Onno Klopp, Moritz Brosch, and Karl Hillebrand, whose works cannot for various reasons be considered as representative of Imperial German historiography,[1] belonged to the same age group as Pauli and others treated in ch. 8. Among historians born between 1830 and 1850, only Heinrich von Treitschke and Lujo Brentano[2] could even remotely be described as men with a deep

[1] All were *Privatgelehrte* (private scholars) who spent most of their mature lives outside the area which became the *Reich*. While they wrote in German, their viewpoints were strongly colored by the unusual circumstances under which they wrote. All, incidentally, could be regarded as Anglophiles, although Brosch was less committed (or, more precisely, more inconsistent) than the other two. Their works were voluminous, but Hillebrand, with his cultural essays, wrote the least. Readers interested in the views of Brosch may consult the 1967 Yale doctoral dissertation, 'The German Historians and England', by the present author. For a further description of the works of Klopp and Hillebrand, see the bibliography.

[2] Lujo Brentano (1844–1931) was a leading economic historian who taught chiefly at Breslau, Strasbourg, and Munich. (See Biographical Appendix.)

curiosity about England. Others, such as Hans Delbrück, Dietrich Schäfer and Gustav Schmoller,[1] became involved in questions touching on England chiefly *after* the turn to *Weltpolitik* – and largely because of it.

The two decades 1850–70, however, witnessed the birth of a remarkable crop of writers about England. These included specialists who devoted most of their scholarly energies to the subject, such as Felix Liebermann, Erich Marcks, Wolfgang Michael, Ludwig Riess, and Felix Salomon. Arnold Oskar Meyer, born in the 1870s, may be counted with this generation.[2] Furthermore, the debate arising out of the Anglo-German power and economic rivalry attracted some noted non-specialists from this generation of historians, notably Otto Hintze, Max Lenz, Hermann Oncken, and Gerhard von Schulze-Gaevernitz,[3] as well as a host of non-professional writers.

The reactions and subjects of debate characteristic of the second, later period will be treated in ch. 10. At that time, the political and psychological insecurity of the German professorate concerning the future of the *Reich* drew them back into politics, even though they fought to maintain a stance at least 'above the parties'. The earlier period, which coincides roughly with Bismarck's tenure as Imperial Chancellor, did not lie under quite the same cloud. To some degree, undeniably, political determinants on scholarly behaviour relaxed, despite the continued fretfulness of some men like Treitschke and the

[1] Hans Delbrück (1848–1929) was a professor at the University of Berlin and was also prominent as a publicist and political thinker. Dietrich Schäfer (1845–1929) ended his teaching career at Heidelberg and Berlin and was active in propaganda work for the creation of a German fleet. Gustav Schmoller (1838–1917) taught economic and administrative history chiefly at Berlin and exercised great influence on legal and political policies of the Prussian government. (See Biographical Appendix.)

[2] Felix Liebermann (1851–1925) was a private scholar who did much to shed light on medieval English sources. Erich Marcks (1861–1938) taught history at a number of universities, beginning and ending with Berlin, and was Historiographer of Prussia. Wolfgang Michael (1862–1945), who was a professor of history at the University of Freiburg im Breisgau, achieved a considerable reputation in England for his work. Ludwig Riess (1861–1928) taught principally at the University of Berlin. Felix Salomon (1866–1928) was a professor at the University of Leipzig. Arnold Oskar Meyer (1877–1944) taught at several universities before ending his career at Berlin. (See Biographical Appendix.)

[3] Otto Hintze (1861–1940), probably the greatest authority on the history of the Hohenzollerns, taught chiefly at Berlin. Max Lenz (1850–1932) was a professor of history at Hamburg and Berlin; he did much to revive the 'spirit of Ranke' in historical writing. Hermann Oncken (1869–1945) was a professor of history chiefly at Heidelberg and Berlin. Gerhard von Schulze-Gaevernitz (1864–1943) taught economic history at the University of Freiburg in Breisgau. (See Biographical Appendix.)

general cultural pessimism of many others about the *Reich*. As Klaus Schwabe has aptly stated it:

The conviction was widely held [after 1871] that, in an era when the *Reich* seemed adequately secure against foreign and domestic threats, the professor could fulfill his civic duties most competently in the field of 'science'—no matter how narrow this might be. For times of crisis, however, they did not yet let such an attitude stand. In such moments their claim to leadership again became timely, and even the Wilhelmine scholars latently clung to it: in such times the politically conscious professorate again became ready to resume its place as political mentor of the people, from which it had been displaced as a result of the failure of the 'forty-eight' revolution.[1]

The prolific writers on England of the 1850s and 1860s tended to follow this formula: the non-experts on England went back to their main interest (e.g. Sybel); the experts wrote less, certainly fewer tendentious articles, contributing little to any new interpretations or debates. The successor generation to these men did not immediately materialize. As a result, the 1870s and, even more noticeably, the 1880s offered a comparatively negligible amount of fresh writing on England by Imperial German historians. With somewhat stronger reservation, the same claim may be made for the period after the First World War as well, as will be elaborated in the final chapter.

The simple explanation for this bell-curve of interest is that England, or at least English history, had ceased to interest German historians once their utopian political hopes had been blown away by the hurricane of Bismarckian *Realpolitik*, and that a flickering revival took place before World War I because of various international tensions. Such an explanation, however, fails to account for some uncomfortable facts. It seeks to crystallize German domestic political history as though little changed after 1871. It implies that the Anglo-German rivalry was a rational and predictable outcome of German unity, with psychological and cultural motives playing only secondary roles, and with war as the outcome. It does not account for men like Treitschke, who mounted vicious attacks on England long before the era of German *Weltpolitik*, nor for those who defended England during it. It crudely approximates some of the changes in attitudes toward England as a political organization and as an economic and diplomatic actor, but it does not tell the

[1] Klaus Schwabe, 'Die politische Haltung der deutschen Professoren im ersten Weltkreig', *Historische Zeitschrift*, 193 (1961), p. 602f.

strange story of the erosion and collapse of the cultural ideal of England in German minds.

In order to find a more subtle explanation, it will be necessary to go into greater detail in the following chapters. The first of these deals overwhelmingly with Treitschke. His case is one of the most unusual and instructive in the story of the German view of England; a large amount of information about him is available; and few other men of his generation happened to compete for attention in describing England to the German reading public. The purpose of allotting him especially close scrutiny is not to exaggerate the representativeness of his opinions about England, which were extreme: it is rather to analyze the nature of his motives and his mental transformation, which form a sort of model for the problem as a whole. What went on in Treitschke's mind within his lifetime happened in German thought about England in general over a much longer period and for comparable reasons. Even though Treitschke was too much a 'political professor' to suit many of his retiring, 'scientific' colleagues after 1871, his very sense of the fragility of the *Reich*, his remedies, and his position on England tell much about the dilemmas of the academic middle class in the Bismarckian and, even more, Wilhelmine eras.

CHAPTER 9

TREITSCHKE AND THE REJECTION OF ENGLAND

The chorus of praise for English models, especially political models, reached its highest crescendo in Germany during the 1850s, as noted in the last chapter. Though conservative historians held up England's traditional anti-French foreign policy for greatest praise, liberals still preferred to investigate those domestic institutions to which they ascribed England's most distinguished accomplishment, stable political liberty. Liberal hopes for Germany were wedded to the liberal view of England. In the 1850s and 1860s, as Fueter said, 'The unproven assumptions of liberal historical writing could be founded basically on only one example, the smooth functioning of the English constitution.'[1]

One voice in this chorus not yet heard is Heinrich von Treitschke's. The tenor of Treitschke's youth merely echoed the rich bass of Dahlmann and Gneist. 'Admiration,' wrote the young *Dozent* in his maiden article in the *Preussische Jahrbücher*, 'is the first feeling which the study of English history calls forth in everyone.' Using the common rhetoric of the day, he praised the English as 'the Romans of the modern age'.[2] The political genius of the English interested Treitschke most strongly, for, as he noted, 'Each of our parties again and again uses the English example to prove its program, and it seems the [English] constitution exercises an irresistible and inevitable power of attraction.'[3] The admiration was misplaced among the conservatives, who stupidly admired the mere traditional surface of the system, whereas only the liberals, among whom Treitschke counted himself, appreciated the deep instructive truths of the English constitution.

When Treitschke's voice deepened with age, however, it growled

[1] Fueter, *Historiographie*, p. 501.

[2] Heinrich von Treitschke, 'Grundlagen der englischen Freiheit', *Preussische Jahrbücher*, I (1858), p. 368.

[3] *Ibid.*, p. 366.

with the suspicion and hatred of England for which Germany's most eloquent historian became famed and feared. More dramatically than any other German historian he veered from his 'first feeling' on English history through disillusionment to an irrational dislike of everything English. The practitioners of causation *post hoc ergo propter hoc* have even linked Treitschke's invective with World War I, assuming that an Anglo-German war could have occurred only in the poisoned climate which Treitschke helped to create. Clearly a parallel existed between the political and intellectual currents that turned Treitschke's toasts to gall in the 1870s and those typical of the imperialistic German Anglophobia of the 1890s. Historians have justly pointed to Treitschke's early advocacy of German naval and colonial expansion to explain his growing hostility to England. Nevertheless, some disturbing doubts arise if one accepts this explanation as total. First, the international conflicts between Britain and Germany did not force a major re-evaluation of England in the minds of many other historians until after the launching of a serious German naval challenge to Britain late in the 1890s – after Treitschke's death. Second, one must consider Treitschke's lifelong fascination with constitutional law and politics: throughout his life he showed a deep concern for the domestic politics of Germany and other lands, and he was one of the keenest constitutional observers of Britain in Germany.[1] Treitschke consciously used the English constitutional example to advance his domestic political aims in Germany during the decades before the *Reichsgründung*, but his domestic political reasons for later heaping abuse on England have not been so strongly emphasized. Like Diedrich in Heinrich Mann's *Der Untertan*, Treitschke considered himself first and foremost a 'national' man: to be 'national' meant not only to close ranks behind the *Reich's* foreign policy, but to struggle against the 'enemy within'. In Treitschke's later years, his constant fears for the viability of the *Reich* prompted him to fight England both as the foreign rival and as the ideological weapon of the *Reichsfeind* (enemy of the *Reich*).

Because more has been written about Treitschke than most other German historians, it is possible to pursue his career somewhat more closely than in the other cases in the hope of finding clues to the motivations behind the late nineteenth-century rejection of England. This is not to say that Treitschke's case is typical. But the extremes of

[1] See Lamer, *Der englische Parlamentarismus*, *passim*.

Treitschke's attitudes do encompass the limits of most other thinkers (except for the most fervently uncritical worshippers of England). The changing motives behind these extremes also encompass the forces acting on other historians.

Treitschke was born in 1834 and grew up in feeble health. By the time he entered the University of Bonn in 1851, the will power for which he later became noted was already being taxed by unusual demands – increasing deafness and strained relations with his father, a Saxon army general and loyal supporter of Saxon particularism, over Heinrich's nationalist leanings.

At Bonn after 1851, Treitschke absorbed and altered for his own use the nationalism, whiggish liberalism, and admiration for English political institutions espoused by his favourite teacher, Dahlmann. Treitschke told his father that Dahlmann had urged him to study the English constitution, but he needed no further encouragement: 'I derive great pleasure from it because it is a subject which necessarily awakens admiration and enthusiasm.'[1]

To explain his enthusiasm, one must understand Treitschke's emotional needs at the time. He despised the waste and vapidity both of German student life and of most levels of German society, dominated, it seemed, by conformistic and morally questionable practices.[2] As he was to do often in later life, Treitschke diagnosed the situation, decided what was wrong, and clung to his critical attitude with all his considerable will power or, as Walter Bussmann calls it, his moral 'conviction'. Alienated from his immediate milieu, Treitschke idealized a German community with which he could feel identity and busied himself writing poetry about it. He also sought a source of political ethics to guide his critique of German politics and society.

This ethical guidance also came from Dahlmann, whose integrity had clashed often with the arbitrariness of German political life that Treitschke so despised.[3] Yet Dahlmann's life had ended in political failure. For evidence that men could act politically out of moral conviction and still succeed, for a symbol of an *effective* political ethic, Treitschke turned to England. Even after he left Dahlmann's side to

[1] Heinrich von Treitschke, *Briefe*, ed. Max Cornicelius, 2nd edn., 3 vols. (Leipzig, 1914–18), letter dated Bonn, 28 February 1852, I, 115.

[2] Treitschke, letter to R. Martin, dated Göttingen, 27 January 1856. *Ibid.*, I, 338f.

[3] See Walter Bussmann, *Treitschke, Sein Welt- und Geschichtsbild* (Göttingen, 1952), pp. 26ff.

study and later teach at the Saxon University of Leipzig, Treitschke continued to deepen his interest in English history.[1] What impressed him most was the way Englishmen stood up for what they believed and, unlike the despised manipulators of German court politics, placed life and fortune in the service of liberty. Treitschke's emotional needs thus induced him to mistake Whig history for English history: Macaulay's *History of England* was a 'splendid book, a magnificent conception of history', Treitschke enthused; he 'could think for hours about a single phrase tossed out by Macaulay'.[2] The English historian, whose judgment was swift and simple, now reinforced Treitschke's belief that 'conviction' was a sufficient basis for both action and scholarly judgment. He sought out analogies in history – a technique encouraged by his Leipzig economics teacher, Wilhelm Roscher[3] – and particularly in English history. Macaulay's *History* provided many examples from the seventeenth century of opposition to political wrongs. 'The English principle of immediate redress of every wrong from above is not only, as Macaulay says, the pillar of English freedom and the pride of every Briton,' he wrote, 'but also the necessary result of a good national education.'[4]

Treitschke's belief in this symbolic moral value of English history overrode his reservations about certain tendencies in English thought. In his doctoral thesis, guided by Roscher, he criticized Adam Smith and the natural-law conception of an unfettered market economy. Treitschke believed the needs of state and society, not the 'invisible hand', should determine the operations of the market. The 'spirit of Manchester', as contemporary German usage labeled English free-trade ideology, threatened to denigrate human welfare and its protector, the state, in favor of impersonal economic forces. Nevertheless,

[1] It is probable, but not certain, that Treitschke's lecture notes for a comparative history of the English and French state, now located in the Treitschke *Nachlass*, *Deutsche Staatsbibliothek*, East Berlin, originated about this time. They show little of the hostility Treitschke later felt toward England. Their conclusions about modern English history, after a fleeting and thoroughly unoriginal sketch of the middle ages, corresponded largely with those of Dahlmann, Gneist, and the national-liberal historians. Treitschke also made some interesting mistakes in his constitutional analyses: he confused 'nobility' and 'gentry' and sought to prove that eighteenth-century England had been ruled by the 'nobility' by including in it such names as Pitt, Fox, and Burke. (See 'Vergleichende Geschichte', *Nachlass* Treitschke, Fach VII, unten, 76–9.)

[2] Treitschke, letter to his father, dated Leipzig, 21 January 1853, *Briefe*, I, 153.

[3] Andreas Dorpalen, *Heinrich von Treitschke* (New Haven, 1957), p. 20.

[4] Treitschke, letter to R. Martin, Göttingen, 10 February 1856, *Briefe*, I, 339.

Treitschke admitted that free-trade doctrine could be useful in the right historical circumstances and supported it in contemporary Europe. Despite his mild rebuke to Smith for excessive materialism, he by no means identified the ruthless pursuit of mammon as the chief attribute of England, as he later would.

Having finished with his doctorate, Treitschke took up university teaching in history at Leipzig and a full commitment to the struggle for national unity under Prussia, making no attempt to separate these roles. He and his political allies, the successors to the old Gotha party (advocates of a *kleindeutsch*, hereditary, constitutional monarchy in 1849–50), worked for the liberalization of the Prussian state, a process which they hoped would make 'moral conquests' for Prussia all over Germany. The direct channel for Treitschke's activism was the journal *Preussische Jahrbücher*, founded specifically to popularize the *kleindeutsch*, liberal cause.

Treitschke's very first article in the *Jahrbücher* in 1858 brought together his hopes for a liberal program in Germany and his admiration for the English concept of citizenship. Neither the national nor the liberal state could exist without the forced development of the public virtues, which Treitschke believed had flourished in England for centuries; the private virtues, limited to the moral systems of family, friendship, and perhaps fellow workers or colleagues, were too highly valued by Germans for the taste of Treitschke and the liberal nationalists.[1] Treitschke was no more objective about English history than he was about Prussia: both served his hopes for the political development of Germany. His wish to accentuate the positive side of English history excluded critical approaches. He closed his mind to the cynical but not altogether unfounded criticisms of English parliamentary government written by the influential London correspondent of the liberal *National-Zeitung*, Lothar Bucher. At a time when only Britain, among the major European states, offered an example of a genuine constitutional monarchy, Treitschke felt compelled to attack the 'great unscrupulousness' of Bucher's reports, chiefly because they might confuse the public about the value of a parliamentary regime in Prussia.[2] If the path to a unified German state passed through a genuine

[1] For a discussion of 'public' and 'private' virtues and their antagonism in German history, see Ralf Dahrendorf, *Society and Democracy in Germany* (New York, 1967), pp. 299ff.

[2] Treitschke, letter to H. Bachmann, Dresden, 12 August 1855, *Briefe*, I, 310.

constitutional monarchy, as most German liberals then believed, then Treitschke was more than willing to praise the highly successful English version of it.[1]

A stress on the symbolic value of English 'character', institutions, and political ideas underlay all of Treitschke's early articles on England and the English. Two of his articles, on Milton and Byron, touched Treitschke's own interest in combining poetry with political commitment; two more enthusiastically popularized Gneist's description of English local self-government; and a fifth one directed the *Jahrbücher* readers to the conception of freedom embodied in John Stuart Mill's *On Liberty*. That two of these subjects – Mill and Milton – had already been treated by Macaulay indicates Treitschke's continued admiration for that author's Whig conception of history. And like Macaulay, Treitschke used the forum of his reviews chiefly to air his own ideas at length.

Treitschke's articles on Milton and Byron (1860 and 1863) stressed the political rather than the poetic side of his subjects. Milton's struggle for religious and political liberty, his willingness to take public responsibility for his personal moral convictions, especially the supremacy of law over royal authority, all ignited Treitschke's enthusiasm. Treitschke praised Milton for the 'unique combination of artistic genius and civic virtue which we admire in him'.[2] He likewise praised the Puritans for their moral and political earnestness: they provided a model for German readers in that they, too, were a patriotic middle class attempting to uphold traditional Germanic religious, personal, and political liberty against imported French notions of centralized autocracy. No matter what the class origin of the Puritan leaders, because of their association with the native Anglo-Saxon (as opposed to French or Latin) culture, they passed in Treitschke's opinion as representatives of the whole nation. That there was more to Milton and Puritanism than this hardly concerned Treitschke: he wished to hold up political and ethical values to his readers, not present the confusing jumble of real events.

[1] As if foreshadowing his later surrender to Bismarck's pseudo-parliamentary *Reich*, Treitschke also conceded privately that he would accept even a dictatorship as long as it would establish German unity under Prussia. But he did this in 1854, despairing of the immediate possibility of a constitutionalist victory. See Treitschke's letter to H. Bachmann, Heidelberg, 10 November 1854, *Briefe*, I, 260.

[2] Treitschke, 'Milton', *Preussische Jahrbücher*, VI (1860), p. 420.

Similarly, Treitschke underlined those traits in Mill and Byron which he hoped the Germans would imitate. In most cases, resistance to the pressure of public opinion, the willingness to risk unpopularity rather than surrender one's values, appealed to Treitschke. He regarded 'personal independence' and a desire for 'living according to one's own preference, for inner, personal, civil liberty' as traits which both 'Germanic' people shared.[1] Indeed, Mill might have chuckled to hear himself described as 'a loyal son of those true Germanic middle classes which, since the days of Richard II, for good or for bad, by their earnest love of truth or by their somber fanatical faith, have excellently represented the internal core, the spiritual labor of [their] land.'[2] Above all Mill reinforced Treitschke's belief that civil liberties, particularly the right to think and speak freely, must precede any meaningful political liberty. Where Treitschke departed from Mill was in appointing the state as guardian of the individual's rights against church and society.

For it was characteristic of German liberalism in the 1850s and 1860s to press for a bigger and more powerful state. Treitschke criticized Mill as well as the older school of German liberalism going back to Humboldt as old-fashioned: the main threat to liberty was no longer the state, but the conformistic pressure of public opinion, against which the state might serve as a bulwark.[3]

On the other hand, a bigger state threatened to extend the evils of a burgeoning centralized bureaucracy over German life. For this danger, too, Treitschke found an *English* answer in the work of Gneist.[4]

What mattered to Treitschke was the compulsory involvement of the citizen in affairs of state which Gneist described. The results were healthy not only for local political life, but as preparatory training for parliamentary life and the inculcation of a feeling of belonging to the state. The mechanical bureaucratic state created by Frederick the Great had proved inadequate in defending Germany in 1806, and Treitschke did not want to see the future German national state suffer from the same weakness. The English example here offered another solution. Treitschke left no doubt that he was advocating the intro-

[1] Treitschke, 'Die Freiheit', *Preussische Jahrbücher*, VII (1861), p. 382.

[2] *Ibid.*, p. 381.

[3] *Ibid.*, p. 386f.

[4] Treitschke reviewed both Gneist's major volumes, *Geschichte der...Aemter* and *Die heutige englische Communalverfassung* in his articles, 'Die Grundlagen der englischen Freiheit', *Preussische Jahrbücher*, I (1858), 366–88 and 'Das Selfgovernment', *Preussische Jahrbücher*, VI (1860), 25–53, respectively.

duction of a similar system in Germany. To be sure, he raised a few criticisms of Gneist, and he emphatically did not wish to see the mere introduction of *superficial* copies of specific English institutions. To copy the forms without the essence of English institutions seemed worse than useless. It was this essence of which Treitschke spoke when he claimed that 'a lasting improvement of the German state will not be reached until the political ideas of [Gneist's] book become the prejudices of all'.[1] Even though the younger generation of moderate German liberals, increasingly impressed after 1848 with the need to build on the historical traditions of the past, were becoming skeptical about the possibility of importing foreign institutions, 'in practice they could not escape from the English example'.[2]

Treitschke closed a five-year burst of articles on England still stressing the peculiar qualities of English national character. He upheld the controversial Lord Byron not only for his good poetry, but for the warm love of personal liberty and patriotism which, according to Treitschke, motivated it. At the same time, he sharply criticized the 'Tory mediocrities' who had governed England at the time. Despite his many harsh words about the English Tories, however, Treitschke in 1863 still believed that the post-1815 regime represented only a short aberration in England's long and glorious history. He regarded the British reform movement of the 1830s as healthy, since it restored the essential spring of British politics, the two-party system. 'In those very years of paralysis, the indestructible vital energy of the English people was quietly producing the healthy germs of a new political development', wrote Treitschke. With the revival of the two-party system, the way stood open for parliamentary reform, Catholic emancipation, and free trade, all movements more consonant with English greatness than the regime of the 'mediocrities' following the great Pitt.[3] This sketch of recent British history roughly coincided with that of other national liberal writers such as Pauli.

Why did Treitschke's youthful literary tributes to England drop off after 1863? His energy was being increasingly absorbed by historical and journalistic work concerning the lively German political situation; furthermore, he began research for a work which, when it finally

[1] Treitschke, letter to J. Klee, Leipzig, 27 January 1860, *Briefe*, II, 72.

[2] Elisabeth Schurig, *Die Entwicklung der politischen Anschauungen Heinrich von Treitschkes* (Dresden, 1909), p. 63.

[3] Treitschke, 'Lord Byron', *Historische und politische Aufsätze*, I (Leipzig, 1864), 325.

appeared sixteen years later, proved to be his masterpiece – the *German History in the Nineteenth Century*. As the action and hope of the sixties replaced the immobility and despair of the fifties, the study of England sank somewhat in importance. English institutions and history had kept alive the hopes of many German liberals in the dark post-1848 days. Now, in the heat of battle, Treitschke and most nationalists and liberals turned their attention inwards. For Treitschke this did not mean a revolution of opinion so much as a decline of relevance. The English, he said in 1863, seemed to be 'an infinitely great people the better one gets to know it'. Nevertheless, he continued on a new note, 'I would not trade our German misfortune for English glory. I see more and more clearly: if there will ever be a truly free state, one of inwardly free men, it can be none other than a German one.'[1]

Throughout his twenties, in effect, Treitschke was strongly attracted to the standard image of England propagated by Dahlmann, Gneist, and the young national liberals. His personal interest in literature had acquainted him with most of the great English authors from Shakespeare to Byron and Scott. Treitschke also spoke of the common 'Germanic' elements in British and German history and touched on the old theme that German political history had merely made a wrong turn from the road of English law. He laid less stress on 'blood' and religion, however, than the preceding generation. While admiring the triumph of Parliament in England since the seventeenth century, Treitschke, perhaps more than other liberals, emphasized the continuity of English history – especially in the tradition of a strong, relatively liberal state, and a national character bold and persistent enough to keep it so. As an opponent of disengaged 'historicism', Treitschke sought unchanging types and firm certainties (such as 'national character') in the past. Like other post-Gneistian liberals, Treitschke dwelt more upon the infrastructure (local self-government and the social base of the state) than upon the workings of parliament, crown, foreign policy, or empire building. At this period, the local roots of England's freedom and energy interested the young author far more than any number of her fleets and colonies. Firm civil and political liberties, the supremacy of law, the full development of individual personality, the selfless responsibility of the ruling classes, moderation even in revolution – all these were traits which Treitschke ascribed to England. That

[1] Treitschke, letter to W. Nokk, Leipzig, 15 February 1863, *Briefe*, II, 254.

he also mentioned the 'Jewish hardness' of the Puritan ethic, as well as scattered arrogance, hypocrisy, dogmatism, and the preponderance of pragmatism over ethical *Bildung* shows Treitschke was not a blind admirer of Britain. But his pains to explain away much that he found irritating shows he *was* an admirer.

Treitschke's virtual silence on England during the last half of the 1860s allows no sound theories about changes in his early view of England. He did, however, change his view of political strategy and ethics. Initially an opponent of Bismarck's unconstitutional regime in Prussia, Treitschke rebuked the indulgent attitude of Duncker and the *Preussische Jahrbücher* toward the minister-president. Yet even as a critic of the Prussian government in the constitutional struggle, Treitschke kept his faith in Prussia's mission as the welder of German unity. Prussian annexation of Schleswig-Holstein in 1864, the hated 'Welf' state of Hanover in 1866, and Alsace-Lorraine in 1871 found Treitschke's passionate approval.

At the same time, he wrote little about England. What he did write in his letters and articles indicated mild dissatisfaction with the stance of the English government towards the German unity movement. Many Germans had expected Britain to lend active support to German unity and were surprised when, instead, England tried to uphold the London Protocol of 1852 in Schleswig-Holstein and remained neutral in 1866. Nevertheless, he apparently did not blame England for its behavior and expressed his continued admiration. He hoped for a quick end to diplomatic estrangement: as he wrote to an old English friend from his Leipzig days, 'mutual recriminations are not the tone in which two great, civilized peoples should communicate with each other'.[1]

Treitschke's disappointment at contemporary English foreign policy then yielded to concern over internal change. In the years of the founding of the North German Confederation and the German Empire, Treitschke was doing some hard thinking about the best state form for the new nation, or rather about the tolerable alternatives within the centralized state which Treitschke had always favored. In the wake of the Second Reform Bill of 1867, which even Derby called a 'leap in the dark', Treitschke concluded the English state was undergoing a crisis. English self-government, which Treitschke still hoped to see elaborated

[1] Treitschke, letter to Joseph A. Crowe (British consul in Leipzig), Freiburg, 23 November 1864, *Briefe*, II, 360.

in Germany, seemed to be yielding to bureaucratization. The two-party system, under the impact of an increased suffrage, seemed to be undergoing considerable strain. Aristocratic rule, which Treitschke's aesthetic elitism had always favored, appeared to be declining in the face of the mass vote. Treitschke, like other national liberals, regretted all these departures from what he considered the traditional good English state. England's internal difficulties, he assumed, explained her unenergetic foreign policy. Despite his worries about the fate of his idealized model state, however, Treitschke nevertheless believed in the seemingly *built-in* capacity of the English constitution for adjusting to new stresses. He wrote:

> Since the Reform Bill the leadership of party government has become incomparably more difficult, as all English politicians admit...Abroad, the esteem of the realm has sunk because of a foreign policy shy of deeds, and all friends of freedom miss England's voice in the council of peoples. But it does not follow that the pessimists are right to predict England's inevitable decline. One should not give up hope that the much-proven wisdom of this aristocracy, having withstood so many storms in the past, will find ways and means of making peace with the new powers of the middle class and the workers.[1]

In other writings of the same period, Treitschke generally elaborated earlier, favorable opinions of English politics and history.[2]

Yet the unification of Germany under the Prussian monarchy posed new problems for Treitschke which eventually had to influence his view of England. Germany had been unified less by the liberals than by Bismarck's national revolution from above. The weak position of the *Reichstag* and the lordly one of Emperor and Chancellor fell far short of liberal demands and, of course, the English model. Treitschke disapproved of the loose, federal structure of the Empire, but he had to choose between supporting the new national state with all its defects or joining the opposition. To insist on a parliamentary, centralized state analogous to England seemed unwise, for Treitschke was very pessimistic about the ability of the *Reich* to withstand even criticisms designed to strengthen it. The *Reich* was imperfect, but at least it existed.

[1] Heinrich von Treitschke, 'Das constitutionelle Königtum in Deutschland' (1869–71), *Historische und politische Aufsätze*, III, 500.

[2] See, for example, Treitschke's essays, 'F. C. Dahlmann' (1864), *ibid.*, I, 348–434, and 'Frankreichs Staatsleben und der Bonapartismus' (1865), *ibid.*, III, esp. pp. 100 and 395.

Having given his allegiance to the Prussian-German *Machtstaat* (power state) and to Bismarck, Treitschke defended them with the boisterousness of the inwardly insecure. Since the liberal advocates of the *Rechtsstaat* continued to invoke the standards of an idealized English constitution, Treitschke became more critical of their ideal. While the first *Reichstag* debated on the future form of the German nation-state in 1867, Treitschke expressed first doubts about the usefulness of English-style parliamentary government. Referring to a recent book on nineteenth-century England, Treitschke remarked, 'It is instructive to see how little the old parliamentary machinery was able to satisfy the demands of modern administration; that leads me to broader thoughts...'[1] What kind of thoughts he meant became apparent by 1869, when the man who had set such great store by parliamentary government attacked attempts to tie the hands of the new German executive with parliamentary strings. Tossing aside Montesquieu and Gneist, Treitschke eagerly embraced Bagehot: *one* power of government must predominate over all others, he argued. In England, the 'aristocracy', after long training in self-government, had become responsible enough to rule the state (through Parliament) in a benign way. In Germany, by contrast, no social class could be entrusted with such power without the danger of its ruling in its own interests. Thus, Treitschke, advancing the classical Prussian myth of monarchy and taking up the doctrines of Stahl, argued for a preponderant monarchy strong enough to balance and stand above class interests. 'To set up an English monarchy, which can neither harm nor create anything as a model for us Germans, when we already have a robust crown – one not desecrated by Stuart sins or Welf [Hanoverian] follies – that is like encouraging a healthy man to cut off his leg so he can clump around, showing off his splendidly carved peg leg.'[2] Prussia's military success against two of the three continental great powers had shown Treitschke that a state which fell short of liberal ideals could still generate the power needed to make the German nation-state viable.

As a supporter of a militarily strong Germany, Treitschke found he had to repudiate England on another quarter, as well – the economic.

[1] Treitschke, letter to W. Wehrenpfennig, Kiel, 26 June 1867, *Briefe*, III, 158. The book was Reinhold Pauli's *Geschichte Englands seit den Friedensschlüssen.*

[2] Treitschke, 'Das constitutionelle Königtum', p. 459. This article represents the summation of Treitschke's political and constitutional thought at the end of the 1860s.

He added to his earlier suspicions of 'Manchester economics' a complaint about the pacifism espoused by Cobden and Bright. 'It is an unhealthy situation,' he wrote, 'when we talk ourselves into an economist's love of peace, which contradicts German idealism and might brake the forward movement of our [national] revolution.'[1] Treitschke declared this sort of unmanly merchant pacifism, bred by a commercial ethic, to be responsible for the decline of great powers like the Netherlands.[2]

In random references to England in the late 1860s, Treitschke shifted emphasis from the seventeenth to the nineteenth century, from the liberty of the English constitution to its contemporary troubles, from its sturdy political ethics to its materialistic opportunism. One could argue that the nineteenth-century Prussian sources Treitschke was now using for his *German History* and greater maturity account for the shift. Certainly these factors played some role in Treitschke's quiet jettisoning of old parts of his descriptive vocabulary. But his first really searing condemnation of England, one in which all his repressed suspicions broke through, speaks volumes about his first motivation: it appeared in an article written during the Franco-German war of 1870.[3]

Treitschke, furious with the Gladstone government for its neutrality in the war, took English behavior as evidence that cowardice, hypocrisy, and the worship of mammon had finally conquered all sense of English honor.

> We had hoped...that the birthplace of parliamentary life would save itself from the fate of all commercial peoples [*Handelsvölker*]. We thought that the great memories of a glorious history, the wisdom of a politically experienced nobility, the sense of justice of a free people would dam the flood of Manchester theory, which washes away the moral values of life. This hope seems deceptive, for the island realm seems already to have glided down that downhill path which Carthage and Holland trod.[4]

Going beyond criticism of Gladstone alone (whom many Germans, including Bismarck, dismissed as a hypocritical, pious *poseur*),

[1] Treitschke, letter to G. Freytag, Heidelberg, 9 January 1870, *Briefe*, III, 259.
[2] Heinrich von Treitschke, 'Die Republik der Vereinigten Nederlanden', *Preussische Jahrbücher*, XXIV (1869), 43–101, 191–255.
[3] Heinrich von Treitschke, 'Die Feuerprobe des Norddeutschen Bundes', *Preussische Jahrbücher*, XXVI (1870), 240–53.
[4] *Ibid.*, p. 249.

Treitschke made historical generalizations about the long-range tendency of British policy. He was trying to 'unmask' England: if she could cover with rhetoric the weakness and greed she showed in the crises surrounding the Franco-Prussian war, then she could have, indeed must have, acted similarly in the past. Treitschke's hope that England would base her policy on support of Germany's liberal and national movements had proven illusory, and his harsh words reflected bitterness. As usual, however, Treitschke turned a political decision into a moral failing and generalized it for all time. England's political ethic no longer held any convincing appeal once it failed to work for the German national cause.

England played a small role in Treitschke's thought and writing immediately after 1870. After moving to Berlin in 1874, he found life, work, and politics more integrated and demanding than ever. Despite his now total deafness and other personal misfortunes, he hurried with characteristic energy from the lecture hall to the *Reichstag* (where he held a seat from 1871 to 1884) to the offices of the *Preussische Jahrbücher*, which he edited. Now that the *Reich* existed, Treitschke reconciled himself to its deficiencies and defended it with a will. The field he chose more and more often from the mid-1870s was that of foreign relations. Whether to turn attention from internal dissensions to foreign threats or because Germany could really not afford to be complacent about its precarious international position, Treitschke directed attention outward.

From the mid-1870s onward, Treitschke mounted a campaign to discredit historic English foreign policy, especially toward the German state. The two-sided argument held that England had used the Germanies as continental foils and that the motive had always been simple greed. His research in the Prussian archives (which he used exclusively)[1] resulted in several articles and the *Deutsche Geschichte*. For the rosy myth of Anglo-German *Waffenbrüderschaft*, forged in battles against France in the eighteenth and nineteenth centuries, Treitschke substituted the idea that Britain's 'sly and violent policy of commercial self-interest passed for a heroic fight for the ultimate good of humanity'.[2]

[1] Treitschke's reaction to the British policy of keeping their state documents closed was characteristic: instead of suspending judgment before seeing them, he eventually charged the British government with hiding the truth lest it shatter the Anglophile position throughout Europe. See his *Deutsche Geschichte im neunzehnten Jahrhundert*, 5 vols. (Leipzig, 1879–94), v, 30f.

[2] Heinrich von Treitschke, 'Preussen auf dem Wiener Kongress', *Preussische Jahrbücher*, XXXVI (1875), p. 674. Other instalments in this long article appeared in *Preussische Jahr-*

Prussia, in this account, had always been the true bearer of Germany's (and humanity's) interests. 'With the progress of my historical studies,' he wrote to a friend, 'I gain more clarity about England and its perpetually inimical policies toward Germany.'[1] The political uses to which such historical arguments could be put came close behind the discovery of the arguments themselves. The long international crisis which began in 1875[2] prompted Treitschke to demonstrate historically that England could not be trusted. 'We have had very unpleasant experiences with England's friendship since the Seven Years' War', he cautioned; 'Russian policy would have to commit unheard-of stupidities to make Germany consider dropping the hand of its tested friend in order to fall into the embrace of a disloyal ally dominated by outmoded ideas.'[3] Treitschke put forward the somewhat strange argument that Germany and Russia now represented young nations based on a new model. Britain and Turkey, on the other hand, represented atavisms resisting the inevitable triumph of the nation-state in Europe. To document this, Treitschke presented a complete distortion of England's role in recent European history:

> She was enthusiastic about the wickedness of North American slave traders; she was the screaming, though—thank God!—cowardly counsel behind Denmark's domination of Schleswig-Holstein; she venerated the *Bundestag* and the Welf kingdom [Hanover]; she permitted the French attack on united Germany, when she could have prevented it, and lengthened the war by selling France arms.[4]

bücher, XXXVII (1876), 133–65 and 281–326. 'Commercial self-interest', which I have used to convey the sinister contextual meaning of one of Treitschke's favorite pejoratives, is a translation of *Handelspolitik*.

1 Cited by Max Cornicelius, 'England in Treitschkes Darstellung und Urteil', *Internationale Monatsschrift*, X (1915), p. 87, from an unpublished letter to T. Nöldecke, July 1876.

2 The diplomatic crisis began in April with the appearance of newspaper articles, probably inspired by Bismarck, which raised the possibility of a new Franco-German war. The first of these articles was placed secretly in the *Kölnische Zeitung* by Ludwig Karl Aegidi, who was Bismarck's press secretary and one of Treitschke's oldest friends. See Erich Eyck, *Bismarck and the German Empire*, paperback edition (New York, 1964), and Dorpalen, *Heinrich von Treitschke*, p. 204. The crisis returned in the form of the Eastern Question later in the year and persisted until the Berlin Congress in 1878. Treitschke's article appeared just weeks after Bismarck had unsuccessfully sounded the British government on working together.

3 Heinrich von Treitschke, 'Die Türkei und die Grossmächte', *Preussische Jahrbücher*, XXXVII (1876), p. 712. The 'outmoded ideas' referred principally to Britain's policy of keeping the Ottoman Empire intact.

4 *Ibid.*, p. 674f. Since Treitschke actually knew how the French 'attack' on Germany had come about, one cannot excuse these charges on the grounds of ignorance. See Dorpalen, *Heinrich von Treitschke*, p. 163.

Sensing that such bitterness contrasted sharply with his earlier Anglophilia, Treitschke attempted to explain his conversion in terms of an awakening from naïveté. 'What German liberal did not dream in earlier days of a national alliance between free England and free Germany!' he wrote. 'It took a long series of disappointments before we finally learned that the foreign policy of a state is not solely or predominantly determined by its internal constitutional situation.'[1] How ironic that he now accepted the opinion of Lothar Bucher, whose gloomy and bitter articles from London had seemed so dangerous and malicious to Treitschke twenty years earlier.

Treitschke also had calculated motives for discrediting the alliance value of Britain. As he wrote prophetically to a friend during the Eastern Crisis of 1876, 'As soon as we break with Russia, a Franco-Russian alliance will arise, and we would have the honorable job of beginning a struggle allied with the two cadavers Austria and Turkey; it would cost the life, not of ourselves, but quite certainly that of the imperial-royal [Austrian] majesty. For a politician, I believe, that is enough said.'[2] Such an alliance system, Treitschke thought, could also force Germany to 'pull England's chestnuts out of the fire' without giving her any meaningful aid in return. His own research, his insight that an English alliance would tend to tie Germany's hands without giving her much in return, and his fear of liberalization of the *Reich* constitution as a price for Anglo-German cooperation all led him to agitate against such a permanent connection. On the other hand, Treitschke sometimes went beyond merely urging Germany to avoid alliance and darkly hinted at actual hostilities with England. The first time, in 1876, Treitschke seemed untroubled by the prospect of war: England, he believed, was 'weaponless' and in decline.[3] But even then, Treitschke regarded France as the instigator of any future war; England would be only a secondary power drawn in by French wiles.

The political uses of Treitschke's historical myth of permanent English enmity found new uses in the 1880s. Britain indeed (and understandably) gave less than full support to Treitschke's favorite causes, a modest German colonial empire and a modest fleet to protect it. Instead of honest irritation and mistrust of the English attitude,

[1] *Ibid.*, p. 673.

[2] Treitschke, letter to Alfred Gutschmidt, Berlin, 5 August 1876, *Nachlass* Treitschke, Schrank 1, Kasten 2, 40.

[3] Treitschke, 'Die Türkei und die Grossmächte', p. 712.

however, Treitschke showed a malicious desire to re-evaluate his earlier, more favorable opinion of Britain's role in the world. In the 1860s Treitschke had spoken approvingly of England's 'cultural mission' in the colonies;[1] in the eighties he mocked his own words. 'In the halls of Parliament,' he wrote, 'one heard only shameless British commercial morality, which, with the Bible in the right hand and the opium pipe in the left, spreads the benefits of civilization around the world.'[2] 'We have already settled accounts with Austria, France, and Russia,' he warned, 'and the last reckoning with England will probably be the longest and hardest; for here we encounter a policy which for a century had steered unresisted for the goal of maritime world domination.'[3]

Treitschke probably knew, as Bismarck certainly did, that colonies and navies for Germany were chiefly useful for their domestic nationalist propaganda value, especially as rallying points for parts of the bourgeoisie. The navy and the colonies were distinctively bourgeois in tone.[4] In his younger days, Treitschke had not demonstrated the same degree of enthusiasm for fleets and colonies as other national-liberal admirers of England (for instance Dahlmann and Pauli). He discovered the usefulness of these institutions at about the same time he discovered England's perfidy in her commercial and diplomatic relations with the continent, that is, only after 1870. A fleet and a colonial empire, no matter how small, would be national institutions, not just Prussian undertakings; and Treitschke favored any move toward greater centralization of the *Reich*. In order to justify them, however, Treitschke found the manufacture of British bogeymen more effective than French ones. Furthermore, their existence would tend to drive a wedge between any future Anglo-German alliance and thereby encourage the continued tie to 'Germany's trusted friend', Imperial Russia. Finally, whatever Treitschke's personal motives in unmasking England's foreign policy, many of his writings on the subject in the *Preussische Jahrbücher* smacked unmistakably of tendentious support of the latest

[1] See his remarks on the English in India, dating from 1866, in his *Zehn Jahre Deutscher Kämpfe* (Berlin, 1874), p. 170.

[2] Treitschke, *Deutsche Geschichte*, IV, 381.

[3] Heinrich von Treitschke, 'Die ersten Versuche deutscher Kolonialpolitik', *Preussische Jahrbücher*, LIV (1885), p. 564f. Treitschke was thus supporting Bismarck's colonial marriage with France and contributing to the hue and cry of danger from abroad which Bismarck was making to win the 1884 *Reichstag* election. See A. J. P. Taylor, *The Struggle for Mastery in Europe, 1848–1918* (Oxford, 1954), p. 293.

[4] See Jonathan Steinberg, *Yesterday's Deterrent* (New York, 1965) p. 59.

twist in Bismarck's foreign policy. Treitschke's inexhaustible warnings against England in the 1880s and 1890s revealed only one change in his attitude of 1870: Britain had recovered from its impotence to become a major threat. The British hypocrisy he attacked late in his life was the cunning of the strong, not the lies of the weak.

Treitschke never went so far in 'unmasking' English domestic politics, and his usual method of dealing with the subject was passing over or limiting what he had said in his youth. Nevertheless, because the *Reichsfeinde* and reformers continued to use the English example to press for political change in contemporary Germany, Treitschke did have to contradict himself at times. As he drifted totally into the camp of Bismarck in the 1870s, he broke his ties with the National Liberal Party in the *Reichstag* and generally voted with the Free Conservatives, whom he once called 'the Bismarck party *à l'outrance*'. His unqualified support for such measures as tariff protectionism and military preparedness brought him into conflict with opponents employing 'English' examples. Free traders, for example, still drew heavily on English laissez-faire doctrine and on the success which it had allegedly brought to the English economy. Left-wing critics of big German armies pointed to England's ability to get along without a massive military establishment. With these questions of the 1870s and 1880s in mind, one can better understand why Treitschke went out of his way to pass harsh judgments in the later volumes of his *German History*. Free-trade doctrine, one reads there, was merely an economic Trojan horse with which England hoped to invade and exploit the continental market; liberalism, merely a poisonous export intended to divide and paralyze continental powers in the face of ruthless British imperialism. With increasing vigor in the1880s, Treitschke carried on through the *Preussische Jahrbücher* a campaign to discredit parliamentary government and its chief representative, Great Britain. Given the vague hopes of many Germans that the accession of Friedrich III and his English wife would herald liberalization of Germany's political constitution, the campaign had the understandable motive of preventive action. Articles by Treitschke and his co-editor, Hans Delbrück, repeatedly depicted parliamentary doctrine as *passé*: it had done its job but had now become dangerous to the German state.[1]

[1] See Hans Schleier, 'Treitschke, Delbrück und die "*PJ*" in den 80er Jahren des 19. Jahrhunderts', *Jahrbuch für Geschichte*, 1 (1967), 147ff.

In a typical perverse distortion of the history of 'constitutional' government in Prussia in the 1850s – a notably reactionary period – Treitschke wrote in 1886:

Prussia in those days was ruled for the first time (and hopefully for the last) strictly by the principles of parliamentarism, even though its constitution was not yet really fixed; the ministers were supported by a devoted majority in both chambers, filled all important offices exclusively with their political friends and showed the world what happens to a monarchical bureaucratic state when it falls under the curse of constitutional party rule.[1]

With such sophistic arguments Treitschke sought to place parliamentary government in the most unfavorable light compared to the Prussian way, with its monarchy, bureaucracy, and army, supposedly standing 'above politics', serving the welfare of all. In his later lectures and books, words of approval[2] only rarely bobbed to the surface from the broad stream of invidious comparisons between England and the *Reich*. Treitschke did not absolutely declare that England had ceased to be a free state, but he now listed numerous qualifications; freedom was the exclusive preserve of the aristocracy, it had arisen by political accident rather than through some innate talent of the British, it usually ran on a shocking amount of corruption, and its best elements – for example, self-government and two-party rule – had declined drastically since 1832. The old Treitschke damned parliamentary reform just as the young Treitschke had damned the Tories.[3] With the British allowing themselves to be tyrannized by 'public opinion',[4] Germany was now the 'freer' of the two states.

One would be unfair to Treitschke if one left the impression that all of his later ideas on England were distorted. He was often able to see the realities of British politics, for example, more clearly than other experts who were still describing the English constitution in the glowing

[1] Treitschke, 'Max Duncker,' *Preussische Jahrbücher*, LVIII (1886), p. 497. Also see Treitschke's (unprinted) article, 'Parlamentarische Erfahrungen der letzten Jahre' (1886), *Nachlass* Treitschke, Fach II, Oben, as well as Hans Delbrück, 'Die englische Wahlreform', *Preussische Jahrbücher*, LVI (1884), p. 287, and 'Notizen', *Preussische Jahrbücher*, LV (1885), p. 105, attacking Gneist, as well as Conrad Varrentrapp, 'Zur Erinnerung an Friedrich Christoph Dahlmann', *Preussische Jahrbücher*, LV (1885), pp. 500–3.

[2] See Heinrich von Treitschke, *Die Politik*, ed. by Max Cornicelius, 5th edn., 2 vols. (Leipzig, 1922), I, 152, on England and ancient Rome. The original edition came out only after Treitschke's death; since the lectures were composed and altered over the years, they contain some inconsistencies in approach to England.

[3] Treitschke, *Deutsche Geschichte*, IV (1889), 24.

[4] Treitschke, *Die Politik*, I, 173, 184.

if unrealistic terms of Montesquieu or Blackstone.[1] Yet the force driving Treitschke to question the system was his desire to denigrate the exemplary value of the English constitution. Insofar as he had any good words to say about England in *Politics*, a book based on his popular Berlin lecture series, they touched on 'old England', the irrevocably lost world of the pre-reform era.

For the 'new England', with a creepingly democratic franchise added to its system of governmental responsibility to Parliament, now became an example even for radical political reformers. First in the hands of such 'socialists of the chair' as Lujo Brentano in the 1870s, then later among the leading theoreticians of German Social Democracy such as Kautsky and Bernstein,[2] England became an object of study and admiration with far-reaching implications for German politics and social reform. This phenomenon was more characteristic of the moderate left, which openly advocated cooperation and reconciliation of the growing industrial proletariat and the 'progressive' bourgeois elements, than of those still faithful to the idea of class warfare. From the viewpoint of Treitschke, who took a prominent part in the literary campaign against socialism, socialist revolution and moderate advocacy of a British-style parliamentary democracy were equally repellent.

A further indication that Treitschke's fear of the domestic political consequences of German Anglophilia, rather than any cool and objective sobering-up from youthful overenthusiasm motivated his about face lies in his choice of language. The emotion-charged slogans which one finds in his youthful writings on England – political and civil liberty, a hard-working, responsible aristocracy, the 'magnificent one-sidedness' and self-confidence of British character – and his youthful heroes – Cromwell, Milton, William III, Pitt, Byron – vanished. But more significantly, their place was taken by words such as ignorance, arrogance, inhumanity, hypocrisy, and crass, selfish materialism ex-

[1] Lamer, *Der englische Parlamentarismus*, 'Schlussbetrachtung'.

[2] Kautsky commented in 1893 that recent developments in the English constitution offered great hope for the socialist cause. 'Already the proletariat is in a position to influence internal politics in its favor—in Parliament and through the agency of Parliament. With giant steps the day nears on which the all-powerful English Parliament will be a tool of the dictatorship of the proletariat'. Karl Kautsky, *Der Parlamentarismus, die Volksgesetzgebung und die Sozialdemokratie* (Stuttgart, 1893), p. 104. Eduard Bernstein, who like Kautsky had spent considerable time in England, went so far as to propose parliamentary power as *the* line of socialist tactics in preference to revolution in his *Die Voraussetzungen des Sozialismus und die Aufgaben der Sozialdemokratie* (Stuttgart, 1899).

pressed in the petty vocabulary of commerce and backed by naked force. A rogue's gallery composed of Castlereagh, Canning, Palmerston, Gladstone, and the entire House of Hanover replaced the earlier hall of fame. The term 'Germanic', which he had previously used to underscore the common origins and cultural heritage of the two peoples vanished from Treitschke's vocabulary; later he distinguished between competing 'Anglo-Saxon' and 'Teutonic' cultures.[1] Thus Treitschke, in correcting a sentimental and unsound credulity about Anglo-German affinity, went to the other extreme and propagated a myth of perpetual rivalry.

The once constant motive discernible in all of Treitschke's thought, including that on England, was his nationalism. It explains both his youthful liberalism and his mature conservatism. His thoughts on government, economy, international relations, and even ethics had to be arranged to harmonize with his overriding desire for the *kleindeutsch* nation-state. When the mechanisms of English central and local government, free trade, the 'natural alliance' of freedom-loving peoples led by England, and English civic responsibility ('public virtue' rather than 'private virtue') promised to propel Germany along the road toward unity, Treitschke advocated studying, respecting, and adapting them. When a German nation-state did arise, however, it depended on maximum bureaucratic and royal power, with minimum popular participation on any level, on protection for agrarians and industrialists, on ruthlessly keeping the other powers slightly more at odds with each other than with Germany (while Germany kept a free hand), and on increasing regimentation in public life. Then Treitschke argued for rejecting England's example. He fell silent about ancient English ties, through 'blood' and religion, and stressed instead national and cultural differences and an imaginary English apostasy to materialism.

In some respects there is a certain inevitability in Treitschke's choices. Once one accepts the nationalist motivation of most of his opinions, one can see quite valid reasons for both his Anglophilia and his rejection of it. In the 1850s Treitschke favored constitutional monarchy and 'self-government' in local communities because they both promised to give an interest in society to passive citizens. Prussia was supposed to liberalize itself politically so as to make 'moral

[1] Dahlmann, among others, had used the terms 'Anglo-Saxon' and 'Germanic' interchangeably.

conquests' among the non-Prussian educated and propertied classes who sought a greater public role. A parliament would presumably aid a united Germany as it had the South German states after 1815 – to integrate newly-won territories into one realm. Self-government would prepare the higher citizenry for its political duties as electors and parliamentarians. Treitschke, like many other German liberals, had little use for democracy, so the aristocratic character of English constitutional institutions pleased him. Finally, it had not yet become apparent that the British cabinet after the 1832 reforms had indeed definitely turned the monarchy into the figurehead which Bagehot later called it. When German liberal nationalists like Treitschke embraced the English constitution, they did not realize that one of the parts they insisted on, an effective royal prerogative, had virtually been removed.

Free-trade doctrine also served its purpose as a nationally integrative force, as historians of the *Zollverein* have pointed out. But once a national market had been created by invoking free trade, and once German agrarians discovered that cheap American wheat was destroying their home and export markets, nationalists went along with protectionism. Nor, it should be recalled, had Treitschke ever proclaimed free trade an eternal doctrine: national interest, not Manchester gospel, appeared to be the governing consideration. It was also politically useful to tell consumers who suffered from protection – and especially the rising working class – that English free trade doctrine was a mere mask to open markets to the greedy exporters of London. The nation needed an army to defend it, and no Prussian army could function without the *Junker* and the peasants whose livelihood would be ruined by Manchester doctrine.

Treitschke's nationalist motives in reversing himself on England's worth as an ally are also tangled with partly valid reasons. Britain was the only great power which offered to support constitutionalism, at least in theory, during Treitschke's young manhood. The rhetoric must not have been completely convincing in the light of Palmerston's aloofness to German unity during 1848–9, but it was less depressing than the overt and active hostility of the other great powers. The German nationalist movement needed England more than England needed it, if only for psychological support. There was, on the other hand, more than a grain of truth in Treitschke's later allegations that an Anglo-German alliance would simply involve Berlin in faraway English troubles. Unfortunately Treitschke's rhetoric carried him away: to fight the old liberal notion of a 'natural alliance' he manufactured a 'natural enmity'.

This rhetoric appealed to the Pan-German propagandists who quoted salient passages from Treitschke in order to lend the respectability of the Historiographer of Prussia to their expansionist propaganda.[1] Treitschke, who thought much as Bismarck did on the limitations and possibilities of Germany's foreign policy, could never have approved the one-sided emphasis of the Pan-Germans on unilateral naval and colonial competition with England. But it is equally true that Pan-German distortions of English history carried on Treitschke's method (whether one speaks of his earlier or later writings) of tailoring historical truth to suit the needs of an imagined national good. Treitschke had made his new myths about England in response to the living needs of the German nation, as he conceived of them; but the myths outlived their original function as well as their creator. Treitschke used extreme means to free himself and many of his countrymen from exaggerated and twisted notions about a country they had long accepted as a model. That process in itself may have been salutary and was probably inevitable. It is quite possible that a heightened degree of xenophobia helped the new *Reich* overcome some of its internal tensions and international insecurity in the first decades of its existence. Yet in the skilled hands of propagandists who had quite different national aims, Treitschke's words about England became weapons that created a deep suspicion on both sides of the North Sea.

[1]For a sample see Ernst Graf zu Reventlow, *Der Vampir des Festlandes* (Berlin, 1915). The National Socialists also listed Treitschke's *German History* as one of the 100 most important works for their party bookstores.

CHAPTER 10

IMPERIALISM AND ANGLO-GERMAN ESTRANGEMENT

Despite the public adulation of a generation of students which thronged to hear Treitschke lecture at Berlin, despite the echo of his biting and hostile words about England in the public press and private conversation,[1] despite the 'conversion' of a few scholarly Anglophiles to Treitschke's viewpoint,[2] Treitschke evidently failed to carry the majority of the historians' guild with him into the rabid Anglophobe camp during his lifetime.

On the other hand, it is an index of the loosening grip of Anglophile myths that very few of Treitschke's contemporaries actually took up a defense of English history. Oddly, there were very few men of about Treitschke's age who paid attention to English affairs. Men older than he (such as Gneist and Ranke) lived on into the last decades of the century but did not respond to Treitschke. Judging by a few inconclusive remarks in their private correspondence, one is tempted to describe their attitude toward England after German unification as one of slight bewilderment. The group of active students of England which came

[1] 'Newspaper wars', a fairly common phenomenon in the Germany of Wilhelm II, were declared on Britain from time to time. One of the most serious outbreaks concerned the Kaiser's Krüger telegram and the British campaign against the Boers. As Pauline Anderson has pointed out in *The Background of Anti-English Feeling*, much of this sentiment grew out of the economic interest groups (like the *Bund der Landwirte*) which became prominent features of German political life at this time. Judging by the better novels of the period, such as Theodor Fontane's *Der Stechlin* and Heinrich Mann's *Der Untertan* (the latter completed before World War I, despite its publication date), references to England, ranging from ironic-ambivalent to hostile, were common in Prussian society.

[2] A prominent example of such a conversion is the article by the aged Max Duncker, 'Preussen und England im siebenjährigen Krieg' (1885), in his *Abhandlungen aus der neueren Geschichte* (Leipzig, 1887), 76–109. Treitschke was so impressed by this piece of 'proof' of complete British perfidy againt Prussia that he took the rare step of not only adding his own emphatic marginalia, but of preserving a copy in his private records, now the Treitschke *Nachlass*.

after Treitschke tended to follow a strictly impartial and sometimes even purely antiquarian approach to their subject.

Treitschke alone could not provoke them into departing from the 'neo-Rankean' ideals of impartial scholarship which were held up by more and more historians as preferable to Treitschkean passion.[1] Yet there was another reason for this aloofness: England no longer held the symbolic meaning of yore. Whatever the cause, for a few years, primarily the 1880s and the first half of the 1890s, it appeared that German historical scholarship had largely freed itself from its fascination with England and English history. These years constitute the first phase to be discussed in this chapter. These also happened to be the years when the ideal of raising themselves above and out of politics dominated the German professors,[2] after England had lost most of its usefulness as a constitutional model and before the Anglo-German strains caused by Imperial Germany's search for 'world politics' and a 'future upon the waters' of the globe.

From the moment in June 1897 when Tirpitz took command of the Imperial Naval Office, however, a second phase began in the writing of English history in Germany. Tirpitz, who 'records gratefully his own debt to Treitschke, "that wonderful man...at whose side I sat scratching notes on bits of paper"',[3] had great and well-placed confidence in the authority of the German professorate and managed to put it to good propagandistic use. From then until about 1910, German historians (as well as economists, sociologists, and other social scientists) were drawn back into a political and didactic discussion of England's past (and future). More and more students of England abandoned their previous stance and aligned their viewpoint with Germany's historical rationalization of *Weltpolitik*. A few, to be sure, vocally resisted this trend, and their resistance might be considered a third phase, but they belonged to a distinct and dwindling minority. By the time of the Second Moroccan Crisis (1911) German historians

1 Even those historians who tried to get beyond the politically charged historical writings of the post-unification era could not escape the Prussian school's heritage—worship of the power-state. Even 'neo-Rankeans' like Max Lenz and Erich Marcks were grounded in 'the intellectual basis of precisely that trend of propagandistic political history from which they wished to distance themselves by turning to Ranke's objective historical observation'. Hans Heinz Krill, *Die Rankerenaissance*: *Max Lenz und Erich Marcks* (Berlin, 1962), p. 256.

2 See Klaus Schwabe, 'Zur politischen Haltung der deutschen Professoren', p. 601.

3 Steinberg, *Yesterday's Deterrent*, p. 41f., citing Alfred von Tirpitz, *Erinnerungen* (Leipzig, 1920), p. 96.

had largely laid the groundwork for the gross distortions of both German and English history characteristic of wartime 'scholarly' propaganda.

I DETACHED EXPERTISE

The character of the German view of English history in the two decades before 1897 may be dealt with briefly.[1] On the whole, the three major tendencies of German historiography during the late nineteenth century passed the England experts by. They were little affected by the triumph of the Droysen–Treitschke school, which made history into a celebration of the triumphant Prussian state. Instead, they carried on in the Rankean tradition of Olympian detachment, albeit not with Ranke's skill and power. The second major development of German historiography in the Bismarck era, the 'intensive cultivation' of economic history,[2] extending economic causal explanations even to political and religious phenomena, also had little impact on Germany's professional English scholars of the 1890s. Third, the engagement of history professors in the German drive for world power after 1897 did not so much capture them as confuse them and drive them into hiding.

Such a position was typical of Pauli's contemporary and successor in the great Heeren project on the entire history of England, Moritz Brosch, who clung to life until 1907. What is more surprising is that it was also typical of the younger generation born between 1850 and 1870. If Brosch's inability to clarify the issues in the English past which most puzzled Germans after 1897 is understandable in light of his age, that of Felix Liebermann, born in 1851, is not. While Brosch had been out of touch with current German affairs, living most of his life in Venice, Liebermann, the brother of the famous impressionist painter, led a quite cosmopolitan life in both England and Germany. But Liebermann was first and foremost a passionate archive searcher, and he shunned the teaching profession altogether. His editorial work opened many important sources on medieval English history: but he rarely wrote narrative and never took positions on questions of modern (especially contemporary) English history.

[1] For a full account, see the author's 1967 Yale doctoral dissertation, 'The German Historians and England: A Study of 19th-century Views', available through University Microfilms, Ann Arbor, Michigan.

[2] Fueter, *Historiographie*, p. 601.

The inadequate quality of Brosch's writing[1] and the lack of narration from Liebermann typified the decline in quantity and contemporary relevance of German historical writing about England by the end of the century. To be sure, a younger generation of English history scholars had been trained. Wilhelm Busch[2] (a student of Maurenbrecher), Ludwig Riess (taught by Delbrück), Erich Marcks (influenced by Mommsen and Baumgarten), and Wolfgang Michael lectured and wrote about England. Max Lenz had begun his scholarly career with English studies. But Lenz quickly entered other fields than English history. Riess, one of the most promising students of medieval England, left Germany for Tokyo after attempting to revise the Gneistian view of the English medieval constitution. Busch, after a brilliant beginning as an expert on the Tudor era, turned his attention to patriotic themes in German history. At the very time when these specialists could have entered the public debate in Germany with some reasoned words about English history, they abandoned the field. Furthermore, their specialized, monographic approach could not have satisfied the public's need for comprehensive views. Significantly, even the monographic studies tended to avoid some of the areas which had been most interesting to German constitutionalist professors at mid-century, particularly constitutional development. The nineteenth century was studiously avoided. Michael, Marcks, and (later) Felix Salomon did much-needed work in the eighteenth century, and Marcks, along with Busch and Marcks's student Arnold Oskar Meyer, did useful work in the sixteenth.[3] When they did concern themselves with seventeenth-century material, they focused on the charismatic leader Cromwell, reflecting the preoccupation of post-Bismarckian Germany with political titans rather than parliamentary government.[4]

[1] See the reviews of his *Geschichte von England* in the *Historische Zeitschrift*, LXX (1893), 369–72, and LXXII (1894), 124f.

[2] Willhelm Busch (1861–1929) was a professor of history principally at Tübingen and Marburg. (See Biographical Appendix.)

[3] Wilhelm Busch, *England under the Tudors. King Henry VII*, tr. by A. M. Todd (New York, 1965), from his *England unter den Tudors* (Stuttgart, 1896), the first and, regrettably, last of Busch's projected volumes on the dynasty. Erich Marcks, *Königin Elisabeth von England und ihre Zeit* (Bielefeld and Leipzig, 1897). Arnold Oskar Meyer, *England and the Catholic Church under Queen Elizabeth*, tr. by J. R. McKee (London, 1916), from *England und die katholische Kirche unter Elisabeth und den Stuarts* (Rome, 1911). The projected part on the Stuarts never appeared.

[4] Wolfgang Michael, *Cromwell*, 2 vols. [vols. 50–1 of the *Geisteshelden* series] (Berlin, 1907). Also see Michael's more scholarly article, 'Oliver Cromwell und die Auflösung des langen Parlaments', *Historische Zeitschrift*, LXIII (1889), 56–78. Compare Moritz Brosch, *Oliver*

Another index of the problematics of solid, non-tendentious English studies is the number of major narrative projects begun and then abandoned. Brosch's volumes in the Heeren series constituted the last successfully completed project of its sort. Busch, Meyer, and Salomon began and then broke off promising planned projects; Michael, though he completed his multi-volume project, did so only after a delay of many years and then after World War I. In most cases, the treatment England received at the hands of the experts was not exclusive: for Michael, for example, the Hanoverian succession was a bigger problem than an English domestic matter. For Meyer and Marcks, the 'problem' of the Reformation was as important as the peculiar traits it took on in England.

A final, though not necessarily conclusive index of the isolation of English studies from current academic relevance is the decline of teaching by the men best qualified to explain English history. Brosch did not teach, nor did Liebermann. Riess taught for many years outside Germany, which he left for obscure reasons. He may have had difficulty finding a comfortable position, for other historians of England (or anyone who ran against the current of accepted orthodoxy in teaching and scholarship) had great difficulties making a good career in late Imperial Germany. The fact that at least three well-known historians of England in Imperial Germany were Jews (Liebermann, Riess, and Salomon) undoubtedly played some role in their teaching careers; but the fact that German antisemitism was almost always allied with German Anglophobia just intensifies suspicion that they were systematically kept from the highest positions in the German educational establishment.[1] Whether because historians of England turned to other topics or were blocked in their way up the ladder of the imperial

Cromwell und die puritanische Revolution (Frankfurt/Main, 1886). English historiography, too, produced a revision toward a conservative, practical, nationalistic, and statesmanlike Cromwell in Gardiner's writings. Samuel Gardiner's multi-volume work on seventeenth-century English history includes the *History of the Great Civil War, 1642–1649*, 4 vols. (London, 1893), *History of the Commonwealth and Protectorate, 1649–1656*, 2 vols., 2nd. edn. (London, 1897), and *Oliver Cromwell* (London, 1909).

[1] See Richard S. Levy, 'Anti-Semitic Political Parties in the German Empire', Yale Ph.D. dissertation, 1969. Levy has pointed out some of the more bizarre interpretations of English history among the antisemites: to prove that modern England has been ruled by Jews, they attempted to show that Disraeli (a clear case) had alternated with 'William Glattstein', who had attempted to cover his Jewish origins by Anglicizing his name to 'Gladstone'. See Levy, p. 299. Both Riess and Salomon ended long and productive careers as mere *ausserordentlich* (associate) professors – a remarkably low rank considering their publications and achievements.

professional hierarchy, it can be safely said that no German historian of this generation achieved great heights of fame and institutional recognition on the basis of studies of English history – in contrast to the careers of Pauli and Gneist.

Aside from the quantitative decline in work on England in the two decades before 1897, and despite the general tendency of German scholarship to approach the same conclusions about English figures as the major English historians themselves,[1] one can still find a few variants and peculiarities marking the works of the England specialists as German in origin. Above all, the works of the neutral specialists underlined the decline of interest among Germans in the political heritage of English constitutionalism, the cultural bond of reformed Christianity, and the perception of an irrational tie of 'blood' and 'race'.

A sign of the Germans' decreasing need of constitutional dogmas drawn from English examples may be found in the works of Riess, which argued against Stubbs's theory of the origins of Commons. Riess implied that the popular house had arisen more as a lower echelon of royal administration than as a means of giving the people a say in government: delegates from the people could report misdeeds of sheriffs to the king and then return to explain royal policy to the constituencies.[2] Riess's theory opened a long debate on whether Commons was the child of rebellion or royal authority. Like Gneist (with whom he disagreed on other points), Riess favored the theory of royal authority. German historiography now found fully unsatisfactory the older theory of a freedom-loving people wresting control from the monarchy step by step. The enthusiasm of previous generations of liberal scholars had misled them about the origins of Parliament, and Riess's painstaking study set out to show that responsibility for government had to be in effect forced upon an unwilling populace. The implications of such an argument for contemporary German constitutional life were clear, if

1 A perusal of the English and German historical reviews of the period shows how interdependent the research of German and British scholars on English history had become. Honorary degrees for German scholars abounded, German works were translated in unprecedented quantity, and German scholars began to read English works with respect and concurrence.

2 Ludwig Riess, *Geschichte des Wahlrechts zum englischen Parlament im Mittelalter* (Leipzig, 1885). The version cited here is *The History of the English Electoral Law*, translated by K. L. Wood-Legh (Cambridge, 1940), pp. 3ff. Riess defended his thesis, which he wrote under Delbück, in 'Der Ursprung des englischen Unterhauses', *Historische Zeitschrift*, LX (1888), 1–33.

not necessarily intended by the author: another historical argument in favor of the claims of popular sovereignty and parliamentary rule was called into question. The blessings of strong monarchical rule were also praised by Busch in his treatment of Henry VII.[1]

The same standards of *Realpolitik* which served Busch in assessing Henry VII also aided the German historians of later sixteenth-century England. The emphasis fell most heavily on the development of the monarchical state rather than on parliamentary institutions or the religious Reformation. Arnold Oskar Meyer and Marcks, for example, treated the church reforms of the sixteenth century as political rather than spiritual phenomena and congratulated the Tudors less for breaking with Rome than for raising the state to a point high above the squalls of religious controversy. Marcks implied that the German Reformation had filled the spiritual vacuum of the 'political' English one.[2] Meyer found that the 'real' Reformation had struck deeper and different roots in the English people than in the German. 'If the Reformation means something concerning the revival of religious life of a nation and leaves its stamp for centuries upon the national character, then the reformers of England were the Puritan Ironsides with their sword and Bible. The religious movement associated with their name has made a deeper impression on the souls of the people than the Reformation succeeded in making in any other country, not even excepting the land of Luther. The heritage of the Puritans, even to this day, is among those characteristics which differentiate the English from other nations.'[3] Thus Meyer, despite many flattering statements about the Puritans, joined the tendency of contemporary German historical writing to emphasize what divided German and English religious history (Puritanism) instead of what united it (Protestantism). This distinction later inspired 'the thesis of Troeltsch, which, by overevaluating the Puritan element in English history, set up an antithesis between West European and German thought, called English thought "secularized Calvinism", saw German thought as "secularized Lutheranism", and correspondingly identified English and even Anglo-Saxon thought as steeped

[1] Busch, *England under the Tudors*, pp. 7, 246.

[2] Marcks, *Königin Elisabeth*, p. 9.

[3] Meyer, *England and the Catholic Church*, p. 6. Although Meyer's work appeared long after the 'turning point' of 1897 and was colored by the Anglo-German rivalry, in spirit he belonged to the pre-rivalry Anglophile experts on England. He did not participate in the debates about English foreign policy.

in normative natural law,...German thought as organic and dynamic...'[1]

The general decline of invocations of the Germanic heritage supposedly common to both England and Germany may also be illustrated with references to the writings of Germany's non-committed English scholars. Busch, for example, flatly insisted that the English state had originated more in Norman than Germanic forms,[2] thus jettisoning the older notion (so fundamental to those who believed Germany could successfully adapt English traditions) that English law was simply Germanic law properly developed. When Liebermann, in one of his few narrative works, attempted to uphold the continuity between Germanic (Anglo-Saxon) and post-Norman institutions,[3] other German historians refused to accept his argument.[4] The time had passed in Germany (and in England as well) when stress on the Germanic elements of English culture had taken first place.[5] Since references to the influence of 'race' on history were always fairly nebulous and difficult to document, one cannot take them very seriously as an academic matter. But as an index of how close the German scholarly community felt to England in an era when 'race' was still taken seriously as a form of kinship, the declining acceptability of *das Germanische* as a causal explanation in English history is important. Whereas early nineteenth-century historians had sought an ultimate secular cause of England's greatness that could also apply to Germany, historians at the end of the century sought to make England seem as different and as remote as possible.

No matter how non-normative and detached most German scholarship about England's cultural and constitutional life was from about 1880 to 1897, it still tended to follow the Rankean conception of England's traditional role in international relations. The specialists spent far less time on England's foreign relations than Ranke had, but they agreed with him that England in the modern era had sought chiefly to uphold the European balance. In comparison to Treitschke's

[1] Dockhorn, *Der deutsche Historismus in England*, p. 192.

[2] Busch, *England under the Tudors*, p. 2.

[3] Felix Liebermann, *The National Assembly in the Anglo-Saxon Period* (Halle, 1913), p. 90.

[4] See Ernst Heymann, 'Felix Liebermann', *Zeitschrift der Savigny-Stiftung für Rechtsgeschichte, Germanische Abteilung* [N.S.], XLVI (1926), p. xxxvi.

[5] For a discussion of the rising 'Celtophilia' in England around 1900 and its emphasis on common ties to France, see Schramm, 'Englands Verhältnis zur deutschen Kultur', pp. 146–9.

accusations, such a position was in fact rather apologetic for England. Michael, for example, described the motives of early eighteenth-century English policy as 'protecting Europe against French domination'.[1] Occasional critical remarks, though a healthy sign of independence, contrasted with the down-the-line defense of English policy by former historians. Yet they were mild compared to the sinister allegations of many other historians after 1897.

There was one exceptional man among scholars specializing in English history before 1897 who did retain some of the older habit of invoking examples from across the North Sea to solve current German problems. Furthermore, he moved in the new stream of interest in economic history. Lujo Brentano, who was a figure somewhat isolated by his faith in classic economic liberalism *and* deep concern for the working classes, spent much of his life describing English attempts to achieve social reconciliation without a planned economy. Brentano indeed owed his unique position in German economic science to his early experiences in England. He shed the conservatism of his patrician German Catholic family in favor of the liberalism he discovered among British Catholics.[2] Despite his belief in a free economy, Brentano participated actively in the *Verein für Sozialpolitik* (Social Policy Association), an organization founded in 1872 'to bring about compromise between the conflicting interests...of the various social classes of the people',[3] that is, to prevent socialist revolution by timely social reform. For this reason Brentano, despite his liberal ideas, was lumped together with less liberal reformers as *Kathedersozialisten* (socialists of the chair.)[4]

From the very beginning of his career, Brentano argued that the best agency for reconciling the laboring masses to existing capitalist society

[1] Wolfgang Michael, *The Beginnings of the Hanoverian Dynasty*, ed. by Sir L. Namier, tr. by A. and G. E. McGregor (London, 1936), p. 225. The work is the first volume of *Englische Geschichte im achtzehnten Jahrhundert*, 5 vols. (Hamburg, 1896; Berlin, 1920, 1934 and 1937; Basel, 1955). Only vol. I appeared before World War I. See also Michael's articles, 'Walpole als Premierminister', *Historische Zeitschrift*, CIV (1910), 504–36, and 'Die Entwicklung der Kabinettregierung in England', *Zeitschrift für Politik*, VI, No. 2 (1913), 549–93.

[2] Werner Barich, *Lujo Brentano als Sozialpolitiker* (Berlin, 1936), p. 8.

[3] Franz Boese, *Geschichte des Vereins für Sozialpolitik, 1872–1932* (Berlin, 1939), p. 1.

[4] See James Sheehan, *The Career of Lujo Brentano* (Chicago, 1966), pp. 55–61, for a discussion of Brentano's relations with the other *Kathedersozialisten* and their detractors. Also see Gerhard Wittrock, *Die Kathedersozialisten bis zur Eisenacher Versammlung 1872* [*Historische Studien*, No. 350] (Berlin, 1939), pp. 95–120, and Abraham Ascher, 'Professors as Propagandists: The Politics of the Kathedersozialisten', *Journal of Central European Affairs*, XXIII (1963), 282–302.

lay in labor unions on the English model. His first major work[1] inaugurated his long struggle to reclaim the working man's spontaneous role in economic life. The reactivation of medieval guilds in the form of labor unions, as Brentano saw it, provided the antidote to more radical and less proven theories by Marxist and neo-mercantilist proponents of a state-guided economy.[2] Brentano believed these guilds were reviving fastest in precisely that country which had the greatest respect both for organic development and the free interplay of economic forces in society – England.[3] His tours of English factory districts evoked admiring comments on the organizational genius of the English workers. In their union activities he saw the solution to industrial and social problems not only of England but of Germany and Europe. England, he asserted, was 'the country which serves as the model of all our economic development and is ahead of us by several decades in all social phenomena'.[4] Brentano viewed the German method – the carrot of state workers' insurance or the stick of anti-socialist laws – as wholly inferior to what he considered successful English methods of reintegrating the working class and the nation.

Brentano's belief in the direct applicability to Germany of English industrial and social experience hardly represented the majority view of German economic scientists. A few men, such as Gerhard von Schulze-Gaevernitz, followed his lead.[5] But Brentano's fellow economic historians often twitted him for believing in England's relevance to Germany or, even worse, regarded him 'solely as the historian of English labor unions' rather than an English-schooled prophet of German social engineering, as he saw himself.[6] The revived 'national historical school' of political economy, in particular, resented Bren-

[1] Lujo Brentano, *Die Arbeitergilden der Gegenwart*, 2 vols. (Leipzig, 1871–2): I, *Zur Geschichte der englischen Gewerkvereine*; II, *Zur Kritik der englischen Gewerkvereine*.

[2] *Ibid.*, I, vi–vii.

[3] *Ibid.*, p. vii.

[4] Brentano, 'Die englische Chartistenbewegung', *Preussische Jahrbücher*, XXXIII (1874), p. 433. See also Brentano, *Die christlich-soziale Bewegung in England* (Leipzig, 1883).

[5] See Gerhard von Schulze-Gaevernitz, *Social Peace. A Study of the Trade Union Movement in England*, tr. by C. M. Wicksteed, ed. by G. Wallas (London, 1893). The German original was *Zum sozialen Frieden*, 2 vols. (Leipzig, 1890). Schulze-Gaevernitz' solution to the social problem, like Brentano's, drew heavily on English experience. Socialist revisionists, represented by Eduard Bernstein, also idealized the English example, although it proposed a political solution (democracy) to an economic and social problem. See Bernstein's testimonial to the vanguard role of English labor in *Sozialismus und Demokratie in der grossen englischen Revolution*, 2nd edn. (Stuttgart, 1908).

Lujo Brentano, 'Entwicklung und Geist der englischen Arbeiterorganisationen', *Archiv für soziale Gesetzgebung und Statistik*, VIII (1895), p. 75.

tano's assumption that other nations would develop economically in the same way, as well as his idealization of the English model of social harmony in an industrial age.

II ECONOMIC HISTORY AND ENGAGED NON-EXPERTISE

Much more characteristic of the view of England among German economic historians than Brentano's was that of Gustav Schmoller. To be more specific, Schmoller had paid little attention to England: the strong Prussian orientation of the 'new' school of historic political economy narrowed the range of its adherents. Considering the fact that List was taken to be the major inspiration for the new school, however,[1] a certain anti-'Manchester' bias and a consequent critical outlook on English economic development were virtually inevitable. Schmoller perceived the heritage of Smithian economics, the idea of a free, international economy, as a major challenge to the protectionist principles adopted by Bismarck's *Reich* in 1879. Until 1897, however, neither he nor most of the other proponents of German neo-mercantilism spent much time on England. Aside from an occasional attack on Smith for failing to understand the essential role of 'the great centralized states and economies for the advancement of culture',[2] Schmoller and the national-historical economists remained comparatively aloof from discussions of England. They at first enjoyed the luxury of indifference to England which List's generation had been unable to afford.

From 1897 onwards, however, Schmoller became more interested in bringing into public view certain aspects of English history, especially recent history. There had already been signs that the German professorate, sensing the lack of leadership in Germany under Wilhelm II, was beginning to drift back into public life, particularly to support the imperialist cause. Max Weber, for example, argued that the foundation of the *Reich* 'would have been better left undone if it meant the conclusion rather than the starting point of German *Weltmachtpolitik* (world power politics)'.[3] Not the creation of a bigger navy after

[1] Gustav Schmoller, 'Was ist uns Friedrich List' (1889), in *Charakterbilder* (Munich and Leipzig, 1913), pp. 135–7. Exact scholarship distinguishes between an 'older' (List) and a 'younger' (Schmoller) 'historical school'.

[2] Schmoller, 'Adam Smith' (1907), *Charakterbilder*, p. 133. This article, though written after 1897, merely repeated earlier sentiments.

[3] Max Weber, *Gesammelte politische Schriften* (Munich, 1921), p. 29.

Tirpitz' appointment in 1897, but the form and justification of that navy brought Germany to the 'turning point of German–English relations'.[1] The 'risk fleet', unlike the previous conceptions of the Imperial Navy, would be directed specifically at England. In order to convince a sceptical public that the 'risk fleet' was actually necessary to national defense, Tirpitz enlisted the aid of the historians. To be sure, anti-English feeling was already running high in Germany as a result of the Boer War;[2] but it was the sustained propaganda effort for the fleet, rather than the transitory public vogue for pro-Boer sentiments, that encouraged a new interpretation of English history in Germany after 1897. Not only did German experts on England begin to falter or join (however feebly at first) in the chorus of imperialistic propaganda after that date; the conjunction of hostility toward England and advocacy of the German fleet was actively created by historians.

In view of the nature of the Anglo–German rivalry, which was acted out in terms of naval, commercial, and colonial ambitions on a global stage, it was logical that the economic historians – up to then rather indifferent to English history – should appear in the midst of the re-evaluation of the English past. When Tirpitz sought a trustworthy professor who would bring both expertise and academic prestige to his newly-founded propaganda organ, the News Bureau in the Imperial Navy Office, he turned first to Schmoller for advice.[3] Schmoller obligingly provided not only the name of Ernst von Halle, a Berlin *Dozent* who became coordinator of academic propaganda for the News Bureau,[4] but an increased degree of literary activity himself.

In a series of articles in the late 1890s, the prolific Schmoller laid out the basic revision of English commercial and naval history which others took up later. His argument differed from the angry accusations of the older Treitschke in the coolly 'scientific' manner in which he presented his case. This calm and scholarly tone marked much of the professorial writing on England thereafter, even though the content

[1] See Otto Becker, 'Die Wende der deutsch-englischen Beziehungen', *Festschrift für Gerhard Ritter zu seinem 60. Geburtstag* (Tübingen, 1950).

[2] Anderson, *Anti-English Feeling*, p. xv. For an example of the misgivings which England's Boer policy aroused among her staunchest friends in German academic circles, see Johannes H. Voigt, 'Die Auseinandersetzung zwischen Theodor Mommsen und Max Müller über den Burenkrieg', *Geschichte in Wissenschaft und Unterricht*, XVII (1966), 65–77.

[3] Wolfgang Marienfeld, *Wissenschaft und Schlachtflottenbau in Deutschland, 1897–1906*, Supplement No. 2, *Marine Rundschau* (1957), p. 79. Schmoller had been one of Tirpitz' revered teachers.

[4] *Ibid.*

sometimes bordered on the outrageous. The tone of course belonged to the 'scientific' self-image of the economic historians, as it did to the neo-Rankean self-image of the more traditional historians. The Machiavellian, matter-of-fact, and often amoral manner in which they now approached English history tended to convince where an impassioned and pseudo-ethical approach would have been put down as mere partisanship. The mood of realism, so hard to convey in the retelling, likewise marked off the boundary between most scholarly propagandists and the hot-headed Anglophobe polemicists of the First World War who spoke much the same words.

Schmoller's general line of argument was that Germany, by losing itself in the ideological side of international economic relations, had blinded itself to the 'natural' policy of all British governments (except during the 'interlude' of the free-trade era) – to strive with every possible weapon toward the expansion of its national economy. Germany and the whole world had been 'taken in' by English free trade doctrine, which was merely another cynical English tool for opening new markets and crippling the infant economies of other nations.[1] The realities of politics, Schmoller believed, had finally forced England to abandon the small fleet, the anti-colonial posture, and the free trade doctrine of the mid-nineteenth century.[2] Having eliminated the rivalry first of Spain and then of France, England began the 'pursuit of the *fata morgana* of a world trade monopoly'.[3] This, and not the balance of power, had been England's chief aim. Especially since the days of Disraeli, Schmoller maintained, English *Handelspolitik* and *Machtpolitik* (power politics) worked inseparably.[4] This much Treitschke had argued.

Yet Schmoller discerned the beginnings of an English drive to supremacy as early as the sixteenth century. The century from Elizabeth to Cromwell had begun 'the bold and aggressive flight which remained typical of English trade policy through the Napoleonic era.'[5] Reversing earlier interpretations, Schmoller characterized England's European

[1] Schmoller, 'Die wirtschaftliche Zukunft Deutschlands und die Flottenvorlage' (1899), *Handels- und Machtpolitik*, ed. by Schmoller, Max Sering, and Adolf Wagner (Stuttgart, 1900), pp. 20ff.

[2] *Ibid.*, p. 23.

[3] Schmoller, 'Fürst Bülow und die preussisch-deutsche Politik im Frühjahr 1907', *Charakterbilder*, p. 99.

[4] Schmoller, 'Zukunft Deutschlands', p. 19.

[5] Schmoller, 'Die englische Handelspolitik des 17. und 18. Jahrhunderts', *Schmollers Jahrbuch*, XXIII (1899), p. 1217.

wars, including those against Louis XIV and Napoleon, as aggressive. The Revolutionary and Napoleonic wars, he said, constituted not an attempt 'of the French Revolution to fill Europe with its "spirit"' nor a drive by '"the conquering beast", as German patriots called Napoleon I, to subordinate Europe to himself', but rather 'the final act in the world-historical struggle between England and France for the best colonies and domination of the world'.[1] The idea that England had been fighting for a principle of self-determination and internal 'freedom', the favorite causal explanation of early-nineteenth century historians, held as little significance for Schmoller as the traditional idea of a balanced English constitution.

For Schmoller's idea of English internal politics was no more flattering. From the seventeenth through the nineteenth centuries, he said, England had been ruled by 'two cliques of noble families...In the basic political questions – the limitation of the monarchy, the exploitation of state power and finances for the ruling noble families, self-government, the extension of colonial power, etc. – they were on the whole united.'[2] Only the 'personal dictatorship' of a man like Pitt could hold the system together and resist some of its 'gross abuses'. He noted with satisfaction that party rule had become so difficult after 1832 that the parties had been forced to give considerable power to a 'professionally trained bureaucracy' similar to Prussia's.[3] Like Hegel, Schmoller admonished admirers of English parliamentary government to stop demanding its introduction in Germany. Instead of the enlightened royal *Beamtenstaat* (bureaucratic state), parliamentary government in Prussia might lead to control by the feudal aristocracy![4]

In some respects, however, Schmoller consciously favored copying Britain. Naturally he rejected the supposed aims of English policy – domination of the seas, world trade monopoly, and control of as much of the world as possible. But he showed great admiration for the wealth, trade, and economic soundness resulting from Britain's 'dominance of world trade'.[5] He also demanded that Germany take up the defense of the balance of power against English encroachment. 'We wish to strengthen ourselves against possible and threatening mistreatment on

1 Schmoller, 'Die Wandlungen in der europäischen Handelspolitik des 19. Jahrhunderts', *Schmollers Jahrbuch*, XXIV (1900), p. 372.

2 Schmoller, 'Fürst Bülow', p. 105.

3 *Ibid.*

4 *Ibid.*, p. 101.

5 Schmoller, 'Zukunft Deutschlands', p. 4.

the high seas and in the field of world and colonial trade so that the great powers will see in us a bastion of peace and a protector against force.'[1] Germany, not England, would hold the balance of power and thereby copy even the international role which previous generations of historians had assigned to England. As Dehio put it, 'Germany learned...from the English rival and cut out for herself a role in world affairs which actually resembled the one England had carried out for centuries in her European policy: resistance to hegemony on behalf of a multitude of free states – for the little states and against the big ones.'[2] Here the German imitation of England reached its most ironic twist.

Other authoritative scholars backed some of Schmoller's arguments with the prestige of their specialized historical knowledge. Among the signers of a public appeal from the founders of the *Freie Vereinigung für Flottenvorträge* (Free Association for Navy Lectures) were, among others, the names of Schmoller, Hans Delbrück, Erich Marcks, Max Lenz, Otto Gierke, Adolf Harnack, and Dietrich Schäfer – all noted historians, many experts on England. Other historians who stood out in the pro-navy agitation in the years just after 1900 included Hintze and Michael as well as Brentano.[3] Of course one did not have to be an Anglophobe to like the navy, especially as long as the German Navy Bills of 1898 and 1900 foresaw only a comparatively modest challenge to British might. But the enthusiasm of men like Brentano and Marcks for the fleet effectively meant that they would keep silent about the historical exaggerations of their political allies, such as Schmoller. Many of them later regretted their aid, and none went as far as Dietrich Schäfer.

Schäfer, the son of a Bremen dockworker, was an expert on the sea by upbringing and a remarkable anomaly among German professors of the period because of his humble birth. He was one of the most active members of the Navy League, which after 1900 became so insistent on stepping up the tempo of keel-layings that it began to embarrass the navy itself.[4] Schäfer was Germany's leading authority on Hanseatic history. Unlike historians from Möser to Pauli, he portrayed the successful assault of Elizabethan England on the enfeebled Hanseatic League as the opening shot of a campaign which ended by hobbling

[1] *Ibid.*, p. 33.

[2] Ludwig Dehio, 'Gedanken über die deutsche Sendung, 1900–1918', *Historische Zeitschrift*, CLXXIV (1952), p. 489.

[3] Marienfeld, *Wissenschaft und Schlachtflottenbau, Anhang 4.*

[4] *Ibid.*, p. 83.

German commerce and penetrating the German market with its Trojan horse, Hamburg.[1] His writings essentially followed lines laid out by Schmoller, depicting with sympathy such 'underdogs' as Louis XIV, who had allegedly aimed only at breaking the Anglo-Dutch preponderance at sea,[2] and other victims of 'a long chain of legislative, diplomatic, and bellicose measures which aimed solely at assuring England the unchallenged dominance of the seas'.[3] As against Holland in the seventeenth century, Schäfer warned, Britain had now proclaimed *Germania delenda est*. The attacks of Nelson on Copenhagen and Jameson on the Boers should convince all that England never holds back on scruple.[4] Schäfer in one breath doubted if an English alliance (much discussed around 1900) would work at all and warned against its working so well as to 'draw us into a war' which would bleed Germany white on the land and fatten England overseas.[5]

The agitation carried on by Schäfer within the Navy League and his late outspokenness during World War I in behalf of large German annexations[6] mark him as an unusually determined and clearly motivated re-interpreter of English history. The next question is how the less clearly biased professors evaluated his (and Schmoller's) 'economic' revision of English history. Despite the initial enthusiasm of many academics for the Imperial Navy in the nineties and the widespread annexationist sentiments of the early war years, few German historians equalled Schäfer's propagandistic zeal. Indeed, professors joined the Free Association for Navy Lectures because it was moderate and untainted with the corruption of heavy industry lobbying that they associated with the Navy League.[7] Nevertheless, no matter how conscientiously many professors withstood co-option by the German 'military-industrial complex', they felt compelled to speak out *as*

[1] Dietrich Schäfer, 'Deutschland zur See' (1897), in *Deutschland und England* (Leipzig, 1915), pp. 33–6.

[2] *Ibid.*, p. 56.

[3] *Ibid.*, p. 50.

[4] *Ibid.*, p. 104f.

[5] *Ibid.*, p. 99.

[6] Schäfer and Hans Delbrück drifted into polar opposition to each other over the 'war aims debate' in Germany. Schäfer, showing remarkable consistency, pursued a *Siegfrieden* (peace by victory) with large annexations; Delbrück, with increasing support from others as the war wore on, advocated a *Verständigungsfrieden* (peace by agreement) with no western annexations and few in the east. See Schwabe, 'Politische Haltung', pp. 615–17; also Gustav Wolf, *Dietrich Schäfer und Hans Delbrück, nationale Ziele in der deutschen Geschichtsschreibung seit der französischen Revolution* (Gotha, 1918).

[7] Marienfeld, *Wissenschaft und Schlachtflottenbau*, p. 85. Delbrück, for example, resigned from the Navy League for this reason; even Schäfer recognized the 'selfish intentions' of many of its members.

historians to clarify the background of the great issues Germany was facing, including her relations to England. Very quickly after 1897, attention shifted to Germany's external relations with England and more recent English history. The historians who brought about this change of focus were not, however, the 'specialists' on England. The inaugurators of a new view of England were more often than not experts in completely different fields. While they spoke and wrote for a German public eager to learn something about an increasingly popular subject, the majority of 'experts' on England remained silent. Had the debate raged only around contemporary British foreign policy, such silence should have been understandable, for most German scholars evidently agreed that that policy was sinister to some extent. But the debate often raged around English history as well. The central problem for the historian was whether this sinister quality was typical and continuous or atypical and momentary. Could Germany simply wait until the present international situation changed and then reassert her request for an enlarged world role? Or was English resistance to this request so deeply ingrained in the policy traditions and 'national character' of the English that a conflict would be inevitable?

Four men in particular may be compared for a good cross-section of answers to these and related questions about England's historic policies. Max Lenz, Hans Delbrück, Otto Hintze, and Hermann Oncken were all non-experts on England who took more than a passing interest in questions of English foreign relations. By training they went back to quite different 'schools': Delbrück, Lenz, and Lenz's student Oncken, to the Rankean (via Sybel, Noorden, and others); Hintze, to the 'Prussian' school of Droysen, augmented by Schmoller. There certainly were differences among them, and they perceived themselves as continuing grand traditions.[1] But many of the differences had been blurred by counterinfluences: Treitschke had some influence on Lenz, and Schäfer on Delbrück. Schmoller appears to have been a pervasive influence on almost everyone. They shared many fundamental presuppositions, such as a fairly uncritical loyalty to the Hohenzollerns and their foreign policy. At the same time, they could be quite open in private about mistakes they perceived in official policy, especially on such great questions as the treatment of the working class, Germanization

[1] Lenz and Erich Marcks, whose attempts to revive the spirit of Ranke are fully described in Krill, *Die Rankerenaissance*, were not the only leading historians to regard themselves as renewers.

of minorities, and even Tirpitz' increasingly hazardous naval program just before the war. It is of course no accident that these four professors who leap to the eye as representatives of the new curiosity of previously uninterested historians about England, taught at Berlin. That university was more closely co-ordinated with the political life of the nation than any other. With Schmoller there to channel influence for Tirpitz, and with the addition of Schäfer as well after 1903, it virtually became the academic center of discussion about England as well.

Since all four Berlin professors more or less subscribed to the vague aims of German *Weltpolitik* and addressed themselves to English history chiefly because of that, the context in which they viewed England was usually global and maritime. They all agreed that England's foreign policy could only be understood by devoting primary attention to her overseas commitments, not only recently, but throughout the modern era. With varying intensity they denied that the balance of power in Europe had always been England's *aim*: some, like Delbrück, could still regard it as a real concept, but one which played only a *secondary* role in British policy;[1] others, such as Oncken and Hintze, presented the balance of power as an ideological mask covering England's real intent, keeping Europe in a turmoil so that England could conquer the world with no opposition.

Delbrück increasingly saw the danger of Germany's opposing the balance of power as a mere English trick. Up to a point, his writings as editor of the *Preussische Jahrbücher* advocated naval and colonial expansion in emulation of Britain. But after 1907 (like Max Weber a short time before), he saw the limits to Germany's strength. He broke his connections with the Pan-Germans, backed down from his extreme support of *Weltpolitik*, and advocated both a policy of co-operation with Britain on colonial questions and the scaling down of further naval building so as not to provoke a conflict.[2] In private, Delbrück could worry that 'Tirpitz' policies will plunge us into war with England and lead us in the steps of Napoleon'.[3] Likewise, he was most cautious in his prewar lectures at Berlin in describing English policies and statesmen

[1] See Hans Delbrück, 'Deutschland und England' (1904), in *Vor und nach dem Weltkrieg* (Berlin, 1926), 50–60.

[2] Annelise Thimme, *Hans Delbrück als Kritiker der wilhelminischen Epoche* (Düsseldorf, 1955), pp. 106, 112. Also Delbrück, 'Morokko-Kongo Handel – Reichstagswahlen – Rüstungen' (1911), *Weltkrieg*, pp. 352–61.

[3] Hans Delbrück, letter to Hermann Oncken, Berlin, 6 March 1912, in *Nachlass* Delbrück, *Deutsche Staatsbibliothek*, East Berlin, x, *Korrespondenzausgang.*

of the past. His ideas harmonized more with those of Sybel and Ranke than those of Treitschke and Droysen.[1] Nevertheless, in his capacity as editor and writer of the *Preussische Jahrbücher*, which Treitschke had made into a pillar of support for the Hohenzollern empire, Delbrück played into the hands of the revisionists of English history. While he rejected talk of an English drive to 'encircle' Germany, he could not shake off the suspicion that England really was stumbling toward a world hegemony. 'It is completely true', he wrote in the *Jahrbücher*, 'that Germany opposes English aspirations in many places in the world and is the main obstacle in the way of the whole world becoming English.' He added that 'nothing is further from German policy than the idea of bringing England to her knees', nor was Germany hostile. On the contrary, like a friend giving good advice, Germany was seeking by her opposition to awaken the 'good' England from a delusion dating at least from Waterloo: 'they [the English] had gotten used to the idea of making the whole world English... and are convinced of their right to rule.'[2] Such support as this for official ideology reached opinion-makers through the *Jahrbücher*, whereas Delbrück's mild lectures and private letters did not.

Lenz, Oncken, and Hintze had fewer reservations about keeping apart their historical and propagandistic work. They were also (though in varying degrees) more inclined to use force for Germany's success, rather than cooperation with Britain. The justification for such a role varied. Hintze claimed (like Schmoller) that 'the meaning of German *Weltpolitik* is not striving for world dominance but for the balance of power in the world system of the future'.[3] A more sinister justification of force, bordering on the German fear of 'encirclement', surfaced in the writings of Oncken and Hintze.[4]

[1] See Hans Delbrück, *Weltgeschichte. Vorlesungen, gehalten an der Universität Berlin 1896/1920*, 5 vols. (Berlin, 1925–31). [2] Delbrück, 'Deutschland und England', pp. 59, 53.

[3] Otto Hintze, 'Imperialismus und Weltpolitik' (1907), *Historische und politische Aufsätze*, 4 vols. (Berlin, 1908–9), IV, 159.

[4] See Hermann Oncken, 'Deutschland und England. Heeres- oder Flottenverstärkung? Ein historisch-politischer Vortrag' (Heidelberg, 1912), and Hintze, 'Die Seeherrschaft Englands, ihre Begründung und Bedeutung', *Neue Zeit- und Streitfragen*, IV, 9 (1907), p. 27. Hintze and Oncken spoke of 'isolation' of the enemy as the traditional English weapon against the main enemy, preferring to describe the action in diplomatic terms. The stronger and more emotionally charged word, 'encirclement', had a military ring to it, implying an invasion from all sides – a thought which certainly also occurred to many German thinkers. Hintze, for one, described rather accurately in 1907 just what the English tactics in the next war would be (p. 14f.). But 'encirclement' assumed a British strategy to lead, co-ordinate and even launch a crushing defeat of Germany.

The modes of refashioning the English past to fit the German present used by Oncken, Lenz, and Hintze varied somewhat, but the variations were unimportant. Hintze, the student of Schmoller, was usually the most inclined to a sweeping revision and toward full support of the Germany Navy. Lenz, a conscious renewer of Rankean 'objectivity', limited his revision to the period since 1815 and kept out of the foreign policy debates altogether between 1902 and 1914.[1] Oncken, Lenz's student, fell somewhere between, but followed Delbrück in calling for no navy increases in 1912.[2] For Hintze, imperialistic drives had motivated English statesmen since the seventeenth century. A conscious, state-directed mercantilism underlay all Britain's actions abroad, despite the interlude of Cobden's influence and the 'slogans' of free trade, peace, and the European balance.[3]

Lenz and, to a lesser degree, his student Oncken refused to go as far as Schmoller and Hintze in revising English history. The influence of Ranke held Lenz back from reading aggressive imperialism into *all* English history, although he felt compelled to discount Ranke's Anglophilia.[4] Even so, Lenz followed Ranke's defense of English foreign policy up to 1815. The struggle with revolutionary France, which Hintze regarded as a struggle for control of the seas, appeared to Lenz 'just as in the sixteenth and seventeenth centuries, a struggle for principles upon which the English national state rested: not only economic survival was in question; parliamentary, Protestant Great Britain would have dissolved and the Romance-Catholic world of both hemispheres filled with new energy if Napoleon had attained his goal'.[5]

With 1815, however, Lenz's tone and attention became sharper. The socio-political structure of England appeared disastrously outmoded thenceforward, as the turmoil in England after 1815 showed. 'The social inequalities which came to bear in this crisis went back to the preceding century and were even then crasser than under the French *ancien régime*,' he claimed.[6] The foreign policy of England's ruling noble clique in the early nineteenth century 'appeared daily...more

[1] See Willy Schenk, *Die deutsch-englische Rivalität vor dem ersten Weltkrieg in der Sicht deutscher Historiker* (Aarau, Switzerland, 1967), p. 43.
[2] Oncken, 'Deutschland und England', p. 41.
[3] Hintze, 'Imperialismus and Weltpolitik', p. 154ff. Also see 'Die Seeherrschaft Englands', pp. 20, 27, and 13 on *Handelspolitik* and English enmity to Germany.
[4] Max Lenz, 'Die grossen Mächte', *Deutsche Rundschau*, CII (1900), p. 75.
[5] *Ibid.*, p. 281f. Cf. Hintze, 'Seeherrschaft Englands', pp. 31ff.
[6] *Ibid.*, p. 280.

repellent'.[1] Lenz joined the revisionists in speaking of England's 'betrayal' of the Concert of Europe and accused Canning and Palmerston of encouraging uproar in Europe solely in order to weaken opposition to her global expansion. The liberal sympathies of England for Greek, Italian, and South American independence movements appeared to Lenz as a mere cynical cover for England's jealous monopoly over Mediterranean and Atlantic sea and trade lanes. Of course much of what Lenz said was true; but he said it with a harshness born of disenchantment. 'The phrases with which the [English] ministers inaugurated the change [at Verona] sounded wonderful', he noted bitterly: '... all these were declamations like those which Chamberlain and his pious colleague Balfour used to gain the support of public opinion for their plundering attack on the Transvaal.'[2] Moderate and 'Rankean' as he tried to be, Lenz could not judge English policy of the 1820s without reference to the 1890s.

To the reader today, inured to the hysterical slanders of Hitlerite and Cold War abuse of history, the historical revisionism of the Berlin professors may seem mild indeed. Much of it was plausible, most of it was sincere, and all of it was well-meant. Certainly the cool, Machiavellian unmasking of naked self-interest in England's historic foreign policies was an act of scholarly correctness. Few can quarrel with the argument that Germany in 1900 was receiving a share of world power disproportionate to her importance or that England was failing to take positive action to correct German resentments. One can furthermore credit many of the 'Navy Professors' with enough political insight to foresee what could happen if they followed Tirpitz all the way to a full 'risk fleet' and to pull back from a risk they considered too great.

Nevertheless, one must point out three important faults in the Berlin non-experts of England who reinterpreted English history in the name of political agitation. First, they carried back into remote times a number of concepts which had validity only for their own time, if even then. By generalizing from certain tendencies such as imperialism, ideas of neo-mercantilism, and the build-up of the British fleet, they ascribed rationality, clarity, and planning to remote ages of English history which had never known them. As Jonathan Steinberg has

[1] *Ibid.*, p. 282.

[2] *Ibid.*, p. 283. For a look at Lenz's more journalistic denunciations of the Boer War, see 'Zur politischen Weltlage', *Die Woche*, II (1900), 703–6 and 'Der Zusammenbruch in Transvaal', *ibid.*, 973–5.

pointed out, such backward projections resulted in distortions of history which ultimately became policy. For example, by constantly referring to 'Copenhagen', that is, the British attack on the Danish fleet in 1807, German historians encouraged false analogy-building in German military planning, giving rise to a *weltpolitische Angst* about such an attack on the German fleet – the 'Copenhagen complex'.[1] Examples of such anachronisms abounded, even among historians who should have had no reason to fall into them. Even in the impressive work of A. O. Meyer, one of the most careful 'experts,' English navalism appeared as such a constant feature of English history that the mighty Spanish Armada of 1588 sank to the level of a pathetic undertaking with little chance of success against confident ancestors of Admirals Blake and Nelson.[2]

The second fault lay in the way the reinterpretation of English history was put forward. To the reading public, but especially the educated and influential 'public' at which their writings were aimed, the words of the Navy Professors came endorsed by all the prestige of the German – especially the Berlin – university elite. In a country where professional journalism enjoyed the lowest esteem, where political parties and *Reichstag* deputies were widely regarded as lobbyists for special interests, the university professor could scarcely be challenged, except by the governing bureaucracy itself. And the third mistake hung together with the bureaucracy's power to censure. Speaking out on politics in Wilhelmine Germany could be recommended to 'non-political' professors only as long as they supported the general lines of official policy. The inducements for speaking out against it were considerably less. Silence, for the prudent man, was not only respectable from the academic point of view; it was almost a national duty, if one happened to disagree. In most cases, the lines were probably not drawn between enthusiastic support and bitter, silent rejection of official policy, however. A more genuine dilemma for many professors was that they were unsure of themselves. Why should a scholar who knew the distortions of the Navy Professors for what they were stand up and object? Their writings, one could argue, are not meant for serious debate among specialists, but for the general

[1] Jonathan Steinberg, 'The Copenhagen Complex', *Journal of Contemporary History*, III (1966), 21–44.

[2] Meyer, *England and the Catholic Church*, p. 328.

public. Besides, much of what they said was reasonable, and to correct them would seem unpatriotic, especially since many of the experts on England themselves tacitly supported the aims of the Imperial government. There is enough evidence to suggest that many original Navy Professors – those willing to leave the ivory tower after 1897 to campaign for the fleet and *Weltpolitik* – grew increasingly doubtful that they had done the right thing. Their solution, too, was to fall silent in public, rather than risk their careers by opposing something in which they half-believed anyway. To correct misinterpretations of English history, considering the predominantly contemporary motivations behind them, would be to cast doubt on one's loyalty to these motivations; and this few professors wished to do.

III THE REACTION OF THE EXPERTS

The reaction of the professional students of England to all this revisionism was, in most cases, oblique if not silent. Politically speaking, the lines were clearly drawn. The head of the rapidly expansionist Pan-German League, Heinrich Class,[1] wrote a popular *German History* in 1910 which dealt with England in very much the same spirit as the Berlin professors of history.[2] Eduard Bernstein,[3] who dabbled in English history himself, spoke for the right wing of German socialism in denouncing the distortions of English history engineered by nationalist writers and dismissed as nonsense the notion that England had historically blocked German unity and economic growth. 'The English peril', he insisted, was 'a superpatriots' myth'. England's supposed policy of encirclement was a German catchword to twist England's natural defensive reaction against German militarism into an offensive posture.[4] Bernstein's highly reasonable analysis of the

[1] Heinrich Class (1868–1953) was a publicist and head of the right-wing nationalist Pan-German League. (See Biographical Appendix.)

[2] Einhart [pseudonym for Heinrich Class], *Deutsche Geschichte* (Leipzig, 1910). The book enjoyed great popularity and reached its thirteenth edition (with 125,000 copies) by 1926. Although he dealt with England only in passing, Class's indebtedness to Treitschke and Schmoller was clear. Yet Class was more emotional than the professional historians, and it is clear he had a great admiration for a 'country of Germanic stock' (p. 98) and the self-confident 'national character' of the English. See Alfred Kruck, *Geschichte des alldeutschen Verbandes, 1890–1939* (Wiesbaden, 1954), p. 24f.

[3] Eduard Bernstein (1850–1932) was the leading 'revisionist' theorist of the German Social Democratic Party. (See Biographical Appendix.)

[4] Eduard Bernstein, 'Die englische Gefahr und das deutsche Volk', [pamphlet] (Berlin, 1911).

problem fell into the category of 'disloyal' propaganda; Class's work, motivated by the views of the right, moved in the same conceptual sphere as that of the Berlin professors. How could the experts on England choose sides, especially if they, too, were members of the respected professorial establishment?

In the majority of cases, the German specialists took no side at all, at least not publicly. Liebermann, Busch, Meyer, Michael, and Riess continued to write in the decade and a half before the war, but they either wrote nothing about England (Busch, Riess) or they produced monographs admirable for their judiciousness, praised by foreign scholars, and wholly irrelevant to the revisionist arguments of the Berliners (Liebermann, A. O. Meyer, Michael). While they consistently refused to engage themselves in the controversy about English foreign policy, however, their own monographic research reached conclusions which did not essentially contradict the basic ideas and presuppositions of the revisionists. German specialists generally stressed the importance of the monarchical state in English history where their predecessors had stressed individualism, the sometimes chaotic nature of English liberty, or the role of local government and aristocracy. The rise of a small power to great eminence under Elizabeth and Cromwell, rather than the religious struggles or the emergence of a powerful Commons, fascinated the men who had grown up under Bismarck.[1] A. O. Meyer, for example, believed that Elizabeth's greatest accomplishment was to make religious conflicts secondary to national unity and that the defeat of the Armada by concerted English effort showed 'loyalty was the ruling passion of Elizabethan England'.[2] Certainly the phrase was true of Wilhelmine Germany; but hardly of Elizabeth's day. Considering the influences causing German historians to stress the state-building activities of the Tudors, it comes as no surprise to find an inordinate amount of interest in Cromwell, who became the center of attention for students of the seventeenth century. Revolution, parliamentary struggles, and charters of liberty now interested the professional historians far less than the charismatic, morally guided leader. For Michael, to take one example, Cromwell could do no wrong; he praised what he thought were the essential good qualities of the era incorporated in his hero – religiosity, concern for the people, military

[1] See, for example, Erich Marcks, *Königin Elisabeth*, p. 13 *et passim*.
[2] Meyer, *England and the Catholic Church*, p. 328.

spirit, and strong nationalism.[1] Michael openly admitted one of the attractions of his subject: 'The German reader will find many traits in the nature of the Puritan hero which remind him of the founder of the German Empire.' Like Cromwell, Bismarck had 'stood in pious modesty before God and ascribed the greater part of his work to a higher power'.[2] The state-building wisdom of the political hero, whether Tudor prince or Puritan commander, appeared to outstrip that of parliamentary representatives and common people. It was certainly no accident that so many German specialists in early-modern English history, once they abandoned their original field, gravitated to Bismarck studies.[3] Of course much of what the specialists said accorded with perfectly respectable English research on the same subject, and at no time had contact with English scholars been richer or more frequent. But Marcks's preference for biography, followed by many of his contemporaries, smacked of a revival of Carlylian hero-worship, a tendency which reached its highest and most sophisticated expression in Max Weber's ruminations on charismatic leadership. The point is that the pre-March liberals' fascination with resistance, revolution, and liberty from overly-demanding 'state-formers' had all but vanished from all German writings about England.

Not all experts on England stood aside from the controversy about England, paralyzed by uncertainty, indifference, or the belief that professors should, after all, be 'above politics'. One, Erich Marcks, became involved from the first, and he perhaps shared many of the doubts and inner conflicts felt by the majority of England specialists. He vacillated considerably, from early defense of England's historic foreign policy to late conversion to the revisionist stance. Another, and indeed the chief defender of England throughout, was Felix Salomon.

Marcks's career was a restless flight from one field of research to another. He never finished his excellent biography of Bismarck, for example. Before studying Bismarck, he began and then abandoned a promising career as the historian of French Protestantism. Yet this very fickleness and inner uncertainty seemed typical of the other experts on England. Like the Navy Professors, Marcks had to choose between the demands of impartial, scientific research and those of a

[1] Michael, *Cromwell*, I, 34. See also pp. 18, 216, 238, *et passim*.

[2] *Ibid.*, I, vi.

[3] Busch, Marcks, and Meyer all published important studies on Bismarck after they had begun to abandon or branch out from exclusive interest in the Tudor–Stuart period.

form of literature, and thus of culture, which sought to associate itself with the life of the German state. Marcks consciously set out to continue many of the elements of Ranke's thought – the critical method, the *Primat der Aussenpolitik*, the concentration upon the Reformation era, the tension between the Romance and Germanic peoples, the interaction of politics and religion, the essential continuity of the international objectives of the great powers. But he gradually went over to stressing the differences among the Germanic peoples and in the special virtue of the Prussian–German power state.[1] Ranke had provided a framework for Marcks: but 'the dynamic foundation was still the intellectual-political heritage of Heinrich von Treitschke'.[2]

Marcks's first major essay on English history, for example, elaborated a Rankean assumption that sixteenth-century England had best conformed to the Germanic 'cultural type'. Elizabethan England seemed to him 'the most powerful representative of the national, Protestant-Germanic principle as opposed to the universalistic, Catholic-Romance principle of Phillip II's Counterreformation'.[3] In 1900, reacting to Anglophobe propaganda, Marcks engaged in a defense of England based on exactly this historic cultural and political community of England and Germany throughout modern times.[4] Nevertheless, such cultural-ideological ties seemed less important than the Treitschkean concept of the state. For six years later, in analyzing Pitt, one of the figures most fascinating to this generation of German historians, Marcks turned about and applied a peculiarly Prussian historical ruler to the English past: he made the state the giver of life to the nation. Pitt, he said, typified the best traits of English national character formed under Elizabeth and continued 'to Chamberlain and Rhodes'.[5] These traits included 'economic daring and economic sobriety together; activeness, hard work, and a sense for the real and concrete; coarse national pride; political integration but, at the same time, free personal development of the individual, his powers, rights, and inward life; hard aggressiveness, ruthless use of power; and an earnest, deep-working cultural effort, all directed, advised, and ordered by a state [!] in living

[1] See Krill, *Rankerenaissance*, pp. 43, 45, 52, 60.
[2] *Ibid.*, p. 257.
[3] *Ibid.*, p. 57.
[4] Marcks, *Deutschland und England in den grossen europäischen Krisen seit der Reformation* (Stuttgart, 1900).
[5] Marcks, 'Der jüngere Pitt und seine Zeit' (1906), in *Männer und Zeiten*, 2 vols. (Leipzig, 1911), I, 147.

contact with its members'.[1] These traits, so typical of imperialism, were stated in terms vague enough to make England's aggressive quest for power and the central role of the state in directing it seem permanent since 1588. In a social-Darwinian way, Marcks admired these 'national character traits', but even England's admirers now agreed on the fundamental aggressiveness of the English state.

Marcks's description of the Anglo–French struggle from 1680 to 1815, for example, reflected his gradual conversion to Berlin revisionism. He described the world-wide duel purely in terms of *Machtpolitik*, dropping the traditional Rankean theory that England's wars against France executed a just 'European mission'. 'It was a struggle for political and economic power,' Marcks wrote, 'fought with all means – political, military, economic; first England removed the threat of Louis XIV's predominance, then she went over to ever-widening and increasingly successful attacks.'[2] The conquest of Canada, India, and other colonial territories appeared to Marcks as the product of conscious and well-directed efforts of state policy rather than as a 'fit of absense of mind', as Seeley had called it.

Even this most pro-British of scholars could no longer defend the constitution of mid-eighteenth-century England. Far from being the harmonious system described by Montesquieu, it was 'a swamp'.[3] The 'idea of the state' had gotten lost in the corrupt scramble of the aristocracy for money and power. It was Pitt's triumph – and that of his father Chatham – to restore the 'idea of the state' to prominence and rescue England.[4]

Marcks still owed enough to Ranke to depict the English struggle against the French Revolution as a struggle between the Englishman's (e.g. Burke's) Germanic love of organic development and the 'French-Romance,...thoroughly un-Germanic' revolution.[5] Yet England's greatest sacrifices were made not only for principles, but for 'fame, colonial possessions, and profits' that 'flowed in wide streams to the mistress of the seas'.[6] In 1900 Marcks had pointed heavily to Anglo–German cooperation in defeating the common danger of Napoleonic dominance; now he insisted that England had emerged in 1815 with the whole world at her feet and Germany with nothing. 'It is not easy for today's Germany to follow English celebrations [of the defeat

[1] *Ibid.* [2] *Ibid.*, p. 125. [3] *Ibid.*
[4] *Ibid.*, p. 127. [5] *Ibid.*, p. 139. [6] *Ibid.*, p. 144.

of Napoleon I] with joyful participation: too much has come between the two great Germanic peoples', he noted.[1] If Marcks still admired England, it was not because of her internal political constitution or because of common battles fought long ago, but because of her self-confident, nationalistic, gross drive for world power. Ranke's *Primat der Aussenpolitik* had been taken up, stretched out of its European context, and misused to apply the concepts of late nineteenth-century imperialism to earlier times.

By 1910 Marcks completely avoided mentioning the common goals and mutual aid connecting England and Germany; instead he identified imperialism as the basis of Britain's foreign policy since 1588.[2] Even in England's successful defense of its coasts against the Armada he saw the first signs of English aggressiveness. Approaching revisionism, he spoke of England consistently covering her back with continental allies, conquering the seas, and fighting her decisive battles at sea. 'Behind this struggle stood a strong and awakened national consciousness, a grimness in which the drives of acquisition and power, of freedom and religion were strangely mixed, but in such a way that political motives won out.'[3] Only ten years before, he had expressed the relief to German Protestants, not England's imperial gain, as the fruits of 1588.[4] Only in nuances did Marcks's review of English history in 1910 differ from that of the revisionists.[5]

Marcks ended by describing Germany as the only threat to England's supremacy in colonial and naval spheres.[6] He accepted the myth of England's 'encircling' Germany – 'the familiar grounds of England's ancient political methods'.[7] Here indeed 'one receives striking proof of what narrow, passive dependence on momentary official political currents the historical writing of the neo-Rankeans could get into – even with the best of intentions'.[8]

Only one expert on English history really fought back at the process of revision undertaken in the wake of Germany's imperial course – Felix Salomon. Fortunately he answered Marcks's later writings with

[1] *Ibid.*, p. 123.
[2] Marcks, 'Die Einheitlichkeit der englischen Auslandspolitik von 1500 bis zur Gegenwart' (1910), *Männer und Zeiten*, II, 235–63.
[3] *Ibid.*, p. 239.
[4] Marcks, 'Deutschland und England', p. 206.
[5] Marcks, 'Einheitlichkeit', p. 240f. See also pp. 243f., 254, and 256f.
[6] *Ibid.*, p. 254.
[7] *Ibid.*, p. 256.
[8] Krill, *Rankerenaissance*, p. 189.

equal measures – a Pitt biography and a sketch of historic English foreign policy[1] – so that a direct comparison is possible.

Where Marcks showed a preference for England's intellectual history and external relations, Salomon's Pitt biography clung closely to internal political and economic developments. Like Marcks, he congratulated Chatham and Pitt for rejuvenating the English state, 'which had been too much weakened by the usurpation of the Whig oligarchy'.[2] In contrast to Marcks, however, Salomon, a historian of German parties, grasped the necessity for powerful economic interest groups in English politics. The Walpole Whigs used their oligarchic rule and corruption to bring about a valuable harmony between the state and the newly powerful merchant class.[3] Salomon was one of the few German historians who drew sociologically sound conclusions from Gneist's theories. Gneist and his followers saw manipulation of the state by an economically motivated group as reprehensible; to Salomon it was the natural extension of Gneist's privilege-sacrifice theory to an age of commercial revolution. If the merchant had become the major economic factor and taxpayer, as he had in eighteenth-century England, why should he not have the formal privilege of directing state economic policy?

Although Salomon ably defended the peculiar nature of English politics in his Pitt biography, he hardly spoke of foreign policy except to claim that peace, the maintenance of the territorial *status quo*, and the balance of power were Pitt's permanent goals.[4] Soon, however, Salomon felt obliged to challenge the distortions of English history which the Anglo–German rivalry was stimulating. Since the end of the medieval wars with France, Salomon argued, England had assumed a 'purely defensive' position in foreign affairs.[5] The security of the realm, including control of the channel, the independence of the Netherlands, and the freedom of England's trade there, was the only aim of Tudor policy.

When England became a colonial power in the seventeenth century, she did so on the initiative of private citizens, not government policy.[6]

[1] Felix Salomon, *William Pitt der Jüngere*, vol. I, *Bis zum Ausgang der Friedensperiode (Februar 1793)* (Leipzig and Berlin, 1906). The promised second part never appeared. Also 'Die Grundzüge der auswärtigen Politik Englands vom sechzehnten Jahrhundert bis zur Gegenwart', *Zeitschrift für Politik*, III (1910), 429–97, especially p. 429.

[2] Salomon, *Pitt*, I, 110f.

[3] *Ibid.*, p. 52f.

[4] *Ibid.*, II, 447.

[5] Salomon, 'Grundzüge', p. 441.

[6] *Ibid.*, p. 442.

Cromwell's attack on the Dutch, it is true, was aggressive; but 'he approached the thinking of militant Puritanism, which Elizabeth had refused to represent, and he recommended a militaristic policy of power and conquest' that was foreign to English history.[1] By contrast, Charles II abandoned England's defense for French money. Had not England overthrown the Stuarts in 1688, neither England nor Europe would have been safe. Like Ranke, Salomon spoke of England's 'European mission' against France in the eighteenth century.[2]

German historians since Treitschke had often singled out one instrument of English hypocrisy in her dealings with other countries: a quick change of government could extricate England from the firmest foreign commitments, as when England abandoned Austria at Utrecht or Frederick the Great in 1762. Salomon attempted to dispel the myth of England's untrustworthiness. He urged German historians to see matters from the quite valid viewpoint of the English themselves. Then they would see, for example, that Utrecht was a fair and reasonable settlement, that England had to align herself against Prussia in 1740 because of the Franco-Prussian axis, and that England had as much right to drop Prussia in 1762 as Prussia had to abandon her allies in 1742.[3]

Salomon likewise dismissed England's so-called striving for hegemony of the oceans as mere Anglophobe propaganda. Far from pressing the wars against revolutionary and Napoleonic France to her own advantage, England had been handicapped in carrying out her European mandate for the balance of power by the greed of her continental allies.[4] 'What England demanded for herself in 1815 was comparatively little.'[5] English foreign policy at Vienna tried, as always, to uphold the balance of power.

Touching on English policy since 1870, Salomon became only slightly less determined in his defense. He firmly denied that Britain had ceased to pursue peace and the balance of power, or that she had kept Europe in turmoil in order to carry on undisturbed conquest of the colonial world.[6] Salomon questioned the truth of charges that England was 'encircling' Germany and denied the possibility of a British attack. 'The assumption that England planned to beat down one power after the other and even climb upon their shoulders is erroneous', he de-

[1] *Ibid.*, p. 446.
[2] *Ibid.*, p. 449.
[3] *Ibid.*, pp. 453, 458.
[4] *Ibid.*, p. 462.
[5] *Ibid.*, p. 464.
[6] *Ibid.*, p. 476.

clared.[1] The English, he said, were oblivious to the idea that power is an end in itself.

The sharp alignment on one side or another of the great debate on English history was thus quite one-sided. One set of historians, by far the largest, revised English history so that world imperialism became its theme. A handful met the attack head on but attracted little attention. Meanwhile the men best equipped to discuss English history either fell silent or wavered between their patriotic duty and their sympathy for England. Many of them shared the dilemma of Brentano, whose 'role in the campaign for naval expansion and... deep-seated Anglophilia were clearly in conflict'.[2] At best they could pretend there were 'two Englands', as Gneist had: Brentano in the end could only hope that the England of Cobden might replace that of Chamberlain.[3] Those who tried to steer a middle course frequently earned themselves only scorn. Brentano himself complained of English articles 'in which I, whom people of Germany scold for being an Anglomaniac, am characterized as an enemy of England'.[4]

The poisonous air of rivalry predictably stimulated the growth of certain viewpoints on English history while stifling others. Practically nobody wrote about the libertarian tradition of England after 1900; German historians might criticize specific policies of their government, but they no longer demanded an 'English constitution' or even used English political history as an arsenal of examples.[5] Having attained civic liberties and a species of parliamentary representation, German historians no longer keenly sought English lessons. As for the idea that England was 'the protector of the oppressed peoples', as Max Lenz noted, the Boer War shattered such romantic notions.[6] To explain

[1] *Ibid.*, p. 496.

[2] Sheehan, *Brentano*, p. 181.

[3] *Ibid.*, p. 182.

[4] Brentano, *Mein Leben im Kampf um die soziale Entwicklung Deutschlands* (Jena, 1931), p. 273.

[5] This is not to say that nobody paid any attention to English domestic politics. Max Weber – to whom, however, few listened – had a keen appreciation of many aspects of English political practice. Many of those professors associated with Naumann's 'National Social' movement approved quasi-democratic reforms in Germany and were open to suggestion from England. Yet Weber and the Naumann circle were also tragically committed to German imperial aims as their primary solution to national problems. Thus their concern with English political institutions, while producing many germinal ideas for later scholarly reflection, paled in comparison to their public advocacy of a foreign policy of confrontation or at least forcible compromise with England.

[6] Lenz, 'Zur politischen Weltlage', p. 705.

England's world success, men like Schmoller and Marcks stressed not the liberty of the English people but the iron discipline of the consolidated English state.

Other old themes of English history vanished less completely than the libertarian ones, but even they were transformed. Protestantism and Germanic 'blood', for example, continued to rate occasional mention; but religion and race served as secondary explanations of England's ruthless and successful imperialism. Schäfer, Marcks, A. O. Meyer, and Hintze, for example, still stressed England's religious and racial heritage but redefined it in such a way that English Protestantism meant Puritanism, an ethical system considered at variance with Germany's. Schulze-Gaevernitz, after conversion to Schmoller's view of English history, attempted to explain the elements of English national psychology which generated such expansive energies. Like so many other German scholars, he greeted Max Weber's speculations about the connection between Protestantism and capitalism as the answer.[1] Schulze-Gaevernitz seized upon English Puritanism as the cultural basis of English aggressiveness and economic success.

What emerged was the following picture: the aggressiveness of the Puritan revolutionaries, the authors of the Navigation Acts and of a trade war with Holland, typified English foreign policy at all times. Puritanism assured the English of their destiny to rule the world as 'God's chosen people'. 'Despite Bentham and Ricardo', Schulze said, 'the idea of the chosen people and the need to prove oneself actively in the outside world is not dead.'[2] He cited Rhodes as a contemporary example of the aggressive Puritan spirit. We have noted that Salomon pointedly underlined the aberrance of English foreign policy under the Puritan revolutionaries; Schulze, along with most other writers, insisted on its typicalness.

Puritanism furthermore appeared as the prime factor of English cultural integration, overshadowing the 'racial kinship' of Germany and England[3] and contrasting sharply with the German form of religion.[4] The term 'Anglo-Saxon', used by previous generations of German historians to denote a closely related branch of the German family, now began to mean England and the United States *as opposed*

[1] Gerhard von Schulze-Gaevernitz, *Britischer Imperialismus und englischer Freihandel zu Beginn des zwanzigsten Jahrhunderts* (Leipzig, 1906), p. 10. Also see his *England und Deutschland*, 3rd edn. (Berlin, 1911).

[2] *Ibid.*, p. 60. [3] *Ibid.*, p. 8. [4] *Ibid.*, pp. 65ff.

to Germany. The sharp decline in invocations of England's Germanic nature during this period indicates the end of Germany's identification with England rather than a decline in the relevance of racial inheritance, for racial doctrines probably gained ground in the university faculties.[1]

Even on the relatively rare occasions when England's Protestant-Germanic heritage was cited as an element contributing to her undeniable greatness, another factor still outweighed it: the state. The state, according to Schmoller and Hintze, for example, had laid its hand on the unformed English community and nurtured it to power. Of the opposite, formerly predominant view – that the freedom of the English from excessive state interference made England great – little trace remained.

Furthermore, commitment to the primary importance of the state and, as Kehr has suggested, the confusion of the state-idea with the current political form[2] determined the rise of Anglophobia among the German historians of this period. The Prussian school, on the heels of the Prussian state itself, had triumphed in 1871. The heirs of the Prussian school envisioned a higher goal for the Prussian–German state than its own bureaucrats ever could, and even those historians – like Marcks and Lenz – who consciously carried on in Ranke's footsteps committed themselves to the state extolled by Treitschke. Insofar as they still admired the English state, they egregiously misunderstood it by representing it as omnipotent and ubiquitous in English life. The new historically-oriented discipline of economics, whose meteoric rise reflected Germany's rapid industrialization, inaugurated this statist interpretation of the past. It sought and found mercantilism everywhere. The economic historians, above all, revived the didactic use of historical examples for the instruction of the present age. They reinterpreted the past – including the English past – in terms attractive to an expansive, imperialist generation. Their theories about English history attained dominance among German intellectuals as a promising generation of highly-skilled, objective specialists in English history fell silent. Delbrück once remarked that Treitschke's idea of a 'final reckoning' with England 'converted many a disciple and follower among the German people'.[3] Not Treitschke's words, but the national

[1] See Mosse, *Crisis of German Ideology*, ch. 10.

[2] Eckart Kehr, *Schlachtflottenbau und Parteipolitik 1894–1901* [*Historische Studien*, No. 197] (Berlin, 1930), p. 360.

[3] Delbrück, *Weltkrieg*, p. 222.

interests he represented and the means he approved in serving them swayed the minds of the German historians who followed him.

In the last decades before 1914, Germany – and Europe as a whole – embarked on an adventure of international scope which encouraged the recasting of her traditional image of England. The last time Germany's fate had depended so heavily on international developments had been the era of the French Revolution, when another profound change in her historians' view of England had occurred. The wars of unification in the 1860s, by contrast, had taken place chiefly within the German-speaking world, and at that time her historians had hesitated out of liberal sentiment from fully endorsing the actions of the Prussian state. By 1914, as in 1815, a large measure of unanimity about what England stood for characterized German historiography. In both cases the determining factor was the historians' commitment to a political ideal.

CHAPTER II

EPILOGUE

I THE DECLINE OF INTEREST IN ENGLAND

When World War I broke out, German officialdom quickly capitalized on the widespread sense of national crisis and solidarity by proclaiming a *Burgfrieden* (end to partisanship). Internal political disputes were to be put aside in order to close ranks for the international conflict ahead. The German academic elite, sensing that the imperial bureaucracy lacked the talent and means to give the war a 'deeper' meaning, rushed to fill the gap and take up again its duty as moral leader of the nation.[1] From the beginning, historians played a major role in defining Germany's 'mission' in terms ranging from high abstractions about culture to concrete ideas about territorial war aims.[2]

Although the imperial leadership and the general public may have been surprised by the English entry into the war,[3] German historians, as we have seen, had psychologically conditioned themselves to expect and explain Britain's intervention as a logical consequence of her pre-war politics. Thus their wartime polemics involved only a shift of their previous writings into a more popular and simplistic tone. Brentano, Hintze, Lenz, A. O. Meyer, Marcks, Michael, Oncken, Schäfer, and Schmoller, to name only a few, took part in the wartime polemics against England. The men who had written about England before the

[1] Schwabe, 'Politische Haltung der deutschen Professoren', p. 602f.

[2] Werner Sombart, for example, attempted to define the 'heroic' German cultural type by contrasting it to the English in his *Händler und Helden; patriotische Besinnungen* (Munich and Leipzig, 1915). Even Schmoller found his assertion that English character had always been absolutely determined by 'commercial spirit' somewhat 'one-sided'. (See Schmoller's review, *Schmollers Jahrbuch*, XXXIX (1915), No. 4, p. 402f.) Sombart's book was one of many which tried to answer the question, 'What values are we fighting for?' with a *Kulturtypenlehre* (theory of cultural types). For a brief discussion of the 'ideas of 1914', see Fritz Fischer, *Griff nach der Weltmacht* (Düsseldorf, 1961), ch. V. For a discussion of two opponents in the war aims controversy, see Wolf, *Dietrich Schäfer und Hans Delbrück*.

[3] Fischer, *Griff nach der Weltmacht*, ch. II.

war, however, seemed relatively restrained when compared to such newcomers as Sombart and the influential Berlin ancient historian Eduard Meyer, who brought to press the zealous teachings of the newly converted.[1] Even though polemical, these writings often granted the kind of grudging respect to a formidable enemy which had characterized Treitschke's later writings. Yet the predominant tenor, as in Treitschke's work, was one of denunciation and vilification. Indeed, critics of the lopsided conclusions of such works often used 'Treitschkean' as a descriptive adjective. As a poignant indication of the potency of war psychosis, however, those historians who could not agree with such distortions responded not with counter-polemics but with the less forceful weapon of chilly receptions in their reviewing columns; and even there they felt compelled to moderate their criticisms on the grounds of the authors' warm and commendable patriotism.[2]

With the passing of the war and, concomitantly, the state which the 'spirit of Treitschke' had striven to uphold, German historians quickly lapsed into a state of relative indifference toward England. Those older historians who still continued to write about their specialty may have felt rather superfluous in such a climate: Sir Lewis Namier actually had to rebuke Michael, whose works were being translated into English, for wishing to write a special preface 'apologizing' for his interest in English history.[3] Most of the books about England appearing in the interwar years fell into three categories: textbook treatments, discussions of England's relations with the non-western world, and investigations of what went wrong in Anglo-German relations before World War I.[4] Many of the titles produced under the Weimar Republic

[1] See Eduard Meyer, *England. Seine staatliche und politische Entwicklung und der Krieg gegen Deutschland* (Stuttgart and Berlin, 1915). Ironically, the more moderate historians who joined in the polemics against England were often attacked for being too *mild* in their judgments. As Willy Andreas wrote to Arnold Oskar Meyer in 1916, 'I have protected you here [in Rostock] against the charge of Anglomania, which is incidentally totally incomprehensible to me when I reflect about how many flies you found in the soup of English parliamentarism [in one of Meyer's wartime pamphlets].' (Willy Andreas, letter to A. O. Meyer, Rostock, 22 May 1916, *Nachlass* Meyer, *Niedersächsische Landesbibliothek* Göttingen, Cod. MS. A. O. Meyer, Folder 12.)

[2] See, for example, Felix Liebermann's review of Eduard Meyer's *England* in the *Historische Zeitschrift*, CXVII (1916), pp. 327ff., and C. Jentsch's review of Sombart's *Händler und Helden* in the *Grenzboten*, LXXIV (1915), No. 2, 62ff., which, like Schmoller's review, mentioned the irresistible 'spirit of Treitschke'.

[3] Sir Lewis B. Namier, letter to Wolfgang Michael, London, 7 August 1935, *Nachlass* Michael, *Universitätsbibliothek* Freiburg-im-Breisgau, Kasten 1.

[4] Examples of textbook treatment are Gustav Wendt, *England, seine Geschichte, Verfassung und staatliche Einrichtungen* (Leipzig, 1923); Wilhelm Dibelius, *England*, 2 vols. (Stutt-

attempted to dispel war-inspired animosities with a more understanding and sympathetic approach to English history. The relatively soft line of Britain toward defeated Germany, as in the Ruhr crisis, undoubtedly encouraged historians to rediscover England as the 'holder of the balance' against France.[1] Indeed, most of the interwar historical literature dealing with England appeared in the years between the Ruhr crisis and 1929, an era of relative prosperity and diplomatic reconciliation with Britain. The era of Hitler, however, witnessed a further sharp decline in historical works on England.[2]

Hitler's personal ideas about England, which have recently been studied,[3] developed almost parallel to the trends of German historical writing. Beginning about 1919 with the theory that England was Germany's natural enemy because of economic and colonial rivalry, Hitler regarded England from the viewpoint of Count Reventlow and other Anglophobe wartime polemicists. He soon added a charge that the Jews had ruined the country. Under the influence of the Ruhr crisis of 1923, however, he reverted to the notion that England sought to uphold the balance of power in Europe so as to concentrate her energies on overseas rather than European problems. If Germany could become strong enough to be *bündnisfähig* (alliance-worthy) and at the same time renounce naval and colonial aspirations, England

gart, 1923); Paul Hartig *et al.*, *Handbuch der Englandkunde*, 2 vols. (Frankfurt/Main, 1929–30); Hugo Preller, *Englische Geschichte* (Berlin and Leipzig, 1934); Bernhard Guttman, *England im Zeitalter der bürgerlichen Reform* (Stuttgart, 1923); Karl Brinkmann, *Englische Geschichte seit 1815* (Berlin, 1924); Felix Salomon, *Englische Geschichte von den Anfängen bis zur Gegenwart* (Leipzig and Berlin, 1923); Ludwig Riess, *Englische Geschichte hauptsächlich in neuester Zeit* (Berlin, 1926), and – on a higher level – Lujo Brentano, *Eine Geschichte der wirtschaftlichen Entwicklung Englands*, 3 vols. (Jena, 1927–9); all designed to acquaint the German public with a country which – it was consciously recognized – Germans had not been fully told about. Various titles on the Empire may be found in the *Bibliographie zur Geschichte des britischen Weltreiches in der Nachkriegszeit*, No. 10 of *Bibliographische Vierteljahreshefte der Weltkriegsbücherei* (Stuttgart, 1936). Diplomatic works include Rothfels, *Bismarcks englische Bündnispolitik*; Friedrich Meinecke, *Geschichte des deutsch-englischen Bündnisproblems, 1890–1901* (Munich, 1927); Gerhard Ritter, *Bismarcks Verhältnis zu England und die Politik des 'Neuen Kurses'* (Berlin, 1924); and his *Die Legende von der verschmähten englischen Freundschaft 1898/1901* (Freiburg, 1929); Max Lenz, *Deutschland im Kreis der Grossmächte, 1871–1914* (Berlin, 1925); and Hermann Kantorowicz, *Der Geist der englischen Politik und das Gespenst der Einkreisung Deutschlands* (Berlin, 1929) [the most pro-English of the diplomatic interpretations].

1 See Erich Marcks, 'England und Frankreich während der letzten drei Jahrhunderte', *Geschichte und Gegenwart* (Berlin, 1925), pp. 5–48.

2 See the rather slim list in Ado Jürgens, *Ergebnisse deutscher Wissenschaft* (Essen, 1939), covering the period 1933–8.

3 A. V. N. van Woerden, 'Hitler, Duitsland en de Engelse Wereldmacht', *Tijdschrift voor Geschiedenis*, LXXVII (1964), 403–38.

might strike a bargain to allow German hegemony on the continent.[1] Only later, in his 'second book', did Hitler develop a third view to resolve the inner contradiction in his own argument – why should England allow German hegemony if she pursued the balance of power? In his third view, Hitler announced that England would not attack just any preponderant continental power, but only one which threatened England's extra-European interests – so the Dutch and French in earlier centuries and Wilhelm II in World War I.[2] Perhaps because of the Nazis' abiding anti-intellectualism, German attacks on English policy and history during the Second World War fell mostly to party hacks; historians stayed out of Anglophobe propaganda work to a far greater extent than in 1914–18. Very few significant works on England by historians appeared during the war.[3] Instead, as a concession to slightly increased curiosity about England after the war broke out, writings on England by such deceased authors as Marcks and Treitschke were 'edited' and republished.[4] Only in a few unfortunate cases did reputable historians lend their names to thoroughly uncritical polemics against England.[5]

The decline of the German historians' interest in England continued even after the collapse of the Third Reich. Almost all histories of England printed in Germany between 1945 and 1949 were translations or revised editions of older works.[6] An authoritative report on major publications on English history in the decade after 1950 found only one German title worth mentioning – the final volume of Wolfgang Michael's *Englische Geschichte im achtzehnten Jahrhundert*.[7]

[1] This is perhaps the most famous of Hitler's several attitudes toward England. See Adolf Hitler, *Mein Kampf*, tr. by Ralph Manheim (Cambridge, Mass., 1943), pp. 664ff.

[2] Van Woerden, 'Hitler, Duitsland en de Engelse Wereldmacht', *passim*.

[3] See entries 5287–5336 in Gerhard Ritter and Walter Holtzmann, *Die deutsche Geschichtsschreibung im zweiten Weltkrieg* (Marburg, 1951).

[4] Marcks, *Englands Machtpolitik*, ed. and introduced by Willy Andreas (Berlin and Stuttgart, 1940); Treitschke, *England, der Brandstifter Europas*, ed. by W. Schneider for the NSDAP (Nuremberg, 1941).

[5] See, for example, Hermann Oncken, 'Deutschland und England', *Marine-Rundschau*, XLVI (1941), pp. 69–80. Here Oncken accused England of having unleashed World War II.

[6] See Richard Mönning, *Amerika und England im deutschen, österreichischen und schweizerischen Schrifttum der Jahre 1945–1949* (Stuttgart, 1951). The attempt to find themes in English experience which were relevant to postwar Germany had ceased to motivate German historians; typical minor exceptions were Johannes Tralow, *Cromwell. Der Untergang einer Diktatur* (Goslar, 1947), and Alois Winbauer, *Oliver Cromwell. Das Experiment der Diktatur in der englischen Geschichte* (Heidelberg, 1946).

[7] See Christopher Howard, 'Literaturbericht über englische Geschichte der Neuzeit Veröffentlichungen 1950 bis 1959', *Historische Zeitschrift*, *Sonderheft* I (Munich, 1962), pp. 88–122.

In the face of this evidence, it seems clear that the period of the most intense German interest in England ended with the First World War. After that time, England virtually ceased to be a problem, a special concept, or a model for German historians – with few exceptions.

The German intellectuals' search for an ideal commonwealth, one bigger and better than the particularist reality they knew in the eighteenth century, drew them at first toward England. The English state, with its strong traditions of justice, civic liberty, and security of property seemed preferable to any other existing regime in Europe; most Germans preferred it to the unrealizable abstractions of the French, particularly after they saw how those abstractions worked out in practice. Of course they idealized England in the process, seeing only freedom and dignity where there was in fact much misery and injustice. In order to set up their ideal, unified commonwealth they often placed hope in England as the natural protector of 'international justice'; here, too, they idealized England and unaccountably overrated her desire to encourage a united Germany. Because particularism often develops into nationalism via the intermediary community myths of common religion and race, England could for a time occupy an honorable place in the minds of German nationalists. Not all nationalism was integral nationalism. Until the mid-nineteenth century, such terms as 'English', 'Anglo-Saxon', 'Saxon', and 'German' [*Germane*, not *Deutscher*] were virtually interchangeable in references to England. Indeed, this somewhat careless disregard of the great differences between English and German cultural traditions seems to have been an essential presupposition for erecting an English-style political system: if imported constitutions were to work at all, they must at least have origins in similar tribal law, as the historical school of jurisprudence implied.

Once the Germans established their commonwealth in 1871, however, the English ideal became superfluous. Furthermore, they established it without direct English aid and, some said, against English opposition. The existence of a nation-state required a closer definition of what was 'German' – especially since millions of German-speaking people lived outside it. The now-predominant Prussian school thus glorified the Prussian–German state and forgot about the more cosmopolitan traditions of German cultural nationalism. The English libertarian political model having become useless and (as it drifted toward democracy) even dangerous, German historians began denying its applicability to Germany. They furthermore replaced the 'old', admirable England with a 'new', aggressive and barely European, let alone Germanic one. Both 'Englands' bore only a pale resemblance to the real one, of course; nor did the speed with which the new image replaced the old in German historical writing correspond to the much slower pace at which England was really changing. England was not less free nor much more aggressive in 1900 than in 1800, but in German historical writings about England, lavish adjectives for 'aggression' had replaced lavish adjectives for 'freedom'. The Anglo-German naval rivalry intensified the search for a specific German culture – as in the attempts to portray English and German Protestantism in quite different terms. Yet given the almost inevitable need of new nation-states for a virulent integral nationalism, one must ask if the political unification of Germany would not eventually have brought about the same result without a direct clash. The cultural climate which Meinecke associated with *Weltbürgertum* (cosmopolitanism) produced one historical ideal image of England; the one associated with the *Nationalstaat* (nation-state), quite another. The men who lived at each end of the nineteenth century – and each generation in between – followed a similar historiographical tradition in seeking to use the English past for their own purposes. In that fact, it would seem, lies the reason for the rise and fall of the German view of England.

II SOME REMARKS ON MOTIVATION

There can be no doubt that politics helped mold German thoughts and representations of England. In some periods, as before 1815 and after 1897, Germany's role in international politics deeply influenced what her historians said about England. In times of peace, when political or social reform most agitated the historians' minds, England appeared less as an ally or enemy than as a model for the moderate elements which wished political or social change without violent revolution. To some extent, naturally, England performed both functions at once, as in the periods 1789–1815 and 1850–70: those who sought English intervention in the name of German political integrity or unity often urged the adoption of English-inspired institutions of government as well. Yet, as we have seen, one period (1830–48) was dominated by concern with constitutional reform at home; another (1890–1914), with the struggle to expand abroad. These overriding concerns left their indelible stamp on the writing about England of these generations. One cannot otherwise explain the vast gulf which separates Raumer's description of England from Schmoller's, for example. In each generation a different political outlook singled out Britain for praise: at the time of the French Revolution, the Burkean conservative reformers; in the 1840s and 1850s, the liberal constitutionalists; after 1900, the social reformers.

Here one might object. An explanation of the vicissitudes of the German view of England solely in terms of changing political influences, one could argue, is dangerously vague and one-dimensional. The historians themselves changed over the century. Even though they owed much to such gifted amateurs as Möser and Niebuhr, German historians increasingly established their discipline as an academic one. As historical method became increasingly complex and specialized, historians devoted more and more time to study and less to politics. Historians after Dahlmann and Treitschke became more 'objective', perhaps, and less engaged politically. After 1870, German historians for the first time expressed broad satisfaction with the existing political order. To be sure, after a time some abandoned objectivity to become close supporters of imperial foreign policy and, after 1897, severe critics of England. Yet a critical attitude, no matter how motivated, is certainly more useful to the historian than uncritical and well-meaning adulation.

To settle the question of primary determinants of scholarly thought, we need something which does not yet exist – a sound psychological theory of perceptions based on a comprehensive sociology of knowledge and capable of extension to the past. What is known about German scholars in the nineteenth century (and that is little indeed) indicates a fairly uniform background in social class and social status rising with time. As historians more and more became professors, and as professorships became more and more desirable and difficult to attain, the social background of Germany's interpreters of England became richer, wealthier, more similar, and more exclusive. The demands of a developing profession left successive generations of scholars with less time to pursue other interests, such as politics or non-historical intellectual pastimes. Thus on the surface one could justify any number of clichés to explain the changes in interpretation. 'Non-political' professors at the end of the century may have had less didactic use for English historical myths than previous generations. Wilhelmine sons of the middle class, striving to achieve some sort of status equality with the aristocracy, may have been less indulgent toward the commercial and 'civilian' values which they perceived in the English state and society than were the fiercely proud bourgeois of early nineteenth-century Germany, who sought outside support for their struggle against the nobility and high-born functionaries of the German states. The secularization of thought, which swept the German academic subgroup of the bourgeoisie before any other, may have contributed to a decline in the relevance of England to Germans: by the early twentieth century, when Protestantism was taken seriously only for its 'ethic' and the normative values it supplied, the fact that England and Germany had both revolted against Rome did not ignite the imagination of North German professors. There is some truth in all these statements, but they do not really explain much.

Intellectuals perceive things differently from most men and are not so tightly bound to the totems and taboos of their society. Nevertheless, periods in history when old thought patterns have been abandoned and new ones not yet established leave the intelligentsia even less bound than usually. If Karl Mannheim is right in saying that 'the decisive fact of modern times...is that [the] monopoly of the ecclesiastical interpretation of the world which was held by the priestly caste is broken',[1] then one might well seek in the early nineteenth century in Germany the end of that break. For several generations, the intellectuals no longer constituted a closed caste but a competitive one. Writings on England reflected this competition: whereas before little had been written or known about England, from the late eighteenth century onwards an enormous amount of literature appeared. Much of it was inaccurate, but most of it had to be: it served as a weapon in the struggle for the establishment of new values, especially political and social values, in a rapidly-developing area with an increasingly national culture. Especially at times when the *status quo* had cracked or was barely holding up under sustained pressure, as in the Napoleonic era and the 'hungry 'forties', English history became more mythical but at the same time more useful to those who wished to increase the pressure. The second half of the nineteenth century, one could argue,

[1] Mannheim, *Ideology and Utopia*, p. 11.

witnessed a gradual closing off of options – in the nature of political organization, economic organization (both industrial and agricultural), and, finally, if one can use such a term, the organization of knowledge. The creation of the Prussian–German empire, a national industrialized economy, national pressure groups, and fairly fixed political allegiances (whether pro or contra) were all signs of this closing of options; so was the reassertion of a claim to ultimate intellectual authority by the university professors, who became the closest thing to a 'priestly caste' that German society has known since the days of the French Revolution. Of course only some of the professors perceived the 'national mission' as the gospel which they must interpret, and even these were not uncritical in their perceptions of the realities of the German national state. But it was clearly the German national state which provided the secular standpoint from which they judged past and present.

This does not mean that simple nationalism determined the change in view of England described here. Dahlmann, an Anglophile, was no less nationalistic than Treitschke and probably a great deal more so than many of the Navy Professors themselves. Likewise, 'liberalism' and even 'socialism' provided very different bases for judging English history, depending on which generation one happens to read. The English flag flew alongside virtually every political banner in nineteenth-century Germany at some time or another.

If a theory of perception is ever devised to fit the changing view of England among German historians, it would have to take into account not only high and abstract primary allegiances to church, state, and philosophies of man, but local and temporary allegiances as well. Often the diligent historian must confess the difficulty of ascertaining such provincial but important allegiances: the information is not and never will be available. It is clear that 'Anglophobes' such as List and Schäfer represented 'German industry' in its struggle for a native economy able to withstand English competition, but List's South German textile manufacturers and Schäfer's North German agrarians and shipbuilders did not share exactly the same view of England. For an 'Anglophile' like Ranke, stress on the common heritage of Protestantism happened to coincide with the Anglo–Prussian church alliance sought by Friedrich Wilhelm IV; for an 'Anglophile' like Marcks, stress on the divergent nature of German and English Protestantism coincided with the semi-official drive to justify German *Weltpolitik* as a superior cultural mission – a campaign which ended in the World War I banalities about Western 'civilization' versus German *Kultur*. But in the end these may indeed be coincidences, not motives – in fact, the problem is exactly to establish the higher motivation of coincidence. It is unlikely, for example, that Ranke wrote what he did about England just to please the Prussian monarch, even though he did become Historiographer of Prussia. The real test of a theory of perceptions is to establish contemporary cultural motivation behind such a coincidence.

There are some factors which one can rule out in a theory of perception, at least in this case. The study of English documents and writings by English historians did not play the chief role in the German historical view of England. German scholars pioneered the critical use of documents and actually aided the English in putting their documentary house in order. The German specialists on England, at least in the latter half of the century, usually knew all the major English works of history, judging by references in their works and the available inventories of their libraries. But documents and secondary works were usually consulted for facts, not interpretations. Like scholars everywhere, the Germans assumed that their stance, lying outside the shibboleths of another culture, gave them a chance for objectivity. They could think and write as no Englishmen could. The English appreciated this distance to the point of translating numerous German works of historical scholarship, but they tended to translate only the more innocuous writings about themselves. What was perhaps characteristic of German historical scholarship was the insistence by many 'Anglophile' writers that, despite hostile reviews in the English press, they actually were representing the 'true' English past to hostile audiences on both sides of the Channel. They often refused to admit that the same distance which allowed them a different perspective moved them from the position of giving an inside description.

Another factor which must be ruled out of a theory of perception is the concept of an international body of agreed truth. Certainly many foreign scholars could agree with the late nineteenth-century German view of England as an aggressive, hypocritical power obsessed by a Puritan heritage of conquest in the name of higher values. Likewise many European scholars shared the opposite view of England in the early nineteenth century. But such an interpretation requires a total abandonment of the sociology of knowledge and the postulate that intellectuals are subject to certain local environmental and temporal influences. It implies that scholars everywhere not only receive and read materials in several languages throughout their adulthood, but that they give them equal credence. It requires that they attend the same kind of school, have identical ambitions, identical ideals, and identical resentments. Even in the German academic world, closeknit as it was, such combinations were impossible. Indeed, it is astonishing that so many late nineteenth-century historians agreed on a basic view of England, a view much more complex and devoid of platitudes than that of their earlier predecessors.

Only by cutting themselves off from regional allegiances, by moving from one university to another, as they did, and by reading and believing a national press more than ever before, could they achieve any degree of national agreement. Even then, their agreement ended as soon as the discussion moved from contemporary Anglo-German relations to the question of past English affairs. The German historians of the late nineteenth century looked to Berlin more than any previous scholars. To be 'called to Berlin' was the ultimate flattery for a German professor, and the signals which emanated from that small building *Unter den Linden*, a few hundred feet from the royal palace and state ministries, reached out to the provinces in a new way after 1871. Not only was it hierarchically unwise to contradict a Berlin professor; the Berlin historical and economic professorate led the country in reevaluating English history. A century which began with the predominance of Göttingen in English studies ended with the predominance of the Imperial capital.

A theory of perception, then, cannot ignore the rise and fall of regional centers of perception. For one word which fell in Berlin about England, ten words would have to fall in Leipzig or Freiburg to offset it. In fact few words fell in the provincial capitals. Just as Berlin had the diplomatic monopoly of relations with the outside world, the university there exercised a sort of intellectual monopoly over interpretation of English history. Michael's students in Freiburg or Salomon's in Leipzig would learn much more about England; but it was Berlin which attracted the students, and a chance remark by Schmoller would gain wider currency than a book by a provincial professor. Perceived from Berlin, the world at the turn of this century was a hostile world, composed of European nations and the U.S.A. struggling for position.

Germany, endorsed by most German historians, sought to widen its power and influence in the world. Under the circumstances, it appeared inconsistent for a German historian to claim that England's dominance of a quarter of the globe was a rather haphazard outgrowth of several accidental factors. Wedded as they were to the aims of the new Hohenzollern empire, they felt called upon to justify what amounted to an attack on England's position in the world. Why they had wedded themselves to the Hohenzollern plan is a matter to be settled by a theory of perception, just as much as the reason for several generations before them wedding themselves to a variously-defined 'internal opposition' to the *status quo* in the German states. In the last analysis, the view of England among German historians varied *most* in relation to political priorities. These priorities happened to have conditioned the view of nineteenth-century German historians more than any other consideration, and it is probably for that reason that history enjoyed such high public esteem among Germans seeking political education. At the same time, German historians, knowing their place in the political life of the nation, consistently showed a heightened awareness of their role as prophets to their people. The uses they made of English history no doubt dignified and denigrated it to levels it did not deserve, but they used it in ways which raised history above the level of dead men and moldering paper. Their perceptions were based on a noble but implausible dream: that scholars can influence the course of history as well as describe it. Insofar as a theory of historical perception will ever have validity, it must start from this problem: how can the scholar divorce his view of the past from his vision of the future?

BIOGRAPHICAL APPENDIX

BIBLIOGRAPHICAL ESSAY

INDEX

BIOGRAPHICAL APPENDIX

(Note: I should like to express my debt to the *Allgemeine Deutsche Biographie*, the *Neue Deutsche Biographie*, the *Deutsches Biographisches Jahrbuch*, Kürschner's *Deutscher Gelehrtenkalender*, and Hellmuth Rössler and Günther Franz's *Biographisches Wörterbuch zur deutschen Geschichte*, which provided considerable information concerning men who have found no biographers.)

ARCHENHOLTZ, Johann Wilhelm von (1743–1812). Protestant. Born near Danzig and educated at the Berlin Cadet School, Archenholtz entered the Prussian army in 1759 and attained the rank of captain by his retirement in 1763. He traveled abroad until 1780 and lived ten years in England. He was appointed lay canon in Magdeburg Cathedral in 1780, a position which allowed him to start a literary career. He purchased an estate near Hamburg in 1792 and lived there the rest of his life. Archenholtz edited several journals in Hamburg, including the *Annalen der brittischen Geschichte*, *The British Mercury*, and *Minerva*.

BERNSTEIN, Eduard (1850–1932). Jewish. The son of a lower middle class Berlin family, he worked as a bank clerk before joining the SPD in 1872. He became secretary to Karl Höchberg, the editor of *Die Zukunft*. Persecution drove him to Zürich in 1878. There, from 1881 on, he edited and smuggled to Germany *Der Sozialdemokrat*. Deported in 1887, he made his way to the political haven of London and worked there as a contributor to *Die Neue Zeit* and the *Sozialistische Monatshefte*. Fabianism served to deepen his growing conviction that democracy rather than revolution would provide the best means of improving the workers' lot. Having returned to Germany in 1901, he led the right wing of the SPD and served in the *Reichstag* (1902–6, 1912–18, 1920–8). He followed the USPD in its split with the SPD during the war.

BLUNTSCHLI, Johann Kaspar (1808–81). Protestant. Of Zürich artisan background, Bluntschli studied law under Savigny in Berlin from 1827. He then became Professor of Roman Law in Zürich (1833–48). A reformer in Swiss politics, he was influential in the later codification of Swiss law. He then became Professor of Law in Munich (1848–61). There he edited the liberal *Staatswörterbuch*. Bluntschli succeeded Mohl as Professor of Law in Heidelberg in 1861. He represented the university in the

Baden Upper House until 1873, when he became president of the Lower House.

BRENTANO, Lujo (1844–1931). Catholic. Brentano was the nephew of Clemens and Bettina Brentano and the son of a Catholic religious writer of Aschaffenburg (Bavaria). He studied economics under Engel at Berlin; after completion of his studies (1868), he went to Britain to study working conditions. He was deeply impressed by the liberal viewpoint he found there. He began his fight for the integration of labor unions into the economy as a means of improving the workingman's position in society. English historic developments in that field became a major source of his rhetorical weapons. Returning to Germany, he taught economics at Berlin (1871–2) and became Professor of Economics at Breslau (1872–82), Strassburg (1882–8), Vienna (1888–9), Leipzig (1889–91), and finally Munich (1891–1916). While he had no sympathy for the harsh attitude of Manchester doctrine toward the working class, he was, in contrast to Schmoller and other colleagues in the *Verein für Sozialpolitik*, a free-trader and polemicist for the free economy. He became a moderate supporter of fleet agitation after 1900.

BUCHER, Lothar (1817–92). Protestant. The son of a schoolteacher in Pomerania, Bucher studied law under Savigny and philosophy under the Hegelians at Berlin (1835–8). He held Prussian legal offices in Cöslin (Pomerania) from 1838 to 1848. Bucher was a member of the Prussian National Assembly in 1848 and the Prussian Lower House in 1849 (left center). Sentenced to jail in 1850 for appealing to citizens not to pay taxes to an unconstitutional government, he fled to London, where he lived as a journalist (1850–61). Bucher wrote chiefly for the liberal *National-Zeitung*. He returned to Berlin under amnesty in 1861. He then served as go-between in Bismarck's talks with Lassalle and became a minor official in the Prussian Foreign Office (1864–86). Turning away from his youthful liberalism, Bucher aided Bismarck in various ways – drafting the first (unsuccessful) bill against the socialists, writing occasional articles in support of Bismarck's policies, etc. After 1890 he helped Bismarck write his memoirs.

BUNSEN, Christian Karl Josias von (1791–1860). Protestant. The son of a retired soldier, Bunsen studied theology and philology at Marburg, Göttingen, and Jena. Through his former teacher, Niebuhr, he entered the Prussian mission in Rome and collaborated in Niebuhr's studies of Roman history. He later pursued a career in the Prussian foreign service in Rome. After a period of disfavor because of his handling of the Cologne church dispute in 1838, he became Prussian ambassador to London through the favor of Friedrich Wilhelm IV in 1842. He was mildly liberal in 1848 and worked to convert the British government to the Prussian position on Schleswig-Holstein. For his advocacy of a 'western' orientation of Prussia before the Crimean War, he was recalled and retired. Until his death he worked in Heidelberg and Bonn as a private scholar. Bunsen was ennobled in 1857.

BUSCH, Wilhelm (1861–1929). Protestant. Born in Bonn as the son of a university professor, Busch was educated there and at Göttingen (*c.* 1880–4). He studied history under Maurenbrecher, who directed him to English studies. Busch taught history at Göttingen (1884–6) and Leipzig (1886–90) before being appointed Professor of History at Leipzig (1890–3), Dresden (*Technische Hochschule*, 1893–4), Freiburg (1894–6), Tübingen (1896–1910), and finally Marburg (1910 on). He lived in Marburg until the end of his life. After turning away from English history as a speciality, he made the struggle for German unity (1848–71) and Bismarck his main interests.

CLASS, Heinrich (1868–1953). Protestant. The son of a notary near Mainz, Class went to school in Mainz and thereafter studied law at the universities of Berlin (where he was impressed by Treitschke), Freiburg, and Giessen. After practical training in the law in Mainz he became an attorney (1895). Soon he became attracted to the antisemitic and racist *Deutschbund* and, in 1897, started agitating for the Pan-German League in Rhine Hesse. He did much to inculcate the Pan-Germans with their antisemitism. Rising rapidly in the organization, he became the deputy of the chairman, Ernst Hasse (1904) and finally chairman himself (1908–39). His annexationist propaganda, sometimes written under pseudonyms, was sufficiently aggressive to be embarrassing to the Imperial government before the war; after 1914 he figured prominently in the annexationist War Aims Movement and the Fatherland Party. Under the Weimar Republic he flirted with right-wing disloyal opposition to the state but lost influence under the Hitler regime's *Gleichschaltung* (coordination).

DAHLMANN, Friedrich Christoph (1785–1860). Protestant. Born in Wismar (Mecklenburg) in a family of government officials, Dahlmann studied classical literature at Copenhagen, Halle, and Wittenberg (1802–10). He taught classics at Copenhagen (1811–12). Soon, however, he was made Professor of History at Kiel (1812–29), although he had no previous historical training. He published *Kieler Blätter* with Welcker and involved himself with the cause of Schleswig-Holstein's 'historic' resistance to innovations by the Danish ruler. As Professor of History at Göttingen (1829–37), Dahlmann associated himself with the cause of constitutional monarchy. Dahlmann was removed from the faculty in 1837 as a result of his protest, with six other professors, against the suspension of the Hanoverian constitution. Eventually he obtained an appointment as Professor of German History and Political Science at Bonn (1842 on). After election to the National Assembly of Frankfurt in 1848, he became a leader of the right-center *Kasino Partei*. Although he brought about the fall of the Central Authority (the government) for approving the Malmö armistice with Denmark in 1848, he failed to form his own ministerial government.

Dahlmann approached constitutionalism from the right wing, that is, with respect for historical institutions. Born a Swedish citizen, he found his way to a moderately liberal German nationalism spawned on the Danish frontier of Germany and dependent upon Prussia for its realization.

DELBRÜCK, Hans (1848–1929). Protestant. He was born on Rügen Island (Pomerania), the son of a family of bureaucrats and teachers. After studies at Greifswald, Heidelberg, and Bonn (under Sybel, Noorden, and Schäfer), he tutored Prince Waldemar of Prussia (1874–79) and edited Gneisenau's papers (until 1882). Delbrück taught history at Berlin, first as a lecturer (1881–95), then as a professor (1895 on). Delbrück's controversial theories about military history held back his academic advancement. His fame came more from his journalistic writings in the *Preussische Jahrbücher*, which he edited (1889–1919). He considered himself an enlightened conservative, recognizing moderate change as necessary to the preservation of the standing order. He was affiliated with the Free Conservative Party and sat in the Prussian House of Deputies (1882–5) and the *Reichstag* (1884–90). He led the moderate wartime opposition to annexationism against its academic champion, Dietrich Schäfer, his old teacher.

DROYSEN, Johann Gustav (1808–84). Protestant. Droysen was born in Treptow (Pomerania) as the son of a pastor. After studying philosophy and philology under Hegel and Böckh at Berlin (1826–9), Droysen taught first in a *Gymnasium* (1829–33), then at Berlin. At first his speciality was classical history, but he developed a keen interest in contemporary problems as well. As Professor of History at Kiel (1840–51) he became involved in the fight of German nationalists against Danish integration of the Elbe Duchies. He represented the duchies in the Frankfurt Assembly of 1848, where he was active as a member of the right center and an advocate of a Prussian, Little German solution to German disunity. He retired from active politics after 1850 but remained a vocal champion of Prussia in his chairs at Jena (1851–9) and Berlin (1859–84). Droysen's works in the 1850s and later dealt with Prussian history, and he was one of the chief architects of the Prussian political mystique.

EICHHORN, Johann Gottfried (1752–1827). Protestant. The scion of a long line of Württemberg pastors, Eichhorn's background and training (at Göttingen, 1770–4) made him receptive to theological concerns. His major work as Professor of Oriental Languages at Jena (1775–88) and of Philosophy at Göttingen (1788 on) was accomplished in the field of biblical criticism. But he lectured history at Göttingen as well.

ENGELS, Friedrich (1820–95). Protestant. Born into a wealthy family of Wuppertal manufacturers, Engels became an opponent of the capitalist system. As a business trainee in Bremen (1838–41), he read the poetry of the Young German authors and the critiques of religion by Schleiermacher and Strauss. His family heritage of pietism having been cast aside, he was open to the teachings of the Young Hegelians of Berlin, where Engels devoted his free time from military service to learning. From 1842 to 1844 Engels lived in England, working in his family's business interests in Manchester. His first years in England offered opportunities for observing the effects of industrialization on working-class society, and his observations were shocking enough to turn him from utopian to revolutionary communism by 1844. He met Marx shortly thereafter and began the literary collaboration and friendship which lasted until Marx's death. He visited England periodically in the 1840s and lived in Manchester and London permanently after 1849. Engels achieved high standing as a military expert, and he contributed many articles to English newspapers in this field. Despite his long residence in England, he did not find close contact with the English working-class movement.

GENTZ, Friedrich von (1764–1832). Protestant. The son of the director of the Prussian mint, Gentz followed the family tradition of state service after attending the University of Königsberg (1783–5). His career went slowly, and he abandoned it as he discovered talents as a journalist in himself. Gentz's first great success was his translation (with commentary) of Burke's *Reflections on the Revolution in France* in 1793, a work which had converted him from his previous admiration for the revolution. From 1794 to 1802 he elaborated his anti-revolutionary ideas as a Berlin journalist. He visited Britain during the calm months after the signing of the Treaty of Amiens; his best expectations were more than fulfilled by what he saw. His pro-English stand made him unwelcome in neutral Prussia, however, and he finally took service with the Austrian government in 1802. In Vienna he unfolded his full powers as a publicist enemy of Napoleon. The failure of the Austrian uprising against French dominion in 1809 shook him deeply. Thereafter he developed into a close collaborator of Metternich, for whom he worked until his death. Gentz founded the *Neue deutsche Monatsschrift* and the *Historisches Journal* in Berlin as well as the *Wiener Jahrbücher der Literatur* in Vienna. He was one of the creators of political journalism in the German-speaking world.

GERLACH, Ernst Ludwig von (1795–1877). Protestant. The son of a high Prussian civil servant, Gerlach studied law at Berlin, Göttingen, and Heidelberg before entering the Prussian service himself. From an early association with the nationalist Father Jahn he moved into the circle of moderate conservatives around the *Politisches Wochenblatt* in the 1830s and on to the circle of extreme conservatives around the *Kreuzzeitung* by 1848. As a legitimist and supporter of strict religious orthodoxy, he became a leader of the extreme right in the Prussian House of Deputies in the 1850s. He ended his political career as a right-wing critic of Bismarck in the Prussian lower house and the *Reichstag*.

GERVINUS, Georg Gottfried (1805–71). Protestant. Born in Darmstadt into a family of artisans and minor officials, Gervinus was originally intended for a commercial career. By teaching himself, however, Gervinus qualified for university training at Giessen and Heidelberg (1825–30). Schlosser was his mentor in history, but his main interest lay in literature. His original and controversial writings on German literary history earned him an appointment first at Heidelberg (1830) and then at Göttingen (1835). His involvement in the protest by Göttingen professors against the suspension of the Hanoverian constitution in 1837 resulted in expulsion from the country. Returning to Heidelberg, Gervinus founded the *Deutsche Zeitung*, a liberal paper, in 1847. Although elected to the Frankfurt Assembly, he was disappointed by it and by the incapacity of the German bourgeoisie which the assembly reflected. After a trip to England in 1850 on behalf of Schleswig and Holstein, he began to turn his political hopes to the democratic countries (e.g. America and England), which he believed would crush continental autocracy. His writing thereafter incorporated these hopes at the cost of historical objectivity. Like his teacher Schlosser, he outlived his own popularity.

GNEIST, Rudolf von (1816–95). Protestant. Born in Berlin as the descendant of soldiers and lawyers, Gneist studied law at Berlin, where he heard Savigny and Hegel. On completion of his studies he became first a *Dozent* in law at his alma mater (1839), then a professor (1845). A reformer from the start, he was one of the major opponents of Stahl's teachings within the university. Gneist propagated his ideas about administrative reform in his Berlin classroom (he attained the rank of full professor only in 1858); as *Stadtverordneter* (city councillor) of the city of Berlin (1845–9 and 1858–75); in the Prussian House of Delegates (1859–93); and in the *Reichstag* (1867–84). Although he was an outspoken foe of socialism, Gneist sympathized with the working class: he was one of the founders of the *Verein für Sozialpolitik* and served for a quarter of a century as chairman of the *Zentralverein für das Wohl der arbeitenden Klassen* (Central Association for the Welfare of the Working Classes). His reform ideas ultimately bore some fruit in the Prussian *Kreis* legislation of 1872.

HÄUSSER, Ludwig (1818–1867). Protestant. Born in Alsace of a clerical family, Häusser studied history at Heidelberg and Jena (1836–39). Schlosser was one of his teachers. He taught all his life at Heidelberg, starting as a *Dozent* in history in 1840. He aided Gervinus in editing the *Deutsche Zeitung*, the voice of moderate German liberalism before 1848. He sat in the Second Chamber of Baden during the Revolution of 1848 and represented Baden at the Erfurt Parliament in 1850. In 1859 he renewed his leadership of the pro-Prussian, Little German party in the South German state. Finally he was appointed to the First (or Upper) Chamber (1860–5). Häusser's main political fame derived from his propagation in South Germany of the Prussian solution to German unification – a cause unpopular with Southern particularists. His writings, chiefly on German history, reflected his political sympathies.

HEEREN, Arnold Hermann Ludwig (1760–1842). Protestant. Although the son of a pastor, Heeren early absorbed from the environment of his native Bremen an interest in the world of trade. At Göttingen (1779–84) he abandoned theology for classical philology and history taught him by Heyne and Spittler. Adam Smith and Montesquieu also influenced him deeply through their writings. Aside from travels in Europe (1785–7) he spent all his life teaching at Göttingen, first as a philosopher, then as an historian. He founded the highly successful series *Geschichte der europäischen Staaten* in 1829. Raumer, Bunsen, and Bismarck were among his students.

HEGEL, Georg Wilhelm Friedrich (1770–1831). Protestant. The son of a Württemberg civil servant, Hegel was educated at the theologically oriented Tübinger Stift (1788–93). After passing his theological examination he served as a private tutor in Bern and Frankfurt/Main (1793–1800). In 1801 he entered the academic world as a *Dozent* in philosophy at Jena. The French invasion of 1806 led to Hegel's flight from that university. He worked as a newspaper editor in Bamberg until he found a position as rector of the Nuremberg *Gymnasium* (1808–16). Following a brief appointment to Heidelberg (1816–18), Hegel, whose works had by this time founded his fame, moved to Berlin where he remained thereafter.

HINTZE, Otto (1861–1940). Protestant. Born, trained, and employed all his life in Prussia, Hintze limited himself largely to the study of the Hohenzollern monarchy. After a short period of study at Greifswald in his native Pomerania, Hintze moved to the University of Berlin in 1880. He studied under Droysen, then fell under the influence of Schmoller. After devoting several years to editing the *Acta Borussica*, he joined the faculty of Berlin University in 1895 and taught there until his retirement in 1920.

HUBER, Victor Aimé (1800–69). Protestant. Born into a literary family, Huber was educated in Fellenberg's experimental school at Hofwyl and at Göttingen (1816–20). In his university days he changed from the study of medicine to literature but finally took a degree in medicine (Würzburg, 1820) which he never used. The historical bent of his uncle, A. H. L. Heeren, had impressed him at Göttingen, and he spent more time mastering the modern Romance languages and English than studying medicine. He was so dissatisfied with the illiberal conditions of Germany and the narrowness of academic life that he embarked in 1821 on several years of travel. He met many men of the liberal opposition in Paris during a half year there (1821) and showed great enthusiasm for the Spanish Revolution. He spent two years in Spain and Portugal, then a half year in England, before returning to Germany in 1824. After a period of unsuccessful studies and further travel to Paris and London, he worked as a schoolteacher in

Bremen (1828–33). During the 1820s Huber's political convictions, stimulated by romantic ideas, became less rational and more conservative. England, as the leading producer of liberal ideology, declined in his estimation. Huber re-entered the academic world as Professor of Literature and History first at Rostock (1833–6), then at Marburg (1836–43), and finally at Berlin (1843–51). His appointment to Berlin was motivated more by his promise as a conservative publicist than by his academic fame. After a trip to inform himself about working conditions in Belgium, England, and France, Huber returned to Berlin and founded the magazine *Janus* in 1845. Its articles against industrial abuses and constitutionalism, written mostly by Huber, failed to attract much attention, and only secret subsidies from the Prussian government could keep it going until 1848. Although Huber wrote for the *Kreuzzeitung* in 1848, he soon discovered that its backers were 'false' conservatives, more concerned about their power position than the plight of the poor. Quitting Berlin in 1851, Huber moved to the tiny town of Wernigerode where, except for travels throughout Europe, he remained thereafter, devoting himself to the study and propagation of working-class self-help methods.

LAPPENBERG, Johann Martin (1794–1865). Protestant. The son of a leading Hamburg physician, Lappenberg, like many other Hamburgers, went to England to finish his education. He became disillusioned with the study of medicine in Edinburgh, however, and tutored to support himself during the two years of his first British voyage (1813–15). Returning to Germany, he sought his career in law, studying at Berlin and Göttingen (1815–16). After another trip to England, he worked several years as a lawyer in Hamburg. As Hamburg's chargé d'affaires in Berlin (1820–3), however, he became more conservative and fell under the influence of Jakob Grimm. When an opportunity arose to direct the Hamburg Archives, he readily took the challenge. The work made him into a competent historian. He remained Archivist of Hamburg until shortly before his death.

LENZ, Max (1850–1932). Protestant. Lenz was the son of a Prussian official. He studied under Sybel and Erdmannsdörffer at Bonn and Greifswald (1869–74) and served in the Franco-Prussian War. The first part of his career, at Marburg (1876–88), was devoted primarily to Reformation studies based on the local archives. His biography of Luther (1883) made him famous enough to be called to Berlin (1890–1914) after an interlude at Breslau. He finally helped establish the reputation of the new University of Hamburg (1914–22) and retired to Berlin. Lenz tried to restore the spirit of Ranke to German historical writing. Many of his themes were borrowed from this great man, whom Lenz never met personally. Still, Lenz was too much a child of the *Reich* to escape from the influence of his teacher Sybel and of Treitschke and Lamprecht.

LIEBERMANN, Felix (1851–1925). Jewish. The scion of a wealthy Berlin manufacturing family, Liebermann was originally destined for business. After spending two years in a yarn-exporting company in Manchester (1871–3), he quit commerce for historical studies, studied under Waitz and Pauli at Göttingen (1873–5), and settled into the life of a private scholar. He occupied himself chiefly with collecting and editing medieval sources, especially English ones. He traveled to England frequently for his research, and his reputation there earned him honorary degrees from both English universities.

LIST, Friedrich (1789–1846). Protestant. The son of a well-to-do tanner in Reutlingen (Württemberg), List became a teacher of government at Tübingen (1818) despite his rather limited formal education. His journalistic activities on behalf of Württemberg constitutionalists and free traders eventually led to conflict with the government in 1819. After resigning his office, List got elected to the state diet but was prevented from taking his seat by government chicanery. After several years of wandering outside Württemberg, he returned in the hope of a pardon; he was told to leave or face jail. Thereupon (1825) List and his family migrated to Pennsylvania, where he learned about and propagandized the advantages of protectionism while making a small fortune himself. In 1832 he went to Leipzig as United States Consul. In succeeding years he traveled throughout Germany, proposing his dream of a national rail system and founding the liberal *Staatslexikon* and the *Eisenbahnjournal.* Amid his travels he wrote the *National System of Political Economy* (1841), the definitive nineteenth-century plea for protectionism. After his unsuccessful mission to England in 1846, he fell into despondency and took his own life.

MARCKS, Erich (1861–1938). Protestant. The son of a Magdeburg architect and a Huguenot mother, Marcks showed from the start of his career a cosmopolitan breadth of interest. After studying ancient and modern history at Strasbourg, Bonn, and Berlin under Baumgarten, Nissen, and Mommsen, he traveled in France and England (1886–7) collecting archival materials in modern history. Finally he began teaching at Berlin in 1887 with Treitschke's support. His range of successive interests went from the French Huguenots and the English Reformation to the life of Bismarck. He left Berlin for Freiburg in 1893, then served as professor at the universities of Leipzig (1894–1901), Heidelberg (1901–7), Hamburg (1907–13), Munich (1913–22) and Berlin (1922–8). He also served as president of the *Historische Kommission* in Munich and shared with Meinecke the honor of being Historiographer of Prussia. He tried to combine political history in the manner of the Prussian school with the objectivity and universal viewpoint of Ranke. He was regarded as one of Germany's best historical stylists.

MARX, Karl (1818–83). Born in a Rhineland rabbinical family converted to Protestantism in the post-Napoleonic persecutions, Marx began his studies at Bonn in 1834 with the intention of following in his father's career as a lawyer. His acquaintances with Young Hegelians in Berlin turned his purpose; his dissertation, finished at Jena in 1841, served notice of his political views by arguing against the right to existence of the state. His lectureship at Berlin was denied on political grounds, so he edited the left-liberal *Rheinische Zeitung* (1842) until his position became untenable. In Paris (1843–5) and Brussels (1845–8), he developed into a revolutionary communist. After the tumult of the 1848 revolution, which saw him in Paris and Cologne, he fled to London and settled there in great poverty to write his major theoretical works. From the early 1860s on he participated in the organization and leadership of various international workers' associations. He remained largely isolated from the English people among whom he lived, including the workers.

MEYER, Arnold Oskar (1877–1944). Protestant. The son of a Breslau professor, Meyer studied history at Tübingen, Leipzig, Berlin, and Heidelberg (1895–1900). He closely followed the interests of his teacher Marcks in Reformation England and Bismarck. He made several trips to England before the war and worked in the Royal Prussian Historical Institute in Rome (1903–8) before teaching at Breslau (1908–13), Rostock (1913–15), Kiel (1915–22), Göttingen (1922–9), Munich (1929–35) and finally Berlin (1935 on).

MICHAEL, Wolfgang (1862–1945). Protestant. The son of a Hamburg physician, Michael spent two years in England (1887–9) after his historical studies at Leipzig, Freiburg, and Berlin. He spent his entire career teaching quietly at Freiburg until the Nazis revoked his right to teach in 1937. His major work, *Englische Geschichte im achtzehnten Jahrhundert*, appeared over a fifty-year period.

MÖSER, Justus (1720–94). Protestant. The son of the director of the Chancellery of the Bishopric of Osnabrück, a church state which alternated between Protestant and Catholic control and consequently had experienced little of the innovations introduced by territorial princes, Möser grew up with a great respect for the older and healthier traditions of a rural German society which he imagined to have stood at the beginning of German history. After study at Jena and Göttingen (1740–2), he entered the civil service of his native state and rose to great eminence as a spokesman for the absentee government in London. He is remembered chiefly for his patriotic writings which criticized the French Enlightenment.

MOHL, Robert von (1799–1875). Protestant. The son of a high Württemberg civil servant and teacher, Mohl grew up in a rationalistic and liberal atmosphere. Following paternal wishes he studied law at Tübingen (1817–19), which he found dull, and Heidelberg (1819–21), then a leader in law. He taught at Tübingen (1824–45) and attempted to introduce French constitutional concepts into his law course. After a dispute with the Württemberg government, he quit Tübingen, dabbled a bit in politics, then accepted a post at Heidelberg (1847–61). Having studied English parliamentary institutions and police methods during a trip in 1847, Mohl was in a good position to serve as Minister of Justice for the revolutionary national government of Frankfurt in 1848. He ended his fruitful career as Baden's representative to the *Bundestag* (1861–5).

MÜLLER, Johannes von (1752–1809). Protestant. Müller's father, a church official in Schaffhausen, Switzerland, sent his son to Göttingen to study theology (1769–71). But young Müller was more impressed by history as taught by Schlözer. After a futile attempt at teaching languages in his native town, Müller first roamed through French Switzerland to escape the narrow atmosphere of Schaffhausen (1772–80), then, in 1780, moved to Germany. He worked in Berlin, then as a librarian in Kassel (1782–3), but, dissatisfied, he returned to Switzerland for three years. Finally, however, he entered the service of the electoral bishop of Mainz (1786–92) until French occupation drove him out. He then served the Austrian state in Vienna (1792–1804) and the Prussian state in Berlin (1804–7). In 1806 he was appointed Historiographer of the House of Brandenburg; typically for his unstable life, the following year found him serving the head of the Westphalian vassal state, Jérôme Bonaparte. He died in the office of General Director of Studies in the Kingdom of Westphalia. As a private scholar Müller rose to great popularity not only in Germany but abroad. His wide interests and many friendships made him privy to the inner circle of German cultural life in his lifetime.

MURHARD, Friedrich Wilhelm August (1779–1853). Born into a wealthy Protestant family of Kassel, Murhard led a privileged life, studying mathematics at Göttingen (1795–7) and visiting the orient (1798–9). He then lived as a private scholar in his native city, producing travel notes (1800–8) and helping edit the Westphalian *Moniteur* under King Jérôme Bonaparte. After 1813 he began a career as a liberal journalist and frequently faced arrest and harassment. When not in Kassel, he traveled a great deal. He edited the polite radical *Allegemeine politische Annalen* in the 1820s, succeeded Martens in editing the *Recueil général des traités* (1842) and contributed to Rotteck and Welcker's *Staatslexikon*.

NIEBUHR, Barthold Georg (1776–1831). Protestant. Born in Copenhagen and raised in Holstein as the son of an outstanding Danish family, Niebuhr studied law at the University of Kiel (1794–6) before moving easily into the position of private secretary to the Danish Finance Minister (1796). After taking a year off to study and travel in England (1798–9), he began his career as a Danish civil servant and rose to the post of Director of the Bank and Exchange Office in Copenhagen by 1804. Greater opportunities soon beckoned, however, and Niebuhr entered the Prussian civil service in 1806 (on Stein's invitation) as a finance expert. Refusing the portfolio of Finance Minister under the Hardenberg regime in 1810, he turned to lecturing Roman history at the new University of Berlin. During the excitement of 1813 he went to Holland to serve the Prussian government as plenipotentiary in subsidy negotiations with the British. From 1816 he represented Prussia in Rome. After the reaction set in in Berlin, he resigned and spent the last years of his life lecturing at the University of Bonn (1823–31). Although he virtually taught himself history, Niebuhr pioneered in the new historical-critical method in his *Roman History* (1811–32). In spite of critical methods, he idealized the early history of Rome as comparable to the state of the 'free peasantry' of his North Sea pasturelands. In his later lectures he held up this ideal against the 'mechanical' principles of the French Revolution, which he detested.

NOORDEN, Karl von (1833–83). Protestant. The son of a prosperous professional family, Noorden studied history at Bonn, where he graduated in 1863. After teaching several years at Bonn, he accepted a professorship at the provincial university of Greifswald (1868), then moved up to Marburg (1870), Tübingen (1873), Bonn (1876), and Leipzig (1877). Noorden was perhaps one of the last important German historians who followed the study of linguistics (Bonn and Marburg, 1851–5) before turning to history. His private studies with Ranke in Berlin (1856) turned him to history, and it was after that experience that he worked under Sybel's guidance in Bonn to become a critical historian. He traveled widely, stopping in London (1867) for research on his masterly history of the War of Spanish Succession.

ONCKEN, Hermann (1869–1945). Protestant. Born in Oldenburg, Oncken studied under Max Lenz in Berlin (1890–4) and then returned to work in the archives of his native province (until 1898). After a lengthy period as *Dozent* in Berlin (1898–1905) and a year teaching at Chicago (1905–6), he returned for a short stay at Giessen (1906) before becoming Professor of History at Heidelberg (1907–23). His interwar career included several years at Munich (1923–8) and Berlin (1928–34). His liberal sympathies and his attempt to revive Rankean objectivity in such works as *Cromwell* brought him to grief with the Nazis. His last writings on England, which went against the spirit of his earlier beliefs, appeared only after he was seventy.

AULI, Reinhold (1823–82). The son of a North German pastor, Pauli grew up in the Atlantic-oriented city of Bremen. He was educated in Berlin, first at school (1841–2), then at the university (1842–6), where Ranke taught him method. He also studied one year at Bonn with Dahlmann. Then Pauli went to England, where he lived as a tutor and private scholar (1847–50). He continued his historical hobby while serving as private secretary to Ambassador Bunsen in London (1850–2). Bunsen's failure to win

English support for Prussian aims in Schleswig-Holstein ended his and Pauli's official careers, and Pauli returned to Germany to teach. After two years of lecturing without pay at Bonn and Munich (1855–7), he received a call to Rostock, where he remained for two years. Pauli took Duncker's chair at Tübingen (1859–66) until his pro-Prussian sympathies in the 'war of brothers' made him unwelcome in that South German city. After an interlude at Marburg (1867–70), Pauli gladly taught at Göttingen for the rest of his life. His work on the Heeren series came about through a family friendship with Lappenberg. His accomplishments brought him honorary degrees from Oxford and Edinburgh. He was the last great general interpreter of English history to the educated German public.

RANKE, Leopold von (1795–1886). Protestant. The son of a lawyer and scion of a family of Thuringian pastors, Ranke attended the Christian-humanist school at Schulpforta and, thereafter, the University of Leipzig (1814–18). There Ranke studied theology and philosophy with the intention of becoming a minister. He always brought to his historical studies his youthful awareness of God's presence in the world. After beginning as a schoolteacher in Frankfurt/Oder, he wrote his great *Histories of the Romance and Teutonic Peoples* (1824). That work brought him to Berlin in 1825, and there he remained, actively teaching, until 1871. He was named Historiographer of Prussia in 1841. Shortly thereafter he traveled to England (1843) and married Clara Graves of Dublin. His *English History* was the product of research in England in 1858, 1862, and 1865.

RAUMER, Friedrich Wilhelm Georg von (1781–1873). Protestant. Born on the Elbian estate of Wörlitz (near Dessau) which his father leased, Raumer was quickly drawn to Prussia, where his family had influential relatives. After attending school in Berlin (1793–8), he studied law and political science at Halle and Göttingen, then entered the Prussian civil service in 1801. He rose to the rank of Councillor in the Finance Ministry (1810) but soon abandoned the civil service for a professorship in political science and history at Berlin from 1819. He founded the *Historisches Taschenbuch* series in 1830 and visited England in 1835. In 1848 he sat as a right-center delegate in the National Assembly and later in the Prussian House of Lords.

REVENTLOW, Count Ernst zu (1869–1943). Protestant. The scion of a North German noble house, Reventlow served in the Imperial Navy. After a trial on charges of insulting the Emperor, he resigned his commission and embarked on a journalistic career. Reventlow criticized Tirpitz' naval building program as too small and too slow. He wrote much about naval and colonial questions and became noted as a Pan-German agitator. He shared the leadership of the North German *Deutschvölkische Freiheitspartei*, a group similar to the Nazi party in the 1920s, before joining the Nazis and sitting in the Reichstag.

RIESS, Ludwig (1861–1928). Riess was born in Deutsch-Krone (in the Netze-District). He studied history under Delbrück at Berlin and received his doctorate in 1884. After teaching briefly, Riess left Germany to teach at the University of Tokyo, where he lectured on English constitutional history. He returned to Germany in 1902 and spent the rest of his career at the University of Berlin. He was still a professor extraordinarius at the time of his death, despite numerous books and his editorship (1909–13) of Schulthess' *Europäischer Geschichtskalender*.

ROTTECK, Karl von (1775–1840). Catholic. The son of a Freiburg doctor raised into the nobility by Joseph II, Rotteck soon became caught up in the rationalism of the Enlightenment. He left the church and studied law at Freiburg University (1790–7). He thereby alienated himself from his family's political conservatism and adopted the principles of natural law as his lifelong creed. He greeted the ideas of the French Revolution with approval, although he deplored the violence and bloodshed which accompanied their implementation. Rotteck became Professor of World History at Freiburg upon graduation. Although he lacked professional training in history, he learned so well that he could eventually publish a *World History* which sold phenomenally well. In 1818 he finally began teaching his real subject at Freiburg: natural law and political science. He represented the university in the First (Upper) Chamber of the Baden Diet from its first session (1818) until 1824. Rotteck, who represented a moderate form of French constitutional doctrine, soon brought the displeasure of even the relatively liberal ruler of Baden upon himself. In 1831 he entered the Second Chamber of the Diet as leader of the opposition. Because of measures taken against him by the Baden government and the *Bundestag*, his real public effectiveness derived from his editorship (with Welcker) of the *Staatslexikon*, the political Bible of pre-March German liberalism.

SALOMON, Felix (1866–1928). After schoolyears in his native Berlin, Salomon studied history at the University of Berlin under Koser, Bresslau, and Treitschke. He wrote his doctoral dissertation in 1890 under Koser on Scottish history. He traveled to England, did archival work for several years after 1890, and took up teaching at the University of Leipzig only in 1895. He remained there the rest of his life and received in 1915 the new title of Professor of West European History, which did not, however, bring an ordinary professorship with it.

SCHÄFER, Dietrich (1845–1929). Protestant. The son of a Bremen port worker, Schäfer struggled through a poor youth to become a schoolteacher (1863). A patron sent him to the university after he had acquired sufficient qualifications. He studied history at Jena, Heidelberg (where Treitschke impressed him deeply) and, after volunteering for the Franco–Prussian War, at Göttingen, where he received his doctorate in 1872. Returning to Bremen to teach in a *Gymnasium*, Schäfer took up the study of Hanse history and edited the *Hanserezesse*, a project founded by Lappenberg. This work remained his lifelong interest, even though he left the North Sea in 1877 to accept an extraordinary professorship at Jena. He subsequently taught at Breslau (1885–8), Tübingen (1888–96), Heidelberg (1896–1903), and Berlin (1903–21). Schäfer was active in the agitation for a big German fleet and was close to the expansionist thinking of the Pan-German League. He led their efforts to mobilize academic support for a maximalist war aims program in World War I. The Independent Committee for a German Peace was the body Schäfer created for this purpose; Delbrück led another camp of professors against it.

SCHLÖZER, August Ludwig von (1735–1809). Protestant. The descendant of two pastoral families, Schlözer studied theology at Wittenberg, then philology at Göttingen. Abandoning plans to take up the ministry, he traveled through Sweden and Russia for nearly fifteen years before returning to teach history and other fields at Göttingen. From 1769 to the 1790s he was one of the most popular lecturers and editors of Germany.

SCHLOSSER, Friedrich Christian (1776–1861). Protestant. Born in Jever on the North Sea as the son of an unsuccessful lawyer, Schlosser spent a somewhat unsettled childhood. He followed the poor students' recourse – studies in theology (at Göttingen, 1794–7) and many years as a private tutor (1797–1810) before receiving his doctorate at Giessen in 1810. He then taught school in Frankfurt (1810–14) until the end of French rule brought his school to an end. After an interval as city librarian in Frankfurt, he finally received a professorship at Heidelberg (1817). He wrote history in the spirit of the German Enlightenment and as a moral judge over the past. His works, particularly his *World History*, captured the public fancy to such an extent that new editions appeared even after the turn of the twentieth century. He represented the last formidable opposition to the critical method introduced by Ranke.

SCHMOLLER, Gustav von (1838–1917). Protestant. The son of a Württemberg civil servant, Schmoller entered the civil service of his native state as a statistician after completing his political and historical studies at Tübingen (1857–61). Although he had studied history under Duncker, his degree was in political science, and it was in that field that he taught once he abandoned the civil service. After a period at Halle (1864–72) he went to the newly refounded German university at Strasbourg for ten years. Although he believed strongly in the leadership role of the state, he quarreled with those (like Treitschke) who wished to make no concessions to the working class. When Bismarck turned to a paternalistic economy guarded by the state, Schmoller fitted better into the faculty of the University of Berlin (1882 onwards) because of his views. From 1884 he worked in the Prussian State Council. He also founded and edited the influential *Jahrbuch* which came to bear his name as a tribute to his influence on Prussian legal and administrative thought. Schmoller represented the University of Berlin in the Prussian House of Lords in 1899, but he did not engage actively in party politics. He preferred to work indirectly – through such organizations as the *Verein für Sozialpolitik* – for his political and social aims.

SCHULZE-GAEVERNITZ, Gerhard von (1864–1943). Protestant. The son of a professor in Breslau, Schulze studied economics at the University of Heidelberg; after travels in England (1886–91) and studies in Moscow (1892–3), he took up teaching at the University of Freiburg (1893–1926).

SPITTLER, Ludwig Timotheus von (1752–1810). Born in Stuttgart as the son of a Protestant clergyman, Spittler attended the theologically-oriented Tübinger Stift (1771–5). After travels in Germany during 1776, he returned to Tübingen to teach in the Stift. In 1778 he was called to teach philosophy at Göttingen, but in 1779 he became Professor of Civic History. He returned to Württemberg in 1797 to enter the civil service; in 1806 he was made Minister and Director of Studies in Württemberg.

STAHL, Friedrich Julius (1802–61). Brought up in the strict Jewish orthodoxy of his merchant father's home in Würzburg, Stahl converted to Lutheranism when he went to study law at Erlangen University (1819–25). After a period of suspension for belonging to a *Burschenschaft*, Stahl began teaching at the University of Munich in 1827. He soon fell under the influence of Schelling. In 1832 Stahl became Professor of Law at Würzburg and, in 1834, at Erlangen. He represented the university in the Bavarian Parliament, but his political activities soon prejudiced his career. Accordingly Stahl took a drop in rank to go to Berlin in 1840 as a *Dozent*. He soon became an outspoken leader of the divine-right reaction. In 1848 Stahl helped found the conservative organ, *Kreuzzeitung*. In 1849 he represented the extreme right in the Prussian First (Upper) Chamber; he also opposed the Prussian government's plan of German unification at the Erfurt Parliament of 1850. Stahl pressed hard for revision of the Prussian constitution, which seemed too liberal for him, and he was one of the proponents of a Prussian House of Lords.

SYBEL, Heinrich von (1817–95). Protestant. Born in Düsseldorf in a family of middle-class civil servants, Sybel studied under Ranke in Berlin (1834–8). In 1840 he began teaching at the University of Bonn, where his senior colleague Dahlmann inspired him with many liberal political ideas. He became Professor of History at Bonn in 1844, then moved to Marburg (1845–56) and Munich (1856–61). During the German Revolution he served in the Frankfurt Pre-Parliament and in the Diet of Electoral Hesse as a moderate constitutionalist. He also attended the Erfurt Parliament. Withdrawing from politics during the 1850s, Sybel founded the great German journal of scholarly history, the *Historische Zeitschrift*, in 1859. Becoming more active politically after the revival of the national movement in 1859, Sybel moved to Bonn in 1861 after political squabbles with the Bavarians and was elected to the Prussian House of Delegates (1862–4) as an enemy of Bismarck's policies. Only after 1866 did he gradually reconcile himself to the Chancellor. He sat in the Constituent Reichstag of 1867 and again in the Prussian lower house (1874–9). He moved to Berlin to become director of the Prussian State Archives in 1875.

TREITSCHKE, Heinrich von (1834–96). Protestant. Born in Dresden as the son of a Saxon general, Treitschke studied at Bonn (1851), Tübingen, and Heidelberg before taking his degree at Leipzig (1854). While at Bonn he had been deeply impressed by Dahlmann. In the 1850s he became convinced that the failure of 1848 had been the inadequate use of Prussian power to unify the nation. Treitschke's early deafness did not hinder him from pursuing an academic career. After teaching at Leipzig, he moved to Freiburg (1863–6), then after a brief period in Berlin in 1866, to Kiel (1866) and Heidelberg (1867–74). Meanwhile Treitschke was editing the *Preussische Jahrbücher*, in which he had been involved since its beginnings in the late 1850s. From 1874 on, Treitschke taught at the University of Berlin. He sat in the Reichstag (1874–84), first as a right-wing National Liberal, then, increasingly, as a Conservative. He finally became an opponent of all liberal and socialist causes and a moderate antisemite. In 1886 Treitschke was named Historiographer of Prussia. He ceased editing the *Jahrbücher* after a dispute with such comparatively liberal editors as Hans Delbrück.

VINCKE, Ludwig von (1774–1844). Protestant. The son of an old noble family of Westphalia, Vincke followed his father in joining the Prussian civil service after his law studies at Marburg, Erlangen, and Göttingen (1792–5). After initial training, he was appointed to administrative posts in Minden, his native town (1798), then in East Frisia (1803) and Münster (1804–6). Vincke fled to England in 1806 as his province and estates came under French control. There he was deeply impressed by English local self-government, and his observations influenced Stein's Nassau Memoir on the reorganization of Prussia. In 1813 he returned to his native Westphalia on the heels of a German army to take over as governor; after 1815 he administered Westphalia in the civilian office of Province President. He was admitted to the Prussian State Council in 1817, and he maintained his high position despite the Prussian reaction.

WELCKER, Karl Theodor (1790–1869). The son of a Hessian Protestant minister, Welcker studied law at Giessen and Heidelberg, after which he taught at Giessen (1813–14). In 1814 he was called to a professorship at the University of Kiel, where he and Dahlmann edited the liberal and nationalist *Kieler Blätter*. He subsequently taught at Heidelberg (1817–19) and Bonn (1819–23). During this last period he stood trial for being a liberal-nationalist 'demagogue', but he was acquitted. Welcker thereupon moved to the more liberal environment of Baden and taught from 1823 on at Freiburg, where he met Rotteck. As a member of the Baden Diet after 1831, he mediated between the radical liberalism of Rotteck and the more conservative variety of such North Germans as Dahlmann. In 1832 he was removed from his chair on account of his liberal political views. He worked then on the *Staatslexikon* and continued editing it after Rotteck's death. He sat with the moderate left in the National Assembly of 1848 and then represented Baden as plenipotentiary to the Frankfurt government. Until the advent of Schwarzenberg in Austria, he supported a Great-German solution to national unity.

BIBLIOGRAPHICAL ESSAY

PRIMARY SOURCE MATERIALS

UNPUBLISHED MATERIALS

Private papers were left by a large number of the authors examined in this study. Several of these *Nachlässe* are quite large and generally informative. Most are less extensive, full of lacunae, and sometimes poorly ordered. In several cases the literary remains turned out to be useless for this study, damaged in war, or inaccessible because of limits placed on scholarly use by the Interior Ministry of the German Democratic Republic. Nevertheless, I list such *Nachlässe* below as a service to interested scholars.

To mention the more useful collections first: the numerous papers of BRENTANO (*Bundesarchiv*, Koblenz) contain mostly manuscripts and letters *to* Brentano but little personal information. The DAHLMANN *Nachlass* (*Deutsche Staatsbibliothek*, East Berlin) contains large quantities of lecture notes, manuscripts, official documents concerning Dahlmann's political activities, and correspondence, mostly to Dahlmann. About a quarter of the correspondence was lost after 1945. A list of Dahlmann's library holdings sheds considerable light on his intellectual development. The papers of DELBRÜCK (*Deutsche Staatsbibliothek*, East Berlin), which appear not to have been used fully by scholars, are impressive, containing materials relating to Delbrück's autobiography, university matters, Imperial political life, and the worlds of publishing and journalism, as well as manuscripts, lectures, notes, and a vast two-way correspondence. The GERVINUS papers (*Universitätsbibliothek*, Heidelberg) contain a rich assortment of letters from Gervinus to prominent friends and associates, as well as materials pertaining to Gervinus' autobiography, poems, and manuscripts.

The *Nachlass* of LIST (*List-Archiv*, Reutlingen) is quite large and well-catalogued, but most of the more interesting materials in it have been published. The extensive papers of A. O. MEYER (*Niedersächsische Staats-*

und Universitätsbibliothek, Göttingen) and MICHAEL (*Universitätsbibliothek*, Freiburg-im-Breisgau) were less useful. Meyer's correspondence after 1920 is not yet open to scholars, so that few letters are available. Michael's remains contain very little in the way of letters or biographical materials. The MOHL *Nachlass* (*Universitätsbibliothek*, Tübingen), on the other hand, is a valuable source for letters to Mohl and memoranda on political questions. Mohl's letters to his family are located elsewhere (*Württembergische Landesbibliothek*, Stuttgart).

With the exception of one or two others, the remaining *Nachlässe* were of little importance. That of PAULI (*Niedersächsische Staats- und Universitätsbibliothek*, Göttingen) contains, in addition to a few letters, chiefly lecture notes. RANKE's *Nachlass* (*Geheimes Staatsarchiv der Stiftung Preussischer Kulturbesitz*, West Berlin) is chiefly an enormous collection of notes and manuscripts; the most important letters and diary entries have been printed – fortunately, considering Ranke's disorderly habits and awful handwriting. The ROTTECK papers (*Stadtarchiv* and also *Universitätsarchiv*, Freiburg-im-Breisgau) include, in addition to manuscripts of mostly printed works, letters which have been published. The TREITSCHKE *Nachlass* (*Deutsche Staatsbibliothek*, East Berlin) contains interesting information, but much of it has been published. Many of the originals of printed letters, in fact, have disappeared from the collection. WELCKER's papers (*Universitätsbibliothek*, Heidelberg) are fragmentary but contain some correspondence.

The group of marginally useful or inaccessible papers is large. I did not use the *Nachlass* of ARCHENHOLTZ (*Staatsarchiv*, Hamburg) because of its fragmentary nature and small size. BERNSTEIN's papers (International Institute for Social History, Amsterdam) promised to shed no new light on an already well-known life. BLUNTSCHLI's political papers (*Zentralbibliothek*, Zürich) and a few letters (*Universitätsbibliothek*, Zürich and Munich), small in scope, were not useful for this study. The fairly thin *Nachlass* of BUCHER (*Deutsches Zentralarchiv* I, Potsdam) and the somewhat more interesting one of BUNSEN (*Deutsches Zentralarchiv* II, Merseburg) may be used only with the permission of the East German Interior Ministry, which I could not obtain. Of CLASS'S *Nachlass*, lost during the war, all that remains is a microfilm of his *Aufzeichnungen* (*Bundesarchiv*, Koblenz). DROYSEN'S papers consist chiefly of manuscripts and letters to Droysen (*Deutsches Zentralarchiv* I, Potsdam) and were not available to me. Letters to his son (*Universitäts- und Landesbibliothek Sachsen-Anhalt*, Halle) and copies of parts of the *Nachlass* meant for publication (*Universitätsbibliothek*, Jena) complete the preserved remains. The DUNCKER *Nachlass*, except for two letters, appears to have been lost in 1945. The ENGELS *Nachlass* (International Institute for Social History, Amsterdam) has been too well publicized to require my visiting it.

The GNEIST *Nachlass* (*Deutsches Zentralarchiv* II, Merseburg) contains personal papers and correspondence, but I was not allowed to see it. HEEREN's papers (*Niedersächsische Staats- und Universitätsbibliothek*, Göttingen), consisting of partly illegible and poorly ordered lecture notes and manuscripts of printed works, was of no use. HINTZE's literary remains (*Deutsches Zentralarchiv* II, Merseburg), like those of HUBER (*Deutsches Zentralarchiv* I, Potsdam), were closed to me. Most of LAPPENBERG's papers have disappeared. Some of LENZ's papers burned during the war; what is left (*Deutsche Akademie der Wissenschaften*, East Berlin) was not available to me. I did not consult the Johannes von MÜLLER papers (*Stadtbibliothek*, Schaffhausen), since a large part of his correspondence has been published. The NIEBUHR papers share the location and (hopefully temporary) inaccessibility of Lenz's; some others, also closed to me, are in Merseburg (*Deutsches Zentralarchiv* II). The papers of NOORDEN (*Universitätsbibliothek*, Leipzig) and ONCKEN (*Staatsarchiv*, Oldenburg) appeared relatively unpromising for this study and were not consulted. The papers of RIESS (*Politisches Archiv des Auswärtigen Amtes*, Bonn) proved to be only fragments of memoranda about Japan. SCHÄFER's papers are assumed to have burned during the war. SCHLOSSER's *Nachlass* (*Stadt- und Universitätsbibliothek*, Frankfurt-am-Main) contains only a few unimportant letters. SCHMOLLER's papers (*Deutsches Zentralarchiv* II, Merseburg) require permission which I could not obtain. SYBEL's remains (*Deutsche Staatsbibliothek*, East Berlin) were not very useful. The VINCKE papers, spread out over three locations (*Staatsarchiv*, Münster; *Staatsarchiv*, Osnabrück; *Stadt- und Landesbibliothek*, Dortmund) contain little of direct biographical importance.

PUBLISHED MATERIALS

Among the primary sources for this study – all published – are autobiographies, memoirs, and letters, political encyclopedias and general treatises on government, narrative histories ranging from universal down to national scope, travel literature, and monographs and articles dealing with special aspects of English internal politics, relations with the outside world, economic and social development, and culture.

AUTOBIOGRAPHIES, LETTERS, AND MEMOIRS

Generally speaking, memoirs and letters provided only limited insights into attitudes toward England, but they often corroborated statements made in other writings by the same author and threw some light upon motivations and contexts of those statements. Eduard BERNSTEIN's *Aus den Jahren meines Exils* (Berlin, 1913) shows how the man who began as a co-worker of Engels in England evolved into a revisionist under the influence of English Fabianism. The *Reden*, *Briefe*, and *Erinnerung und Gedanke*, vols. X–XV of

Die gesammelten Werke, 19 vols. (Berlin, 1924–35), of Otto, Prince von BISMARCK, constitute the major sources of his views of England, which varied considerably with the occasion and the format of his remarks. Johann Kaspar BLUNTSCHLI's *Denkwürdiges aus meinem Leben*, edited by Rudolf Sayerlen, 3 pts. (Nördlingen, 1884) reveals more about the great law professor's role in Swiss and German affairs than his attitude toward England. Lujo BRENTANO's *Mein Leben im Kampf um die soziale Entwicklung Deutschlands* (Jena, 1931) is a rich mine for the social historian, reflecting the author's intense personal involvement with the 'social question', his indebtedness both to Cobden and the English labor movement, and his nascent irritation at the English for abandoning Cobden's principles. The interesting collection of materials on and by Lothar BUCHER in *Ein Achtundvierziger: Lothar Buchers Leben und Werke*, 3 vols. (Berlin, 1890–4) is somewhat marred by the unsystematic and partisan editing of Heinrich von Poschinger. Christian Karl Josias von BUNSEN's *A Memoir of Baron Bunsen, Drawn Chiefly from Family Papers by His Widow*, 2 vols. (Philadelphia and London, 1868) vividly demonstrates the closeness of Anglo–Prussian relations during the reign of Friedrich Wilhelm IV despite disagreements on commercial questions and Schleswig-Holstein. The temper of the Anglophile, constitutional 'pre-March' liberalism is reflected in letters of Friedrich Christoph DAHLMANN and Georg Gottfried GERVINUS published by Eduard Ippel as *Briefwechsel zwischen Jakob und Wilhelm Grimm, Dahlmann und Gervinus*, 2 vols. (Berlin, 1885–6). Hans DELBRÜCK's *Erinnerungen, Aufsätze, Reden* (Berlin, 1902) contains only hints showing his relatively objective attitude toward England. Likewise the letters in *Ignaz Döllinger und Lord Acton. Briefwechsel, 1850–1890* (Munich, 1963), edited by Victor Conzemius, disappoint the searcher for South German Catholic attitudes toward England.

The letters of two of the most uncompromising members of the Prussian school, Johann Gustav DROYSEN's *Briefwechsel*, edited by R. Hübner, 2 vols. (Stuttgart and Berlin, 1929) and Max DUNCKER's *Politischer Briefwechsel aus seinem Nachlass* (Stuttgart, 1923) say little about England but speak vividly of the contemporary political philosophy of the authors. *Karl Friedrich Eichhorn, Sein Leben und Wirken nach seinen Aufzeichnungen, Briefen, Mitteilungen von Angehörigen, Schriften*, edited by Johann von Schulte (Stuttgart, 1884), is one of those rare candid collections which open many doors on the inner workings of German academic life. Friedrich von GENTZ showed his early enthusiasm for England in vol. II of *Briefe von und zu Friedrich von Gentz*, edited by F. K. Wittichen, 3 vols. (Munich and Berlin, 1909–13); his later disappointment emerges from vol. III of the same collection and in *Briefe von Friedrich von Gentz an Pilat*, edited by Karl Mendelssohn-Bartholdy, 2 vols. (Leipzig, 1868), and *Aus dem Nachlass des Grafen Prokesch-Osten*, 2 vols. (Vienna, 1881). That a romantic Prussian conservative need not be an enemy of England is evidenced in Ludwig von GERLACH's *Aufzeichnungen aus seinem Leben und Wirken 1795–1877*, edited by Jakob von Gerlach, 2 vols. (Schwerin, 1903). Georg Gottfried GERVINUS chronicled his own life in 1860, later published as *Leben von ihm selbst* (Leipzig, 1893). Arnold Hermann Ludwig HEEREN, another 'original' among German historians, gave a charming account of his life in 'Biographische Nachrichten über den Verfasser', in *Historische Werke*, 15 vols. (Göttingen, 1821–6), I. The ambivalence of the Little German historians toward England – and their tendency to think little about a power only marginally involved in their hopes – emerges from the letters in *Deutscher Liberalismus im Zeitalter Bismarcks. Eine politische Briefsammlung*, edited by Julius Heyderhoff and Paul Wentzcke, 2 vols. (Bonn and Leipzig, 1925–6). Robert von MOHL's *Lebenserinnerungen, 1799–1875*, 2 vols. (Stuttgart and Leipzig, 1902), like the EICHHORN materials, reveals much about German academic life. Biographical materials and letters of Adam MÜLLER appear in his *Ausgewählte Abhandlungen*, edited by Jakob Baxa (Jena, 1921). Johannes von MÜLLER's *Briefe an Freunde*, vols. XXXVIII–XL of his *Sämmtliche Werke*, edited by J. J. Müller, 40 vols. (Stuttgart and Tübingen, 1831ff.) suffer from the manner in which they are printed and edited. NIEBUHR's letters appeared in an edition by Dietrich Gerhard and William Norvin, *Briefe*, 2 vols. (Berlin, 1926–9). The best source on Reinhold PAULI is his *Lebenserinnerungen nach Briefen und Tagebüchern*, edited by Elisabeth Pauli (Halle, 1895).

The rich collections of diaries and letters by Leopold von RANKE, the *Briefe* in vols. LIII–LIV of Ranke's *Sämmtliche Werke*, 54 vols. (Leipzig, 1868–90), *Neue Briefe*, edited by Bernard Hoeft and Hans Herzfeld (Hamburg, 1949), *Das Briefwerk*, edited by Walter Peter Fuchs (Hamburg, 1949), and the *Tagebücher*, edited by Fuchs and Theodor Schieder (Munich and Vienna, 1964) were particularly valuable, because this most cautious of historians expressed his sentiments more profusely in private than in his works. Neither Friedrich von RAUMER's *Lebenserinnerungen und Briefwechsel* (Leipzig, 1861) nor Karl von ROTTECK's *Briefwechsel*, vol. V of his *Gesammelte und nachgelassene Schriften mit Biographie und Briefwechsel*, edited by Hermann von Rotteck, 5 vols. (Pforzheim, 1841–3) reveals much more about their views of England than their writings. Dietrich SCHÄFER produced an autobiography, *Mein Leben* (Berlin, 1926), at the end of his career. *Aus August Ludwig Schlözers öffentliches und Privateleben von ihm selbst beschrieben*, edited by Beyer-Fröhlich (Leipzig, 1934) is more revealing about SCHLÖZER's view of Russia than of England. Heinrich von TREITSCHKE's correspondence, in *Heinrich von Treitschkes Briefe*, edited by Max Cornicelius, 3 vols. (Leipzig, 1912–20) and *Briefe Heinrich von Treitschkes an Historiker und Politiker vom Oberrhein*, edited by Willy Andreas (Berlin, 1934), gives valuable insights into the author's character and motives. The background of German views of English self-government can be found in Ludwig von VINCKE's *Briefwechsel zwischen Stein und Vincke*, edited by Heinrich Kochendörffer (Münster, 1930).

ENCYCLOPEDIAS AND TREATISES ON POLITICAL THEORY

The need of the German middle class for popular instruction in constitutional theory and practice explains the publication and widespread influence of the advanced liberal *Staatslexikon oder Encyclopädie der Staatswissenschaften*, edited by Karl von ROTTECK and Karl WELCKER, 18 vols. including *Supplement* (Altona, 1835–48) and, as it became outdated, the *Deutsches Staatswörterbuch*, edited by Johann Kaspar BLUNTSCHLI and Karl BRATER, 11 vols. (Stuttgart and Leipzig, 1857–70). Although both these political encyclopedias praised England, the different way in which each did so reveals much about changing German political values. Less voluminous treatises on political theory ranged from Friedrich Christoph DAHLMANN's *Die Politik auf den Grund und das Mass der gegebenen Zustände zurückgeführt* (Göttingen, 1835), a moderate liberal bible, to Friedrich Julius STAHL's reactionary *Das monarchische Prinzip. Eine staatsrechtlich-politische Abhandlung* (Heidelberg, 1845). The argument for a protectionist economy put forth in Friedrich LIST's 1841 edition of *The National System of Political Economy*, translated by S. S. Lloyd, new edn. (London, 1904) fell upon comparatively barren ground. The progression of advanced German political thinking in the last half of the century is reflected in Robert von MOHL's *Enzyklopädie der Staatswissenschaften* (Tübingen, 1859), Heinrich von TREITSCHKE's *Politik*, edited by Max Cornicelius, 2 vols. (Leipzig, 1897–8), and Eduard BERNSTEIN's revisionist treatise, *Die Voraussetzungen des Sozialismus und die Aufgaben der Sozialdemokratie* (Stuttgart, 1899). All of these works drew upon English examples.

UNIVERSAL AND EUROPEAN HISTORIES

Because the first good German history of England did not appear until the nineteenth century was already in its fourth decade, the attitudes of German historians had to be sought in world and European histories as well. The early nineteenth-century universal histories – Karl von ROTTECK's *Allgemeine Geschichte vom Anfang der historischen Kenntnis bis auf unsere Zeiten*, 15 vols. (Freiburg, 1812–44), Johann Gottfried EICHHORN's *Weltgeschichte*, 3 vols. (Göttingen, 1817), and Friedrich Christoph SCHLOSSER's *Weltgeschichte für das deutsche Volk*, 19 vols. (Frankfurt/Main, 1844–57) – were didactic Enlightenment stories of civilization which drew upon past events to illustrate their point. While world histories remained popular among the lay readers, respected historians shunned them after mid-century; only when Germany became involved in world politics and Ranke himself had turned to universal history did a revival set in. Such works as Maximilian, Count

Yorck von WARTENBURG's *Weltgeschichte in Umrissen* (Berlin, 1900), Dietrich SCHÄFER's *Weltgeschichte der Neuzeit*, 2 vols. (Berlin, 1922), and Hans DELBRÜCK's *Weltgeschichte. Vorlesungen*, 6 pts. (Berlin, 1925–31) reflected that revival. On the less sweeping level of European histories, the early nineteenth-century historians were more at home. Ludwig Timotheus SPITTLER's *Entwurf der Geschichte der europäischen Staaten*, 2 vols. (Berlin, 1793–4), Arnold Hermann Ludwig HEEREN's *Handbuch der Geschichte des europäischen Staatensystems und seiner Kolonien* (Göttingen, 1809), Johann Gottfried EICHHORN's *Geschichte der letzten drei Jahrhunderte*, 2 vols. (Göttingen, 1804) and its continuations in the third edition, 6 vols. (Hanover, 1817–18) and in *Geschichte des neunzehnten Jahrhunderts* (Hanover, 1817), Johannes von MÜLLER's *Vierundzwanzig Bücher allgemeiner Geschichten, besonders der europäischen Menschheit*, 3 vols. (Stuttgart, 1810–11), and Friedrich Christoph SCHLOSSER's *Geschichte des achtzehnten Jahrhunderts in gedrängter Übersicht*, 2 pts. (Heidelberg, 1823) and subsequent editions all attained high standards and popularity as Enlightenment-inspired treatments of modern history. One of the last and most exhaustive examples of this genre was Friedrich von Raumer's *Geschichte Europas seit dem Ende des 15. Jahrhunderts*, 8 vols. (Leipzig, 1832–50). The dilemma which increasing specialization forced upon writers of European-wide narrative histories was reflected in Georg Gottfried GERVINUS's *Einleitung in die Geschichte des 19. Jahrhunderts* (Leipzig, 1853) and *Geschichte des 19. Jahrhunderts seit den Wiener Verträgen*, 8 vols. (Leipzig, 1853–66), which attempted to organize history under an idiosyncratic democratic ideology. More objective historians faced the problem by severely limiting their chronological focus, as Heinrich von SYBEL did in his *Geschichte der Revolutionszeit von 1789 bis 1795*, 3 vols. (Düsseldorf, 1853–8), later brought up to 1800 with vols. IV–V (Düsseldorf, 1870–4), and Karl von NOORDEN in his *Geschichte des spanischen Erbfolgekrieges*, 3 vols. (Leipzig, 1870–82). Toward the end of the century, Onno KLOPP's *Der Fall des Hauses Stuart und die Succession des Hauses Hannover in Grossbritannien und Irland im Zusammenhange der europäischen Angelegenheiten von 1660–1714*, 14 vols. (Vienna, 1875–88) graphically demonstrated the difficulties of European-wide narrative history even when the author had a distinct (pro-Habsburg) viewpoint and thousands of pages at his disposal.

NARRATIVE HISTORIES OF ENGLAND AND BIOGRAPHIES

The same tendency to specialize which made universal histories unfashionable gave rise to narratives organized on a national level. Johann Martin LAPPENBERG's *Geschichte von England*, 2 vols. (Hamburg, 1834–7), emphasizing Anglo-Saxon cultural continuity even after 1066, was a pioneer work in the remote 'Germanic' phase of England's development. Reinhold PAULI continued Lappenberg's work (a part of the Heeren series of European national histories) in his *Geschichte von England*, 3 vols. (Gotha, 1851–8), which carried the story from 1154 to 1509. Leopold von RANKE, Pauli's teacher, provided an excellent narrative from the Reformation to the Hanoverian succession in his *Englische Geschichte vornehmlich im sechzehnten und siebzehnten Jahrhundert*, 7 vols. and Register (Berlin, 1859–68). All these works gained critical acclaim in England as well as Germany. Pauli, instead of duplicating Ranke's work by continuing his history, leaped to the latest times – up to 1852 – in his *Geschichte Englands seit dem Friedensschluss von 1814 und 1815*, 3 vols. (Leipzig, 1864–75), a thorough, solid, and objective treatment. Only with Moritz BROSCH's *Geschichte von England*, 5 vols. (Gotha, 1890–7) was the Heeren series brought to its conclusion, but Brosch lacked the intense personal involvement in English history and the style which characterized his predecessors. His judgments were confused, inconsistent, and strongly influenced by current events. Ignoring Brosch's efforts, Wolfgang MICHAEL sought in his *Englische Geschichte im 18. Jahrhundert*, 5 vols. (Hamburg, Berlin, and Basel, 1896–1955) to fill the major gap left by Lappenberg, Pauli, and Ranke – the eighteenth century. His work, unlike Brosch's, also found critical acclaim in England despite failings of style and verbosity.

In addition to broad narrative histories, German historians produced many works on special periods and individuals. The demand among feminine readers for historical heroines undoubtedly encouraged such biographies as Johann Wilhelm von ARCHENHOLTZ's *Geschichte der Königin Elisabeth von England* (Leipzig, 1789), Friedrich von GENTZ's *Maria, Königin von Schottland* (Brunswick, 1799), and Friedrich von RAUMER's *Die Königinnen Elisabeth und Maria Stuart, nach den Quellen* (Leipzig, 1836), the only critical treatment. The Germans' awakened interest in the early Germanic inhabitants of England found expression in Georg Gottfried GERVINUS' first work, *Geschichte der Angelsachsen im Überblick* (Frankfurt/Main, 1830). In the politically charged atmosphere of the subsequent decade, Friedrich Christoph DAHLMANN's *Geschichte der englischen Revolution* (Leipzig, 1844) was as much a warning to German monarchs as a history. Although PAULI was an objective historian, one can find in his biographical writings after 1850 some of the political criteria of the national-liberal movement: his laudatory *König Aelfred und seine Stellung in der Geschichte Englands* (Berlin, 1851) stressed the unifying hand of the 'father of the English state' in contrast to the freedom-loving Alfred portrayed by Karl von Rotteck, a cosmopolitan liberal, in his 'Alfred der Grosse', in *Gesammelte und nachgelassene Schriften* I, 93–9. Pauli's *Simon von Montfort, Graf von Leicester, der Schöpfer des Hauses der Gemeinen* (Tübingen, 1867) praised Montfort as a furtherer of 'self-government', about which German liberals in the 1860s were excited. Yet national liberals like Pauli were not yet ready to surrender constitutional liberties as the price of national unification; that became clear from Pauli's article, 'Heinrich VIII und seine neuesten Beurteiler', *Historische Zeitschrift*, III (1860), 97–132. Many of Pauli's vivid biographical portrayals of English figures were collected under the title *Aufsätze zur englischen Geschichte*, 2 vols. (Leipzig, 1869–83). Karl von NOORDEN's best English biographical essays – on William III, Bolingbroke, Swift, and Fox – are available in his *Historische Vorträge* (Leipzig, 1884). Moritz BROSCH also entered eighteenth-century political biography with his *Lord Bolingbroke und die Whigs und Tories seiner Zeit* (Frankfurt/Main, 1883).

The increasing tendency of German historians after Bismarck's unification of Germany to stress forceful, integrating rulers found expression in Moritz BROSCH's disappointing *Oliver Cromwell und die puritanische Revolution* (Frankfurt/Main, 1888), Wolfgang MICHAEL's more convincing *Cromwell*, 2 vols. (Berlin, 1907), and Wilhelm BUSCH's *England unter den Tudors* (Stuttgart, 1892). As the Anglo-German rivalry prompted German Anglophiles to look back wistfully on their 'best friend' among the English, biographical treatments of Carlyle such as Gerhard von SCHULZE-GAEVERNITZ' *Carlyle, seine Welt- und Gesellschaftsanschauung* (Berlin, 1897) were especially welcome. Erich MARCKS, a master of the elegant biographical essay, reminded his countrymen of a more admirable England in his *Königin Elisabeth von England und ihre Zeit* (Bielefeld, 1897). But his inability to keep up his faith in a benign England brought about a darkening of his view in 'Der jüngere Pitt und seine Zeit' (1906), in *Männer und Zeiten*, 2 vols. (Leipzig, 1911), I, 121–53, a work answered by Felix SALOMON's apologetic *William Pitt der Jüngere* (Leipzig, 1906).

The first World War elicited attempts at general treatments of English history slanted to explain the Anglo-German struggle. Of these, Eduard MEYER's *England. Seine staatliche und politische Entwicklung und der Krieg gegen Deutschland* (Stuttgart and Berlin, 1915) is a somewhat extreme example from the Anglophobe camp of academic writers. In reaction to such war-inspired writings, specialists of the 1920s tried to re-educate the German public to view England more objectively. This effort produced such broad but capsulated narratives as Karl BRINKMANN's *Englische Geschichte 1815–1914* (Berlin, 1924), Wilhelm DIBELIUS' *England*, 2 vols. (Stuttgart, 1923), Bernhard GUTTMANN's *England im Zeitalter der bürgerlichen Reform* (Stuttgart, 1923), Paul HARTIG's symposium *Handbuch der Englandkunde*, 2 vols. (Frankfurt/Main, 1929–30), Hugo PRELLER's *Englische Geschichte* (Berlin and Leipzig, 1934), Ludwig RIESS's *Englische Geschichte hauptsächlich in neuester Zeit* (Berlin, 1926), Felix SALOMON's *Englische Geschichte von den Anfängen bis zur Gegenwart* (Leipzig and Berlin, 1923), and Gustav WENDT's *England, seine Geschichte, Verfassung und staatliche Einrichtungen* (Leipzig, 1923). The production of new works on English history by major German historians fell off rapidly thereafter; only occasionally did a new interpretation – such as ONCKEN's implicit challenge to the Nazis, *Cromwell. Vier Essays über die Führung einer Nation* (Berlin, 1935) – appear. Examples of the rather meager production of the period since the Second World War are Rudolf STADELMANN's *Geschichte der englischen Revolution* (Wiesbaden, 1954) and Erich EYCK's *Politische Geschichte Englands. Von der Magna Charta bis zur Gegenwart* (Berlin, 1951).

TRAVEL LITERATURE

Travel literature is a genre to itself, but a few works in this category contain useful historical observations. Johann Wilhelm von ARCHENHOLTZ' *England und Italien*, 2 vols. in 3 (Leipzig, 1785) was, judging by the number of reprinted and pirated editions – not to mention translations – of it, one of the most widely-read early panegyrics to the English way of life. Of related interest are the fashionable journals edited by Archenholtz: *Annalen der brittischen Geschichte*, 20 vols. (Hamburg *et al.*, 1787–91), *The Brittish Mercury*, 17 vols. (Hamburg, 1787–91) – with its German edition, *Der brittische Merkur* – and *Minerva* (Hamburg, 1792–1809). Friedrich von RAUMER's *England im Jahre 1835*, 2 vols. (Leipzig, 1836) attempted to enlighten German readers and dispel many uncertainties about the nature of 'reformed' England. Victor Aimé HUBER's critique, 'Über Friedrich von Raumer's England im Jahre 1835', in *Beiträge zur Kritik der neuesten Literatur* (Rostock, 1837), represented the more negative view taken by some romantic conservatives. Theodor FONTANE's *Bilderbuch aus England*, edited by Friedrich Fontane (Berlin, 1938), presenting observations gleaned from several visits in the period 1844–59, reflects a more ambivalent viewpoint on England than the writings of politically-oriented historians and, for that matter, than *Der englische Charakter, heute wie gestern*, edited by Samuel Saenger (Berlin, 1915), which presents mainly Fontane's negative remarks. Jacob VENEDEY provided in his *England*, 3 vols. (Leipzig, 1845) a typical, though non-scholarly, survey of history and institutions, which, despite the author's generally Francophile position, is full of praise. In HUBER's *Reisebriefe aus Belgien, Frankreich und England im Sommer 1854*, 2 vols. (Hamburg, 1855), one can perceive the beginnings of that author's reconciliation with England, which came to be in his eyes a model for amelioration of social conflicts. Ludwig von OMPTEDA's *Bilder aus dem Leben Englands* (Breslau, 1881) strongly restated the older view that English institutions and habits really constituted a development of the sympathetic 'Germanic spirit' at a time when Germans increasingly regarded English culture as totally foreign. Heinrich Langwerth von SIMMERN renewed Ompteda's point in his die-hard Anglophile work, *Deutschtum und Anglophobie*, 2 vols. (Wiesbaden, 1903–4).

NARRATIVE HISTORIES OF GERMANY

Because they contain views of England which were not fully expressed in other works by the same authors, a few works dealing mostly with German history proved useful. Heinrich von TREITSCHKE's *Deutsche Geschichte im 19. Jahrhundert*, 5 vols. (Leipzig, 1879–94), Dietrich SCHÄFER's sketch of German maritime history, *Deutschland zur See* (Jena, 1897), Heinrich CLASS's *Deutsche Geschichte* (Leipzig, 1910), and Max LENZ's exposition of imperial foreign policy, *Deutschland im Kreis der Grossmächte, 1871–1914* (Berlin, 1925) provided interesting insights.

MONOGRAPHS AND ARTICLES ON ENGLAND – SPECIAL ASPECTS

In addition to the general works listed above, German historians produced copious monographs and articles on limited aspects of English history.

DOMESTIC POLITICAL DEVELOPMENT

The constitution

The progressive development of their views on the whole English constitution may be found in the following works. August Ludwig SCHLÖZER, *Allgemeines Staatsrecht und Staatsverfassungslehre* (Göttingen, 1793) made quite clear the author's view that England enjoyed the most perfect constitution in the world. Also see Friedrich von GENTZ, 'Darstellung und Vergleichung einiger politischen Constitutions-systeme die von dem Grundsatze der Teilung der Macht ausgehen', *Neue Deutsche Monatsschrift*, III (1795), 123–7. Theodor A. H. SCHMALZ, while generally pro-English, attempted (without much success) to counteract the prevailing view of the English constitution with a highly Tory description in his *Staatsverfassung Grossbritanniens* (Halle, 1806). More typical were Karl von ROTTECK, 'Georg Custance's Gedrängte Übersicht der englischen Verfassung', *Gesammelte und nachgelassene Schriften*, II, 93–102, and Friedrich Christoph DAHLMANN, 'Ein Wort über Verfassung', 'Vorrede zur deutschen Übersetzung von DeLolme's Darstellung der Verfassung Englands', and 'Reden in der Paulskirche', in *Kleine Schriften und Reden*, edited by Conrad Varrentrapp (Stuttgart, 1886). Conservative critiques of the 1830s and 1840s include Georg Wilhelm Friedrich HEGEL, 'Über die englische Reform-Bill', in *Sämmtliche Werke*, edited by H. Glockner *et al.*, 21 vols. (Stuttgart, 1958), XX, 471–518, and Victor Aimé HUBER, *Zur vergleichenden Politik I. Die englische Verfassung und ihr 'it works well!'* (Berlin, 1843). Among the most important essays of the pre-March period are Robert von MOHL, 'Das Repräsentativsystem', in *Staatsrecht, Völkerrecht und Politik*, 3 vols. (Tübingen, 1860–9), I, 367–458, and MOHL, 'Über die verschiedene Auffassung des repräsentativen Systems in England, Frankreich und Deutschland', *Zeitschrift für die gesamte Staatswissenschaft*, III (1846), 451–95. See also MOHL's review of

Brougham's *British Constitution* in *Kritische Zeitschrift*, XVIII (1846), 195–215; and his attempts to make use of English practice by translating W. G. Hamilton's *Parlamentarische Logik* (Tübingen, 1828) and Charles Dupin's *Die konstitutionelle Staatsverwaltung oder System der brittischen Staatsverwaltung* (n.p., 1823). Significantly, MOHL's *Die Verantwortlichkeit der Minister in Einherrschaften und Volksvertretungen* (Tübingen, 1837) gives 100 pages to England, but only 22 to France and Germany combined. For the period after 1848, see the following: Lothar BUCHER, *Der Parlamentarismus wie er ist* (Berlin, 1855); Rudolf von GNEIST, *Englische Verfassungsgeschichte* (Berlin, 1882), *Das englische Parlament in tausendjährigen Wandlungen vom 9. bis zum Ende des 19. Jahrhunderts* (Berlin, 1886), and *Budget und Gesetz nach dem konstitutionellen Staatsrecht Englands, mit Rücksicht auf die deutsche Reichsverfassung* (Berlin, 1867); Eduard FISCHEL, *Die Verfassung Englands* (Berlin, 1862); Karl von NOORDEN, 'Die parlamentarische Parteiregierung in England', *Historische Zeitschrift*, XIV (1865), 45–118; and Ludwig RIESS, *Geschichte des Wahlrechts zum englischen Parlament im Mittelalter* (Leipzig, 1885) and 'Der Ursprung des englischen Unterhauses', *Historische Zeitschrift*, LX (1888), 1–33. Typical of the turn against the English parliamentary example are Anonymous (probably Friedrich THUDICUM), 'Parlamentarisches und konstitutionelles System', *Preussische Jahrbücher*, 46 (1880), 630–9; Heinrich von TREITSCHKE, 'Parlamentarische Erfahrungen der letzten Jahre', a printed manuscript intended as an addition to his essays and located in the *Nachlass* Treitschke, East Berlin. For late and generally more favorable views, see Wolfgang MICHAEL, 'Oliver Cromwell und die Auflösung des langen Parlaments', *Historische Zeitschrift*, LXIII (1889), 56–78; Karl KAUTSKY, *Der Parlamentarismus, die Volksgesetzgebung und die Sozialdemokratie* (Stuttgart, 1893); Wolfgang MICHAEL, 'Walpole als Premierminister', *Historische Zeitschrift*, CIV (1910), 504–36, and 'Die Entwicklung der Kabinettregierung in England', *Zeitschrift für Politik*, VI (1913), 549–93; and Felix LIEBERMANN, *The National Assembly in the Anglo-Saxon Period* (Halle, 1913). For one of the last and most subtle critiques of English constitutionalism, see Otto HINTZE, 'Das monarchische Prinzip und die konstitutionelle Verfassung', *Gesammelte Abhandlungen zur allgemeinen Verfassungsgeschichte* (Leipzig, 1941), 349–79.

Self-government

In a more specialized category of English domestic political history, that of 'self-government', one may mention the observations which flowed from Ludwig von Vincke's views in NIEBUHR's 'Vorrede zur Darstellung der inneren Verwaltung Grossbrittaniens', in *Nachgelassene Schriften B. G. Niebuhr's nichtphilologischen Inhalts* (Hamburg, 1842), 462–5. Although Friedrich Christoph DAHLMANN praised one important aspect of English self-government in his 'Ein Wegweiser durch die Geschichte der englischen

Jury', in *Kleine Schriften und Reden*, 337–55, German thinkers did not really return again to self-government as a system until the advent of Rudolf von GNEIST after 1848. His pioneering work on the unique nature of the English aristocracy, *Adel und Ritterschaft in England* (Berlin, 1853), which immediately impressed Max DUNCKER in his 'Feudalität und Aristokratie', in *Abhandlungen aus der neueren Geschichte* (Leipzig, 1887), began GNEIST's long and influential career as the German advocate of an English-style system of self-government. His subsequent monographs – including *Das englische Grundsteuersystem* (Berlin, 1859) and *Die Stadtverwaltung der City von London* (Berlin, 1867), – were absorbed in his definitive *Das heutige englische Verfassungs- und Verwaltungsrecht*, 2 vols. (Berlin, 1857–60) and subsequent editions including a distillation in *Verwaltung, Justiz, Rechtsweg* (Berlin, 1869). The articles of Heinrich von TREITSCHKE, 'Die Grundlagen der englischen Freiheit', *Preussische Jahrbücher*, I (1858), 366–81 and Karl von NOORDEN, 'Zur Literatur und Geschichte des englischen Selfgovernment', *Historische Zeitschrift*, XIII (1865), 1–89, testify to the impact of Gneist on younger historians.

Liberty

In addition to references to English libertarian traditions in broader works, the following pieces addressed themselves specifically to English liberty. Friedrich von GENTZ tried to define the conservative form of freedom he admired about England in his articles, 'Über die politische Freiheit' and 'Über die Moralität der Staatsrevolutionen' in vol. II of his *Ausgewählte Schriften*, edited by W. Weick, 5 vols. (Stuttgart and Leipzig, 1836–8). Heinrich von TREITSCHKE's definitive article, 'Die Freiheit', *Preussische Jahrbücher*, VII (1861), 381–403, both praises and criticizes the English conception of freedom as represented by Mill and illuminates the differences of the German conception. The German tendency to admire English freedom as embodied in an independence of mind which did not, however, paralyze patriotic dedication, is well expressed in Ludwig HÄUSSER's essays on Dahlmann and Macaulay in his *Gesammelte Schriften*, edited by Carl Pfeiffer, 2 vols. (Berlin, 1869–70). The most extreme attempts to discredit English liberty in German eyes were Lothar BUCHER's later writings, exemplified by 'Die englische Rede- und Pressefreiheit und die Fenierprozesse', in *Kleine Schriften politischen Inhalts* (Stuttgart, 1893).

Special problems

Barthold Georg NIEBUHR's little article, 'Über Irrland', in his *Nachgelassene Schriften*, 404–13, shows how much good will the Irish question exhausted among continental Anglophiles from the very beginning of the century. Niebuhr's 'Über Englands Zukunft' (1823) in the same collection reflected the ebb of enthusiasm for England in the period just after 1815. Other Anglophile historians, such as Reinhold PAULI in his 'Irland unter den Tudors', *Historische Zeitschrift*, XXII (1868), 257–69, could bring themselves to apologize for some English policies in Ireland. The subject, being a touchy one, received only infrequent attention. Even Lothar Bucher, who sought to 'unmask' England, usually turned his fire on mainland problems. In his articles 'Zwei Minderer des Reiches' and 'Die Ära Gladstone', in *Kleine Schriften*, he accused Gladstone – a special *bête noire* of Bismarck – of subverting English religious life and encouraging political revolution through reform; his 'Ein böser Geist im heutigen England', in *Kleine Schriften*, identified 'cant' as the contemporary spirit of England. Contrasted to Bucher, the painstaking editor of English sources, Felix LIEBERMANN, seems quiet indeed. His most important work – among many editing tasks – was the arrangement and commentary in *Die Gesetze der Angelsachsen*, 3 vols. (Halle, 1898–1916). One of the most sophisticated explanations of the difference between German and English constitutional development was provided by Otto HINTZE's 'Staatsverfassung und Heeresverfassung', *Staat und Verfassung, Gesammelte Abhandlungen zur allgemeinen Verfassungsgeschichte*, edited by Fritz Hartung (Leipzig, 1941), 42–73.

FOREIGN POLICY

Broad works on Anglo–German relations

Arnold Hermann Ludwig HEEREN's 'Versuch einer historischen Entwicklung der Entstehung und des Wachstums des britischen Kontinentalinteresses', in *Historische Werke*, was a successful early attempt to deal objectively with England's foreign interests as an expression of her economic needs. Leopold von RANKE's highly influential essay of 1833, 'Die grossen Mächte', *Historisch-politische Zeitschrift*, II (1833), 1–51, helped set in the minds of generations of Germans the idea that England always pursued the balance of power as the end of her foreign policy. Ranke's student Reinhold PAULI intensified the master's positive, friendly evaluation of Anglo–German cooperation in such works as *Der Gang der internationalen Beziehungen zwischen Deutschland und England* (Gotha, 1859) and 'Englands älteste Beziehungen zu Österreich und Preussen', in *Bilder aus Alt-England* (Gotha, 1860), 90–117. At the turn of the twentieth century, Erich MARCKS was still using Rankean ideas to defend historic English foreign policy in his *Deutschland und England in den grossen europäischen Krisen seit der Reformation* (Stuttgart, 1900). By that time, however, even the neo-Rankeans had begun questioning Ranke's premises, as in Max LENZ's *Die grossen Mächte. Ein Rückblick auf unser Jahrhundert* (Berlin, 1900). MARCKS, too, negatively revised his earlier opinions of historic Anglo–German relations in *Die Einheitlichkeit der englischen Auslandspolitik von 1500 bis zur Gegenwart* (Stuttgart, 1910). Counterdefenses in the old Rankean vein against the neo-Rankeans – such as that provided by Felix SALOMON in *Die Grundzüge der auswärtigen Politik Englands vom 16. Jahrhundert bis zur Gegenwart* (Berlin, 1910) – became scarce after 1900. What balanced discussion appeared in print tended to be written by amateurs working toward Anglo-German reconciliation, as in the case of Karl BLEIBTREU, *Deutschland und England*, 2nd. edn. (Berlin, 1909).

Specific problems

German discussions of special periods of English foreign relations before 1900 fall roughly into two categories – those which argued strongly for or against English policy and those which approached it with a dispassionate and usually antiquarian intent. Friedrich von GENTZ's spirited support of England's anti-French struggle found expression in his 'Über den Ursprung und Charakter des Krieges gegen die französische Revolution', in *Ausgewählte Schriften*, II, 189–389, and his *Darstellung des Verhältnis zwischen England und Spanien*, vol. III of *Ausgewählte Schriften*. Barthold Georg NIEBUHR's 'Mémoire sur la guerre entre l'Angleterre et la France' (1806), in *Nachgelassene Schriften*, was also a pro-English apology. Heinrich von SYBEL reaffirmed their view of England's positive role in 'Die Erhebung Europas gegen Napoleon I' (1860), in *Kleine historische Schriften*, 243–342. After a long lull in German interest in English foreign policy, Friedrich LIST raised the possibility of basing Germany's power and security on an English alliance in his 'Über den Wert und die Bedingungen einer Allianz zwischen Grossbritannien und Deutschland' (1846), in *Lists gesammelte Schriften*, edited by Ludwig Häusser, 3 vols. (Stuttgart and Tübingen, 1850), II, 435–68. HÄUSSER himself expressed the general *realpolitisch* tone of the 1848 revolutionaries in assessing England's policy toward new nation states, although his 'Deutschland und die Politik der fremden Mächte', *Deutsche Zeitung*, 13 September 1848, is harsher on England than most. Early champions of a German fleet based their argument heavily upon English experience, as Reinhold PAULI did in 'Wie Kriegsflotten entstehen', *Preussische Jahrbücher*, XIV (1864), 506–22. The strain in Anglo-German relations is evident in Heinrich von TREITSCHKE's articles 'Die Feuerprobe' (1870), in *Zehn Jahre deutscher Kämpfe* (Berlin, 1874) and 'Die Türkei und die Grossmächte' (1876) in *Deutsche Kämpfe*, new series (Leipzig, 1896), and, in a more muted tone, in Heinrich von SYBEL's 'Das neue deutsche Reich' (1871), in *Vorträge und Aufsätze* (Berlin, 1874). Thereafter came a trickle of writings which tried to show that England had always been a secret opponent of German victories: Johann Gustav DROYSEN's 'England und Preussen', *Zeitschrift für preussische Geschichte und Landeskunde*, XVII (1880), 502ff., Max DUNCKER's 'Preussen und England im Siebenjährigen Krieg', in *Abhandlungen aus der neueren Geschichte*, and Lothar BUCHER's 'Der Cobdenclub' and 'Stammverwandtschaft und Waffenbrüderschaft mit England', both in *Kleine Schriften*, which argued that free trade doctrine and the foreign policy myth of 'brotherhood in arms' disguised sinister English exploitation of Germany.

The more antiquarian treatments of remote periods of English foreign policy – except for Reinhold PAULI's 'Heinrich VIII als Bundesgenosse Maximilians I und als Bewerber um die Kaiserkrone', in *Aufsätze zur englischen Geschichte*, I – constituted the fruits of doctoral research. Such were the following works: Max LENZ's *König Sigismund und König Heinrich V von England* (Berlin, 1874); Wilhelm BUSCH's *Cardinal Wolsey und die kaiserlich-englische Allianz, 1522–1525* (Bonn, 1886), a continuation of *Drei Jahre englischer Vermittlungspolitik, 1518–1521* (Bonn, 1884); Felix SALOMON's *Frankreichs Beziehungen zu dem schottischen Aufstand 1637–1640* (Berlin, 1890) and *Geschichte des letzten Ministeriums Königin Annas von England* (Gotha, 1894); and Arnold Oskar MEYER's *Die englische Diplomatie in Deutschland zur Zeit Edwards VI und Mariens* (Breslau, 1900).

The Anglo–German rivalry

The objectivity of these young authors became increasingly difficult to maintain as German historians started to revise their view of all past English foreign policy in the light of the Anglo–German rivalry after about 1897. Gustav SCHMOLLER argued in 'Die wirtschaftliche Zukunft Deutschlands und die Flottenvorlage' (1899), in *Handels- und Machtpolitik*, edited by Schmoller, Max Sering, and Adolf Wagner (Stuttgart, 1900), that Germany must copy England's long-standing pursuit of empire and commercial advantages by the unhesitating application of political and military (including naval) force. The Boer War provided an example of ruthlessness which observers like Max LENZ, in his articles, 'Ein Blick ins 20. Jahrhundert', 'Zur politischen Weltlage', and 'Der Zusammenbruch in Transvaal', *Die Woche*, II (1900), Nos. 12, 17, and 23, believed typified English imperialism throughout the nineteenth century and before. Gerhard von SCHULZE-GAEVERNITZ, in his *Britischer Imperialismus und englischer Freihandel zu Beginn des 20. Jahrhunderts* (Leipzig, 1906) and *England und Deutschland*, 3rd edn. (Berlin, 1911), and Otto HINTZE, in 'Imperialismus und Weltpolitik' (1907), in *Historische und politische Aufsätze*, 4 vols. (Berlin, 1908–9), IV, 144–59, took a similar line. Arguing on the more specific grounds of Germany's need for a fleet, such works as Wolfgang MICHAEL's 'Englands Flottenpolitik unter der Republik und der Untergang Hollands', *Beiträge zur Beleuchtung der Flottenfrage*, No. 5 (Munich, 1900), Dietrich SCHÄFER's articles in *Deutschland und England in See- und Weltgeltung* (Leipzig, 1915) – all printed before the war – Otto HINTZE's 'Die Seeherrschaft Englands, ihre Begründung und Bedeutung', *Neue Zeit- und Streitfragen*, IV, 9 (Dresden, 1907), Hans DELBRÜCK's 'Weshalb baut Deutschland Kriegsschiffe?', *Preussische Jahrbücher*, CXXXVIII (1909), 149–61, and Hermann ONCKEN's 'Deutschland und England. Heeres- oder Flottenverstärkung?', in *Historisch-*

politische Aufsätze und Reden, 2 vols. (Munich and Berlin, 1914), I, 121–44, urged Germans to create a huge fleet either to pursue the supposed ruthless methods of English commercial success or to escape the fate at English hands of earlier peoples who had crossed the path of English imperial plottings. Historical examples were, of course, copiously invoked. Similar sentiments are to be found in Hans DELBRÜCK's articles in the *Preussische Jahrbücher*, many of which are reprinted in *Vor und nach dem Weltkrieg. Politische und historische Aufsätze 1902–1925* (Berlin, 1926).

The opposition to these lines of argument was rather feeble. Eduard BERNSTEIN unmasked the 'unmaskers' of English imperial methods in *Die englische Gefahr und das deutsche Volk* (Berlin, 1911). Lujo BRENTANO, who at first sought to distinguish between 'good', Cobdenite and 'bad', Kiplingesque Englishmen in 'Cobdens Argument gegen Flottenvermehrungen', *Die Nation*, XVII (1900), 205–8 and 217–20, later preferred to look upon the Cobdenite period in English history as a glorious but regrettably impermanent departure from the ruthless English norm – such was the general theme of 'Die englische Seeherrschaft und Deutschland' [Vienna] *Neue Freie Presse*, 24 December 1911, and 'Die heutigen Hauptursachen des Krieges', *Die Friedensbewegung*, VII (1912), 95–7.

War literature

The opinions on English foreign policy current among German historians before the First World War required no major changes to serve as contributions to the German war effort. Typical works by historians whose prewar writings appeared in this study were as follows: Lujo BRENTANO, 'England und der Weltkrieg', *Flugschriften des Bundes 'Neues Vaterland'*, No. 6 (1918); Otto HINTZE, 'Die englischen Weltherrschaftspläne und der gegenwärtige Krieg', *Unterm eisernen Kreuz*, XV (1915), also 'Imperialismus und Weltpolitik', reprinted in *Staat und Verfassung* (Leipzig, 1941), 447–59; Erich MARCKS, *Der Imperialismus und der Weltkrieg* (Leipzig, 1916); Arnold Oskar MEYER, 'Deutsche Freiheit und englischer Imperialismus', in *Weltkultur und Weltpolitik*, edited by Ernst Jäckh (Stuttgart, 1916), 'Worin liegt Englands Schuld', *Der deutsche Krieg* (Berlin, 1915), and *Englands Friedensschlüsse* (Berlin, 1918); Hermann ONCKEN, 'Unsere Abrechnung mit England', *Unterm eisernen Kreuz*, VIII (1914); Ernst, Count zu REVENTLOW, *Der Vampir des Festlandes. Eine Darstellung der englischen Politik nach ihren Triebkräften, Mitteln und Wirkungen* (Berlin, 1915); Ludwig RIESS, 'Der Stufengang des deutsch-englischen Gegensatzes', *Der Tag des Deutschen*, V (1917); and Felix SALOMON, *Wie England unser Feind wurde* (Leipzig, 1914) and *Der britische Imperialismus* (Leipzig, 1916).

Postwar interpretations

A few of the more objective postwar treatments of Anglo-German relations are listed among the secondary works in this bibliography. Among more idiosyncratic interpretations – both positive to England – are Erich MARCKS's 'England und Frankreich während der letzten drei Jahrhunderte' (1923), in *Geschichte und Gegenwart* (Berlin, 1925), and Hermann KANTOROWICZ, *Der Geist der englischen Politik und das Gespenst der Einkreisung Deutschlands* (Berlin, 1929). The advent of the Second World War produced a few reversions to pre-1914 thinking in the form of Karl BRINKMANN's *Der englische Wirtschaftsimperialismus* (Berlin, 1940), a new edition of MARCKS's essays (not all of them anti-English) under the title *Englands Machtpolitik. Vorträge und Studien*, edited by Willy Andreas (Stuttgart and Berlin, 1940), Hermann ONCKEN's 'Deutschland und England', *Marine-Rundschau*, XLVI (1941), 69–80, and an edition of TREITSCHKE England-baitings under the title *England, der Brandstifter Europas*, edited by W. Schneider (Nuremberg, 1941).

ECONOMIC AND SOCIAL QUESTIONS

Some of the earliest incisive writing on the English economy and economic doctrine can be found scattered throughout Friedrich LIST's *Schriften, Reden, Briefe*, edited by Erwin von Beckerath *et al.*, 10 vols. (Berlin, 1927–36), particularly for the period 1835–46. The fullest German examination of English economic development – Lujo BRENTANO's *Eine Geschichte der wirtschaftlichen Entwicklung Englands*, 3 vols. (Jena, 1927–9) – appeared after the cut-off point of this work but summarized much of Brentano's prewar writings. It builds up to the free-trade period as the golden age of the English economy. Except for HEEREN, German historians showed little interest in English economic history (apart from the social question) until after the 1840s. Reinhold PAULI's *Der hanseatische Stahlhof in London* (Bremen, 1856) was prompted more by nostalgia at the wrecking of the Steelyard compound than by economic curiosity. With BRENTANO, English economic history received more attention, as in his article, 'Anfang und Ende der englischen Kornzölle', *Münchener Allgemeine Zeitung* 15–16 January 1892. Gustav von SCHMOLLER could view English economics quite objectively – as in his *Skizze einer Finanzgeschichte von Frankreich, Österreich, England und Preussen (1500–1900)* (Leipzig, 1909) – or with the critical eye of a German competitor – as in his tendentious 'Die Wandlungen in der europäischen Handelspolitik des 19. Jahrhunderts', *Schmollers Jahrbuch*, XXIV (1900), 373–82, 'Die künftige englische Handelspolitik, Chamberlain und der Imperialismus', *Schmollers Jahrbuch*, XXVIII (1904), 829–52, and 'Die englische Handelspolitik des 17. und 18. Jahrhunderts', *Schmollers Jahrbuch*, XXIII (1899), 1211–41. Dietrich SCHÄFER's 'Deutschland und

England im Welthandel des 16. Jahrhunderts', *Preussische Jahrbücher*, LXXXIII (1896), 268–81, argued that England's supreme ruthlessness in commerce dated at least from the sixteenth-century encroachments on the German Hanse. Lujo BRENTANO, in *Die Entwicklung des englischen Erbrechts in dem Grundeigentum* (Berlin, 1898), *Die Schrecken des überwiegenden Industriestaates* (Berlin, 1901), and *Das Freihandelsargument* (Berlin, 1901), tried to base economic proposals for Germany on English experience.

The most impressive early German work on the 'social question' in England was Friedrich ENGELS' *Die Lage der arbeitenden Klasse in England* (Leipzig, 1845), which elaborated and documented some themes in the same author's 'Die Lage Englands', and 'Umrisse zu einer Kritik der Nationalökonomie', both in *Deutsch-französische Jahrbücher* (Paris, 1844). From the other end of the German political spectrum came Victor Aimé HUBER's *Über die co-operativen Arbeiter-Associationen in England* (Berlin, 1852), his collected pamphlets under the title *Sociale Fragen*, 7 vols. in 1 (Nordhausen, 1863–9), his 'Die sociale Hebung der arbeitenden Klassen in England', *Deutsche Vierteljahrsschrift*, XXXI (1868), 83–148, and many lesser articles. Heinrich von SYBEL was one of the few German historians to discuss English women's advanced rights in his 'Über die Emancipation der Frauen', in *Vorträge und Aufsätze*. Lujo BRENTANO's interest in economics sprang largely from his youthful enthusiasm for English labor organizations, described briefly in his *On the History and Development of the Gilds, and the Origin of Trade-Unions* (London, 1870) and more elaborately in *Die Arbeitgilden der Gegenwart*, 2 vols. (Leipzig, 1871–2). His subsequent works, such as 'Die englische Chartistenbewegung', *Preussische Jahrbücher*, XXXIII (1874), 431–47 and 531–50, *Die christlich-soziale Bewegung in England* (Leipzig, 1883), and 'Entwicklung und Geist der englischen Arbeiterorganisationen', *Archiv für soziale Gesetzgebung und Statistik*, VIII (1895), 75–139, attempted to break German resistance to cooperation with the labor movement by citing English examples of social progress. Gerhard von SCHULZE-GAEVERNITZ, after his own studies in England, continued Brentano's line of argument in his *Zum sozialen Frieden: Eine Darstellung der sozialpolitischen Erziehung des englischen Volkes im neunzehnten Jahrhundert*, 2 vols. (Leipzig, 1890). The warning voice of hardened anti-labor men can be heard in Lothar BUCHER's 'Die Vorfahren und die Erben der Chartisten', *Kleine Schriften*. Finally, Eduard BERNSTEIN also sought and found English leadership in the modern communist movement in his *Sozialismus und Demokratie in der grossen englischen Revolution*, 2nd edn. (Stuttgart, 1908).

CULTURE

General

Many nineteenth-century German political historians also produced monographs and articles on English culture, some of which still read well today.

Karl von ROTTECK, in a review of RANKE's *Geschichte der romanischen und germanischen Völker, 1494–1535*, in *Gesammelte und nachgelassene Schriften*, II, 371–80, disputed in vain the validity of the dominant notion that Germanic and Romance cultural groups might be used as units of history. Not until quite late in the century did the concept of a Germanic community of nations break down. Adolf Helfferich's *Engländer und Franzosen* (Berlin, 1852) found the Romance nation quite inferior in culture to the 'Germanic' English. Karl Hillebrand's *Aus und über England*, written in 1873 and published as vol. III of his *Zeiten, Völker und Menschen*, 7 vols. (Strasbourg, 1885–1902), contains some of the most intelligent and unbiased German writing on English culture. Unfortunately Hillebrand, a cosmopolitan expatriate, was evidently little read in his homeland. Heinrich Langwerth von SIMMERN's 'Der englische Nationalcharakter', in *England in deutscher Beleuchtung*, edited by Thomas Lenschau, No. 7 (Halle, 1906), attempted to define 'national character' in the Anglophile language of a bygone era. Werner SOMBART's *Händler und Helden; patriotische Besinnungen* (Munich and Leipzig, 1915), though an extreme simplification, better represented the spirit of prewar German thought on English culture than Simmern.

Religion

The predominantly secular historians used in this study wrote few monographs and articles on English religious life. Among those few are Barthold Georg NIEBUHR's 'Kirchliche Verhältnisse in England', in *Nachgelassene Schriften*, Hans DELBRÜCK's 'Über den politischen Charakter der englischen Kirchenspaltung', *Historische Zeitschrift*, XXXVI (1875), 83–106, which explained the Reformation in secular terms, and several works by Arnold Oskar MEYER – 'Der Toleranzgedanke im England der Stuarts', *Historische Zeitschrift*, CVIII (1912), 255–94, and *England und die katholische Kirche vom Regierungsantritt Elisabeths bis zur Gründung der Seminare* (Rome, 1908). MEYER's 'Die sittlichen Triebkräfte des englischen Imperialismus', *Englischer Kulturunterricht*, February 1924, 15–28, argued that religion had always served the English state and also sanctified imperialism as a holy cause.

Universities

Although the English were more likely to study German educational methods than vice versa, Victor Aimé HUBER laid the basis of his reputation as an historian with *Die englischen Universitäten*, 2 vols. (Cassel, 1839–40). Heinrich von SYBEL's 'Die deutschen und die auswärtigen Universitäten', in *Vorträge und Aufsätze*, avoided the common sneering at English universities and pointed out their different and quite valuable aim of educating the whole man.

Literature

Four political historians in particular successfully tried their hand at literary history: Georg Gottfried GERVINUS in *Shakespeare*, 4 pts. (Leipzig, 1849–50), and *Händel und Shakespeare* (Leipzig, 1861); Reinhold PAULI in essays collected in his *Bilder aus Alt-England*; Heinrich von TREITSCHKE in 'Milton', *Preussische Jahrbücher*, VI (1860), 431–6, and 'Lord Byron und der Radikalismus', in *Historische und politische Aufsätze* (Leipzig, 1865); and Felix LIEBERMANN in 'Shaws Bildnis der Jungfrau von Orleans', *Historische Zeitschrift*, CXXXIII (1925–6), 20–40, 'Shakespeares Anschauungen von Staat, Gesellschaft und Kirche in Heinrich VIII', *Sonderausgabe aus Beiträge zur Literatur- und Theatergeschichte* (Berlin, 1918), 13–41, and 'Shakespeare als Bearbeiter des King John', *Archiv für das Studium neuerer Sprachen*, CXLII (1921), 177–202, and CXLIII (1922), 17–46 and 190–203.

OTHER WORKS

In addition to the books and articles discussed above, many German historians referred to England in passing in scattered works which are collected in some of the following editions. Lujo BRENTANO, *Gesammelte Reden und Aufsätze*, new series, 2 vols. (Leipzig, 1923–4); Hans DELBRÜCK, *Historische und politische Aufsätze*, 3 pts. (Berlin, 1886); Johann Gustav DROYSEN, *Politische Schriften*, edited by Felix Gilbert (Munich and Berlin, 1933); Arnold Hermann Ludwig HEEREN, *Vermischte historische Schriften*, 2 vols. (Göttingen, 1821); Friedrich LIST, *Schriften/Reden/Briefe*, edited by Erwin Beckerath *et al.*, 12 vols. (Berlin, 1927–35); Karl MARX and Friedrich ENGELS, *Werke*, edited by the Institut für Marxismus-Leninismus beim Zentralkommittee der Sozialistischen Einheitspartei Deutschlands, 32 vols. (Berlin, 1957ff.), and *On Britain* (Moscow, 1953), a distillation of their remarks from scattered works.

Arnold Oskar MEYER, *Deutsche und Engländer* (Munich, 1937) contains less about England than the title hints. Also see Robert von MOHL, *Die Geschichte und Literatur der Staatswissenschaften*, 3 vols. (Erlangen, 1855–8) and *Staatsrecht, Völkerrecht und Politik*; Justus MÖSER, *Sämmtliche Werke*, 7 vols. (Berlin, 1798–1820); Barthold Georg NIEBUHR, *Politische Schriften*, edited by G. Küntzel (Frankfurt/Main, 1923); Hermann ONCKEN, *Historisch-politische Aufsätze und Reden*, 2 vols. (Munich and Berlin, 1914); Karl von ROTTECK, *Sammlung kleinerer Schriften meist historischen und politischen Inhalts*, 3 vols. (Stuttgart, 1848); Gustav SCHMOLLER, *Charakterbilder* (Munich and Leipzig, 1913); and Heinrich von TREITSCHKE, *Ausgewählte Schriften*, 2 vols. (Leipzig, 1907), *Historische und politische Aufsätze*, various editions culminating in 4 vols. (Leipzig, 1871–97), and *Zehn Jahre deutscher Kämpfe 1865–1874* (Berlin, 1874) with its continuation *Deutsche Kämpfe*.

SECONDARY MATERIALS

The secondary literature used for this work includes treatments of Anglo-German relations from various viewpoints; works on the history of historical writing; contributions to intellectual history; and biographies of the historians discussed in the text.

ANGLO-GERMAN RELATIONS AND ATTITUDES

THE GERMAN VIEW OF ENGLAND AND ITS BACKGROUND

Franz MUNCKER's *Anschauungen vom englischen Staat und Volk in der deutschen Literatur der letzten vier Jahrhunderte*, 2 vols. (Munich, 1918–25) was the first serious attempt to assess the German view of England, but it lacked depth and reached only to about 1840. Bernadotte SCHMITT, in *England and Germany, 1740–1914* (Princeton, 1916), restricted himself to a popular explanation of the Anglo-German conflict; Schmitt and, to a lesser degree, Raymond SONTAG, in his *Germany and England; Background of Conflict, 1848–1894* (New York and London, 1938), described attitudes in general terms without always identifying their spokesmen. In both books the emphasis fell largely on the period 1870–1900 and on diplomatic relations. To an even greater degree than Schmitt and Sontag, Hermann LEVY, in his essay *England and Germany – Affinity and Contrast* (Leigh-on-Sea, 1949), sought more to explain the differences between the two countries than to examine how one viewed the other.

Several other works, by clearly defining their chronological framework and the sources of public opinion, gained thereby in coherence. Eber Malcolm CARROLL's *Germany and the Great Powers, 1866–1914. A Study in Public Opinion and Foreign Policy* (New York, 1938) traces the fluctuating reactions of the press to foreign policy crises. Pauline ANDERSON's *The Background of Anti-English Feeling in Germany, 1890–1902* (Washington, 1939) is still one of the most valuable studies of German political pressure groups, their attitudes toward England, and their attempts to influence foreign policy under the reign of Wilhelm II. Anderson was inspired by Eckart KEHR, whose 'Englandhass und Weltpolitik', *Zeitschrift für Politik*, XVII (1924), 500–26 pointed out the connection between Anglophobia and domestic politics. Ludwig DEHIO's articles, 'Gedanken über die deutsche Sendung, 1900–1918', *Historische Zeitschrift*, CLXXIV (1952), 479–502, and 'Ranke und der deutsche Imperialismus', *Historische Zeitschrift*, CLXX (1950), 307–28, posit a convincing theory: the imperial leadership built up 'new England's' imperialism and navalism as a hegemonial threat to obtain support for a navy which would allow Germany to take up 'old England's' role as holder of the balance. Erich LEUPOLT's *Die Aussenpolitik in den bedeutendsten Zeitschriften Deutschlands 1890–1909* (Leipzig, 1933), less broadly conceived than Carroll's book, amounts to an intensive study of four important periodicals – the *Grenzboten*, *Preussische Jahrbücher*, *Zukunft*, and *Alldeutsche Blätter*. Willy SCHENK's *Die deutsch-englische Rivalität vor dem ersten Weltkrieg in der Sicht deutscher Historiker. Missverstehen oder Machtstreben?* (Aarau, 1967) examines the writings of many of the same Wilhelmine historians discussed in this study and attempts, without complete success, to answer the question posed in the subtitle. Two interesting articles which lay beyond the central purpose of this study were Johannes VOIGT's 'Die Auseinandersetzung zwischen Theodor Mommsen und Max Müller über den Burenkrieg', *Geschichte in Wissenschaft und Unterricht*, XVII (1966), 65–77, and A. V. N. van WOERDEN's 'Hitler, Duitsland en de Engelse Wereldmacht', *Tijdschrift voor Geschiedenis*, LXXVII (1964), 403–38. Among works concerning impressions of Germans traveling in England are Robert ELSASSER's useful *Über die politischen Bildungsreisen der Deutschen nach England* (Heidelberg, 1917), on eighteenth-century observers, and Edward SMITH's superficial *Foreign Visitors in England* (London, 1889), which goes only to 1840.

THE ENGLISH VIEW OF GERMANY

I am indebted for methodological approaches suggested by several good studies of other national images reflected in historical writing. Manfred MESSERSCHMIDT's *Deutschland in englischer Sicht. Die Wandlungen des Deutschlandbildes in der englischen Geschichtsschreibung* (Düsseldorf, 1953) and Manfred SCHLENKE's *England und das friderizianische Preussen, 1740–1763. Ein Beitrag zum Verhältnis von Politik und öffentlicher Meinung in England des 18. Jahrhunderts* (Freiburg, 1963) do for the English attitude toward Germany what this work attempts to do for the reverse. Heinz-Otto SIEBURG's *Deutschland und Frankreich in der Geschichtsschreibung des 19. Jahrhunderts*, 2 vols. (Wiesbaden, 1954–8), uses similar methods for reciprocal Franco-German attitudes. Martin VOGT's 'Das vormärzliche Deutschland im englischen Urteil, 1830–1847', *Geschichte in Wissenschaft und Unterricht*, XVI (1965), 397–413, and Kurt Meine's *England und Deutschland in der Zeit des Überganges vom Manchestertum zum Imperialismus, 1871–76* (Berlin, 1937) are less successful but still interesting attempts at assessing English views of Germany over briefer periods.

ANGLO-GERMAN RELATIONS AND ATTITUDES IN SPECIAL FIELDS

CONSTITUTIONAL THEORY

Theodor SCHIEDER's essays in *The State and Society in Our Times*, translated by C. A. M. Sym (Edinburgh, 1962), count among the most lucid expositions of German party history and clear up many differences between German experience on the one hand and Anglo-American presuppositions on the other. The essays in Ernst FRAENKEL, *Deutschland und die westlichen*

Demokratien (Stuttgart, 1964) also shed some light on these differences, although Fraenkel often overestimates the gullibility of nineteenth-century German theorists about the 'transferability' of English constitutional practice. For a standard comparative work, see Friedrich GLUM, *Das parlamentarische Regierungssystem in Deutschland, England und Frankreich* (Munich and Berlin, 1950). Of the various descriptions of German attitudes toward the English constitution – Friedrich KLENK's 'Die Beurteilung der englischen Verfassung in Deutschland von Hegel bis Stahl' (Dissertation, Tübingen, 1930), Theodor WILHELM's *Die englische Verfassung und der vormärzliche deutsche Liberalismus* (Stuttgart, 1928), and Reinhard LAMER's *Der englische Parlamentarismus in der deutschen politischen Theorie im Zeitalter Bismarcks (1857–1890): Ein Beitrag zur Vorgeschichte des deutschen Parlamentarismus* (Lübeck, 1963) – the last is by far the best. For a sound attack on the old notion that 'French' and 'English' schools grew up in isolation, see F. Gunther EYCK, 'English and French Influences in German Liberalism before 1848', *Journal of the History of Ideas*, XVIII (1957), 313–41. Gerhard A. RITTER's 'Deutscher und britischer Parlamentarismus', *Recht und Staat*, CCXLII–III (1962), deals with the interwar problems of parliamentary government.

DIPLOMATIC RELATIONS

Standard works on European diplomatic history, forced by their international scope to deal chiefly with crises, rarely treat Anglo-German relations before 1870 in a bilateral context. Studies are especially thin for the period before 1848, and what brief treatment one can find among recent general works is usually uninformative. It would be hard to find a duller and more restricted approach to the problem, for example, than that of David B. HORN, *Great Britain and Europe in the Eighteenth Century* (Oxford, 1967). Sir Richard LODGE, *Great Britain and Prussia in the Eighteenth Century* (Oxford, 1923) is a straightforward and commendably sober account of diplomacy. One is forced to cast a broad net and even consider such slender treatments as Ernst SCHRÖDER's *Christian Friedrich von Stockmar. Ein Wegbereiter der deutsch-englischen Freundschaft* (Essen, 1950) and works not specifically about Anglo-German relations. For the period after 1848, one may turn to Werner Eugen MOSSE's *The European Powers and the German Question, 1848–71* (Cambridge, 1958), Hans PRECHT's *Englands Stellung zur deutschen Einheit 1848–50* (Munich, 1925), the conclusions of which contradict the Treitschkean allegation of a monolithic British opposition to German unity, Alexander SCHARFF's *Die europäischen Grossmächte und die deutsche Revolution, 1848–51* (Leipzig, 1942) and Frank WEBER's 'Palmerston and Prussian Liberalism, 1848', *Journal of Modern History*, XXXV (1963), 125–36, and Günther GILLESSEN, *Lord Palmerston und die Einigung Deutschlands* [*Historische Studien*, No. 384] (Lübeck, 1961), which agree with Precht.

Lawrence STEEFEL's *The Schleswig-Holstein Question* (Cambridge, Mass., 1932) and, more pointedly, Johannes VOIGT's 'Englands Aussenpolitik während des deutsch-dänischen Konfliktes 1862–1864', *Zeitschrift der Gesellschaft für schleswig-holsteinische Geschichte*, LXXXIX (1964), 36–212, pilot the reader through the treacherous waters of the German–Danish conflict. Whatever myths might still linger about a supposed anti-German attitude by the British government during that conflict have been conclusively exploded by Holger HJELHOLT's lengthy *British Mediation in the Danish–German Conflict, 1848–50*, 2 vols. (Copenhagen, 1966). For Anglo-German relations during the mid-1860s, one may consult (with considerable reservations) Charlotte SEMPELL, *England und Preussen in der schleswig-holsteinischen Frage* [*Historische Studien*, No. 219] (Berlin, 1932) and (with more confidence) Gerhard BRÜNS, *England und der deutsche Krieg 1866* [*Historische Studien*, No. 221] (Berlin, 1933). Horst MICHAEL adequately describes Bismarck's subsequent relations with England in *Bismarck, England und Europa* (*Vorwiegend von 1866–1870*) (Munich, 1930).

The question raised after World War I about the nature and possibilities of Germany's policy toward England before she became inaccessible to a German alliance is thoroughly discussed in the following works: Gerhard RITTER's *Bismarcks Verhältnis zu England und die Politik des 'Neuen Kurses'* (Berlin, 1924) and *Die Legende von der verschmähten englischen Freundschaft 1898–1901* (Freiburg, 1929); Hans ROTHFELS' *Bismarcks englische Bündnispolitik* (Stuttgart, 1924) and 'Zur Beurteilung der englischen Vorkriegspolitik', *Archiv für Politik und Geschichte*, XII (1926), 599–615; Friedrich MEINECKE's *Geschichte des deutsch-englischen Bündnisproblems, 1890–1901* (Munich, 1927); and – more recently – Sigfried KAEHLER's *Zwei deutsche Bündnisangebote an England, 1880 und 1939* (Göttingen, 1948) and Otto BECKER's 'Die Wende der deutsch-englischen Beziehungen', in *Festschrift für Gerhard Ritter zu seinem 60. Geburtstag*, edited by Richard Nürnberger (Tübingen, 1950). Less interesting and successful are Heinrich G. DITTMAR, *Die deutsch-englischen Beziehungen in den Jahren 1898/99* (Stuttgart, 1938) and Johannes DREYER, *Deutschland und England in ihrer Politik und Presse im Jahre 1901* [*Historische Studien*, No. 246] (Berlin, 1934). The thesis that commercial rivalry alone led to the Anglo-German estrangement, as stated in Ross J. S. HOFFMAN, *Great Britain and the German Trade Rivalry, 1875–1914* (Philadelphia, 1933), was effectively challenged by Angelika BANZE, *Die deutsch-englische Wirtschaftsrivalität* [*Historische Studien*, No. 274] (Berlin, 1935).

On the question of German naval policy and its influence on English relations, Eckart KEHR, *Schlachtflottenbau und Parteipolitik 1894–1901* (Berlin, 1930) and Rudolf STADELMANN, 'Die Epoche der deutsch-englischen Flottenrivalität', *Deutschland und Westeuropa; drei Aufsätze* (Schloss Laupheim/Württemberg, 1948), condemn Tirpitz more severely than Walter HUBATSCH in *Die Ära Tirpitz: Studien zur deutschen Marinepolitik 1890–1918* (Göttingen, 1955). On the political uses of history, see Jonathan STEINBERG, 'The Copenhagen Complex', *Journal of Contemporary History*, No. 3 (1966), 21–44, as well as *Yesterday's Deterrant, Tirpitz and the Birth of the German Battle Fleet* (New York, 1965). The *Bibliographie zur Geschichte des Britischen Reiches in der Nachkriegszeit*, No. 10 of *Bibliographische Vierteljahreshefte der Weltkriegsbücherei* (Stuttgart, 1936), is a bibliographical rather than a critical approach to post-World War I German attitudes toward the Empire.

COMMERCE AND INDUSTRY

Britain's direct example as an industrial model is described in William Otto HENDERSON's *Britain and Industrial Europe 1750–1870* (Liverpool, 1954). Germany's struggle for commercial maturity – sometimes with, sometimes against British policies – is colorfully described in Percy Ernst SCHRAMM's *Hamburg, Deutschland und die Welt. Leistung und Grenzen hanseatischen Bürgertums in der Zeit zwischen Napoleon I und Bismarck* (Munich, 1943) and *Deutschland und Übersee. Der deutsche Handel mit den anderen Kontinenten, insbesondere Afrika, von Karl V bis zu Bismarck. Ein Beitrag zur Geschichte der Rivalität im Wirtschaftsleben* (Brunswick, 1950) as well as in HENDERSON's *The Zollverein* (Cambridge, 1939). For a discussion of List's efforts to combat English free-trade doctrine, see Heinz ROGGE, *England, Friedrich List und der deutsche Zollverein* (Würzburg, 1939). The Germans' acceptance of the English free-trade doctrine, their struggle for it (even against remnants of English mercantilism), and their losing fight to maintain it in the 1870s are respectively investigated in Wilhelm TREUE's 'Adam Smith in Deutschland. Zum Problem des "politischen Professors" zwischen 1776 und 1810', *Deutschland und Europa*, edited by Werner Conze (Düsseldorf, 1951), John CLAPHAM's 'The Last Years of the Navigation Acts', *English Historical Review*, XXV (1910), 480–501 and 687–707, and Ivo Nikolai LAMBI's *Free Trade and Protection in Germany, 1868–1879* (Wiesbaden, 1963).

CULTURE

Two of the most suggestive works on reciprocal influences in German and English culture are Percy Ernst SCHRAMM's 'Deutschlands Verhältnis zur englischen Kultur nach der Begründung des Neuen Reiches', in *Festschrift für S. A. Kaehler*, edited by Walter Hubatsch (Düsseldorf, 1950) and 'Englands Verhältnis zur deutschen Kultur zwischen der Reichsgründung und der Jahrhundertwende', in *Deutschland und Europa*. René WELLEK, in *Confrontations. Studies in the Intellectual and Literary Relations between Germany, England, and the United States during the Nineteenth Century* (Princeton, 1965), brilliantly reveals the differences between English and

German literature in the early part of the century. Walther FISCHER's *Deutscher Kultureinfluss am viktorianischen Hofe bis zur Gründung des Deutschen Reiches* (Giessen, 1951), by contrast, is a meager book. Klaus DOCKHORN, though lacking the lucidity of Schramm and Wellek, makes some interesting suggestions in his *Der deutsche Historismus in England, ein Beitrag zur englischen Geistesgeschichte des 19. Jahrhunderts* (Göttingen and Baltimore, 1950) and *Deutscher Geist und angelsächsische Geistesgeschichte. Ein Versuch der Deutung ihres Verhältnisses* (Göttingen, 1954). No work has yet successfully dealt with the welter of values and feelings surrounding the term 'Germanic', but Marie SCHÜTT, 'Das Germanenproblem in der englischen Geschichtsschreibung des achtzehnten Jahrhunderts', *Brittanica et Americana* V (1960), 7–48, at least indicates some of the dimensions of the question.

HISTORIES OF HISTORICAL WRITING

In this field, which can boast no general work which all agree is definitive, one must pick and choose. Eduard FUETER's *Geschichte der neueren Historiographie*, 3rd edn. (Munich, 1936), the oldest work of its kind still in general use, is impatient with many traditions sacred to German historical thought. Nevertheless it is refreshing and vivid. George Peabody GOOCH's *History and Historians in the Nineteenth Century* (Boston, 1959) is still the best work on the nineteenth century alone, though its organization leaves much to be desired. James Westfall THOMPSON's *A History of Historical Writing*, 2 vols. (New York, 1942) offers little new in the way of analysis but compiles much useful data. Friedrich MEINECKE's *Die Entstehung des Historismus*, 2 vols. (Munich and Berlin, 1936) is primarily a classic in intellectual history. Bernadotte SCHMITT's symposium, *Some Historians of Modern Europe* (Chicago, 1942) sometimes suffers from superficiality but maintains a good average on the German historians – Delbrück, Lamprecht, Marcks, and Schmoller. Fritz STERN's collection with introduction, *The Varieties of History*, sums up many valuable points.

In the more limited field of histories of *German* historiography one may include the old and still marginally useful study by Franz von WEGELE, *Geschichte der deutschen Historiographie* (Munich and Leipzig, 1885), Ottokar LORENZ' highly selective and interpretative *Die Geschichtswissenschaft in Hauptrichtungen und Aufgaben* (Berlin, 1886), Lord John ACTON's still interesting article, 'German Schools of History', *English Historical Review*, I (1886), 7–42, and Georg von BELOW's *Die deutsche Geschichtsschreibung von den Befreiungskriegen bis zu unseren Tagen*, 2nd edn. (Munich and Berlin, 1924), an analysis based on debatable 'school' classifications. Antoine GUILLAND's *Modern Germany and Her Historians* (London, 1915) brings little sympathy to the nationalist attitudes it uncovers among major nineteenth-century German historians. Undoubtedly the best account of German historiography is Heinrich von SRBIK's *Geist und Geschichte vom deutschen Humanismus bis zur Gegenwart*, 2 vols. (Munich and Salzburg, 1950–1). George G. IGGERS' *The German Conception of History* (Middletown, Conn., 1968) is more an analysis of the development of historicism as a *Weltanschauung* than a history of historiography. Dietrich FISCHER, *Die deutsche Geschichtswissenschaft von J. G. Droysen bis O. Hintze in ihrem Verhältnis zur Soziologie* (Cologne, 1966) shows how several late-nineteenth-century historians rejected the 'Western' sociological tradition. Several smaller works consulted for developments after 1920 include Ado JÜRGENS' *Ergebnisse deutscher Wissenschaft* (Essen, 1939), Felix GILBERT's 'German Historiography during the Second World War', *American Historical Review*, LIII (1948), 50–8, Gerhard RITTER's *Die deutsche Geschichtswissenschaft im zweiten Weltkrieg* (Marburg, 1951), Richard MÖNNING's *Amerika und England im deutschen, österreichischen und schweizerischen Schrifttum der Jahre 1945–1949* (Stuttgart, 1951), and Christopher HOWARD's 'Literaturbericht über englische Geschichte der Neuzeit. Veröffentlichungen 1950 bis 1959', in *Literaturberichte über Neuerscheinungen zur ausserdeutschen Geschichte*, *Historische Zeitschrift*, *Sonderheft* I (Munich, 1962).

Among more specialized works are Chaim JAFFE, *Roscher*, *Hildebrand und Knies als Begründer der älteren historischen Schule deutscher Volkswirte* (Wetzikon, 1916), and Andreas KRAUS, *Vernunft und Geschichte. Die Bedeutung der deutschen Akademien für die Entwicklung der Geschichtswissenschaft im späten achtzehnten Jahrhundert* (Freiburg-im-Breisgau, 1963). The latter redresses the balance of institutional responsibility for the rise of modern historiography, which has traditionally been ascribed most heavily to the universities. Finally, one might list Kurt HUNGER's *Die Bedeutung der Universität Göttingen für die Geschichtsforschung am Ausgang des 18. Jahrhunderts* (Berlin, 1933) for a discussion of the English inspiration of Göttingen, Edward DANCE's *History the Betrayer. A Study in Bias*, 2nd edn. (London, 1964), for a warning against the dangers of unconscious presuppositions, and the publications of the Internationales Schulbuchinstitut of Brunswick for trying to point them out in recent European textbooks.

WORKS ON THE HISTORY OF IDEAS AND OPINION

HISTORIES OF POLITICAL THOUGHT

Among the histories of ideas in Germany, only a few deal directly with the development of political and social thought. Friedrich MEINECKE's classic, *Weltbürgertum und Nationalstaat*, 7th edn. (Munich and Berlin, 1928), traces the development of German national ideas through most of the nineteenth century, just as Leonard KRIEGER investigates *The German Idea of Freedom* (Boston, 1957) up to the latter part of the century. Both works are the starting point for any study of German liberal and national thought. Oskar KLEIN-HATTINGEN's *Geschichte des deutschen Liberalismus*, 2 vols. (Berlin, 1911–12) is less a history of ideas than of men, though it is useful for that reason. Works on more specialized areas of political thought are Heinrich HEFFTER's valuable *Die deutsche Selbstverwaltung im 19. Jahrhundert. Geschichte der Ideen und Institutionen* (Stuttgart, 1950) and, for a critique of German views of English self-government, Josef REDLICH's *Englische Lokalverwaltung* (Leipzig, 1901). George Lachmann MOSSE's *The Crisis of German Ideology* (New York, 1964) discusses the evolution of racist thinking in nineteenth-century Germany. Donald ROHR, in *The Origins of Social Liberalism in Germany* (London and Chicago, 1963), shows the impact of the 'social question' on liberal thinking.

Many books have been written to explain the awakening of German political thought at the end of the eighteenth century. Some – such as Fritz VALJAVEC's *Die Entstehung der politischen Strömungen in Deutschland, 1770–1815* (Munich, 1951) and Carlo ANTONI's *Der Kampf wider die Vernunft: Zur Entstehungsgeschichte des deutschen Freiheitsgedankens*, translated by Walter Goetz (Stuttgart, 1951) – emphasize a reaction to the Enlightenment antedating the French Revolution. Others, such as George Peabody GOOCH's older *Germany and the French Revolution* (London, 1927) and Reinhold ARIS' *History of Political Thought in Germany from 1789 to 1815* (London, 1936), stress the impact of the revolution and Napoleonic invasion. The impact of Burke on Brandes, Rehberg, Gentz, and Adam Müller is described in Frieda BRAUNE's *Edmund Burke in Deutschland* (Heidelberg, 1917). Many of the strands woven in these books are brought together in Klaus EPSTEIN's masterful *The Genesis of German Conservatism* (Princeton, 1966). Two other works which transcend the narrow focus on selected thinkers and take up much broader problems are Jacques DROZ, *L'Allemagne et la révolution française* (Paris, 1949), and Henri BRUNSCHWIG, *La crise de l'état prussien à la fin du XVIIIe siècle et la genèse de la mentalité romantique* (Paris, 1947). Both support a description of the German intellectual milieu around 1800 as fluid and in crisis. Both Droz and Wolfgang von GROOTE, in his *Die Entstehung des Nationalbewusstseins in Nordwestdeutschland, 1790–1830* (Göttingen, 1955), argue persuasively that the French revolution created not a modern, exclusive, state-oriented nationalism but a blend of patriotism and cosmopolitanism leading to an ill-defined ambivalence toward foreign models. DROZ's subsequent *Le romantisme allemande et l'état; résistance et collaboration dans l'Allemagne napoléonienne* (Paris, 1966) is a more restricted work which views romanticism as an ideological foundation for political resistance to France.

Hajo HOLBORN's profound 'Der deutsche Idealismus in sozialgeschichtlicher Beleuchtung', *Historische Zeitschrift*, CLXXIV (1952), 359–84, and George IGGERS' 'German Historical Thought and the Idea of Natural Law',

Cahiers d'histoire mondiale, VIII (1964), 564–75, show how German thought developed away from the western empirical, natural-law tradition during the nineteenth century. Friedrich MEINECKE's 'Germanischer und romanischer Geist im Wandel der deutschen Geschichtsauffassung', *Historische Zeitschrift*, CXV (1916), 516–36, argues that the early nineteenth-century idea of a historic community among Germanic peoples constitutes a natural bridge between earlier Enlightenment cosmopolitan thought and the later identification of the nation and the state in Germany. Rudolf STADELMANN's stimulating essay, 'Deutschland und die westeuropäischen Revolutionen', *Deutschland und Westeuropa* (Laupheim/Württemberg, 1948), takes up the problem of the failure of the German reform movement in the nineteenth century. For the relationship between French and German political thought in the 'pre-March' period, see Lothar GALL's *Benjamin Constant. Seine politische Ideenwelt und der deutsche Vormärz* (Wiesbaden, 1963). Peter GILG, *Die Erneuerung des demokratischen Denkens im wilhelminischen Deutschland* (Wiesbaden, 1965) gives a description of socialist, left-liberal, and Catholic political thought toward the turn of this century.

PROFESSORIAL POLITICAL THOUGHT

Although the importance of academic thinkers for German political and social theories is widely recognized, few studies have been undertaken. Here again Friedrich MEINECKE led the way in his 'Drei Generationen deutscher Gelehrtenpolitik', *Staat und Persönlichkeit* (Berlin, 1933). Abraham ASCHER's 'Professors as Propagandists: The Politics of the Kathedersozialisten', *Journal of Central European Affairs*, XXIII (1963), 282–302, points up the material presented by Gerhard WITTROCK in *Die Kathedersozialisten bis zur Eisenacher Versammlung 1872* (Berlin, 1939) and Franz BOESE in *Geschichte des Vereins für Sozialpolitik, 1872–1932* (Berlin, 1939). The period from 1890 on has received most attention. Fritz K. RINGER, *The Decline of the German Mandarins. The German Academic Community 1890–1933* (Cambridge, Mass., 1969) is a model study which illuminates the whole panorama of the political, social, and intellectual forces at work in the German intellectual establishment. Gustav Schmidt, *Deutscher Historismus und der Uebergang zur parlamentarischen Demokratie* [*Historische Studien*, No. 389] (Lübeck and Hamburg, 1964) is a difficult but well-researched investigation of Meinecke, Troeltsch, and Weber's political thought. Dieter FRICKE's 'Zur Militarisierung des deutschen Geisteslebens im wilhelminischen Kaiserreich: Der Fall Leo Arons', *Zeitschrift für die Geschichtswissenschaft*, VII, No. 5 (1960), 1069–1107, is an East German view of the limits of academic freedom under Wilhelm II; Wolfgang MARIENFELD, *Wissenschaft und Schlachtflottenbau, 1897–1906*, *Marine-Rundschau*, *Beiheft* II (April 1957), and Klaus SCHWABE, 'Zur politischen Haltung der deutschen Professoren im ersten Weltkrieg', *Historische Zeitschrift*, CXCIII (1961), 601–34, stress the willingness of the German professors to support their government. SCHWABE's *Wissenschaft und Kriegsmoral. Die deutschen Hochschullehrer und die politischen Grundfragen des ersten Weltkrieges* (Göttingen, 1969) appeared too late to be used for this study, but the 1958 Freiburg University dissertation upon which it is based is a clear and interesting account of the consequences of mixing 'impartial science' and politics. There and in 'Ursprung und Verbreitung des alldeutschen Annexionismus in der deutschen Professorenschaft im ersten Weltkrieg', *Vierteljahresschrift für Zeitgeschichte*, XIV (1966), 105–38, Schwabe subtly distinguishes the many colorations even among professors who were 'for' the war.

PUBLIC OPINION STUDIES

Neither primary nor secondary materials on public opinion proved very useful for this work. Nevertheless, a few secondary works served the function of control in determining how far historians deviated from public opinion. (Very often, they led it.) Eberhard SAUER's *Die französische Revolution von 1789 in zeitgenössischen deutschen Flugschriften und Dichtungen* (Weimar, 1913), Otto TSCHIRCH's *Geschichte der öffentlichen Meinung in Preussen vom Baseler Frieden bis zum Zusammenbruch des Staates, 1795–1806*, 2 vols. (Weimar, 1933–4), Karl WOLFF's *Die deutsche Publizistik in der Zeit der Freiheitskämpfe und des Wiener Kongresses, 1813–1815* (Plauen, 1934), Hans ROSENBERG's *Die nationalpolitische Publizistik Deutschlands vom Eintritt der Neuen Ära in Preussen bis zum Ausbruch des Deutschen Krieges*, 2 vols. (Munich and Berlin, 1935) and *Die nationalpolitische Publizistik Deutschlands von 1866 bis 1871*, edited by Karl Georg Faber, 2 vols. (Düsseldorf, 1963), Otto WESTPHAL's *Welt- und Staatsauffassung des deutschen Liberalismus: Eine Untersuchung über die Preussischen Jahrbücher und den konstitutionellen Liberalismus in Deutschland von 1858–63* (Munich and Berlin, 1919), the BRITISH FOREIGN OFFICE's *German Opinion on National Policy Prior to July 1914*, 2 pts. (London, 1920), and Alfred KRUCK's *Geschichte des Alldeutschen Verbandes, 1890–1939* (Wiesbaden, 1954) were helpful. The history of individual organs of public discussion has been sadly neglected in Germany, but a few works do give some insights. Hans ZEHNTER, *Das Staatslexikon von Rotteck und Welcker* (Jena, 1929) and Wolfgang SCHEEL, *Das 'Berliner Politisches Wochenblatt' und die politische und soziale Revolution in Frankreich und England* (Göttingen, 1964) are better than most such studies.

RELIGION

A small number of books shed some light on the thoughts about England of the German churches. William SHANAHAN's *German Protestants Face the Social Question* (Notre Dame, Ind., 1954) is much more than its title indicates. Otto PFLEIDERER's *Die Entwicklung der protestantischen Theologie in Deutschland seit Kant und in Grossbritannien seit 1825* (Freiburg, 1891) provides many valuable clues to the affinities between German and English religious thought, and Heinrich BÖHMER's 'Die Kirche von England und der Protestantismus', *Neue kirchliche Zeitschrift*, XXVII (1916), 573–614 and 642–61, tells as much about the German wartime viewpoint on English culture as it does about the real differences between German and English Protestantism. Fritz FISCHER's 'Der deutsche Protestantismus und die Politik im 19. Jahrhundert', *Historische Zeitschrift*, CLXXI (1951), 473–518, is informative about the political stance of Protestantism.

UNIVERSITIES

Among the many centennial histories of German universities, few were helpful for this study. Goetz von SELLE's *Die Georg-August-Universität zu Göttingen, 1737–1937* (Göttingen, 1937), however, is exceptional as an intellectual, as well as institutional, history; it furthermore touches on the ties of this most English of German schools to Britain. Friedrich PAULSEN's pioneering *The German Universities and University Study*, translated by Frank Thilly and William Elwang (New York, 1906), which clearly shows its age, still stands alone in a sadly neglected field.

BIOGRAPHIES OF HISTORIANS

Much work needs to be done before a satisfactory body of biographies of major nineteenth-century German historians – not to mention the minor ones – is complete. Archenholtz has been adequately covered by Friedrich RUOF's *Johann Wilhelm von Archenholtz* (Berlin, 1915). Peter GAY's *The Dilemma of Democratic Socialism. Eduard Bernstein's Challenge to Marx* (New York, 1952) is the best appreciation of Bernstein in English. Beyond the numerous Bismarck biographies are treatments by Georg BRODNITZ, *Bismarcks nationalökonomische Anschauungen* (Jena, 1902), Eva Maria BAUM, *Bismarcks Urteil über England und die Engländer* (Munich, 1936), and Veit VALENTIN, 'Bismarck and England in the Earlier Part of his Career', *Transactions of the Royal Historical Society*, 4th series, XX (1937), 13–30. Jacques VONTOBEL's *Johann Caspar Bluntschlis Lehre von Recht und Staat* (Zürich, 1956) is less a biography than a theoretical analysis. Werner BARICH's *Lujo Brentano als Sozialpolitiker* (Berlin, 1936) is too compressed, but James SHEEHAN's *The Career of Lujo Brentano* (Chicago, 1966) is an exemplary treatment of this central figure in German social thought. Bernhard DAMMERMANN's 'Lothar Bucher in England, seine Entwicklung vom Achtundvierziger zum Gehilfen Bismarcks', *Archiv für Politik und Geschichte*, VIII (1927), 186–230, and Karl ZADDACH's *Lothar Bucher bis zum Ende seines Londoner Exils (1817–1861)* (Heidelberg, 1915) are good as far as they go, but a real biography of this lonely and secretive assistant of Bismarck still needs to be done. Bunsen, a key figure in mid-century Prussian diplomatic and church affairs, remains unexamined except in Wilma HÖCKER's *Der Gesandte Bunsen als Vermittler zwischen Deutschland und England* (Göttingen, 1951), a superficial and chronologically limited treatment. Dahlmann deserved and got close attention from Anton Heinrich SPRINGER's *Friedrich Christoph Dahlmann*, 2 vols. (Leipzig, 1870–2) and Hermann CHRISTERN's *F. C. Dahlmanns politische Entwicklung bis 1848* (Leipzig, 1921). Annelise THIMME's *Hans Delbrück als Kritiker der Wilhelmischen Epoche* (Düsseldorf, 1955) does justice to one of the most independent-minded members of the Imperial establishment, even though the author was evidently unable to use the huge Delbrück *Nachlass* in East Berlin. Axel von HARNACK presents a similar view in 'Hans Delbrück als Historiker und Politiker', *Neue Rundschau*, LXIII (1952), 408–26. Gustav DROYSEN's *Johann Gustav Droysen* (Leipzig, 1910) reaches only to 1848. Felix GILBERT's *Johann Gustav Droysen und die preussisch-deutsche Frage*, *Historische Zeitschrift*, *Beiheft* XX (Berlin, 1931) and Günther BIRTSCH's *Die Nation als sittliche Idee: Der Nationalstaatsbegriff in Geschichtsschreibung und politischer Gedankenwelt Johann Gustav Droysens* (Cologne, 1964), which deal chiefly with Droysen's national ideas, disagree on their evolution. Wolfgang HOCK, in his *Liberales Denken im Zeitalter der Paulskirche. Droysen und die Frankfurter Mitte* (Münster, 1957), tries to depict Droysen as a pragmatic politician who did not set great store in philosophy or theory.

Rudolf HAYM's old *Das Leben Max Dunckers* (Berlin, 1891) is still serviceable, but Duncker has received less attention than he deserves. Gustav MAYER's *Friedrich Engels: A Biography*, translated by Gilbert and Helen Highet (New York, 1936), remains a classic; Siegfried BÜNGER's *Friedrich Engels und die britische sozialistische Bewegung, 1881–1895* (East Berlin, 1962) tries to justify Engels' isolation from the English workers.

Friedrich von Gentz has been well covered by Paul SWEET's *Friedrich von Gentz, Defender of the Old Order* (Madison, 1941), Golo MANN's *Secretary of Europe. The Life of Friedrich Gentz, Enemy of Napoleon*, translated by William Woglom (New Haven, 1946), Charles Stephen BUCKLAND's *Friedrich von Gentz' Relations with the British Government during the Marquis Wellesley's Foreign Secretaryship of State (from 1809 to 1812)* (London, 1933), and Paul WITTICHEN's 'Friedrich von Gentz und die englische Politik, 1800–1814', *Preussische Jahrbücher*, CX (1902), 462–501. Gervinus, the opponent of Rankean detachment and the prophet of democracy, received a gentle burial in Leopold von RANKE's own 'Georg Gottfried Gervinus', *Historische Zeitschrift*, XXVII (1872), 134–46. Johannes DÖRFEL's *Gervinus als historischer Denker* (Gotha, 1904) is very short. Not even dissertations – of which Rolf BÖTTCHER's 'Nationales und staatliches Denken im Werke G. G. Gervinus' (dissertation, Cologne, 1935) is one of the better ones – have done justice to this important historian and political thinker. There is still no adequate biography of Gneist, the ubiquitous law professor who deeply influenced

German constitutional and social thought. Eugen SCHIFFER's *Rudolf von Gneist* (Berlin, 1896) is only a memorial speech. Erich MARCKS's 'Ludwig Häusser und die politische Geschichtsschreibung in Heidelberg', in *Heidelberger Professoren aus dem 19. Jahrhundert*, 2 vols. (Heidelberg, 1903), II, 283–354, was the best treatment – by default – of the South German prophet of Prussian–German nationalism until the appearance of Anneliese KALTENBACH's *Ludwig Häusser, historien et patriote (1818–1867)* (Paris, 1965), a thoroughly-documented biography. Heeren, a man who deeply influenced American historians, still wants a biographer; Irene KAHN's dissertation, *Der Historiker Arnold Hermann Ludwig Heeren* (Ludwigshafen, 1939), is the largest critical work devoted to him. Frederick M. BARNARD, *Herder's Social and Political Thought* (Oxford, 1965) was quite useful and to the point for this study. Otto Hintze's name must also be placed on the list of those who lack a complete biography, although one can turn to Fritz HARTUNG, 'Einleitung', to HINTZE's *Gesammelte Abhandlungen*, vol. I (Leipzig, 1941) or to H. WARTENBERG's 'Hintze als Geschichtsdenker' (Dissertation, Berlin, 1953). Ingwer PAULSEN's *Victor Aimé Huber als Sozialpolitiker* (Leipzig, 1931) is still, unfortunately, the best treatment of Huber.

Elard Hugo MEYER's ancient *Johann Martin Lappenberg* (Hamburg, 1867) remains the only biography of one of the fathers of critical English historical studies. Neither Hermann Oncken's 'Gedächtnisrede auf Max Lenz', *Sitzungsberichte der preussischen Akademie der Wissenschaften Berlin* (1933), cxvii–cxxv, nor Hans-Heinz KRILL's *Die Rankerenaissance: Max Lenz und Erich Marcks* (Berlin, 1962) fulfills the function of a Lenz biography. Felix Liebermann's fine, unobtrusive scholarship earned him no more than Ernst HEYMANN's skeletal 'Felix Liebermann', *Zeitschrift der Savigny-Stiftung für Rechtsgeschichte, Germanistische Abteilung*, XLVI (1926), xxiii–xxxiv. Friedrich List's life needs more attention. Margaret E. HIRST, *Life of Friedrich List and Selections from His Writings* (London, 1909) is all too short, while Paul GEHRING, *Friedrich List. Jugend- und Reifejahre 1789–1825* (Tübingen, 1964), is only a partial treatment. In addition one can learn something from Friedrich BAHR, *Die politischen Anschauungen Friedrich Lists, dargelegt an seiner Stellung zu England* (Eibau, 1929), and Erna SCHULZ, 'Friedrich Lists Geschichtsauffassung', *Zeitschrift für die gesamten Staatswissenschaften*, XCVII (1936/37), 290–334. Ludwig SEVIN investigated List's confrontation with England in his articles 'Die Entwicklung von Friedrich Lists kolonialen und weltpolitischen Ideen bis zum Plane einer englischen Allianz 1846', *Schmollers Jahrbuch*, XXXIII (1909), 299–341, and 'Die List'sche Idee einer deutsch-englischen Allianz in ihrem Ergebnis für Deutschland', *Schmollers Jahrbuch*, XXXIV (1910), 173–222.

Erich Marcks, a great biographer himself, has found no biographer: Krill's work is an analysis of ideas, and Karl STÄHLIN's 'Erich Marcks zum Gedächtnis', *Historische Zeitschrift*, CLX (1939), 496–533, is simply a memorial. Isaiah BERLIN's *Karl Marx. His Life and Environment* (New York, 1959) and Franz MEHRING, *Karl Marx* (Ann Arbor, 1962) remain standard. Of some interest for the views of the business community is Joseph HANSEN's *Gustav von Mevissen. Ein rheinisches Lebensbild 1815–1899*, 2 vols. (Berlin, 1906). Peter KLASSEN's *Justus Möser* (Frankfurt/Main, 1936) and Clemens August HOBERG's '"Historische Logik". Ein Beitrag zu Mösers Geschichtsauffassung', *Historische Zeitschrift*, CLVIII (1938), 492–503, are even mistier than the writings and thoughts of their subject. But see also Ernst HEMPEL, 'Justus Mösers Wirkung auf seine Zeitgenossen und auf die deutsche Geschichtsschreibung', *Mitteilungen des Vereins für Geschichte und Landeskunde von Osnabrück*, LIV (1933), 1–76.

Erich ANGERMANN's *Robert von Mohl, 1799–1875. Leben und Werk eines altliberalen Staatsgelehrten* (Neuwied, 1962) is the sort of biography which should exist for every major German historical and legal thinker. Johannes von Müller has been treated by Charles MONNARD in his *Biographie de Jean de Muller* (Paris and Lausanne, 1839), by Edgar BONJOUR in *Studien zu Johannes von Müller* (Basel and Stuttgart, 1957), by Willy ANDREAS in his illuminating 'Johannes von Müller in Weimar', *Historische Zeitschrift*, CXLV (1931/32), 69–89, and by Gordon A. CRAIG in 'Johannes von Müller: The Historian in Search of a Hero', *American Historical Review*, CXXIV (1969), 1487–1502. While both Karl HENKING, *Johannes von Müller, 1752–1809*, 2 vols. (Stuttgart and Berlin, 1909–28) and Karl SCHIB, *Johannes von Müller, 1752–1809* (Schaffhausen, 1967) carefully used documentary evidence, neither is an inspired biography. The best biographical treatment of Niebuhr used to be Dietrich GERHARD, 'Zur Einführung', *Die Briefe Barthold Georg Niebuhrs*, 2 vols. (Berlin, 1926), but Seppo RYTKÖNEN, *Barthold Georg Niebuhr als Politiker und Historiker* (Helsinki, 1968), which appeared too late for me to consult, has received favorable notice. One of the most astonishing gaps in German biography is Ranke's. Only his early years have been covered by Hermann ONCKEN's *Aus Rankes Frühzeit* (Gotha, 1922), Theodor von LAUE's *Leopold Ranke. The Formative Years* (Princeton, 1950), and Conrad von VARRENTRAPP's 'Rankes Historisch-politische Zeitschrift und das Berliner Politische Wochenblatt', *Historische Zeitschrift*, XCIX (1907), 35–119. On a more restricted scale, Gunther BERG, *Leopold von Ranke als akademischer Lehrer* (Göttingen, 1968) is imaginative and revealing. Hermann von ROTTECK wrote a familial biography of Karl von Rotteck which is included in the latter's *Gesammelte und nachgelassene Schriften*; Richard ROEPELL's superficial *Karl Wenceslaus von Rotteck, Antrittsrede* (Breslau, 1883) and Horst EHMKE's *Karl von Rotteck, der politische Professor* (Karlsruhe, 1964), essentially an appeal for a biography, are not substitutes for a critical appraisal of this important political spokesman of the German middle class. Gustav WOLF's *Dietrich Schäfer und Hans Delbrück, nationale Ziele der deutschen Geschichtsschreibung seit der franzö-*

sischen Revolution (Gotha, 1918) is more a historical essay than a critical approach to Schäfer. Frederike FÜRST, *August Ludwig von Schlözer, ein deutscher Aufklärer im achtzehnten Jahrhundert* (Heidelberg, 1928) is interesting. Schlosser seems to have no biographers other than his students, but these were not unequal to the task. Wilhelm DILTHEY, 'Friedrich Christoph Schlosser', *Preussische Jahrbücher*, IX (1862), 373–433, is a full biography in miniature. Schmoller also lacks a biographer, despite his great importance. Fritz HARTUNG's 'Gustav von Schmoller und die preussische Geschichtsschreibung', *Schmollers Jahrbuch*, LXII (1938), 277–302, is brief, specialized, and informative. Joist GROLLE's brief *Landesgeschichte in der Zeit der deutschen Spätaufklärung: Ludwig Timotheus Spittler* (Göttingen, 1963) emphasizes chiefly one aspect of Spittler's contribution to historical writing. Stahl has received quite competent treatment in Gerhard MASUR's *Friedrich Julius Stahl, Geschichte seines Lebens* (Berlin, 1930). Sybel warrants further investigation, but Hellmut SEIER, *Die Staatsidee Heinrich von Sybels in den Wandlungen der Reichsgründungszeit 1862/71* (Lübeck, 1961) is good on his politics in a crucial period for academic liberalism.

Andreas DORPALEN's *Heinrich von Treitschke* (New Haven, 1957) is the fullest biography of Treitschke; Walter BUSSMANN's *Treitschke, sein Welt- und Geschichtsbild* (Göttingen, 1952) is more a psychological interpretation. Paul BAILLEU's 'Heinrich von Treitschke', *Deutsche Rundschau*, LXXXIX (1896), 97–132 and 197–231, provides some interesting insights by a friend. Treitschke's opinion of England has been briefly examined, but not explained, by Max CORNICELIUS in *England in Treitschkes Darstellung und Urteil* (Leipzig, 1915) and Karl HAMPE's 'Treitschke in London', *Internationale Monatsschrift*, X (1915/16), 865–72. Ernst LEIPPRAND's *Treitschkes Stellung zu England* (Stuttgart, 1928), by contrast, is painstaking and judicious. The conclusions of Elisabeth SCHURIG's *Die Entwicklung der politischen Anschauungen Heinrich von Treitschkes* (Dresden, 1909) are represented in Dorpalen's book. In addition, several other works on certain aspects of Treitschke's thought have been suggestive. Walter BUSSMANN, 'Treitschke als Politiker', *Historische Zeitschrift*, CLXXVII (1954), 249–79, Max CORNICELIUS, 'Treitschke und Robert von Mohl', *Deutsche Rundschau*, CLXXXIX (1921), 310–23, Holger HJELHOLT, *Treitschke und Schleswig-Holstein* (Munich and Berlin, 1929), Irmgard LUDWIG, *Treitschke und Frankreich*, *Beiheft* 32 of the *Historische Zeitschrift* (1934), and Hans SCHLEIER, 'Treitschke, Delbrück und die "PJ" in den 80er Jahren des neunzehnten Jahrhunderts', *Jahrbuch für Geschichte*, I (1967), 134–79, all had materials to contribute to the unending debate about the fascinating super-Prussian from Saxony.

Heinrich KOCHENDÖRFFER's *Vincke*, 2 vols. (Soest, 1932–3), the fullest biography, suffers from the *Archivrat* style: too much detail presented with too much affection and too little imagination. Marianne WEBER's *Max*

Weber, ein Lebensbild (Heidelberg, 1950) gives color, and Wolfgang J. MOMMSEN's *Max Weber und die deutsche Politik* (Tübingen, 1959), critical analysis to the life of Germany's greatest sociologist. Karl WILD, *Karl Theodor Welcker, ein Vorkämpfer des älteren deutschen Liberalismus* (Heidelberg, 1913) is lengthy and thorough, though uninspired.

RECENT HISTORIES OF ENGLAND

It has not been my intention in this work to adopt a firm view of English history and then judge German historians by their degree of deviation from it. Nevertheless, some knowledge of the changing interpretations of British historians themselves has been indispensable. To name only a few of the recent works which have given me stimulus: Asa BRIGGS, *The Age of Improvement* (London, 1959); S. G. CHECKLAND, *The Rise of Industrial Society in England* (London, 1964); Archibald S. FOORD, *His Majesty's Opposition, 1714–1830* (Oxford, 1964); Norman GASH, *Politics in the Age of Peel* (London, 1952); and John H. PLUMB, *Sir Robert Walpole*, 2 vols. (London, 1956–60).

INDEX

Index